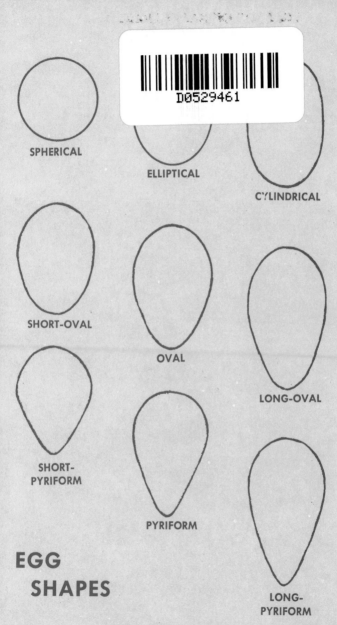

SPHERICAL

ELLIPTICAL

CYLINDRICAL

SHORT-OVAL

OVAL

LONG-OVAL

SHORT-
PYRIFORM

PYRIFORM

EGG
SHAPES

LONG-
PYRIFORM

A Field Guide to
Western Birds' Nests

THE PETERSON FIELD GUIDE SERIES
EDITED BY ROGER TORY PETERSON

1. A Field Guide to the Birds of Roger Tory Peterson

2. A Field Guide to Western Birds by Roger Tory Peterson

3. A Field Guide to Shells of the Atlantic and Gulf Coasts and the West Indies by Percy A. Morris

4. A Field Guide to the Butterflies by Alexander B. Klots

5. A Field Guide to the Mammals by William H. Burt and Richard P. Grossenheider

6. A Field Guide to Pacific Coast Shells (including shells of Hawaii and the Gulf of California) by Percy A. Morris

7. A Field Guide to Rocks and Minerals by Frederick H. Pough

8. A Field Guide to the Birds of Britain and Europe by Roger Tory Peterson, Guy Mountfort, and P. A. D. Hollom

9. A Field Guide to Animal Tracks by Olaus J. Murie

10. A Field Guide to the Ferns and Their Related Families of Northeastern and Central North America by Boughton Cobb

11. A Field Guide to Trees and Shrubs (Northeastern and Central North America) by George A. Petrides

12. A Field Guide to Reptiles and Amphibians of Eastern and Central North America by Roger Conant

13. A Field Guide to the Birds of Texas and Adjacent States by Roger Tory Peterson

14. A Field Guide to Rocky Mountain Wildflowers by John J. Craighead, Frank C. Craighead, Jr., and Ray J. Davis

15. A Field Guide to the Stars and Planets by Donald H. Menzel

16. A Field Guide to Western Reptiles and Amphibians by Robert C. Stebbins

17. A Field Guide to Wildflowers of Northeastern and North-central North America by Roger Tory Peterson and Margaret McKenny

18. A Field Guide to the Mammals of Britain and Europe by F. H. van den Brink

19. A Field Guide to the Insects of America North of Mexico by Donald J. Borror and Richard E. White

20. A Field Guide to Mexican Birds by Roger Tory Peterson and Edward L. Chalif

21. A Field Guide to Birds' Nests (found east of Mississippi River) by Hal H. Harrison

22. A Field Guide to Pacific States Wildflowers by Theodore F. Niehaus

23. A Field Guide to Edible Wild Plants of Eastern and Central North America by Lee Peterson

24. A Field Guide to the Atlantic Seashore by Kenneth L. Gosner

25. A Field Guide to Western Birds' Nests by Hal H. Harrison

THE PETERSON FIELD GUIDE SERIES

A FIELD GUIDE to WESTERN BIRDS' NESTS

of 520 species found breeding
in the United States
west of the Mississippi River

by HAL H. HARRISON

Photographs by the author
unless otherwise credited
Map, endpapers, and logo by
MADA HARRISON

Sponsored by the National Audubon Society
and National Wildlife Federation

HOUGHTON MIFFLIN COMPANY BOSTON
1979

Library of Congress Cataloging in Publication Data
Harrison, Hal H
   A field guide to Western birds' nests.

   (The Peterson field guide series; 25)
   Bibliography: p.
   Includes index.
    1. Birds—Eggs and nests—Identification. 2. Birds—
The West—Identification. 3. Birds—Middle West—Identi-
fication. I. Title.
QL675.H38   598.2'978   79–11330
ISBN 0–395–27629–2

Printed in the United States of America

A 10 9 8 7 6 5 4 3 2 1

For
George and *Gretchen*
of whom I am
very proud

Editor's Note

THIS *Field Guide to Western Birds' Nests* fills a great gap in the popular ornithological literature and every birder who would be well-informed will surely make it part of his field equipment, to be left at home only during those months when birds are not actively nesting.

In the latest edition (1961) of my own *Field Guide to Western Birds,* I included a single line or two about the nest and eggs of each species, a feature that was lacking in my eastern *Field Guide,* but the limitations of space dictated that I could not say more if the book was to remain a size to fit the pocket. Hence this new *Field Guide* by Hal Harrison, the premier nest photographer.

The area covered by this guide is considerably greater than that of my *Field Guide to Western Birds,* extending from the Pacific eastward to the Mississippi instead of the 100th Meridian on the Great Plains. This was dictated by the fact that Mr. Harrison's eastern nest book (1975) stopped at the Mississippi. Therefore, the species coverage — 520 — is much more extensive. Birders who live in the "twilight" zone or in-between zone of the Great Plains need not carry both the eastern and the western books to take care of all possibilities.

I recall a letter that I received from Hal Harrison many years ago, back in the 1940s, when he was a newspaperman in Tarentum, Pennsylvania. He wrote that my own work, and particularly my *Field Guide to the Birds,* had sparked a desire to abandon the world of the press and to seek fulfillment as an interpreter of nature — by lecturing, writing, and photographing birds. In turn he inspired his son, George, who became the distinguished editor of *National Wildlife* and *International Wildlife* magazines and has since published his own books on the delights of bird-watching. To George Harrison and his sister this new *Field Guide* is dedicated by a proud father. Although Hal Harrison filmed a variety of nature subjects over the years and has lectured throughout the country with his films, he has always had a special interest and skill in finding nests, and no one excels him at nest photography.

As any birder knows, it is challenge enough to amass a "life list" of several hundred species *seen.* But, to find their nests — with full clutches of eggs — and to photograph them as Mr. Harrison has done, is a staggering *tour de force.* Actually most birders are not too skilled at finding nests. In most cases there would be an appalling gap between the number of species ticked off on their checklists and the number of nests they have discovered.

Not so long ago it was feared that drawing attention to nests by means of a guide such as this might lead to a resurgence of nest-robbing. Now this fear is no longer valid; egg-collecting is a thing of the past. It was basically a boy's hobby, now disapproved by public opinion, prohibited by law, and replaced by the game of bird-listing or "birding" — collecting sight records and ticking them off on checklists. Bird banding and bird photography are sophisticated spinoffs that appeal to many birders who want to collect something more tangible than names.

At the turn of the century, ornithology went through a phase of collection; birds were collected (shot) and then classified. Eggs were also collected, by professionals and amateurs alike; however, much of the collecting by amateurs contributed little to the science of ornithology. Today the collecting of eggs — or, rather, their shells — would be meaningless. It no longer suits the climate of the times. In the modern context, only research concerned with embryology or with protein analysis (as a taxonomic tool) would justify the taking of eggs.

On the other hand, bird nesting has now come of age with the discovery that hard pesticides of the hydrocarbon complex may affect the calcification of eggs and result in thin-shelled eggs that break or fail to hatch. Monitoring nests has become a highly organized procedure, yielding data important to the concerned environmentalist. These data are gathered and analyzed at the Laboratory of Ornithology, Cornell University, Ithaca, New York, where more than 250,000 nest record cards are now on file.

There are dangers, of course, in careless or too frequent visits to nests. But whether you are a bander, a photographer, a systematic nest observer, or simply an armchair type, this book with its beautiful photographs and informative text will enhance and enlarge your ornithological horizons.

ROGER TORY PETERSON

Preface

To THE casual bird watcher, the finding of a nest with eggs or young is an interesting or exciting event. For more dedicated birders, the discovery of one or more nests is expected on an outing in spring and summer; and for many experienced birders the search for nests has become as compelling as the listing of species observed. Indeed, the hobby of "nesting" has grown in popularity during recent years, and much of the credit must go to the North American Nest Record Card Program, sponsored by the Laboratory of Ornithology at Cornell University, Ithaca, N.Y.

Cornell's Nest Record Card Program (NRCP) has collected data since 1965. There are now more than 250,000 nest records on file. Records received from collaborators in all parts of the United States are edited and verified for accuracy and usability by laboratory personnel. For species for which over 1000 records are on file, data are stored in a computerized memory bank for efficient retrieval and use.

Hundreds of enthusiastic amateur and professional field ornithologists annually contribute thousands of cards to the NCRP. When a nest is found, the observer records information on the species, location, habitat, and reproductive history on a nest card provided by the laboratory. Cards are returned directly to Cornell or to one of more than 150 regional centers. These data are available to any qualified researcher interested in various aspects of reproductive biology.

With the publication of *A Field Guide to Birds' Nests East of the Mississippi River* in 1975, the author hopes he has made birding more interesting by supplying a quicker and more accurate means of identifying nests. That volume and the present one are intended as companions to Roger Tory Peterson's eastern and western *Field Guides* to bird identification.

A rather ambitious project started by the author about 20 years ago led to the undertaking of the eastern *Field Guide*. The original plan was to photograph all the breeding wood warblers in the United States along with their nests and eggs. That task still remains to be done. However, photographing warbler nests and eggs led to photographing those of other species, and a *Field Guide* evolved. Work on the present guide followed the success of the first.

In tackling the western assignment, the author-photographer faced an even more awesome task than in the East—to find hundreds (even thousands) of nests with eggs to study and photograph. To have done it alone would have required many years, but with the help of kind and interested friends, the project was accomplished in about five. My debt to those who helped is immeasurable. Space does not permit naming them all. There were times when I was indebted to an entire bird club, as when the Eagle Lake Audubon Society in Susanville, California, took me to a mountainous area where I found the only nest with eggs of a Canyon Wren that I have ever seen. There were some faithful friends whose help was so vital and outstanding that I would be remiss if I failed to mention them.

First, as always, is my wife, Mada. Not only was she at my side when I took the photographs, but in many cases it was she who found the nest. It was she who took all the measurements and kept the field notes. It was also Mada who did the initial editing of the text, typed the manuscript, sketched the drawings for the endpapers, and prepared the area map. Her constant encouragement was inspirational. Her dedication equaled my own.

I am grateful, too, for constant help and encouragement from my son, George, and his wife, Kit. They spent time with us every season we worked in the West and contributed much, especially to the photography.

The oological help extended to me by the Western Foundation of Vertebrate Zoology in Los Angeles has been invaluable. Not only did the president, Ed N. Harrison, turn over to me the facilities of the institution, but two staff members, Lloyd F. Kiff and Raymond J. Quigley, were actively involved in my field work. In addition, Mr. Kiff, curator for the foundation, reviewed my texts on eggs and made many valuable suggestions for improving the oological sections of the guide.

Outstanding help in California also came from Diane and Lynn Fuller, Jay S. Dow, Alice E. Fries, Don Bleitz, Dale B. Dalrymple, Stephen I. Rothstein, and personnel of the Honey Lake Wildlife Refuge, especially Charles Holmes, Jr., and Al Lapp.

In Colorado, I had a great many interested and helpful friends. Much cooperation came from students and faculty of Colorado State University at Fort Collins, especially from Clait E. Braun, Ronald A. Ryder, W. Paul Gorenzel, Kenneth M. Giesen, David A. Weber, and Gary Miller. It was Walter D. Graul of the Division of Wildlife who guided much of my activity in the state. Ruth and Warner Reeser and Ted and Lois Matthews tramped the Rockies with Mada and me.

I am indebted to A. D. McGrew, Mary Gray, Wayne Shifflett, and Cruz Martinez for guidance in Texas.

My thanks also must go to Fred Alberico, Griffing Bancroft, Margaret Bancroft, W. Wilson Baker, Barbara Beard, Bill and Jessie Berg, Pete Bloom, Tom J. Cade, Roger Cobb, Mrs. LeRoy Collins, Allegra Collister, John Cummings, Kent Dannen, Mr. and Mrs. Robert Engel, Helen Gildred, Jon Gnagy, Ellen Gorenzel,

Joseph A. Grom, Ladislav Hanka, Grant Heilman, Dave and Betty Hollister, Robert Hudson, Doug Irwin, Joseph R. Jehl, Ronald M. Jurek, Julie Kiff, Leo Kirsch, Douglas A. Lancaster, Roger M. Latham, Ralph H. Long, William J. Mader, Kenneth E. Marshall, Barbara Massey, Donald McCrimmon, Jess and Donna Morton, Jane McNeal, Mary and Jerry Nordstrom, Henry Pelzl, Robert G. Personius, Russell L. Pyke, Melanie Walker Rankin, Donald G. Rose, Sharon K. Schafer, Ralph W. Schreiber, Robert K. Selander, Sydney Smith, Bart Synder, Robert Carrington Stein, Deane Swickard, Kenneth Vierling, Bob Walker, Shirley Wells.

In attempting to update the breeding status of the 520 species in the 22 western states included in this *Field Guide,* the author was confronted with the distressing fact that a number of states are woefully lacking in current publications on the subject. To accomplish an adequate census of what nests where today, the author was helped by a number of knowledgeable ornithologists and bird watchers who accepted the assignment of reviewing and correcting the available material. Among those who were especially helpful, I should like to thank William H. Elder, Walter D. Graul, Mrs. Henry N. Halberg, Joyce Harrell, J. W. Johnson, Richard F. Johnston, Chuck Lawson, Harry B. Nehls, Lewis W. Oring, Peter C. Petersen, Neva L. Pruess, Thomas H. Rogers, Dr. and Mrs. Oliver K. Scott, Esther Serr, P. D. Skaar, George M. Sutton, Max C. Thompson, Charles H. Trost, Dale A. Zimmerman.

General information on the status of species in each of the 22 states was compiled mainly from latest editions of books accepted as "official" for those states. Where such publications were not available, ornithological societies cooperated by furnishing the latest checklists indicating breeding species and their present status within those states. Following are these sources: Allan Phillips, Joe Marshall, and Gale Monson, *The Birds of Arizona*; Florence Merriam Bailey, *Birds Recorded from the Santa Rita Mountains in Southern Arizona*; James A. Lane, *A Birder's Guide to Southeastern Arizona*; Herbert Brandt, *Arizona and its Bird Life*; W. J. Baerg, *Birds of Arkansas*; Douglas James and Frances C. James, *The Seasonal Occurrences of Arkansas Birds*; *Arkansas Audubon Society Field List,* 1974; William Leon Dawson, *The Birds of California* (3 vols.); Arnold Small, *The Birds of California*; Edwin R. Pickett, *Birds of Central California*; Robert D. Mallette, *Upland Game of California*; C. F. Yocom and S. W. Harris, *Birds of Northwestern California*; Howard L. Cogswell, *Water Birds of California*; James A. Lane, *A Birder's Guide to Southern California*; Alfred M. Bailey and Robert J. Niedrach, *Birds of Colorado* (2 vols.); Robert J. Niedrach and Robert B. Rockwell, *The Birds of Denver and Mountain Parks*; The Colorado Field Ornithologists in cooperation with the Colorado Division of Wildlife, *Colorado Bird Distribution Latilong Study*; Allegra Collister, *Birds of Rocky Mountain National Park*; Fred

Mallery Packard, *The Birds of Rocky Mountain National Park*; James A. Lane and Harold R. Holt, *A Birder's Guide to Denver and Eastern Colorado*; Thomas D. Burleigh, *Birds of Idaho*; Idaho State University, *Birds of Idaho Field Check List* (emphasis on se. Idaho); Woodward H. Brown, *An Annotated List of the Birds of Iowa*; Frederick W. Kent and Thomas H. Kent, *Birding in Eastern Iowa*; Richard F. Johnston, *The Breeding Birds of Kansas,* and *A Directory to the Birds of Kansas*; Arthur L. Goodrich, Jr., *Birds in Kansas*; George H. Lowery, Jr., *Louisiana Birds* (3rd ed.); Janet C. Green and Robert B. Janssen, *Minnesota Birds*; Thomas S. Roberts, *The Birds of Minnesota* (2 vols.); The Audubon Society of Missouri, *Checklist of Missouri Birds*; P. D. Skaar, *Montana Bird Distribution*; Aretas A. Saunders, *A Distributional List of the Birds of Montana*; F. W. Haecker, R. Allyn Moser, and Jane B. Swenk, *Check-List of the Birds of Nebraska*; William F. Rapp, Jr., Janet L. C. Rapp, Henry E. Baumgarten, and R. Allyn Moser, *Revised Check-list of Nebraska Birds*; Dr. Esther V. Bennett (comp.), "Nebraska Nesting Survey" (from *The Nebraska Bird Review*); Jean M. Linsdale, *The Birds of Nevada* and *A List of the Birds of Nevada*; John P. Hubbard, *Check-List of the Birds of New Mexico*; J. Stokley Ligon, *New Mexico Birds and Where to Find Them*; Florence Merriam Bailey, *Birds of New Mexico*; Dale A. Zimmerman, *Bird-Finding Localities in Southwestern New Mexico and Southeastern Arizona*; Paul E. Stewart, *Breeding Birds of North Dakota*; Norman A. Wood, *A Preliminary Survey of the Bird Life of North Dakota*; Paul A. Johnsgard, *Waterfowl of North Dakota*; George Miksch Sutton, *Oklahoma Birds*; Ira N. Gabrielson and Stanley G. Jewett, *Birds of Oregon*; Gerald A. Bertrand and J. Michael Scott, *Check-List of the Birds of Oregon*; The South Dakota Ornithologists Union (Nathaniel R. Whitney, Jr., Chairman, Byron E. Harrell, ed.), *The Birds of South Dakota, An Annotated Checklist*; Olin Sewall Pettingill, Jr., and Nathaniel R. Whitney, Jr., *Birds of the Black Hills*; William H. Over and Craig S. Thomas, *Birds of South Dakota*; Harry C. Oberholser, *The Bird Life of Texas* (2 vols.); Roland H. Wauer, *Birds of the Big Bend National Park and Vicinity*; Col. L. R. Wolfe, *Check-List of the Birds of Texas*; James A. Lane, *A Birder's Guide to the Rio Grande Valley of Texas*; Roger Tory Peterson, *A Field Guide to the Birds of Texas*; William H. Behle and Michael L. Perry, *Utah Birds*; William H. Behle, *The Bird Life of Great Salt Lake*; Roland H. Wauer and Dennis L. Carter, *Birds of Zion National Park and Vicinity*; C. Lynn Hayward, Clarence Cottam, Angus M. Woodbury, and Herbert H. Frost, *Birds of Utah* (Great Basin Naturalist Memoirs, no. 1); Earl J. Larrison and Klaus G. Sonnenberg, *Washington Birds, Their Location and Identification*; Stanley G. Jewett, Walter P. Taylor, William T. Shaw, John W. Aldrich, *Birds of Washington State*; Warren A. Hall, L. D. LaFave, J. D. Acton (Spokane Audubon Society), *Daily Field*

Card Birds of Eastern Washington; Philip W. Mattocks, Jr., Eugene S. Hunn, Terence R. Wahl, "A Checklist of the Birds of Washington State, with Recent Changes Annotated" (*Western Birds,* vol, 7, no. 1); Dr. Oliver K. Scott (ed.), *Check List—Birds of Wyoming*; Otto McCreary, *Wyoming Bird Life.*

In addition to the state and regional publications listed above, I made extensive use of the files of *The Condor, The Auk, The Wilson Bulletin, The Living Bird, American Birds, Western Birds,* and *Birding.* Many contributors to these publications have been quoted, and I regret that space limitations make it impossible to name them individually. My thanks are nonetheless sincere.

I am greatly in debt to Arthur Cleveland Bent for his 23 volumes of *Life Histories of North American Birds* published by the Smithsonian Institution. Although recent and more advanced research has sometimes disproved statements made in the Bent series, there is no doubt that this monumental work is the foundation for much of our knowledge of avian biology. In addition to Bent, I made reference to the following: American Ornithologists Union, *Check-List of North American Birds,* 5th ed. (and 32nd and 33rd supplements); *A.B.A. Checklist: Birds of Continental United States and Canada*; Anders H. Anderson and Anne Anderson, *The Cactus Wren*; Frank C. Bellrose, *Ducks, Geese & Swans of North America*; Carl E. Bock, *The Ecology and Behavior of the Lewis Woodpecker (Asyndesmus lewis)*; Clait E. Braun and Glenn E. Rogers, *The White-tailed Ptarmigan in Colorado*; John Bull and John Farrand, Jr., *The Audubon Society Field Guide to North American Birds, Eastern Region*; Derek Goodwin, *Crows of the World*; Frank Graham, Jr., *Gulls, A Social History*; Ludlow Griscom and Alexander Sprunt, Jr. (eds.), *The Warblers of North America*; Mary Louise Grossman and John Hamlet, *Birds of Prey of the World*; Robert Bruce Hamilton, *Comparative Behavior of the American Avocet and the Black-necked Stilt (Recurvirostridae)*; Hal H. Harrison, *A Field Guide to Birds' Nests in the United States East of the Mississippi River*; John Hay, *Spirit of Survival, A Natural and Personal History of Terns*; Paul A. Johnsgard, *Waterfowl of North America* and *North American Game Birds of Upland and Shoreline*; Roger M. Latham, *Complete Book of the Wild Turkey*; John P. S. Mackenzie, *Birds in Peril*; Michael H. and Barbara R. MacRoberts, *Social Organization and Behavior of the Acorn Woodpecker in Central and Coastal California*; Thomas P. McElroy, Jr., *The Habitat Guide to Birding*; Charlton Ogburn, *The Adventure of Birds*; Sigurd T. Olson and William H. Marshall, *The Common Loon in Minnesota*; Ralph S. Palmer, *Handbook of North American Birds* (3 vols.); Roger F. Pasquier, *Watching Birds*; Roger Tory Peterson, *A Field Guide to the Birds, A Field Guide to Western Birds,* and *A Field Guide to Mexican Birds*; Chandler S. Robbins, Bertel Bruun, and Herbert S. Zim, *Birds of North America*; Glen C.

Sanderson (ed.), *Management of Migratory Shore and Upland Game Birds in North America*; Alexander F. Skutch, *The Life of the Hummingbird*; Robert Carrington Stein, *The Behavioral, Ecological and Morphological Characteristics of Two Populations of the Alder Flycatcher, Empidonax traillii (Audubon)*; Gardner D. Stout (ed. and sponsor), *The Shorebirds of North America*; Miklos D. F. Udvardy, *The Audubon Society Field Guide to North American Birds, Western Region*; Lewis Wayne Walker, *The Book of Owls*; David A. Weber, *Blue Grouse Ecology*.

Unless otherwise credited, all photographs in this book were taken by the author. Credit for the use of color photographs is given on the legend page opposite the color plates. The author thanks these excellent photographers for their generosity and is grateful to the following for the use of their black-and-white photographs in the text:

Clait E. Braun: Water Pipit habitat

Kenneth M. Giesen: White-tailed Ptarmigan and habitat

Ed N. Harrison: California Condor, Great Horned Owl

George H. Harrison: Western Grebe habitat, Burrowing Owl, Elf Owl habitat, Screech Owl

Ted and Lois Matthews: Broad-billed Hummingbird

Raymond J. Quigley: Rose-throated Becard, Dipper, Spotted Dove, Golden Eagle, Peregrine Falcon, Ring-billed Gull, Anna's Hummingbird, Long-eared Owl, Black Phoebe, Pintail, Lincoln's Sparrow, Cinnamon Teal, Willet (bird)

Ronald K. Quigley: Prairie Falcon, Killdeer (broken-wing ruse)

Ronald A. Ryder: White-necked Raven.

I should like to express my thanks to members of the Houghton Mifflin staff who helped with the production of this Field Guide, but particularly to James Thompson, Natural History Editor, and Lisa Gray Fisher, Field Guide Copy Editor. Both were most cooperative. Lisa Fisher was particularly understanding and helpful with the problems I encountered in the text. I should also like to thank Richard B. McAdoo, Austin Olney, Carol Goldenberg, Stephen Pekich, and Janice Byer for their help and interest. And to Roger Peterson, a special thanks for his kind *Editor's Note*.

Contents

Editor's Note   vii

Preface   ix

About This Book   xvii

Species Descriptions   1

     Arranged in systematic order; 520 species are described, 153 species are illustrated with black-and-white photographs

Glossary   261

Index   265

Black-and-White Plates

     Endangered Species: California Condor and Peregrine Falcon   opp. 35

     Southern Arizona Birds   opp. 121

     Texas (Rio Grande Valley) Birds   opp. 147

     Minnesota Wood Warblers   opp. 199

Color Plates   grouped after 126

     Photographs of nests of 256 species arranged in systematic order

Map of Area Covered by This Book   xxxii

Endpapers: Markings of Eggs (left); Shapes of Eggs (right)

About This Book

FORMAT of this *Field Guide* follows that of its companion volume, *A Field Guide to Birds' Nests East of the Mississippi River* published in 1975. Included are descriptions of range, habitat, nests, and eggs, with miscellaneous notes for 520 species of birds that breed regularly or occasionally in all or some of the 22 states lying entirely or partly (Minnesota and Louisiana) west of the Mississippi River. Precedent for choosing this geographic approach rather than one involving specific biomes such as mountains, forests, swamps, prairies, etc., was established originally in 1951 with the publication of *A Guide to Bird Finding East of the Mississippi* by Olin Sewall Pettingill, Jr. When a guide to eastern nests was accepted enthusiastically by birders, the present companion volume became inevitable. Indeed, during its preparation, the author continually received letters from Westerners asking "When?"

Species Included: In the eastern *Field Guide,* which includes 285 species nesting in 26 states, perhaps the author was more cautious than necessary in eliminating a number of species not definitely established as regular breeders and others considered rarities (Spotted-breasted Oriole, Fulvous Whistling-Duck, Bachman's Warbler, Ivory-billed Woodpecker, a number of primarily western species, especially waterfowl, and others). The present volume treats all species now known to breed in the West, even casually or rarely (Hook-billed Kite, Marbled Murrelet, Buff-collared Nightjar, Berylline and Lucifer Hummingbirds, Skylark, Black-capped Gnatcatcher, Rufous-capped Warbler, and others). Time after time today's rarity has become tomorrow's common nesting bird. Nesting House Finches in eastern U.S. are a notable example. Cattle Egrets are another. Thus, the list included here is as complete as possible at the time of publication.

Order of Species: Species are in the order designated in the American Ornithologists' Union *Check-List of North American Birds* (5th ed., 1957), and in the 32nd Supplement published in April 1973 (*The Auk,* 90: 411–419) and the 33rd Supplement published in October 1976 (*The Auk,* 93: 875–879). No attempt has been made to anticipate changes in the A.O.U. list. Names, both common and scientific, are in compliance with those accepted at this time by the A.O.U. Most guides for the identification of birds, as well as local, state, and regional checklists, are organized in A.O.U. order. The bird watcher has learned to locate species names quickly in these publications, where species are not arranged in alphabetical order. His familiarity with this system makes the use of the nest guide a simple and convenient extension of an everyday habit.

Subspecies: The oriole nesting in California, which was once called Bullock's, is the same species as the one nesting in Pennsylvania, which was always known as Baltimore, and both are now Northern. The Audubon's Warbler in Colorado is the same species as the Myrtle Warbler in Maine, and both are now the Yellow-rumped Warbler. While subspecies are generally ignored here, it must be conceded that old habits are not broken easily. It might be well to remember that "lumping" species is a decision of the scientists and need not necessarily influence the personal inclinations of the "lister." Subspecies have not ceased to exist and knowledge of various races is never so complete that we should ignore further study. Birding in most cases is a hobby, a personal thing. If you care to note the particular races that you have seen or studied, there is no reason not to do so. Generally, the eggs of the races of species are indistinguishable; nests typically follow the same basic pattern, although materials used in construction may vary according to what is available.

Time of Nesting: Exact time of year when each species nests is not given, principally because it is impossible to be accurate. Not only does the nesting time vary from south to north and from sea level to mountaintop, in the range of the same species, but it varies greatly in the same species in the same geographic location. External factors such as rainfall, temperature, water levels, amount of snowfall, and similar phenomena may influence time of nesting from year to year.

Young in the Nest: The subject of nestling birds and fledglings is a complete study in itself, one that might challenge a researcher-photographer to attempt a field guide to baby birds. However, the subject is outside the province of this book. When the eggs have hatched, a new phase in the bird's breeding cycle has been reached.

Courtship: Only when courtship is involved directly with nest building, as in grebes and in some species of herons, has it been mentioned. Like the study of young birds, this is a subject for independent study.

Illustrations: Of the 209 color photographs taken by the author, most were taken with a $3\frac{1}{4} \times 4\frac{1}{4}$ Crown Graphic with a 135 mm Graflex Optar lens, using groundglass focusing and Strobonar flash. In a few exceptions, a Hasselblad camera was employed. Daylight-type Ektachrome sheet film was used in the Graphic; Kodak Ektachrome X in the Hasselblad for the $2\frac{1}{4} \times 2\frac{1}{4}$ transparencies. Since the problem of movement, so vexing in the photography of live birds, is not encountered in taking pictures of nests and eggs, it was possible to expose at a small aperture (generally f/32) to assure the sharp picture so essential in portraying accurately the markings on eggs.

Measurements: Because of the changeover in the United States to the metric system, all statistics are given in duplicate: U.S. first, followed by the same measurement in metric terms, rounded to the first decimal, except for egg measurements, which are exactly as given by the U.S. National Museum in Bent's *Life Histories.* Equivalents are: 25.4 millimeters (mm) or 2.54 centimeters (cm) per inch; 30.48 centimeters or .305 meter (m) per foot; .914 meter per yard; 1.609 kilometers (km) per mile; .4047 hectares (ha) per acre; 39.37 inches or 3.28 feet per meter; .3937 inch per centimeter.

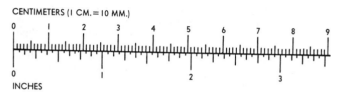

Comparison of millimeter and inch scales.

Bibliography: Space limitations preclude a formal bibliography. Listed in the *Preface* are books and checklists pertaining to the 22 individual states, and other books and periodicals which I used in my work on this guide.

Evolution of Nests: If all birds had the same kind of nest—the same kind of site, same size, same materials, same shape—a guide like this would not be needed. This obviously is not the case, and to learn why nests vary so much, you must first know why birds build nests at all. The necessity arose as birds evolved from cold-blooded (exothermal) creatures into animals that could no longer abandon their eggs to hatch in the heat of their environment. As warm-blooded organisms, they were compelled to supply warmth for their eggs through incubation—transmission of heat from the parent's body. This necessitated the development of protective measures, not only for the exposed eggs, but also for the incubating parent.

Thus nest building became a necessary part of the breeding cycle. It is likely that the first nests were nothing but depressions scraped in the ground. Some may have been in natural cavities among rocks or tree roots, or in hollow trees. Such primitive nests are still used today by many species.

Additional protection may have resulted when the first birds elevated their nests by placing them in vegetation off the ground. They were the first birds to depend entirely upon accumulated materials for holding eggs. Their nests were probably loose platforms of sticks and twigs, the type still built by most herons and related birds.

The ultimate in nest-building evolution is the cupped nest characteristic of many birds, particularly passerines. These vary greatly in adaptation to environment. Although some species, like Robins and grackles, build solid cups of mud and grasses in the forks of trees or on horizontal branches, others, like orioles, vireos, and bushtits, may hang pensile nests on twigs at the ends of branches. Phoebes, Barn and Cliff Swallows plaster their cupped or globular nests to the sides of vertical structures. Bluebirds, wrens, chickadees, Tree and Violet-green Swallows still use cavities as nesting sites and build cupped nests within these cavities. Other cavity-nesting birds like the woodpeckers, some owls, American Kestrels, build no nest of their own within the hollows. Some birds that still nest on the ground have added the protection of cupped or even domed nests like those built by meadowlarks, Water Pipit, Ovenbird, Bachman's Sparrow, Painted Redstart, and Red-faced Warbler. Camouflage of the nest itself has been carried to a high degree by the hummingbirds, gnatcatchers, wood pewees, whose meticulously woven and decorated nests look like part of the structures upon which they are saddled.

Breeding Range

Range here refers only to the *breeding* or *nesting* range of the species solely within the boundaries of the 22 states; many of the species of course also nest elsewhere—east of the Mississippi, in Canada, south of the United States, and even in other parts of the world. The range is adequate to inform the reader where the bird nests in western United States.

The range description in each species account will help in two basic ways. (1) If you find a nest and are trying to identify the owner, the range given will indicate whether the bird you are considering may be expected to nest in the area where your nest is found. For example, you have found a nest in a conifer in Kansas; it seems to fit the description of a Steller's or a Scrub Jay's nest. The range tells you that neither species nests as far east as Kansas. It is probably a Blue Jay's nest. (2) You live in southern Arizona and every fall and winter you see Marsh Hawks coursing over fields hunting prey. You decide you would like to find the nest of this harrier. You already know that it nests on the ground and lays 4–6 pale bluish eggs. The range will tell you that you will waste time looking for it in your part of Arizona. It is a winter resident and typically nests much farther north.

Information under **Breeding Range** is general in scope. The fact that a species nests in South Dakota does not necessarily mean that it breeds in all parts of South Dakota. To narrow the possibilities, consult the *Habitat* section given in the account. South

Dakota is a good example; many species nest in the Black Hills that do not nest in other parts of South Dakota. Biologically and geologically the Black Hills show close affinities to the Rocky Mountains. Thus many Rocky Mountain or western birds reach the eastern limits of their range here (Prairie Falcon, Poor-will, White-throated Swift, Lewis' Woodpecker, Dusky and Western Flycatchers, Violet-green Swallow, Dipper, Canyon Wren, Townsend's Solitaire, MacGillivray's Warbler).

Winter resident birds and birds in migration do not necessarily indicate breeding birds. Some winter birds are also permanent residents—birds that do not migrate but are generally found in the same area the year round; but others, like the Marsh Hawk cited previously, move to different areas when the seasons change. Even permanent resident birds (chickadees, nuthatches, some woodpeckers, Starlings, some hawks and owls, and others) can wander at times in the nonbreeding season, so a Mockingbird might show up at a winter feeding station far north of its normal breeding range.

In some cases the stated breeding range may be unavoidably inaccurate by the time this book is published: many birds continue to extend their breeding range annually. Not only do we have range extensions, but new species continue to enter the United States as nesting birds. In 1977, a Rufous-capped Warbler was discovered with a nest and four eggs in Cave Creek Canyon in the Chiricahuas, Arizona. The nest was found in July and the first sight-record of this species in the United States was established just two months previously. To have this guide as up-to-date as possible at the time of publication, I have leaned heavily on *American Birds,* published by the National Audubon Society, which devotes its entire November issue each year to the nesting season. Information comes from bird watchers everywhere who annually report changes in breeding status of species in their states. This compilation of changes from scattered and often otherwise unobtainable data makes available a review of the current status of nesting birds.

Where it is deemed necessary to define the relative abundance of a species within its range, abbreviations are used after the name of the state involved. Example: N. Dakota (cas.). The abbreviations include: unc. (uncommon); cas. (casual); prob. (probable); poss. (possible); loc. (local); irr. (irregular). Rare is also used.

Habitat

Habitat, as used in the species accounts, refers only to the breeding or nesting habitat of a species within its range in our area and is not concerned with the winter or other nonbreeding habitat of the bird. Even during the breeding season the place where an adult bird is discovered is not necessarily the place where its nest is located. A Common Raven seen visiting a garbage dump at the edge of a small town may be nesting on a ledge of a steep cliff several miles away. Gulls perched on a fishing shack along the ocean may be nesting on an island several miles offshore. A female Ring-necked Duck, feeding with a small flock of waterfowl on an open lake, may have her clutch of eggs hidden in a grassy marsh a mile or more away. A Belted Kingfisher that habitually fishes from the trees bordering a slow-moving stream most likely is nesting in a sandbank some distance away.

In a guide such as this, all the possible habitats that a bird may select cannot be listed, but it is desirable and feasible to describe where a bird is *likely* to place its nest. It is difficult to pinpoint the habitat of some species. One can say definitely that Bank Swallows nest in banks of clay or sand; that American Coots nest in freshwater ponds and marshes; that Piping Plovers nest on sandy beaches; that woodpeckers nest in tree cavities. But where do Starlings nest? And how do you state exactly where one should look for the nest of a House Wren—in a sun-bleached cow skull, in an old boot, a flowerpot, the pocket of a bathrobe, or in a birdbox? Any could be right.

Habitat is closely related to the territory demanded by a breeding bird, and this varies greatly depending upon the requirements of the species. Colonial birds such as pelicans, gulls, terns, many herons, may nest close together. Nests of Cliff Swallows may touch each other. Great Horned Owls may demand a square mile of defended territory and Golden Eagles may claim even more. Certainly the establishment and defense of territory must work to the advantage of the species. Undoubtedly it disperses the population and that prevents overcrowding in favorable habitats. Defense of a territory insures an adequate food supply for the adults and their young, proper shelter, and sufficient nesting material. Defense is always most aggressive nearest the nest.

Nest

While knowledge of the breeding range and habitat of a species is basic to finding and/or identifying the nest, it is also necessary to pinpoint the typical site chosen and to have a detailed description of the nest itself. In the species accounts an order has been followed, depending at times on the amount of information available.

Colony Nesting: Where birds typically nest in colonies, the fact has been noted. The degree to which birds are colonial has been emphasized in such terms as "congested colonies," "loose colonies," "scattered colonies," or "singly." This information will be helpful in that it narrows the search. If a nest is found after the breeding season, the presence of similar nests in the same area would be the only indication of a colony.

Nest Site: The site at which the nest is located is often diagnostic. While some species will choose a variety of sites, many are highly specialized, and this is important in identification. Water Pipits nest on the ground in tundras; Chimney Swifts nest in chimneys, and White-throated Swifts nest in steep cliffs; all woodpeckers nest in tree cavities and so do Prothonotary Warblers; storm-petrels, kingfishers, and Bank Swallows nest in burrows; MacGillivray's Warblers nest in low bushes while Olive, Hermit, and Townsend's Warblers nest high in conifers; orioles build beautiful hanging baskets but Poor-wills build no nest at all.

I have tried to be specific about the site, giving whenever possible such facts as the height above ground, types of vegetation commonly chosen, precise location of a nest when placed in a tree (fork, distance out from trunk, surroundings, and even the appearance of the structure as seen from the ground). This, it is hoped, adds to information concerned with "What nest is this?" or "Where shall I look?"

Nest Description: The nest itself is described in detail. Material used will vary with availability. For some species this has been noted, but readers should bear in mind that Spanish Moss would be no more available to a bird in Montana than spruce needles would be to a bird in the Rio Grande Valley of Texas. The basic structure of the nest of most species is so uniformly true to type that even though the materials used may vary, the format generally does not. An American Robin's nest in Washington or Oregon with mosses built into it still looks very much like a Robin's nest in Arkansas with mud and grasses predominating.

Birds, like people, often display individual traits that defy the rules. There is much truth in the old saying, "Birds never read the books." Consequently, we find a maverick Northern Oriole near a fishing lake that has built its hanging nest of monofilament fishline; a White-necked Raven that used barbed wire for the foundation of its nest on an old piece of farm machinery; a Great Crested Flycatcher that substituted cellophane for snakeskins; a Solitary Vireo near a campsite that constructed the outer part of its basketlike nest from facial tissues and paper napkins. The author found a Western Kingbird's nest in Arizona made largely of mattress felt. In a nearby yard I noticed an old mattress discarded and torn open. A nest found in a cemetery was decorated with plastic flowers. Several nests near a drive-in theatre had dozens of cigarette filtertips in their material. Ticket bits are used near a movie; shavings adjacent to a wood-working shop.

Nest-building Behavior: Most birds build a new nest each year. Some that have more than one brood each season will build a new nest for each brood. Other species, especially birds of prey, will often repair old nests and use them year after year. Confusing at times are species that convert the nests of other species to their own use or even nest simultaneously at the same site. In the former category, the Great Horned Owl using an abandoned hawk's nest comes to mind. A Mountain Bluebird made its home in an old Dipper's nest. Cliff Swallows sometimes convert Bank Swallow burrows to their own use. The author has several times found stick platforms of Mourning Doves placed on top of old Robins' nests. Large nests of magpies, Ospreys, and Golden Eagles sometimes attract tenants to the lower parts of their structures, birds such as American Kestrels, Long-eared Owls, Western Kingbirds, Starlings, and House Sparrows among others, who share occupancy with the large nest builders.

In describing nest construction, I have generally noted the fact that the female builds the nest, or that both sexes build, or that the male accompanies the female as she builds, or, in some species, the male does all the building alone (Wilson's Phalarope, Jacana, and Phainopepla). To find a singing male Lincoln's Sparrow during the nest-building period will not be much help in locating the nest; the female alone is the builder. To follow either a male or female Bushtit or Hutton's Vireo while the nest is being built may be quite rewarding; both actively engage in construction.

Usually a nest is made as inconspicuous as possible—not with you in mind, be assured, but by an instinct that guides the species in hiding the nest from natural enemies that might threaten survival. In some species, this instinct dictates that no nest at all is best. The Common Nighthawk lays its eggs on a gravel roof; the Whip-poor-will places its two eggs on a carpet of leaves on the ground; the killdeer chooses a bed of gravel or cinders to conceal its eggs; all have evolved this way and survived better.

The Brown-headed and Bronzed Cowbirds are different cases. They too build no nest, but the instinct to lay their eggs in other birds' nests has evolved along an entirely different route from that of the killdeers and nighthawks.

Nest Measurements: Where average measurements of a nest are available, they are given in this order: outside diameter, height (distance from top of rim to outside bottom of nest), inside diameter of cup, depth (distance from top of rim to inside bottom of cup). If all these statistics were not found or recorded by the author, those available are given. Where measurements vary from this order, they are self-explanatory.

Eggs

In each species account, information concerning eggs is given generally in the order indicated below by the boldface headings.

Number of Eggs Laid: The total number laid by 1 female in 1 nesting is called a clutch or set. This varies from 1 egg for species like storm-petrels, murres, California Condor (1 egg every 2 years), Black Swift, Band-tailed and Red-billed Pigeons, to as many as 20 for the Bobwhite and almost that many for some of the ducks. The females of a species do not always lay the same number of eggs per clutch. Where variations occur, normal possibilities are given first, followed by the number of eggs commonly laid. For example, a White-necked Raven lays 3–8 eggs, usually 5; a Gray Jay lays 2–5, typically 3–4; Hutton's Vireo lays 4, sometimes 3, rarely 5.

Some species normally have 2 or even more broods each season. It is not unusual for the female of such a species to lay fewer eggs in the second or subsequent clutches than in the first. The American Robin commonly lays 4 eggs in its first set, 3 in the second. Species that normally raise only 1 brood each year will usually make 2 or more attempts to breed successfully if the first nest is destroyed. Like the Common Flicker, the Red-headed Woodpecker is a persistent layer. In 1 experiment, 6 sets of eggs (28 in all) were collected from the same Red-headed Woodpecker cavity in 1 season, after which the pair drilled a new hole in the same tree and raised 4 young successfully (a total of 32 eggs laid).

The same or closely related species nesting in areas widely separated geographically or ecologically may show variations in clutch size. The Horned Lark with its many subspecies is a good example: in the plains, the normal clutch is 2 or 3; more northern and eastern races may lay 4 or 5 eggs in a set; nests on the tundra will normally have 4 or 5. A Screech Owl in Texas typically lays 2 or 3 eggs; the same species in Colorado will commonly lay 4 or even 5. Further examples can be found in the Parulidae (wood warblers). The clutch laid by most members of this large family is 4 eggs, sometimes 5. Three outstanding exceptions are in species that range far north of most Parulidae: Tennessee Warblers commonly lay 6 eggs, sometimes 7; the Cape May Warbler normally lays 6 or 7 eggs; and the Bay-breasted Warbler rarely lays fewer than 5 eggs, sometimes 6 or 7.

One theory advanced to explain this difference is that the southern individual has a more constant or stable food supply for the young and does not "need" to lay large sets of eggs to perpetuate the species. It is also suggested that the more uniform southern climate permits a smaller clutch because the young are subjected to fewer risks from unfavorable weather. Birds nesting on sea islands may have smaller egg clutches than those breeding on the mainland, a concomitant of predator-free conditions and more stable weather, which favor optimal survival rate of young. Species that nest at high altitudes may lay larger clutches because the short summer season leaves very little time to renest for a normal second brood. Tundra-nesting White-tailed Ptarmigans do not normally have 2 broods and do not often attempt a second clutch if the first is destroyed.

It is significant, I think, that owls that nest on the ground, where danger from predation undoubtedly is greater than for owls that nest in trees and in cavities, lay more eggs than their relatives. In our area, this would include the Short-eared Owl (4–9 eggs) and the Burrowing Owl (6–11 eggs). Nesting of the Snowy Owl in the Arctic further confirms the effect of ground-nesting. It commonly lays 7 or 8 eggs, but as many as 13 have been reported. An exception to the hypothesis is the Barn Owl's sets of 5–7 eggs with as many as 11 reported. This species, however, is also vulnerable to predators when it nests in barns, silos, church steeples, and old wells.

It is not uncommon for ducks to lay in each other's nests. The result is often sets of eggs that are abnormally large. A Ruddy Duck typically lays 5–15 eggs with an average clutch of about 8, yet one nest was reported with 80 eggs. Such a nest is referred to as a "dump nest." Clutches of 40 or more eggs have been found in Wood Ducks' nests with as many as 5 hens known to be involved. Four Wood Duck hens are known to have laid in the same nest during 1 day. More than 15 eggs in 1 Wood Duck nest is conceded to indicate a dump nest.

In most species, 1 egg is laid daily until the clutch is complete. Some species lay every other day and occasionally a lapse of several days may occur. Screech Owls usually lay at intervals of 2 or 3 days. A Boreal Owl will lay 3–6 eggs in 8–12 days. Even in species that normally lay daily, a day may be missed during the production of a full set.

Much of the assembled information on clutch sizes comes from old collections in museums. Some egg collectors in the past vied to collect the largest sets of eggs they could find. Small sets, although normal, were not considered desirable, so statistical information on the number of eggs laid by a species may be slanted toward large numbers. A case in point is the Pinyon Jay. In Riverside County, California, I found more complete sets of 3 eggs than I found of any larger numbers. Checking with the Western Foundation of Vertebrate Zoology in Los Angeles, I discovered that in a collection of 45 sets of Pinyon Jay eggs only 3 sets contained 3 eggs; 29 sets had 4 and 13 had 5. I suspect that earlier contributors to this institution had shunned the smaller sets while picking up sets of 4 and 5.

Size of Eggs: Egg sizes are given in millimeters, the standard measurement in oology for many years. Length is given first; the greatest width next. All measurements are average for the species, which means that in the field you may discover eggs both larger and smaller than the sizes given here. The measurements are those published in Bent's *Life Histories of North American Birds* from data recorded in the United States National Museum, Smithsonian Institution, and data taken from other large collections of eggs in public and private repositories.

If you wish to measure eggs, dividers or calipers will be necessary. A millimeter rule would be convenient, although the conversion rule given on p. xix and on the back cover of the book offer assistance. Precision is imperative, especially in measuring small eggs where the differences are slight. Among species included in this guide, the Calliope Hummingbird (av. 12.1 × 8.3 mm) and the Costa's Hummingbird (av. 12.4 × 8.2 mm) lay the smallest eggs; the Trumpeter Swan (av. 110.9 × 72.4 mm) and the California Condor (av. 110.2 × 66.7 mm) lay the largest eggs.

Shape of Eggs: The endpapers have been designed to help you learn the terminology of egg shapes and markings that has been used throughout the *Field Guide*. Egg shapes not only vary from species to species, but they often vary from individual to individual within a species, and may even vary within the same clutch. When this situation may be expected the fact is noted, as with the eggs of Le Conte's Thrasher which are "short- to long-oval, somewhat pointed at smaller end," or the unusually varied eggs of the Black-billed Magpie which are described as "short-oval, spherical, elliptical, or long-oval."

Reasons for variations in egg shapes are not always clear, but probable deductions can be made in many cases. Seabirds that lay a single egg on a precipitous cliff generally lay pyriform eggs (Common Murres). This certainly helps to keep the egg from rolling off of a narrow ledge. An owl that lays its eggs in the comparative security of a tree cavity has no need for such protection, and this is probably why most owl eggs tend to be more or less spherical. A Bobwhite might have a problem successfully incubating 20 round eggs, but the clutch is more manageable when the eggs are decidedly pointed (pyriform) and fit well into a compact area. Most shorebirds lay eggs that are large for the size of the female. They tend to be quite pointed and may be incubated with the pointed ends turned inward, thus using less space. Abnormally small eggs sometimes occur. These tiny yolkless eggs are called "runts." Dwarf eggs are likely to be more nearly spherical than normal eggs. Exceptionally large eggs are not common in wild birds.

Eggshells: The texture of the surface of eggs varies greatly. Most are smooth to the touch but some are granulated and rough, such as the eggs of many raptors. Whatever the texture, all eggshells are perforated with countless minute pores that permit air to reach the growing embryo whose head rests in a breathing pocket at the blunt end. Eggshells may be glossy as in woodpeckers, lusterless as in many of the passerines, or they may be chalky as in grebes and cormorants. Some eggs that are dull when laid may acquire before hatching a slight gloss from contact with the incubating bird's body. When laid, an egg is covered with a glistening film that hardens in the air in about 10 minutes. Shells of most eggs in the nest are partly translucent and appear darker in color than those in museum collections. White eggs, especially those of passerines, when fresh look pink rather than pure white. This condition is caused by the color of the yolk visible through the partly translucent shell.

Egg Colors and Markings: In describing the color and markings of eggs, I have first stated the ground color. The eggs of many widely different species are white (woodpeckers, owls, swifts, Dippers, petrels, kingfishers) but most eggshells are pigmented, and the variation in both ground color and markings is wide. Oologists describe egg hues with a multitude of terms that would require a chart for interpretation: Brussels brown, sayal brown, Prout's brown, hazel, warm sepia, cartridge buff, bister, Saccardo's umber, court gray, greenish glaucous, aniline lilac, Rood's lavender, Quaker drab, Isabella, vinaceous drab, ecru drab, tawny olive, and on and on and on. I decided that the average user of this guide would prefer to have colors stated in more familiar terms even if they lack the nuances of the more elaborate terminology.

Shapes and sizes of markings on eggs are described in 10 general terms that cover well the possible varieties: blotched, spotted, dotted, splashed, scrawled, streaked, marbled, wreathed, capped, and overlaid. Drawings on the endpapers depict these terms, and reference should be made to these illustrations when descriptions are studied. An egg may have one or more of these markings on its shell: the eggs of a Black Vulture as described here are "gray-green, bluish white, or dull white with large blotches or spots of pale chocolate or lavender wreathed or clustered near the large end, overlaid with dark brown blotches or spots"; Common Snipe eggs are "spotted, heavily blotched, scrawled, overlaid with deep brown." In many species the markings tend to be heaviest around the large end, sometimes forming a wreath or cap. During an egg's descent through the oviduct, the large end comes first and often picks up the greater supply of pigment from the cellular walls.

Heaviest pigmentation is generally found in open nests where cryptic colors help protect the eggs from predators and may also protect the embryos from the intense radiation of the sun. White eggs or eggs with little pigment are characteristic of hole-nesting species. Not all cavity-nesting birds lay white eggs, however; chickadees, nuthatches, bluebirds, titmice, and several flycatchers are examples. Since these species also build cupped nests within a cavity, they may still be evolving from a time when they too built nests and laid eggs in the open.

Incubation: The act or process by which a bird applies its body heat to an egg is called incubation. In most species, just before the beginning of incubation the bird develops a brood spot on the ventral surface of its body, a featherless area with an abundant supply of blood vessels that help pass heat from the bird's body to the eggs upon which it sits. Most species develop a single brood patch in the center of the ventral surface, but some species may have 2 or 3 patches. Some alcids, like puffins, razorbills, and Dovekies, have 2 brood spots, one on each side of the body, despite the fact that they generally lay 1 egg.

In researching this phase of breeding behavior, I found more discrepancies and more lack of definite information than for any other subject. In some species there is a dearth of information concerning the part played by the male, female, or both in the incubation process. It is generally true that the female assumes the larger responsibility; but how much the male participates, if at all, is too often a matter of guesswork. The subject is in need of further study in many species.

Length of the incubation period is another subject for which information is often inaccurate or unavailable. To quote accurately the incubation period of any species, one should know first the researcher's definition of "incubation period." Does he mean the time required to hatch a full clutch of eggs, or does he refer to the time necessary to hatch a single egg within a clutch? It seems to me that the most accurate method of determining the incubation period is to mark the last egg laid and then check accurately in days and/or hours the time required for that egg to hatch. In cases in which a bird starts to incubate before the last egg is laid (in some species—Barn Owls for instance—incubation starts with the laying of the first egg) some students calculate the period for the entire clutch, the total number of days the adult spends on the nest incubating. This does not give accurate incubation time for a single egg, and in some species would vary considerably from bird to bird, since all individuals do not start to incubate after laying the same number of eggs. The size of the clutch laid by individual females may also vary, so the time of hatching for a full clutch might be longer or shorter within a species.

Other factors are involved in lengthening or shortening the period of incubation. A very cold wet period may delay hatching for a day or more as compared to incubation during a normal or a favorable warm dry period. The degree of attentiveness (time spent on the nest) of the incubating bird will have some effect on the number of days or hours required to hatch a clutch.

In stating the incubation period for most species, I have given a range of days denoting the shortest to the longest time required to hatch the eggs. Where the period is unknown, I have said so. Where the period is uncertain, I have occasionally given the time as "probable." In some instances where the researchers disagree, I have quoted the periods stated by each.

Notes

There are so many interesting facets in the nesting life of birds that do not fit neatly into any of the above categories that I have used **Notes** as a means of crowding in bits of information that I feel are pertinent. This section could be described accurately as a catchall. Thus it is difficult to summarize here what is included; a bit of everything, I would say. Surprisingly, this section elicited more enthusiastic comments from readers of *A Field Guide to Birds' Nests East of the Mississippi River* than any other part of the species texts.

Sometimes the facts are amplifications of points referred to under **Breeding Range, Habitat, Nest,** and **Eggs;** then again, they may be entirely different from any facts given in those categories. The notes are often concerned with my own experiences, but a multitude of facts were gleaned from the field experiences of others. It is my hope that this conglomeration of tidbits helps to make the book more interesting and informative.

A Field Guide to
Western Birds' Nests

The geographical area covered by this guide embraces
all the contiguous states west of the Mississippi River.
It also includes the portions of Minnesota and Louisiana
that extend east of the Mississippi.

COMMON LOON *Gavia immer*   Pl. 1

Breeding range: Washington, Oregon, cen. Idaho, nw. Montana, nw. Wyoming, n.-cen. N. Dakota, n. and cen. Minnesota.

Habitat: Permanent freshwater lakes, particularly those surrounded by undisturbed wilderness and bordered by marsh vegetation. Edges of small wooded islands are favored.

Nest: As close to water as possible, usually protected from prevailing winds and wave action, but often continuously wet. May be on bare ground, muskrat house, floating bog; commonly is attached to shoreline vegetation. Eggs laid before nest complete. As incubation progresses birds add material, producing a mass of reeds, rushes, grasses, and sticks. Outside diam. 2 ft. (0.6 m) or more; center slightly hollowed.

Eggs: 2, occasionally 1; av. 88.9 x 56.2 mm. Oval to long-oval. Shell thick, somewhat granular; slight gloss. Shades of greenish or brownish olive, usually with scattered spots or blotches of brown or black. Incubation by both sexes, mostly by female; commonly 29 days, starting with 1st egg. 1 brood.

Notes: One bird attends eggs at all times unless frightened by intruder. Incubating bird faces water, slips off nest and dives when disturbed, surfacing many yards away. Same site may be used in succeeding years.

RED-NECKED GREBE *Podiceps grisegena*   Pl. 1

Breeding range: E. Washington (unc.), n. Idaho, nw. Montana, n. and cen. N. Dakota, e. S. Dakota, Minnesota.

Habitat: Freshwater or slightly brackish permanent sloughs, marshes, shallow lakes, and ponds of 10 acres (4 ha) or more.

Nest: Usually solitary, a single pair on 10–30 acres (4–12 ha), but sometimes in loose colonies on larger ponds or lakes. Floating but anchored in or to fringe of emergent plants (rushes, flags, cattails, sedges). A low, flat (slightly above water level), carelessly built mass of rotted vegetation. Male often dives for aquatic plant material and carries it to female at nest. Diam. 2 ft. (0.6 m) with 6-in. (15.2 cm) saucer-shaped depression for eggs.

Eggs: 2–6, usually 3–5; av. 53.7 x 34.5 mm. Intermediate between oval and long-oval. Shell smooth or slightly chalky. Pale blue or buff when fresh; later stained brownish by mud and debris; usually wet. Incubation by both sexes; 22–23 days, starting with 1st egg. 1 brood.

Notes: Very shy; conceal nests well. Often abandon clutches before incubating or before all eggs hatch. Eggs covered with wet plant material when adults not in attendance.

HORNED GREBE *Podiceps auritus*

Breeding range: E. Washington (cas.), s. Oregon (unc.), n. Montana, n. and cen. N. Dakota, ne. S. Dakota (cas.), Nebraska (rare, Cherry Co.), nw. Minnesota.

Habitat: Fresh to slightly brackish permanent and seasonal ponds and lakes where extensive beds of aquatic plants are present; sometimes in shallow river impoundments.

Nest: Nesting pairs widely scattered on larger lakes. Constructed of matted underwater plants (often water milfoil) floating over a bed of submerged vegetation; either in open water or hidden by emergent marsh plants. Both sexes build. Material added during laying and incubation. Outside diam. 10–14 in. (25.4–35.6 cm); inside diam. 4–7 in. (10.2–17.8 cm).

Eggs: 3–6, commonly 4–5; av. 44 x 30 mm. Long-oval to cylindrical. Shell chalky. Dull bluish-white or pale olive-white, often concealed by nest stains and deposits of mud. *Indistinguishable from eggs of Eared or Pied-billed Grebes.* Incubation by both sexes; 24–25 days. 1 brood as far as known.

Notes: Water depths at 11 nest sites in N. Dakota 6–48 in. (15.2–121.9 cm), av. 16 in. (40.6 cm). Most nests were located within 100 ft. (30.5 m) of shore.

EARED GREBE *Podiceps nigricollis* Pl. 1

Breeding range: E. Washington, s. Idaho, Montana south to Mexico (unc. in Arizona); N. Dakota south to Nebraska; w. and cen. Minnesota, nw. Iowa (cas.), se. Texas (rare).

Habitat: Commonly lakes or ponds of 10 acres (4 ha) or more where extensive beds of submerged vegetation are present; also in shallow river impoundments and backwaters.

Nest: In dense colonies, from touching each other to 10 ft. (3.1 m) apart, in more or less open situations. A floating raft of matted aquatic vegetation built by both sexes. Bird shapes nest by sitting on it and piling weeds around itself. Outside diam. 12–14 in. (30.5–35.6 cm); inside diam. 5–6 in. (12.7–15.2 cm); very shallow egg cup at top.

Eggs: 1–6, usually 3–5; av. 43.5 x 30.0 mm. Usually oval. Chalky; bluish or greenish white when first laid, soon becoming permanently stained with buff or brown. *Indistinguishable from eggs of Horned or Pied-billed Grebes.* Both sexes incubate; approximately 3 weeks beginning with 1st egg. 1 brood.

Notes: Author counted 123 nests in compact colony in Lake John Annex, Jackson Co., Colorado in 1977. Nests were in long narrow bed of a water milfoil and were 4–12 ft. (1.2–3.7 m) apart. Eared

LEAST GREBE

Grebes often nest with terns, gulls, coots, but usually exclude other grebes.

LEAST GREBE *Podiceps dominicus* Pl. 1

Breeding range: Permanent resident in s. Texas, principally Rio Grande Valley.

Habitat: Preferably small intermittent ponds and roadside ditches and canals; also lakes and larger inland waterways.

Nest: A cone-shaped mass anchored among emergent plants or in open water $1\frac{1}{2}$ ft. (0.46 m) to over 5 ft. (1.5 m) deep. Both sexes build, using chiefly decayed vegetation and debris. Same nest often used in successive broods. Outside diam. 14–24 in. (35.6–61.0 cm) tapering to 6–8 in. (15.2–20.3 cm), height 4–6 in. (10.2–15.2 cm).

Eggs: 3–6, commonly 4–5; av. 33.9 x 23.4 mm. Elliptical or oval. Shell fairly smooth and chalky. Bluish white or dull buffy white, becoming nest-stained buff or brown. Incubation by both sexes; 21 days beginning with 1st egg. Nest throughout year if weather favorable; probably 2 or 3 broods per year.

Notes: Nest-building continues during incubation; both sexes remodel and make additions daily.

WESTERN GREBE *Aechmophorus occidentalis* Pl. 1

Breeding range: E. Washington, Oregon, California, Idaho, Nevada, ne. Utah, Montana, Wyoming, e. Colorado, N. and S. Dakota, w. Minnesota, s. New Mexico.

Habitat: Usually fairly extensive areas of open fresh or brackish water bordered by tules or other rushes.

Nest: In colonies; hundreds or even thousands on some lakes; closely spaced. A solid mound of dry or sodden vegetation anchored to or built up from surrounding plants or roots in water 2–10 ft. (0.6–3.1 m) deep. Much material brought by male; arranged by female. Outside diam. 18–25 in. (45.7–63.5 cm); inside diam. 7–9 in. (17.8–22.9 cm); height above water 3–5 in. (7.6–12.7 cm).

Eggs: 3–4, sometimes 5–6, rarely 2 or 7; av. 58.0 x 37.5 mm. Elliptical to cylindrical. Shell chalky, lusterless. Dull bluish white or cream; buff or brown from nest stains. Incubation by both sexes; 23 days probably starting with 1st or 2nd egg. Eggs generally wet. 1 brood.

Notes: Western Grebes nest in harmony with other species including gulls, terns, White Pelicans, herons, and other water birds. Klamath Lake and Lake Malheur reservations in California and Oregon were set aside in 1908 to protect grebes from slaughter by plume hunters.

PIED-BILLED GREBE   *Podilymbus podiceps*   Pl. 1

Breeding range: All western states. Permanent resident in many areas.

Habitat: Freshwater ponds, marshes, sloughs, marshy parts of lakes and rivers with open water and aquatic vegetation.

Nest: In water 1 ft. (30.5 cm) or more deep, anchored to or built around or among dead or growing plants. A shallow depression slightly above water level in sodden floating mass of decaying aquatic plant matter. Typically anchored to underwater foundation of rotted plants. Both sexes build. Outside diam. 15 in.

WESTERN GREBE habitat, Bear R. Migratory Bird Refuge, Utah

(38.1 cm); height above water 3¼ in. (8 cm); inside diam. 5⅛ in. (13 cm), depth 2 in. (5.1 cm).

Eggs: 3–10, usually 4–8, laid at irregular intervals; av. 43.4 x 30.0 mm. Elliptical to oval. Shell generally smooth, sometimes slightly chalky; dull or with light luster. Pale blue or green when laid, turning buff or brown during incubation. *Indistinguishable from eggs of Eared or Horned Grebes.* Incubation by both sexes, more often by female; 23 days, beginning with 1st egg. Probably 1 brood.

Notes: Not gregarious but associates and nests with coots, rails, ducks, and other waterbirds. Adults are difficult to catch sight of on nest. Cover eggs with wet debris when not incubating. At 82 N. Dakota nests, water depth ranged 11–37 in. (27.9–94 cm), averaged 25 in. (63.5 cm).

Eggs covered

Eggs uncovered

PIED-BILLED GREBE
Before leaving their nests to feed, grebes conceal their eggs by covering them with surrounding wet vegetation.

FORK-TAILED STORM-PETREL *Oceanodroma furcata*

Breeding range: Washington, Oregon, and California coasts.
Habitat: Islands with soft soil and steep grassy hills.
Nest: In colonies; in burrows dug in turf; rarely, in holes among rocks. End of burrow is enlarged; may have scant lining of grass. Both sexes dig. Burrow up to 8 in. (20.3 cm) deep; entrance diam. at surface 2½–3½ in. (6.4–8.9 cm).
Eggs: 1; av. 33.9 x 25.7 mm. Shell smooth, without gloss. Dull white wreathed with dark dots. Both sexes incubate, exchanging places at night.
Notes: Share islands with other nesting petrels and seabirds.

LEACH'S STORM-PETREL

LEACH'S STORM-PETREL *Oceanodroma leucorhoa* Pl. 1

Breeding range: Pacific coast, Washington to California.
Habitat: Offshore islands in areas of cold water.
Nest: In bank or in open field under stump, rock, or bush. Using feet and bill, male alone digs burrow in 2–3 days. Egg chamber at end of burrow may be lined with grass, rootlets, twigs, bark, dry leaves. Male calls female to burrow; mating occurs inside. Some burrows reused many years. Tunnel usually about 3 ft. (0.9 m) long; may be up to 6 ft. (1.8 m).
Eggs: 1; av. 32.5 x 24.0 mm. Elliptical to nearly oval. Shell smooth, dull. Pure white, cream white; occasionally faintly spotted or wreathed; often nest-stained. Incubation by both sexes; 41–42 days. One bird may incubate 1–5 days without relief. Change at nest made only at night. 1 brood.
Notes: Musky petrel odor strong in nest area. Changing at nest at night often involves hordes of fluttering birds. On ground, seeking or leaving burrow, birds are awkward, stumbling and fluttering. Pairs probably mate for life.

ASHY STORM-PETREL *Oceanodroma homochroa*

Breeding range: Islands off California coast, principally Farallon Is.

Habitat: Rocky shores, piles of loose rock, stone walls, driftwood, turf.
Nest: In natural cavities, particularly under loosely piled rocks; also burrows. Nest cavity rarely lined.
Eggs: 1; av. 29.7 x 22.8 mm. Elliptical to subelliptical. Dull or creamy white; spotless or faintly wreathed with tiny reddish brown dots. Incubation by both sexes; 44 days. Change at nest as complete darkness occurs. 1 brood.
Notes: Musky odor of petrels makes discovery of burrows easy.

BLACK STORM-PETREL *Oceanodroma melania*

Notes: First breeding record in the U.S. was established on the night of July 16, 1976, when a bird was found incubating a single white egg on Sutil I., a tiny islet adjacent to Santa Barbara I., Channel Islands National Monument, California. The nest was in a grotto of a rocky cliff face. A few other Black Storm-Petrels were on the islet at the time.

WHITE PELICAN *Pelecanus erythrorhynchos* Pl. 1

Breeding range: Locally common in Oregon, Nevada, Utah, Montana, Wyoming, Colorado, N. and S. Dakota, sw. Minnesota; Idaho (poss.), California (?); Texas (Gulf Coast). In 1977 about 15 nesting sites known in U.S.
Habitat: Islands in lakes and extensive marshes free of mammalian predators; level, with open areas for takeoff and landing.
Nest: In colonies of a few to several hundred nests as close together as 20 in. (50.8 cm). Vary from bare ground or a slight depression to sizable mounds; usually mounds of debris and earth collected near nest site. Diam. at base about 24 in. (61 cm), may be as big as 36 in. (91.4 cm); height 8–12 in. (20.3–30.5 cm).
Eggs: 1–3, commonly 2; av. 90.0 x 56.5 mm. Oval to long-oval. Shell rough with calcareous deposit which flakes off irregularly. Dull white, smeared and streaked with blood, typically nest-stained and dirty. Both sexes incubate; 30 days, starting with laying of 1st egg. 1 brood.
Notes: An adult attends nest continually during incubation and until young are 3–4 weeks old. Predation by California Gulls may take heavy toll of eggs and chicks, especially when coupled with human disturbance. Future of present colonies threatened by increased demand for water-based recreation.

BROWN PELICAN *Pelecanus occidentalis*

Notes: Build their nests in colonies in trees or on the ground on coastal islands. Normal clutch is 3 eggs; av. 73.0 x 46.5 mm. Oval to long-oval. White; usually blood-stained. Incubation by both sexes; 30 days.

Between 1950 and 1961, the Brown Pelican, official state bird of Louisiana, disappeared entirely as a breeding bird in that state. Flourishing pelican colonies off the Pacific coast of s. California were drastically reduced by 1968. The pelicans ate fish contaminated by DDE. This affected their oviducts, causing thin eggshells which broke. In 1970 the Brown Pelican was placed on the Endangered Species List. Efforts have been made ever since by state and federal agencies and private individuals to implement a recovery plan that would result in viable colonies once again in Louisiana, Texas, and California. A program to stock former colonies in Louisiana with young birds captured at nesting sites in Florida met with mixed success. Since 1972, when the use of DDT was banned in the U.S., nesting results have been more encouraging.

DOUBLE-CRESTED CORMORANT   Pl. 2
Phalacrocorax auritus

Breeding range: Washington, Idaho (unc.), and Montana south to Mexico and Texas; N. Dakota south to Kansas (Barton, Phillips Cos.); Minnesota south to Louisiana. Breeding areas difficult to define; colonies shift because of human disturbance.
Habitat: Coastal islands, cliffs, bays; freshwater lakes, ponds, rivers, sloughs, swamps.
Nest: Mostly in colonies; occasionally solitary; invariably near water. On ground or in trees — nests in a given colony all one or the other. Ground nests built of sticks and coarse material often gathered at water's edge; lining of finer material. Tree nests (up to 36 nests per tree) in dead or live tree at any height and as far out as limb will support; made principally of sticks, with soft lining. Male brings material, female builds, requiring about 4 days. Material added throughout season. Old nests often rebuilt.
Eggs: 3–4, often 5, rarely 2 or 6; northern race (*P. a. auritus*) av. 61.6 x 38.8 mm; southern race (*P. a. floridanus*) av. 58.2 x 36.8; western race (*P. a. albociliatus*) av. 62.9 x 38.8. Long-oval to cylindrical. Shell pale bluish with white chalky surface; soon stained brown. Incubation by both sexes; 25–29 days. 1 brood. Usually 3 years old at 1st breeding.
Notes: Nests filthy with guano, dead fish, dead young.

OLIVACEOUS CORMORANT   *Phalacrocorax olivaceus*

Breeding range: Resident in Louisiana (Cameron Parish), Texas (se. coast). First nesting in New Mexico (Sierra Co., 1972).
Habitat: Freshwater lakes and ponds; coastal islands.
Nest: In colonies. On living or dead trees or bushes, 3–20 ft. (0.9–6.1 m) above water, or on bare ground; of small sticks compactly arranged, lined with twigs or coarse grass.
Eggs: 3–5, commonly 4, similar to other cormorant eggs in shape and texture; av. 53.7 x 33.8 mm.

BRANDT'S CORMORANT
Pl. 2
Phalacrocorax penicillatus

Breeding range: Pacific coast, British Columbia to Baja.
Habitat: Offshore islands, rocks, and coastal headlands.
Nest: In closely crowded colonies on grassy slopes or flat tops of rocky islands; or high on shoulder of rocks. Made of seaweed and sea mosses (sticks not used). Male gathers material, female arranges. Nest may be used more than 1 year. Typical size: outside diam. 22 x 19 in. (55.9 x 48.3 cm), height 5–7 in. (12.7–17.8 cm); inside diam. 10 x 10 in. (25.4 x 25.4 cm), depth 4 in. (10.2 cm).
Eggs: 3–6, typically 4; av. 62.2 x 38.6 mm. *Indistinguishable from eggs of other cormorants of similar size.* Both sexes incubate. 1 brood. Normally eggs never left unattended, especially in presence of chief predator, Western Gull.

PELAGIC CORMORANT *Phalacrocorax pelagicus*

Breeding range: Pacific coast, British Columbia to Baja.
Habitat: Inaccessible precipitous coastal cliffs and islands.
Nest: In colonies on narrow ledges of perpendicular cliffs facing the sea. Mainly of seaweeds, rubbish, grasses, with sticks added occasionally. Both sexes build, one gathering, the other arranging. Nest used in successive seasons and added to until several feet high.
Eggs: 3–5, rarely more; av. 58.3 x 37.4 mm. Elliptical or long-oval. Pale blue or bluish white, often concealed by a thin calcareous deposit; usually nest-stained. Both sexes incubate beginning with 1st egg; 26 days.
Notes: Gregarious but less so than other cormorants. In breeding area, mingles socially with gulls, murres, puffins. Unlike Pelagic, Brandt's, and Double-crested Cormorants, use slopes and level places for rookeries.

ANHINGA *Anhinga anhinga*

Breeding range: Se. Oklahoma (cas.), e. and s. Texas, Arkansas, Louisiana.
Habitat: Sheltered quiet waters of ponds, swamps, freshwater sloughs, marshy lakes, bays, lagoons, tidal streams.
Nest: Mostly in colonies, up to several hundred pairs separated into clusters of 8–12 pairs; often near herons, ibises, and cormorants. In willows, buttonwoods, pond apples, and other aquatic trees and shrubs, 5–20 ft. (1.5–6.1 m) above water or ground. Base of twigs, coarse sticks, dead leaves; lining of leaves or twigs. Male establishes nest site; both sexes build. May use same nest successive years. Outside diam. 18–20 in. (45.7–50.8 cm), height 6 in. (15.2 cm).

Eggs: 4, sometimes 3 or 5; av. 52.5 x 35.0 mm. Oval to long-oval. Shell pale bluish white with chalky coating; becoming glossy and nest-stained during incubation. Incubation by both sexes; 26–29 days, beginning before clutch complete.

GREAT BLUE HERON   *Ardea herodias*   Pl. 2

Breeding range: All western states.

Habitat: Salt- and fresh-water environments, ponds, marshes, streams, bays, rocky ledges, cliffs.

Nest: Generally in colonies, commonly among nests of other herons, in congested communities, often with many nests in one tree. Commonly high in one of a variety of trees; also bushes, rock ledges, sea cliffs, tule rushes, and on the ground. Flimsy to compact platform of large sticks; lined with fine twigs and green leaves. Male brings material to female who places it in nest. Outside diam. 25–40 in. (63.5–101.6 cm).

Eggs: 3–6, usually 4; West Coast (*A. h. hyperonca*) av. 61.3 x 43.4 mm; cen. and w. plains (*A. h. treganzai*) av. 60.1 x 41.9 mm; South (*A. h. wardi*) av. 65.4 x 46.4 mm. Oval to long-oval. Shell smooth or slightly rough. Pale bluish green, unmarked. Incubation by both sexes; 28 days.

Notes: In mixed heronries Great Blue Herons usually nest in highest parts of trees; other herons building below in same trees. 41 Great Blue nests along with nests of 28 Black-crowned Night Herons counted in one giant sycamore in California.

ANHINGA

LITTLE BLUE HERON

GREEN HERON *Butorides striatus* Pl. 2

Breeding range: Washington (cas.), Oregon (unc.), south to Mexico, sw. Utah (rare), Arizona (unc.), e. Colorado (rare), s. New Mexico, N. Dakota (rare); and s. Minnesota south to Mexico and Gulf of Mexico.

Habitat: Great variety: streams, swamps, shorelines (fresh or salt); open marshes, irrigation ditches; woodlands and orchards, often far from water.

Nest: Commonly solitary; occasionally in small colony away from other species (large colonies rare). Site varies from on ground to over 30 ft. (9.2 m) above ground in bush or tree. Flimsy to tightly woven platform of sticks and twigs; may or may not be lined with finer material. Male selects site, starts building. After pairing, male carries material while female builds. Twigs, lining added after laying. Outside diam. 10–12 in. (25.4–30.5 cm); inside diam. 4–5 in. (10.2–12.7 cm).

Eggs: 4–5, 3–9 recorded; av. 38.0 x 29.5 mm. Oval. Shell smooth without gloss. Pale greenish or bluish green, unmarked. Incubation by both sexes; 20 days. Sometimes 2 broods.

Notes: Some nests so shallow and flimsy that eggs can be seen through bottom. In 1975 a Green Heron's nest containing 3 young was discovered in a man-made Wood Duck box on a steel fence post in Ontario.

LITTLE BLUE HERON *Florida caerulea*

Breeding range: N. Dakota (1st nesting recorded in 1976), Kansas (Barton Co.), e. Oklahoma, Texas, Minnesota (unc.), e. Missouri, Arkansas, Louisiana. Also New Mexico (1st nesting recorded in 1975 at Elephant Butte Lake). Range increasing.

11

Habitat: Inland freshwater marshes, coastal bays, saltwater marshes, marine islands.

Nest: In colonies; in homogeneous groups, often near other herons. Placed 8–15 ft. (2.4–4.6 m) above water in low trees and shrubs. Loosely woven platform of twigs and sticks; may or may not be lined with leaves and finer substances. Material gathered by male; female builds in 3–5 days. Outside diam. 16–20 in. (40.6–50.8 cm), height 6–8 in. (15.2–20.3 cm).

Eggs: 3–5, generally 4; av. 44.0 x 33.5 mm. Typically oval. Shell smooth, no gloss. Pale greenish blue, unmarked. *Indistinguishable from eggs of Louisiana Heron or Snowy Egret.* Incubation by both sexes; 22–23 days. 1 brood.

Notes: In a study of 50 nests, 34 had 4 eggs, 9 had 5, 7 had 3.

CATTLE EGRET *Bubulcus ibis*   Pl. 2

Breeding range: Species rapidly extending its range westward; new breeding colonies recorded annually. Presently known to nest in California, N. Dakota (1976), Colorado, Kansas (Barton Co.), Oklahoma, Texas, Minnesota, se. Missouri, Arkansas, and Louisiana. Probably in Oregon, Idaho.

Habitat: Fresh- and salt-water marshes, islands, swamps, ponds.

Nest: Birds highly social. Many nests up to 30 ft. (9.2 m) above ground in willows, elders, buttonwoods, maples, cedars, and other trees. A platform of sticks, twigs, and vines. Pilfering material from other nests common. Male carries material; female builds, taking 3–6 days; roles occasionally reversed. Building continues during incubation. Outside diam. 10–18 in. (25.4–45.7 cm), height 3–9 in. (7.6–22.9 cm).

Eggs: 2–5, commonly 3–4, laid at 2-day intervals; av. 47.5 x 33.7 mm. Oval. Shell smooth, no gloss. Very pale blue or bluish white, unmarked; *paler than eggs of other herons.* Incubation by both sexes; 23–25 days, mean 24. Occasional polygamous matings suspected. 1 brood.

Notes: Nest competition with other herons not significant. In many cases, Snowy Egrets and Louisiana Herons nested successfully within 8 in. (20.3 cm) of Cattle Egret nests.

REDDISH EGRET *Dichromanassa rufescens*

Breeding range: Texas and Louisiana Gulf coasts.

Habitat: In Louisiana, coastal areas near or over salt water; in Texas, dry coastal islands in brushy thickets.

Nest: May be solitary but usually in colonies, often with other species in crowded heronries. Commonly in shrubs or trees. Nest may be flat platform of sticks with little or no lining or an elaborate ground nest of grass with a deep cavity. Building done by both sexes; material added throughout egg-laying.

Eggs: 3–4, occasionally 5; av. 51.0 x 37.6 mm. Oval to long-oval.

Shell smooth, not glossy. Pale bluish green, unmarked. Incubation by both sexes, 3–4 weeks.

GREAT EGRET *Casmerodius albus* Pl. 2

Breeding range: Oregon, California, Arizona, n. Colorado (rare), New Mexico, Kansas (Crowley Co.), e. and cen. Oklahoma, Texas, s. Minnesota, e. and cen. Iowa (unc.), Missouri, e. and s. Arkansas, Louisiana.

Habitat: Swamps, bushy lake borders, ponds, islands; deciduous woods with tall trees; willows, tules; dry islands.

Nest: Solitary or in small to large colonies with other species of herons, cormorants, anhingas. In trees or shrubs usually 10–30 ft. (3.1–9.2 m) above ground. In Texas, in willows, tules; on dry islands in mesquite, huisache, and prickly pear. Generally built of sticks and twigs; may or may not be lined with leaves, moss, finer materials. Larger and more substantial than nests of small herons but *not as bulky as nest of Great Blue Heron.* Diam. approximately 2 ft. (61 cm).

Eggs: 3–4, rarely more; av. 56.5 x 40.5 mm. Long-oval. Shell smooth, little or no gloss. Blue or greenish blue, unmarked. Incubation by both sexes; 23–24 days. 1 brood.

SNOWY EGRET *Egretta thula* Pl. 2

Breeding range: Oregon (Malheur National Wildlife Refuge), s. Idaho, Wyoming (local), Kansas (Barton Co.), e. Oklahoma, se. Missouri, south to Mexico and Gulf of Mexico.

Habitat: Fresh- and salt-water marshes, swamps, willow ponds, islands (wet or dry).

Nest: In colonies, thousands in some heronries, usually with other herons, cormorants, and anhingas. In trees, shrubs, cactus, tules and other bulrushes, above ground or water; occasionally on ground; may be up to 30 ft. (9.2 m) above ground, 5–10 ft. (1.5–3.1 m) typical. Flat, elliptical, loosely woven of slender twigs on foundation of heavy sticks; additional available material often used, including reeds, rushes, dead cane, holly. Building by both sexes, 5–7 days. Male selects territory; both sexes vigorously defend. Outside diam. 1–2 ft. (30.5–61.0 cm).

Eggs: 4–5, sometimes 3, rarely 6; laid about every other day; av. 43.0 x 32.4 mm. Oval. Shell smooth, little or no gloss. Pale greenish blue, unmarked. *Indistinguishable from eggs of Little Blue Heron or Louisiana Heron.* Incubation by both sexes; 18 days, possibly longer. 1 brood.

LOUISIANA HERON *Hydranassa tricolor*

Breeding range: Coastal Louisiana and Texas; also Kansas (Barton Co.).

Habitat: Islands, ponds, sloughs, lakes, bayous, in fresh- or salt-water environments; favors latter.
Nest: Typically in large colonies; sometimes solitary. In mangroves, willows, holly, and other low shrubs and trees; also near ground on barren islands, and in prickly pear cactus, huisache, canes, mesquite (Texas). Low, flat, round or elliptical nest of sticks, twigs; lined with twigs, grasses, weeds.
Eggs: 3–7, commonly 3–4; av. 44.1 x 32.3 mm. Oval to long-oval. Shell smooth, not glossy. Pale greenish blue, unmarked. *Indistinguishable from eggs of Little Blue Heron and Snowy Egret.* Incubation by both sexes; 21 days. 1 brood.

BLACK-CROWNED NIGHT HERON   Pl. 2
Nycticorax nycticorax

Breeding range: All western states; local or uncommon in some.
Habitat: Fresh-, salt-, or brackish-water areas; in shrubs, groves, forests, thickets, reeds, cattails, tall grass.
Nest: In small to very large colonies; close together, usually with other heron species. Nest on ground or above, to 160 ft. (48.8 m) in tall firs or sycamores. Consists of sticks, twigs, reeds with fine lining; varies with availability; very flimsy to substantial. Both sexes build; male most active in gathering material. Building time, 2–5 days. Outside diam. about 2 ft. (61 cm), height to 18 in. (45.7 cm).
Eggs: 3–5, sometimes 1–2, occasionally 6, rarely 7; av. 51.5 x 37.0. Oval to long-oval. Shell smooth, no gloss. Pale blue or greenish blue, unmarked. Similar to Great Egret eggs but slightly smaller. Practically *indistinguishable from eggs of Yellow-crowned Night Heron.* Incubation by both sexes, beginning with 1st egg; 24–26 days. 1 brood.
Notes: Black-crowns often predatory on eggs of other species nesting in same area. Author observed entire colony of Forster's Terns destroyed in Colorado.

YELLOW-CROWNED NIGHT HERON
Nyctanassa violacea

Breeding range: Se. Minnesota and se. Kansas south to Gulf.
Habitat: Bayous, backwaters in swamps and rivers, freshwater ponds, wet or dry islands, forests, isolated groves.
Nest: Usually in small or large colonies. May nest with other herons, but isolated colonies common. Built 1–50 ft. (0.3–15.3 m) above ground or water in variety of trees and shrubs. Nest built of sticks, lined with fine twigs, rootlets, leaves. Both sexes build. Outside diam. about 20 in. (50.8 cm).
Eggs: 3–4, sometimes 5: av. 51.3 x 36.9 mm. Oval, long-oval, or cylindrical. Shell smooth, not glossy. Pale bluish green, un-

YELLOW-CROWNED NIGHT HERON

marked. Practically *indistinguishable from eggs of Black-crowned Night Heron.* Incubation by both sexes.

LEAST BITTERN   *Ixobrychus exilis*   Pl. 3

Breeding range: Oregon, California (unc.), Arizona (unc.), Colorado (rare) and New Mexico; also N. Dakota and Minnesota south to Gulf of Mexico.
Habitat: Mainly freshwater marshes, sedgy bogs; also brackish-water areas; sometimes saltwater marshes.
Nest: Solitary, but high density common in favorable habitat. Generally in cattails, tall grass, dense aquatic vegetation, bushes, woody growth; typically less than 3 ft. (0.9 m) above water or ground. Platform of dead plant material interwoven with living plants. Male probably chooses nest site and does most of building, assisted by female. Outside diam. 5–8 in. (12.7–20.3 cm), height 2–5 in. (5.1–12.7 cm).
Eggs: 3–6, commonly 5; av. 31.0 x 23.5 mm; *smallest heron eggs.* Oval, elliptical, or long-oval. Shell smooth, not glossy. Very pale bluish or greenish, unmarked. Incubation by both sexes, 17–20 days, starting with 1st or 2nd egg. 2 broods; 3 unlikely.
Notes: Adults approach nest by walking through concealing vegetation. When disturbed at nest, bird "freezes," bill pointed skyward, and is well camouflaged.

AMERICAN BITTERN   *Botaurus lentiginosus*   **Pl. 3**

Breeding range: Although it nests in most western states, the American Bittern is rare or uncommon in many areas; possibly absent from Arizona, Louisiana, Arkansas.

Habitat: Freshwater bogs, swamps, wet fields, cattail and bulrush marshes; brackish and saltwater marshes and meadows.

Nest: Mostly solitary, but may be in loose colonies in favorable habitat. On dry ground or on mound 3–8 in. (7.6–20.3 cm) above water or mud among cattails, bulrushes, tall grass; occasionally on a platform in deeper water. A scanty platform or mound of available material: dried cattails, reeds, grasses. Nest becomes more hidden as surrounding green vegetation continues to grow. Female gathers material and builds. Outside diam. 10–16 in. (25.4–40.6 cm).

Eggs: 3–7, generally 4–5, probably laid at irregular intervals; av. 48.6 x 36.6 mm. Oval to long-oval. Shell smooth, slightly glossy. Buffy brown to olive-buff, unmarked. Incubation by female, beginning with 1st egg; 24–28 days.

Notes: Species may be polygynous. When approached at nest, female sits motionless, neck and bill pointed upward; camouflage with surroundings is effective. Author observed nest with 5 eggs in Colorado marsh parasitized by 1 egg of Redhead.

GLOSSY IBIS   *Plegadis falcinellus*

Notes: Uncommon permanent resident in Louisiana. First nesting in Arkansas recorded in 1965 when 3 nests were found in Mississippi Co. For details of breeding biology see *A Field Guide to Birds' Nests East of the Mississippi River*.

AMERICAN BITTERN

WHITE-FACED IBIS *Plegadis chihi*

Breeding range: Oregon (Malheur National Wildlife Refuge), California, Nevada, e. Idaho, n. Utah, Montana (Bowdoin National Wildlife Refuge), cen. Wyoming, Colorado, Kansas (Barton Co., rare), Texas and Louisiana Gulf coasts.
Habitat: Freshwater marshes and sloughs, uncommon in salt marshes.
Nest: Small colonies often associated with herons and egrets. In cattails, tules and other rushes, reeds, bushes, or small trees; usually over water but sometimes on the ground. Well-made platform of dead rushes, tules, twigs; well lined with fine pieces of rushes and grasses.
Eggs: 2–7, commonly 3–4; av. 51.5 x 36.0 mm. Oval to long-oval. Shell smooth or finely pitted with little or no gloss. Deep greenish blue or bluish green, unmarked; *much darker than heron eggs.* Incubation by both sexes; 21–22 days. 1 brood.
Notes: In Texas and Louisiana nesting populations of this once abundant bird have been greatly reduced by the use of pesticides and herbicides by rice farmers.

WHITE IBIS *Eudocimus albus*

Breeding range: Coastal Louisiana and Texas.
Habitat: Fresh- and salt-water marshes, coastal bays, swamps.
Nest: In colonies. In trees, bushes, vines; sometimes touch each other; often in close association with herons, cormorants, anhingas. Well built of dead sticks, live twigs, and leaves broken from nearby vegetation, Spanish Moss (where available); deeply cupped. Material added throughout nesting period. Nest size varies; outside diam. 8–24 in. (20.3–61.0 cm).
Eggs: 2–5, typically 3–4; av. 57.6 x 38.3. Oval to long-oval. Shell smooth or finely granulated. Pale buff, bluish or greenish white, from almost immaculate to heavily spotted and blotched or splashed with shades of brown. Incubation by both sexes; 21–23 days; begins when clutch complete.
Notes: Colony sites often deserted after one or more years.

ROSEATE SPOONBILL *Ajaia ajaja*

Breeding range: Texas Gulf Coast and Louisiana (resident in Cameron and Vermilion Parishes).
Habitat: In Texas on dry coastal islands and spoil banks along Intercoastal Waterway; in Louisiana in marshy areas of willow and buttonwood.
Nest: In colonies, isolated in small groups or joining large colonies of cormorants, anhingas, ibises, and herons. In trees, typically 6–15 ft. (1.8–4.6 m) above water. Somewhat bulky but well built of coarse sticks and lined with twigs and green and dry leaves; deeply hollowed. Both sexes build.

Eggs: 3, often 4, sometimes 2, rarely 5; not always laid on successive days; av. 65.0 x 43.9 mm. Oval to long-oval. Thick shell, roughly granulated, no gloss. Dirty white with evenly distributed spots or blotches of various shades of brown. Incubation by both sexes; about 23–24 days beginning when clutch is complete. Probably 1 brood.

TRUMPETER SWAN *Olor buccinator*

Breeding range: E. Idaho (Fremont Co.), sw. Montana (Red Rocks Lake National Wildlife Refuge), nw. Wyoming (Yellowstone National Park); reintroductions attempted in Washington, Oregon, Nevada, S. Dakota, and Minnesota.

Habitat: Lakes, ponds with cattails, rushes, and submerged aquatic vegetation; also sloughs and open marshes.

Nest: In Red Rocks Lake, solitary in territory of 57–480 acres (23.1–194.3 ha). Elevated above water, often on nest of preceding year or on muskrat house with a cleared moat surrounding it. Available materials used: rootstalks, sedges, bulrushes, cattails. Male brings clumps of marsh plants while female arranges. Outside diam. 6–12 ft. (1.8–3.7 m), av. height 18 in. (45.7 cm); inside diam. 10–16 in. (25.4–40.6 cm).

Eggs: 3–9, commonly 4–6, laid every other day; av. 110.9 x 72.4 mm (based on 109 eggs at Red Rocks Refuge). Oval to long-oval. Shell rough or granulated, more or less pitted. Creamy white or dull white, becoming nest-stained. Both parents in attendance at nest but only female incubates; 33–37 days.

Notes: Trumpeters are monogamous and have strong pair bonds. May remate following season after loss of mate. In 1978, the South Dakota Department of Game, Fish, and Parks reported continuing success with the flock of Trumpeter Swans it established artificially in the early 1960s in the LaCreek National Wildlife Refuge area by transplanting 17 Swans from the Red Rocks Lake Refuge. The new flocks had grown to 191 Swans, and some were nesting as far as 200 miles from the original release site.

CANADA GOOSE *Branta canadensis*   Pl. 3

Breeding range: Washington to Minnesota, south to Nevada, Utah, n. New Mexico, S. Dakota and Missouri; also Kansas (Barton, Crowley, Phillips Cos.), and Louisiana (interior).

Habitat: Great diversity: marshes, dikes, ditch banks, islands, cliffs, muskeg, tundra, man-made platforms.

Nest: Usually on ground near water, often on a low stump, mound, muskrat house; in bulrushes, reeds, cattails. Typically a depression lined with sticks, cattails, reeds, grasses, gathered nearby by female; lined progressively with soft gray down plucked from breast after laying is initiated. Outside diam. 15–37 in. (38.1–94.0 cm); inside diam. 6–13 in. (15.2–33.0 cm), depth $3\frac{1}{2}$–$4\frac{1}{2}$ in. (8.9–11.4 cm).

Eggs: 4–7, commonly 5–6; av. 85.7 x 58.2 mm. Oval to long-oval. Shell smooth or slightly rough, no gloss. Creamy white or dirty white, unmarked when laid, becoming nest-stained. Male stands guard while female incubates; 28 days. 1 brood.

Notes: Canada Geese mate for life. To avoid detection on nest, goose lies flat and motionless with neck outstretched. Geese in Missouri accepted as nesting sites washtubs placed on posts and dead trees at heights of 1–20 ft. (0.3–6.1 m) above water. Over a 3-year period, 51 female geese chose tub sites 79 percent of the time, ground sites 21 percent. Almost 90 percent of 11,786 nests in 34 studies had clutches of 4–7.

BLACK-BELLIED WHISTLING-DUCK (TREE DUCK)
Dendrocygna autumnalis   **opp. p. 147**

Breeding range: Extreme s. Texas. First nesting reported near Phoenix, Arizona, in 1969.

Habitat: Shallow lagoons with floating vegetation and areas of exposed mud; usually a thicket composed of characteristic trees and shrubs near or bordering a freshwater lake or pond with nest trees along border or in openings.

Nest: Preferably in tree cavities; also on ground and in nest boxes. Little or no material added to cavity; most ground nests composed of dead grasses woven into shallow bowls. Trees chosen include live oak, ebony, willow, and hackberry. Av. nest hole opening measures 7 x 12½ in. (17.8 x 31.8 cm); entrances average 8⅔ ft. (2.7 m) above water or ground. Cavities average 23 in. (58.4 cm) in depth.

Eggs: 12–16, laid 1 per day; av. 52.3 x 38.3 mm. Oval or short-oval. Shell smooth and typically not glossy. White or creamy white, often with nest stains. Incubation by both sexes; 25–30 days. Some evidence that 2 broods possible.

Notes: Incubation by male, uncommon in waterfowl, is typical of whistling-ducks. E. G. Bolen found nests in such odd sites as a chimney, a cotton gin exhaust pipe, and a pigeon loft.

FULVOUS WHISTLING-DUCK (TREE DUCK)
Dendrocygna bicolor

Breeding range: E. coastal Texas, s.-cen. and sw. Louisiana; 2 small and casual breeding colonies in California in Fresno Co. and near Salton Sea. Also a Kansas record (see **Notes**).

Habitat: Principally extensive areas of rice fields in Texas and Louisiana; freshwater marshes in California.

Nest: On levees and dikes; also on rafts a few inches or more above water in flooded fields. Constructed of surrounding vegetation, principally rice straw. No down added to the grass-and-weed-lined nest bowls.

Eggs: 10–16, commonly 12–13, laid 1 per day; av. 53.4 x 40.7 mm. Short-oval to oval. Usually smooth and without gloss. White or buffy white, stained with shades of buff. Both sexes incubate; 24–26 days.

Notes: These ducks are careless about laying in each other's nests, using "dump nests" into which large numbers of eggs are laid by more than one female and forgotten. In California, as many as 62 eggs have been found in one nest; 23 in Louisiana. Eggs of this duck have been found in nests of Ruddy Ducks and Redheads. In Elkhart, Kansas, in 1971, a Fulvous Whistling-Duck nested successfully in a children's tree house.

MALLARD *Anas platyrhynchos* Pl. 3

Breeding range: All western states.

Habitat: Principally shallow freshwater potholes, marshes, ponds, sloughs, lakes, bogs; also in upland meadows, hayfields, pastures, forest clearings.

Nest: Usually within $\frac{1}{2}$ mile (0.8 km) of water, sometimes as far away as $1\frac{1}{2}$ miles (2.4 km). Well concealed in dense vegetation, preferably about 2 ft. (61 cm) high; in depression in ground, built up with cattails, reeds, grasses, and other surrounding vegetation. Down added sparingly until just before completion of clutch when female plucks down from her breast to form ring around eggs. When absent, hen uses down to cover eggs. Av. size of 4 nests: outside diam. $11\frac{1}{4}$ in. (28.5 cm); inside diam. $6\frac{1}{8}$ in. (15.5 cm), depth 4 in. (10.2 cm).

Eggs: 6–15, commonly 8–9; laid 1 a day; av. 57.8 x 41.6 mm. Long-oval. Shell smooth, very little luster. Light greenish buff to light grayish buff or nearly white, unmarked. Eggs *almost indistinguishable from eggs of Common Pintail and Northern Shoveler* but average larger than eggs of either species. Incubation by female alone; 26–30 days, av. 28. 1 brood.

Notes: Mallards often seek unusual nesting sites: on limbs or in hollows in trees, old magpie nests, rain gutter on roof of 4-story building, in vines at top of stone wall, in box on barn roof, in accumulated leaves at bottom of window well below ground level, in artificial cone-shaped baskets lined with grass and erected on pipes in Iowa marsh (33 percent used).

MEXICAN DUCK *Anas diazi*

Breeding range: Se. Arizona (loc.), Rio Grande Valley from El Paso, Texas (prob.) to Albuquerque, New Mexico.

Habitat: Meadows and marshes of grass, sedges, and rushes.

Nest: Well hidden on the ground close to water. Built of grasses, lined with down. Very few nests have been observed.

Eggs: 4–9; av. 56.8 x 41.2 mm. White with greenish tinge.

Notes: In 1960, New Mexico Department of Fish and Game began to raise Mexican Ducks in captivity for release in the wild. By

1975, because of this program, the population in Arizona was estimated at 95; in New Mexico, 200–300; in Texas, 100–150. Future still in doubt because constantly expanding agriculture encroaches on habitat. Some ornithologists believe Mexican Duck should be reclassified as a subspecies of Mallard.

MOTTLED DUCK *Anas fulvigula*

Breeding range: Coastal Louisiana and Texas.
Habitat: Salt or brackish meadows at edge of coastal marshes; prairie meadows, fallow rice fields, freshwater marshes.
Nest: On or slightly above ground (often in cordgrass) well concealed with overhead cover of grasses or bushes. Built of weeds, grasses, and leaves; rim of nest and lining of egg cavity of brown down from female's breast.
Eggs: 8–13, av. 10, laid 1 a day; av. 54.9 x 40.5 mm. Oval to long-oval. Shell smooth, sometimes slightly glossy. Creamy white, greenish white, occasionally pale tan. Incubation by female; 25–27 days, av. 26 days. 1 brood.
Notes: Deserts nest readily if disturbed.

BLACK DUCK *Anas rubripes*

Notes: This eastern species is a rare breeder west of the Mississippi R. Nesting records are established in N. Dakota and Minnesota, primarily in northeast (Koochiching and Itasca Cos.). For details of breeding biology see *A Field Guide to Birds' Nests East of the Mississippi River.*

MOTTLED DUCK

GADWALL *Anas strepera*   **Pl. 3**

Breeding range: Washington to Minnesota, south to Mexico, nw.
Nebraska (Sandhills) and n. Iowa (cas.).
Habitat: Islands are favored; marsh dikes, fields, meadows. Less
likely than most other duck nests to be over water.
Nest: Tall, dense vegetation preferred. Built of reeds, grasses,
stems, roots gathered at site; building continues during laying
period; down from female's breast added continually even during
incubation.
Eggs: 7–13, usually 10–12, laid 1 a day; av. 55.3 x 39.7 mm.
Nearly oval. Shell dull creamy white, unmarked; *indistinguishable from eggs of American Wigeon.* Incubation by female; 24–27
days.
Notes: Down feathers in Gadwall's nest are somewhat darker and
larger than in American Wigeon's nest. Redheads, Mallards,
Lesser Scaup, and Common Pintails have deposited eggs in Gadwall nests. A study of 660 Utah nests showed 3 cover types preferred: Hardstem Bulrush (*Scirpus acutus*), brushy willows, and
various forbs. At 381 California nests, nettle highly preferred.
Gadwall excels all other species of dabbling ducks in nest success
(67.5 percent in 2173 nestings).

PINTAIL *Anas acuta*

Breeding range: Washington east to w. Minnesota, south to cen.
California, n. Arizona, n. Texas; casual breeder in n. Oklahoma, n.
Iowa, Missouri, Arkansas, Louisiana.
Habitat: Stubble fields, prairies, hayfields, planted croplands,
weedy field borders, open grasslands with brushy thickets and
adjacent sloughs or ponds. More than most other ducks, Pintails
nest in open areas where vegetation is low or sparse.

PINTAIL

Nest: Sometimes poorly concealed; often far from water. In depression in ground in dry situation, either natural or dug by female about four days before 1st egg laid. Of leaves, sticks, dead grasses, intermingled with down. Outside diam. $7\frac{1}{2}$–14 in. (19.1–35.6 cm), height 3–7 in. (7.6–17.8 cm); inside diam. 7–$8\frac{1}{2}$ in. (17.8–21.6 cm); scrape depth $2\frac{3}{4}$–6 in. (7.0–15.2 cm).

Eggs: 6–12, usually less than 10, laid 1 a day; av. 54.9 x 38.2 mm. Long-oval. Pale olive-green to pale olive-buff. *Almost indistinguishable from eggs of Mallard and Northern Shoveler;* average smaller than eggs of former and larger than latter. Incubation by female; 22–23 days. 1 brood.

Notes: Nests often destroyed by farming operations, particularly in stubble fields, a favorite nesting site. Clutch size averages less than that of other surface-feeding ducks.

GREEN-WINGED TEAL *Anas crecca* Pl. 3

Breeding range: Washington east to Minnesota, south to n. Utah, nw. New Mexico (cas.), nw. Nebraska (Sandhills), Iowa (cas.); rare in Arizona, Kansas (Barton Co.).

Habitat: Islands, borders of freshwater lakes, ponds, and sloughs; mostly upland.

Nest: In dense stands of grass, weeds, and brush; often well concealed by tall grass at base of shrubs or willows. Nest well made in a hollow deeply lined with soft grasses, forbs, twigs, leaves; lined with dark brown down from female's breast. More down added during incubation; used to cover eggs during female's absence. For nest shown on Pl. 3: outside diam. $6\frac{2}{3}$ in. (17 cm), height $1\frac{7}{8}$ in. (4.8 cm).

Eggs: 6–18, commonly 10–12; av. 45.8 x 34.2 mm. Oval or long-oval. Shell smooth with slight gloss. Dull white, cream-white, or pale olive-buff. *Indistinguishable from eggs of other teal.* Incubation by female; 20–23 days, commonly 21. Drakes nearly always abandon mates before incubation begins.

Notes: In approaching nest, hen customarily lands 10–15 ft. (3.1–4.6 m) away and walks to it; but when leaving, flies directly from nest after covering eggs with down.

BLUE-WINGED TEAL *Anas discors*

Breeding range: E. Washington and Oregon, ne. California east to Minnesota and south to Utah, n. New Mexico, Texas, Louisiana. Casual in Arizona, Oklahoma, Missouri, Arkansas.

Habitat: Grasslands, hayfields, sedge meadows, borders of freshwater sloughs, marshes, lakeshores. Midwest nests often in bluegrass, buckbrush, alfalfa, sedge.

Nest: Shallow bowl on dry ground in cover 8–24 in. (20.3–61.0 cm) high; lined with dry vegetation. Down added after 4 or more eggs laid. Surrounding cover usually arched over nest, providing excel-

lent concealment. Av. size of 186 nests: outside diam. 7⅔ in. (19.6 cm); inside diam. 5⅓ in. (13.5 cm), depth 2¼ in. (5.6 cm).
Eggs: 6–15, commonly 10–12, laid 1 a day, av. 46.6 x 33.4 mm. Oval to long-oval. Shell smooth with slight gloss. Dull white, light cream, or pale olive-white; unmarked. *Indistinguishable from eggs of other teal.* Incubation by female; about 24 days.
Notes: Female Blue-winged and female Cinnamon are difficult to distinguish, but, if flushed female joins male, problem is solved.

CINNAMON TEAL   *Anas cyanoptera*   Pl. 3

Breeding range: Washington, Montana, south to Mexico; also Kansas (Barton Co.) and Oklahoma (rare), w. Texas.
Habitat: Marshes, sloughs, wet or dry grassy meadows.
Nest: Dense cover 12–15 in. (30.5–38.1 cm) high is more important for nest site than the species of plants. Dense growth of dead salt grass often chosen. Hollow may be dug; lined with small bits of dead grasses and other vegetation. Down is added as clutch nears completion and during early incubation. Outside diam. 6½– 9½ in. (16.5–24.1 cm); inside diam. 4½–5½ in. (11.4–14.0 cm), depth 2½–3½ in. (6.4–8.9 cm).
Eggs: 4–16, typically 9–12, usually 1 a day; av. 47.5 x 34.5 mm. Oval or long-oval. Shell smooth, slightly glossy. Pale pinkish-buff to almost white. *Indistinguishable from eggs of other teal.* Incubation by female; 21–25 days.
Notes: Identification of female Cinnamon and female Blue-winged Teal difficult but pair bond in former is maintained throughout most of incubation; thus, flushed female may be known by male that joins her. Redheads commonly parasitize Cinnamon nests; eggs of Mallard and Ruddy also found in Cinnamon's nests. Half of 524 nests found in Utah were in Spiked Salt Grass (*Distichlis spicata*); 23 percent in Hardstem Bulrush (*Scirpus acutus*).

AMERICAN WIGEON (BALDPATE)   *Anas americana*

Breeding range: Cen. and e. Washington east to nw. Minnesota, south through e. Oregon, ne. California, n. Nevada, n. Utah, n. Colorado, nw. Nebraska.
Habitat: Islands in lakes; upland sites of grass, weeds, brush; sedge meadows.
Nest: In dry places, often at considerable distance from water, in a hollow, well lined with bits of dry grasses, plant stems, and a large amount of light gray down which increases in quantity as incubation advances.
Eggs: 6–12, commonly 9–11; av. 53.9 x 38.3 mm. Long-oval. Shell smooth and somewhat glossy. Deep cream to nearly white; unmarked. *Indistinguishable from eggs of Gadwall.* Incubation by female, 23–24 days. 1 brood.

RING-BILLED GULL   CINNAMON TEAL
Nesting side by side in California

Notes: Pair bond of short duration. In an Idaho study, 60 percent of the males deserted their mates during 1st week of incubation and remainder during 2nd week. Wigeon is late breeder; very few eggs laid before 1st week of June.

NORTHERN SHOVELER *Anas clypeata*   **Pl. 3**

Breeding range: Washington east to w. Minnesota, south to e. Oregon, cen. and ne. California, nw. Utah, n. Colorado, Nebraska, nw. Iowa, Kansas; casual in Oklahoma, Texas.

Habitat: Shallow prairie marshes with abundant aquatic vegetation and surrounding dry meadows; lakes with open rather than wooded shores; islands.

Nest: In grass around boggy edges of sloughs and ponds. Short grasses often preferred to tall grasses; when short grass not available, hayfields, meadows, bulrushes, and, rarely, salt grasses accepted. Slight hollow in ground; lined with dead grasses and forbs. As incubation advances, quantity of down increases. For nest on Pl. 3: outside diam. $8\frac{2}{3}$ in. (22.1 cm), height $3\frac{2}{3}$ in. (9.4 cm); inside diam. $5\frac{1}{2}$ in. (14 cm).

Eggs: 6–14, usually 10–12, laid 1 a day; av. 52.2 x 37.0 mm. Oval. Shell thin, smooth, very little gloss. Pale olive-buff to pale greenish gray. *Eggs almost indistinguishable from eggs of Mallard and Common Pintail;* average smaller than either. Incubation by female; probably 23–25 days. 1 brood.

Notes: In Montana study, over half of 132 nests in short grasses, 23 percent in tall grasses, and 13 percent in thistles. In Utah, salt grass provided cover for 24 of 37 nests. Upland nesters typically prefer grasses usually under 12 in. (30.5 cm) high and almost never more than 24 in. (61 cm).

WOOD DUCK *Aix sponsa*   Pl. 4

Breeding range: Washington, w. Oregon, n. and cen. California, n. Idaho, w. Montana, cen. Colorado (rare); also cen. and e. N. Dakota and Minnesota south to e. Texas and Louisiana.

Habitat: Slow-moving rivers, bottomland sloughs, and ponds, especially where large trees offer usable cavities.

Nest: In tree cavities 2–65 ft. (0.6–19.8 m) above ground, 30 ft. (9.2 m) or more preferred. Accumulated chips of wood and mouse-gray down from female's breast line cavities. Wood and metal nest-boxes erected especially for Wood Ducks have been highly successful; abandoned nest cavities of Pileated Woodpeckers occasionally used.

Eggs: 10–15, sometimes 6–8; laid 1 a day; av. 51.1 x 38.8 mm. Clutches of 40 or more have been found, but nests with over 15 eggs conceded to be dump nests with more than 1 female laying. Oval. Shell smooth, somewhat glossy. Creamy white, dull white, or pale buff; unmarked. Incubation by female, 28–31 days. 1 brood; 2 have been reported.

Notes: 4 Wood Duck hens known to have laid in same nest during 1 day. Involvement of 5 hens at 1 nest reported. Rarely, 2 females have been found side by side incubating. In some dump nests eggs are never incubated by any of hens involved. In these, nest material includes no down.

REDHEAD *Aythya americana*   Pl. 4

Breeding range: Washington to Minnesota, south to Mexico, Texas, nw. Nebraska, n. Iowa (unc.), Kansas (prob.).

Habitat: Emergent vegetation of large marshes and potholes of prairies and parklands; large sloughs with deep water surrounded by extensive areas of cattails, bulrushes, reeds.

Nest: Usually over standing water in emergent vegetation, sometimes on islands or other dry areas. Heavy, deep basket of rushes or cattails supported by growing plants, resting on matted dead stems; lined with bits of dry cattails mixed with much down. Down *whiter* than that of Canvasback.

Eggs: Difficult to determine normal clutch size because many hens lay in nests of other Redheads or other species. Normally 9–14, laid 1 a day; av. 61.2 x 43.4 mm. Oval to long-oval. Shell smooth and glossy. Pale olive-buff to pale cream-buff. *Similar to eggs of Mallard but larger and more glossy.* Incubation by female; av. 24 days. 1 brood.

Notes: Redheads parasitize Canvasback nests more than any others. In the Bear R. marshes, Utah, in 1 year Redheads laid eggs in 70 percent of Mallard nests, 79 percent of Cinnamon Teal nests. Redheads strongly prefer Hardstem Bulrush beds for nesting; cattails 2nd choice; sedges 3rd.

RING-NECKED DUCK *Aythya collaris*

Breeding range: Isolated, limited, and local breeding in ne. Washington, s. Oregon, ne. California, Idaho, Montana, nw. Wyoming, Nevada, n. Colorado (rare), e. and cen. N. Dakota, S. Dakota, Nebraska.

Habitat: Sedge-meadow marshes and bogs, shallow freshwater marshes, sweetgale bogs. Cover type for 411 nests: sedge, sweetgale, leatherleaf.

Nest: In dry or semi-dry situations close to open water; rarely over water. Nest building accompanies rather than precedes egg laying. No scrape is made and no bowl is formed until 3rd or 4th egg is laid. Down is added to platform of nesting material.

Eggs: 6-14, av. 9, in 423 completed clutches; laid 1 a day; av. 57.5 x 39.8 mm. Oval to long-oval. Shell smooth, slightly glossy. Olive-gray, olive-brown, light buffy brown, creamy buff; much variation in color, but nearly always constant in given clutch. *Indistinguishable from eggs of Lesser Scaup.* Incubation by female, starting with laying of last egg; 25-29 days, av. 26. 1 brood.

Notes: In Minnesota Ring-necked ranks 3rd, behind Blue-winged Teal and Mallard, in number of breeding birds in state. Males remain with mates until 4th week of incubation, sometimes until hatching.

CANVASBACK *Aythya valisineria*   Pl. 4

Breeding range: Ne. Washington, se. Oregon, ne. California, nw. Nevada, s. Idaho, n. Montana, nw. Wyoming, cen. Colorado (unc.), N. Dakota, S. Dakota, Nebraska (Sandhills).

Habitat: Shallow prairie marshes, ponds, sloughs, potholes, surrounded by cattails, Hardstem Bulrush (*Scirpus acutus*), and other emergent vegetation with enough open water for easy take-offs and landings; little if any wooded vegetation around shoreline.

Nest: Usually over water 6-24 in. (15.2-61.0 cm) deep. Nest bulky; constructed by female using previous year's growth of plant material gathered at site; sometimes on muskrat house, seldom on dry ground. Resembles Redhead nest in size and shape but nest down differs, being *pearly gray.*

Eggs: Normally 7-12, often increased by addition of several eggs of other species, especially Redhead; laid 1 a day; av. 62.2 x 43.7 mm. Oval to long-oval. Shell smooth with slight gloss. Grayish olive or greenish drab. Incubation by female beginning with laying of last 2 or 3 eggs; 24-29, av. 25 days. Males desert hens as soon as clutch complete.

Notes: When Redheads lay in Canvasback nests, host clutches are reduced in size due presumably to depressing effect upon ovulation. Desertion appears to be far greater cause of nest loss in Canvasbacks than in most other ducks. Important reasons for desertion are flooding and intrusion by parasitic Redheads or other Canvasbacks. Nest parasitism caused 64 percent of 42 nest failures at Malheur Lake, Oregon.

LESSER SCAUP *Aythya affinis*   Pl. 4

Breeding range: Washington to nw. Minnesota, south to n. California, n. Utah, ne. Colorado, Nebraska (Sandhills), ne. Iowa; also Arizona (White Mts.).
Habitat: Upland areas adjacent to lakes, sloughs, marshes, potholes; low islands, moist sedge meadows.
Nest: In dry situations but within 3–50 yds. (2.7–45.7 m) of water. Almost never over water, usually in cover 13–24 in. (33–61 cm) high. Hollow scooped in ground, lined with dark down mixed with dry grasses. As eggs are laid, rim is built up with surrounding vegetation and more down. Typically uses *less down* than most other ducks.
Eggs: 6–15, commonly 9–11; laid 1 per day; av. 57.1 x 39.7 mm. Oval to long-oval. Shell smooth and slightly glossy. Shades of olive-buff. *Indistinguishable from eggs of Ring-necked Duck.* Incubation by female, 21–27 days, av. 24.
Notes: Male normally deserts hen when incubation begins, but sometimes remains until middle of incubation period. Largest nesting concentrations are in marshes of Hardstem Bulrush (*Scirpus acutus*) bordering lakes.

COMMON GOLDENEYE *Bucephala clangula*

Breeding range: Montana, Wyoming (Yellowstone National Park), N. Dakota (Turtle Mts.), ne. and n.cen. Minnesota.
Habitat: Watered areas having marshy shores with adjacent stands of old hardwood trees to provide nesting sites.
Nest: Natural cavity in tree at height of 6–60 ft. (1.8–18.3 m). Inside cavity a rounded depression in rotted wood or chips with down added. No preference for type of tree nor size of cavity as long as it's large enough to conceal bird. Man-made nest boxes used readily, especially those placed 18–20 ft. (5.5–6.1 m) above ground along lakeshores.
Eggs: 7–12, often 9; laid every other day; av. 59.7 x 43.4 mm. Long-oval. Shell thin with dull luster. Pale green or olive-green; various colors often in same nest. *Indistinguishable from eggs of Barrow's Goldeneye;* may average smaller. Incubation by female; 27–32 days, probably most often 30. 1 brood.
Notes: Where cavities are scarce, joint layings by 2 or more females may occur, with over 30 eggs deposited.

BARROW'S GOLDENEYE *Bucephala islandica*

Breeding range: Cascade Mts. of Washington, Oregon, and n. California; also Sierras of cen. California; w. Montana (Flathead Valley), nw. Wyoming (Yellowstone and south).
Habitat: Wooded areas near relatively shallow lakes and ponds having extensive beds of submerged vegetation.
Nest: Commonly in cavities in live or dead trees, in nest boxes; rarely, in holes in ground or in old crow nests (British Columbia). Probably no material brought to nesting cavity but it is profusely lined with white down.
Eggs: 6–15, commonly 10; laid at irregular intervals; av. 61.3 x 44.0 mm. Oval to long-oval. Smooth with slight gloss. Deep lichen-green to pale grass-green. *Indistinguishable from eggs of Common Goldeneye;* average slightly larger. Incubation by female; 32–34 days (based on 10 clutches, from laying of last egg to time when all hatched). 1 brood.
Notes: When natural cavities scarce, deserted holes of Pileated Woodpeckers or Common Flickers often used. Cavity of latter must have been enlarged by natural decay.

BUFFLEHEAD *Bucephala albeola*

Breeding range: Uncommon or rare in Washington, Oregon, and n. California; e. Idaho, nw. Montana, nw. Wyoming, N. Dakota (Turtle Mts.).
Habitat: Wooded shores of lakes and ponds.
Nest: In tree cavities excavated by woodpeckers, particularly flickers; preference given to trees near or standing in water. Most nests 2–10 ft. (0.6–3.1 m) above ground, some up to 23 ft. (7 m) in aspen and 49 ft. (15 m) in Douglas Fir. Nothing added to cavity but nest down. Entrance sizes suitable for Buffleheads remarkably small: $2\frac{1}{2}$ –3 in. (6.4–7.6 cm). Interior diam. about 6 in. (15.2 cm), depth of cavity 10–14 in. (25.4–35.6 cm).
Eggs: 6–14, usually 10–12; laid irregularly; av. 48.5 x 34.7 mm. Bluntly oval to nearly oval. Shells smooth and slightly glossy. Ivory yellow to pale olive-buff. Incubation by female; 28–33 days, commonly 29–31. 1 brood.
Notes: Nest boxes have been erected for Buffleheads but intensity of use varies, probably in relation to availability of tree cavities and abundance of breeding birds.

HARLEQUIN DUCK *Histrionicus histrionicus*

Breeding range: Western mts.: Washington, Oregon, California (prob.), along Idaho-Montana border south to nw. Wyoming.
Habitat: Islands or shores of cold, fast-flowing mountain streams often surrounded by forests.
Nest: On ground, under bushes, or among rocks. A thin layer of

grasses, occasionally with twigs and leaves; lined with white down.
Eggs: 4–8, commonly 6; laid at intervals of 1 or 2 days; av.
57.5 x 41.5 mm. Short to long-oval, some quite pointed. Shell
smooth and slightly glossy. Light buff or cream-colored. Incubation by female, 28–29 days.
Notes: Not hole nesters, but Harlequins sometimes use sheltered
cavities, usually close to water.

WHITE-WINGED SCOTER *Melanitta deglandi*

Notes: Evidence of nesting in the U.S. by this boreal-subarctic
breeder apparently is confined to records in N. Dakota. Although
it nested regularly at Devil's Lake between 1900 and 1920, the
species became rare or absent until broods were observed in
McHenry Co. in 1936 and at Des Lacs and Lostwood Refuges,
Burke Co., in 1952, 1953, and 1955. Nonbreeding birds often summer in Washington.

RUDDY DUCK *Oxyura jamaicensis*   Pl. 4

Breeding range: E. Washington to Minnesota, south to s. and
cen. California, Arizona (cas.), New Mexico (cas.), s. Texas, nw.
Iowa.
Habitat: Permanent freshwater or alkaline marshes large or small,
with open water and adequate nesting cover.
Nest: In tall reeds, bulrushes, cattails; normally 7–8 in. (17.8–
20.3 cm) above water and attached firmly to growing reeds.
Sometimes built on muskrat house, feeding platform, or old nest of
American Coot. Basketlike, woven from nearby dead or live
plants; interwoven with and matching surrounding vegetation;
sparsely lined with down. A sloping pile of reeds may be added to
form runway between water and nest. Av. outside diam. 12 in.
(30.5 cm); inside diam. 7 in. (17.8 cm), depth 3 in. (7.6 cm).
Eggs: 5–15; av. for 312 nests, 8; laid 1 a day, sometimes in 2 or
even 3 layers; av. 62.3 x 45.6 mm (surprisingly large for size of
bird). Short-oval to long-oval. Shell *thick, rough, and granular* — much more so than eggs of other ducks. White or creamy
white, becoming nest-stained. Incubation by female; commonly
23–24 days; sometimes begins before laying of last egg.
Notes: Dump nests common; 80 eggs reported in one such nest.
Ruddies lay in nests of Redhead, Canvasback, grebes, gallinules,
American Bittern, American Coot, and others.

MASKED DUCK *Oxyura dominica*

Notes: This Mexican species may be extending its breeding range
northward. Since nesting records for Texas were established in
1967 (Chambers Co.) and in 1968 (Brooks Co.) both males and
females have been observed in s. Texas during the breeding season.

RUDDY DUCK parasitized Canvasback nest (3 white eggs are Ruddy's).

HOODED MERGANSER   *Lophodytes cucullatus*   Pl. 4

Breeding range: Washington, w. Oregon, n. California, n. and e. Idaho, w. Montana (poss.), nw. Wyoming (poss.), n.-cen. N. Dakota, n. Minnesota, south through Mississippi River Valley; Texas (Fort Bend Co., 1977).
Habitat: Wooded freshwater streams, wooded shorelines of lakes, swamps, where clear water for foraging and tree cavities for nesting are available.
Nest: Normally in tree cavities near water similar to those preferred by Wood Ducks. Man-made nest boxes, erected primarily for Wood Ducks, have had surprisingly frequent occupancy by mergansers. Nest lined with debris in cavity mixed with down from female's breast. May use same site year after year.
Eggs: 6–15, typically 10–12, laid every 2 days; av. 53.5 x 44.9 mm. Oval or almost round. Smooth, quite glossy. Pure white; *resembles white egg of domestic chicken.* Larger than eggs of Wood Duck. Common Goldeneye eggs pale green and longer. Incubation by female; 31 days.
Notes: Frequently lay in Wood Duck nests and vice versa. Only way to determine which duck began nest is by species that finally incubates. In Missouri, 61 clutches contained eggs of both species; 27 were incubated by mergansers, 32 by Wood Ducks, and 2 were unincubated. Eggs of mixed clutches normally hatch about the same time.

COMMON MERGANSER   *Mergus merganser*

Breeding range: Washington, w. Oregon, n. and cen. California, Idaho, w. Nevada, w. Montana, w. Wyoming, cen. Colorado, ne. and n.-cen. Minnesota. Has nested in Arizona.

Habitat: Wooded areas preferably near fresh water, lake borders, islands; inland rather than coastal.

Nest: Usually in tree cavities, at any height; in holes in banks, beneath boulders, cliffs, under dense matlike bushes, occasionally in buildings. Sometimes in man-made boxes. Trash in cavity mixed with down from female's body. Ground nests usually bulky; of dead forbs, fibrous roots, moss. Same site may be used year after year.

Eggs: 6–17, commonly 9–12; probably laid irregularly; av. 64.3 x 44.9 mm. Oval. Shell thick; little or no luster. Pale buff or ivory-yellow, unmarked. Incubation by female; probably about 32 days. 1 brood. Drake leaves mate after eggs are laid.

Notes: When flushed from nests, Common and Red-breasted Merganser females are hard to distinguish. Down of Common Merganser's nest is much whiter than that in Red-breasted nest; colors of eggs different. If nest is in tree cavity, it is *not* a Red-breasted's nest.

RED-BREASTED MERGANSER   *Mergus serrator*

Notes: Nests in ne. Minnesota, principally along shores of Lake Superior. Unlike Hooded and Common Mergansers which usually nest in tree cavities, this species *nests on ground.* Clutches vary from 5–11, commonly 8–10. Eggs oval, olive-buff; incubated by female for about 30 days.

TURKEY VULTURE   *Cathartes aura*   **Pl. 4**

Breeding range: All western states; resident in South.

Habitat: Remote areas in precipitous cliffs, caves, hollow stumps or logs, dense shrubs.

Nest: Little or no nest; eggs laid on ground, on gravel of cliffs, or on rotted chips or sawdust in logs and stumps.

Eggs: Typically 2, rarely 1 or 3; av. 71.3 x 48.6 mm, *smaller than Black Vulture eggs.* Elliptical or long-oval. Shell smooth or finely granulated; little or no gloss. *Dull white or creamy white;* handsomely marked with irregular spots, blotches, and splashes of bright brown. Incubation by both sexes "very close to 30 days" (Jackson from Bent), "41 days" (Pennock from Bent); "probably between 5 and 6 weeks" (Grossman and Hamlet).

Notes: Unusual nesting sites recorded: abandoned pigsty in woods; floor of old neglected barn; snag of dead tree with nest 14 ft. (4.3 m) below entrance; 6 ft. (1.8 m) below ground surface in rotted stump; natural cavity in live beech tree, 40 ft. (16.1 m) above ground.

BLACK VULTURE   *Coragyps atratus*

Breeding range: Resident in se. Kansas (poss.), s. Missouri (rare), e. Oklahoma, e. and s. Texas, Arkansas, Louisiana.
Habitat: Open country interspersed with woodlands and thickets.
Nest: None. Eggs laid on bare ground; bottom of stump, hollow log, in dense thickets, under large boulders, caves; rarely in hollow trees.
Eggs: 1–3, typically 2; av. 75.6 x 50.9 mm; *larger than Turkey Vulture eggs.* Oval to long-oval. Shell smooth, not glossy. *Gray-green,* bluish white or dull white with large blotches or spots of pale chocolate or lavender wreathed or clustered near large end, overlaid with dark brown blotches and spots. Some eggs almost without spots. Incubation by both sexes; variously stated to be 28–41 days or 39–41 days (Grossman and Hamlet), 28–29 days in 21 nests (Baynard), 38 days (Stewart), 39 days (Thomas).
Notes: Nesting area sometimes decorated with bright bits of trash — bottle caps, broken glass, piece of comb, and so forth.

CALIFORNIA CONDOR   **opp. p. 35**
Gymnogyps californianus

Breeding range: Present population of this endangered species is perhaps as few as 30 birds nesting principally in the Sespe Wildlife Area of Los Padres National Forest, Ventura Co., California.
Nest: On bare floor of cave or among boulders.
Eggs: 1 every 2 years; av. 110.2 x 66.7 mm. Long-oval. Shell finely granulated, without gloss. Plain greenish white, bluish white, or dull white. Both sexes incubate; "at least 42 days, and probably more" (Grossman and Hamlet), "said to be 29 to 31 days" (Bent), 56 days (Koford).
Notes: To save this species, a program of captive breeding has been discussed at the San Diego Zoo, but how offspring can be restocked in the wild is unresolved. In recent report of Condor Recovery Team, the following judgment was made: "The species can probably never achieve completely secure status, but continuous rigorous protection and management might maintain a small but stable population." The objective is to maintain a population of at least 50, but the latest report of the Fish and Wildlife Service (December 1978) stated that no more than 30 (adults and juveniles) are believed to survive.

WHITE-TAILED KITE   *Elanus leucurus*   **Pl. 4**

Breeding range: Resident in Oregon (Benton Co., 1977), California, s. Texas, Louisiana (first nest reported in 1976 in Bossier Parish). Range extension noted in recent years.
Habitat: Open, cultivated bottomland with scattered trees; grassy

CALIFORNIA CONDOR nest and single egg in Sespe Condor Sanctuary, Ventura Co., California.

PEREGRINE FALCON nest and eggs in remote California mountainous wilderness.

foothill slopes interspersed with oaks and other trees; orchards, windbreaks.

Nest: 15–59 ft. (4.6–18.0 m) above ground in oak, willow, eucalyptus, cottonwood, or other deciduous tree. Bulky, deeply hollowed, of small fine twigs lined with dry grass, forbs, rootlets. Nests often used in succeeding years.

Eggs: 3–6, commonly 4–5; av. 42.5 x 32.8 mm. Oval. Shell smooth but not glossy. White or creamy white ground color often concealed by profuse markings of rich browns over washes or splashes of brighter browns. Incubation probably by both sexes; "not less than 30 days" (Pickwell).

SWALLOW-TAILED KITE   *Elanoides forficatus*

Breeding range: Uncommon summer resident in Louisiana, nesting principally in the Atchafalaya Swamp.
Habitat: Swamps or along forested rivers.
Nest: Near top of tall tree. Sticks and twigs interspersed with Spanish Moss and leaves; has slight depression.
Eggs: 2; av. 46.7 x 37.4 mm. White, boldly blotched or spotted with shades of brown. Incubation by both sexes, mostly female; about 28 days.

HOOK-BILLED KITE   *Chondrohierax uncinatus*

Notes: First successful nesting in U.S. of this neotropical raptor reported in the Santa Ana National Wildlife Refuge, Texas, May 1976. Two eggs hatched, 1 nestling disappeared but the other fledged successfully. This species is a resident in Mexico, Central America, and South America.

MISSISSIPPI KITE   *Ictinia mississippiensis*

Breeding range: Summer resident in e. Colorado (rare), sw. and s.-cen. Kansas, se. Missouri (rare) south to Mexico and Gulf of Mexico; unc. in New Mexico.
Habitat: Normally prefers forests of tall trees; in Texas and Oklahoma may seek stands of low mesquites.
Nest: Typically at great height, 30–135 ft. (9.2–41.2 m) in treetops, often in Sweetgum, cottonwood, pines, where dense foliage hides nest from ground. In mesquite, only 4–6 ft. (1.2–1.8 m) above ground. Bulky shallow saucer of coarse sticks and twigs, flat on top, with thick lining of live twigs with green leaves attached. Both sexes build. Size varies with location; diam. 10–25 in. (25.4–63.5 cm).
Eggs: 1–2, rarely 3; av. 41.3 x 34.0 mm. Oval to short-oval. Shell smooth, no gloss. White or pale bluish white, usually unmarked. Incubation by both sexes; 31–32 days.

Opposite: Endangered Species: California Condor and Peregrine Falcon.

GOSHAWK *Accipiter gentilis* Pl. 5

Breeding range: Uncommon throughout most of its range from Washington to w. Montana, south to n. and cen. California, Arizona, n. and w. New Mexico; also n. Minnesota.

Habitat: Heavily wooded, remote wilderness areas, often mountain forests.

Nest: Usually in tall trees as high as 75 ft. (22.9 m) from ground. Nest placed in crotch or on limb against trunk. Bulky nest of large sticks; slightly hollowed, lined with bark chips, evergreen sprigs; commonly feathers and down in and around nest. May use other hawk nests as base; often occupies same nest year after year. Outside diam. 3–4 ft. (91.4–121.9 cm), height 18–35 in. (45.7–88.9 cm).

Eggs: 3–4, sometimes 2, rarely 5; not always laid on successive days; av. 59.3 x 45.6 mm (western race). Oval to long-oval. Shell rather tough, granulated or pitted. Pale bluish white or dirty white, typically unmarked. Occasionally eggs are sparsely brown-spotted. Incubation "said to be about 28 days" (Bent), "probably is four weeks" (Bendire), "Incubation (36–38 days) almost entirely by the hen, begins with the second or third egg" (Grossman and Hamlet).

Notes: Goshawks fiercely defend nest; have been known to harass and even attack persons near nest tree.

SHARP-SHINNED HAWK *Accipiter striatus*

Breeding range: Local, uncommon, or rare in all western states.

Habitat: Dense groves of trees with heavy canopies.

Nest: Usually in conifer but occasionally in deciduous tree (cottonwood, maple, oak). In Utah, 18 of 27 nests were in conifers in midst of deciduous stands. 20–60 ft. (6.1–18.3 m) above ground, av. 30–35 ft. (9.2–10.7 m). A broad platform of sticks and twigs, built on limb against tree trunk, unlined or lined with chips of bark. Prefers new nest annually, but sometimes repairs old one. Nest large in proportion to size of bird: outside diam. 24–26 in. (61–66 cm), height 7 in. (17.8 cm); inside diam. 6 in. (15.2 cm), depth 2–3 in. (5.1–7.6 cm).

Eggs: 4–5, often 3, rarely 6; may be laid on alternate days; av. 37.5 x 30.4 mm. Spherical or short-oval. Shell smooth, not glossy. Dull white or pale bluish white, with large blotches or splashes of rich brown concentrated at either end or forming a wreath midway. Incubation by both sexes, mostly female, beginning when clutch complete, "about 3 weeks, perhaps 21 to 24 days" (Bent), "30 days after the last egg was laid" (K. Tuttle), "lasts 35 days" (Meng), 30–34 days (Platt; Snyder and Wiley).

COOPER'S HAWK *Accipiter cooperii* Pl. 5

Breeding range: Local throughout western states but uncommon to rare in many areas.

Habitat: Deciduous and coniferous woodlands.

Nest: Placed 20–60 ft. (6.1–18.3 m) above ground in upright crotch of deciduous tree or next to trunk on horizontal limb of conifer. Substantial structure of sticks and twigs always *lined with chips or flakes of outer bark;* not decorated with greenery as often as nests of buteo hawks (see Plate 5). Usually builds new nest annually but may repair old one or build on old squirrel or crow nest. Both sexes build. Outside diam. 24–28 in. (61.0–71.1 cm), height 7–8 in. (17.8–20.3 cm) (nests in crotches higher but not so wide); depth 2–4 in. (5.1–10.2 cm).

Eggs: 4–5, sometimes 3, rarely 6; deposited at intervals of 1–2 days; av. 49.0 x 38.5 mm. Short-oval to oval. Shell smooth, not glossy. Bluish white when fresh, fades to dirty white; sometimes scattered pale spots. Incubation by both sexes, mostly female; 24 days (Bent), 35–36 days (Meng). May start before clutch complete.

RED-TAILED HAWK *Buteo jamaicensis* **Pl. 5**

Breeding range: All western states.

Habitat: Deserts to mountaintops, open country to cliffs with commanding views of surrounding country. Food supply may govern habitat more than available nesting sites.

Nest: In trees (cottonwoods, sycamores, conifers) to height of 120 ft. (36.6 m) or more above ground; in desert Saguaros (Arizona); on rocky cliffs; in abandoned nests of Golden Eagle, Common Raven; in shrubs or small trees (paloverde, ocotillo, mes-

RED-TAILED HAWK

quite). Well made of sticks and twigs, lined with inner bark, evergreen sprigs, or fresh green foliage. Green sprigs renewed during incubation. Both sexes build. *Larger than nest of Red-shouldered Hawk;* outside diam. 28–30 in. (71.1–76.2 cm); inside diam. 14–15 in. (35.6–38.1 cm), depth 4–6 in. (10.2–15.2 cm).

Eggs: 2–3, occasionally 4; laid at intervals of 1 or 2 days; av. 59.2 x 46.4 mm (western race). Oval or long-oval. Shell finely granulated or smooth, without gloss. Dirty white or bluish white, usually with varying arrangements of spots or blotches in shades of brown. More heavily marked than Swainson's; less heavily than Red-shouldered's. Incubation by female; 28 days (Bent), 34 days (Grossman and Hamlet), 32–35 days (Fitch, Johnson, Wiley).

RED-SHOULDERED HAWK *Buteo lineatus* Pl. 5

Breeding range: Discontinuous. Nebraska south through Texas; Minnesota south through Mississippi Valley to Gulf of Mexico. Western range: California, along Central Valley and southern coast to Baja.

Habitat: River-bottom woodlands surrounded by open meadows, wet pastures, and grain fields; borders of swamps.

Nest: Often close to tree trunk, usually 20–60 ft. (6.1–18.3 m) from ground; av. 35–45 ft. (10.7–13.7 m). No preference in kind of tree although oak, willow, sycamore, and cottonwood often used. Well built of sticks and twigs; lined with strips of inner bark, fine twigs, dry leaves, sprigs of evergreen, feathers, down. *Resembles nest of Red-tailed Hawk but smaller.* Outside diam. 18–24 in. (45.7–61.0 cm), height 8–12 in. (20.3–30.5 cm); inside diam. 8 in. (20.3 cm), depth 2–3 in. (5.1–7.6 cm).

Eggs: 3, often 4, occasionally 2, rarely 5; av. 54.7 x 43.9 mm. Oval to short-oval. Shell smooth, no gloss. Dull white or pale bluish with variety of brown spots, blotches, or streaks. More heavily marked than Red-tailed eggs. Incubation by both sexes; about 28 days, 33 days (Snyder and Wiley). 1 brood.

Notes: Very consistent in returning to same territory or nesting site annually.

BROAD-WINGED HAWK *Buteo platypterus*

Breeding range: N. Dakota (Turtle Mts.), Nebraska (Missouri R.), e. Kansas (rare), e. Oklahoma, e. Texas (poss.), and n. Minnesota south to Louisiana.

Habitat: Dry forests, wooded hillsides, mostly deciduous forests near small ponds, streams; occasionally conifers.

Nest: Typically in main crotch or on supporting branches against tree trunk 24–40 ft. (7.3–12.2 m) from ground. Small, poorly built of sticks, dead leaves; lined with strips of inner bark, chips of outer bark (pine, oak); often decorated with green leaves and sprigs. Usually new annually but occasionally a rebuilt crow, hawk, or

BROAD-WINGED HAWK

squirrel nest. Outside diam. 15–17 in. (38.1–43.2 cm), height 5–12 in. (12.7–30.5 cm); inside diam. 6–7 in. (15.2–17.8 cm), depth 1–3 in. (2.5–7.6 cm).

Eggs: 2–3, sometimes 1 or 4; av. 48.9 x 39.3 mm. Nearly oval to long-oval. Shell finely granulated. Dull white, creamy white, bluish white; many variations in color, shape, and size of blotches, splashes, and spots, mostly shades of brown. Both sexes incubate, but male's share is minimal; 28 days or longer; 30–38 days (Olendorff).

Notes: Number of eggs in each of 406 clutches: 15 clutches of 1 egg, 183 of 2, 190 of 3, 18 of 4.

SWAINSON'S HAWK *Buteo swainsoni* Pl. 5

Breeding range: Summer resident in Washington east to N. Dakota, south to Texas; se. Minnesota, Iowa (rare), w. Missouri (cas.). Highly migratory.

Habitat: Wide open spaces, prairies, plains, deserts; absent in densely timbered mountain regions; at home in wooded areas along lowland water courses.

Nest: Usually a bulky, *unsightly mass* of sticks, sagebrush, thistle, brambles; may be lined with green willow sprigs, green forbs, grass, wool. Typically 6–30 ft. (1.8–9.2 m) above ground, sometimes to 75 ft. (22.9 m); 1 California record "100 ft. up in giant yellow pine" (Dawson). In Saguaro in Arizona; in Joshua Tree in California; sometimes on abandoned nests of Black-billed Magpie. For nest on Pl. 5: outside diam. $46\frac{7}{8}$ in. (119 cm), height $9\frac{3}{8}$ in. (23.9 cm); inside diam. $7\frac{7}{8}$ in. (20.1 cm), depth $3\frac{1}{8}$ in. (7.9 cm). **Eggs:** 2–3, rarely 4; av. 56.5 x 44 mm. Short-oval to oval. Shell smooth or finely granulated. Pale bluish or greenish white when fresh, fading to dull white; some immaculate, others more or less sparsely spotted with various shades of brown. Rarely heavily marked. Incubation by female, possibly some help from male; about 28 days (Bent), 34–35 days (Fitzher).

Notes: 7 nests observed by author in Colorado were partly or entirely constructed externally of Russian Thistle. In the Pawnee National Grasslands of e. Colorado, this raptor appeared to favor trees in windbreaks as nesting sites.

ZONE-TAILED HAWK   *Buteo albonotatus*

Breeding range: Local in Arizona, s. New Mexico, w. Texas.
Habitat: In giant cottonwoods along rivers and canyons.
Nest: In top of large cottonwood. Of large sticks lined with green leaves of cottonwood attached to twigs.
Eggs: 1–3, commonly 2; av. 55.6 x 43.5 mm. Oval, short-oval. Smooth or finely granulated. White or bluish white, usually unmarked, sometimes sparingly marked with small lavender or brownish spots. Incubation 35 days (Newton).
Notes: Heavily marked eggs likely to indicate nest of Black Hawk (*Buteogallus anthracinus*).

WHITE-TAILED HAWK   *Buteo albicaudatus*

Breeding range: Casual in s. Texas, (Rio Grande Valley). Formerly a rare nester in s. Arizona and s. California.
Nest: Usually in tops of thick clumps of thorny bushes, sometimes catclaw. Of coarse and fine sticks, lined with grass and green leaves.
Eggs: 1–3, commonly 2; av. 58.9 x 46.5 mm. Dull white or pale bluish; often spotted with brown, sometimes unmarked.
Notes: Incubating bird usually leaves nest when intruder is far away, disappears, or hovers high in sky overhead.

FERRUGINOUS HAWK   *Buteo regalis*   Pl. 5

Breeding range: Washington to N. Dakota, south to Oregon (cas.), Arizona, New Mexico, nw. Oklahoma; Texas (poss., last nesting reported in 1966).
Habitat: Timber belts in barren, treeless plains and grassy prairies; cliffs and rocky outcrops.
Nest: In large dead or live trees of various kinds or on the ground

on hillsides, buttes, cliffs, or rocky pinnacles. Usually large accumulations of sticks, rubbish, sage bark, sod, cow dung; lined with dried grass, roots, well dried chips of dung. May be used successive years; become large as eagle nests. Use of large chunks of horse or cow dung is common. Both sexes build. Outside diam. 24–42 in. (61.0–106.7 cm); height also varies with age of nest and amount of repeated repair, 3 ft. (0.9 m) or more.
Eggs: 3–4, sometimes 2–5, rarely 6; av. 61.2 x 48.0 mm. Oval or long-oval. Shell smooth or finely granulated. White, creamy white, or pale bluish white; boldly marked with blotches or spots of rich brown; some nearly or completely immaculate. Incubation by both sexes; about 28 days (Bent), 33 days (Angell).
Notes: In study of 27 nests in S. Dakota, 12 were on the ground on hilltops; 13 were in tall cottonwoods; 2 were on haystacks. In Utah: 60 percent in trees; 31 percent on ground.

GRAY HAWK *Buteo nitidus*

Breeding range: S. Arizona. Reports of nestings in New Mexico appear erroneous. Probably bred formerly in Rio Grande delta, Texas.
Habitat: Stream bottoms of mesquite, cottonwood.
Nest: Somewhat flimsy shallow platform of twigs, mostly green, up to 70 ft. (21.4 m) above ground.
Eggs: 2–3; av. 50.8 x 41.0 mm. White or pale bluish white, almost always *unmarked*. Incubation 32 days (R. Glinski).

HARRIS' HAWK *Parabuteo unicinctus*   Pl. 5

Breeding range: S. Arizona, se. New Mexico, s. and cen. Texas. Nest with young found in Meade Co. State Park, Kansas, in 1962.
Habitat: River woodlands, mesquite forests, Saguaro–paloverde deserts, brushy flatlands.
Nest: In mesquite, Spanish Bayonet, Saguaro, paloverde, ironwood, hackberry, cottonwood, ebony, or other trees. Platform of sticks, twigs, forbs, roots; lined with green shoots, leaves, grass, bark. Female builds, occasionally assisted by male.
Eggs: 1–4, often 2–3, rarely 1; av. 53.7 x 42.1 mm. Oval. Shell smooth, no gloss. Dull white, usually unmarked. Incubation by both sexes; 33–36 days, av. 35; may start with 1st egg or later. Sometimes 2 broods per year. In one Arizona nesting, female laid 3 clutches in one season; 2 succeeded, 1 failed.
Notes: Harris' Hawks nest in pairs and also trios in which extra hawk is nest helper. In Saguaro–paloverde desert in Arizona, William J. Mader observed evidence of polyandry at 23 (46 percent) of 50 active nests. Both males copulated with same female and also helped bring prey to nest.

BLACK HAWK   *Buteogallus anthracinus*

Breeding range: Summer resident in s. Arizona, sw. New Mexico, s. Texas; first recorded nest in Utah in 1962.
Habitat: Heavily wooded canyons and arroyos, river-bottom forests; usually near water.
Nest: In tree. Large nest of sticks lined with fine green leaves, grass.
Eggs: 1–2, occasionally 3; av. 57.3 x 44.9 mm. Oval or short-oval. Dull white, spotted with dull or light brown; some nearly immaculate. *Very similar to eggs of Zone-tailed Hawk.* Incubation 34 days (Schnell).
Notes: Less common in U.S. than Zone-tailed Hawk.

GOLDEN EAGLE   *Aquila chrysaetos*   **Pl. 5**

Breeding range: Washington to Montana, south to Mexico; also N. Dakota (badlands), w. S. Dakota, Nebraska (cas.), Oklahoma (Cimarron Co.) and Texas (rare).
Habitat: Mountains and rangelands.
Nest: Placed in trees or in commanding position on rocky cliffs. Tree nests 10–96 ft. (3.1–29.3 m) above ground. Huge structure of sticks, roots, stems, brush, rubbish; lined with grasses, forbs, dead and green leaves, mosses, lichens. Birds often build 2 or more nests and use them alternately. New nests often quite small but added to from year to year become bulky. Outside diam. 5–6 ft. (1.5–1.8 m), height 4–5 ft. (1.2–1.5 m).
Eggs: 1–3, commonly 2, laid at 2–3 day intervals; av. 74.5 x 58.0 mm. Short-oval to oval, rarely long-oval. Shell thick, finely to coarsely granulated. Dull white, cream-buff; variation in type and color of markings; usually shades of brown, frequently overlaid with darker browns. Often 1 egg in clutch immaculate. Incubation mostly by female, beginning with 1st egg. 28–35 days (Bent), 41 days in Texas (Mitchell), 44–45 days in captivity (Vokle), 43–45 days (Gordon). 1 brood.
Notes: Size of territory of 19 pairs in Montana study ranged 66.3–74.2 sq. mi. (171.7–192.2 sq. km) per pair; distance between nests 1.0–10.5 mi. (1.6–16.8 km). Eagles probably mate for life. American Kestrels and Western Kingbirds known to nest in lower parts of Golden Eagles' nests.

BALD EAGLE   *Haliaeetus leucocephalus*

Breeding range: Rare, uncommon, and local from Washington to n. Minnesota, south to Mexico; casual or rare in Mississippi Valley; rare or absent from Central Plains.
Habitat: Open areas, forests, mountains, buttes; typically near lakes, rivers, seashores.
Nest: An eyrie, preferably in fork near crown of large tree; species

GOLDEN EAGLE

BALD EAGLE

of tree not as important as size, shape, and distance from other nesting eagles. Nests also built on rocky cliffs or pinnacles, often inaccessible. Both birds build an immense pile of large sticks, branches, cornstalks, rubbish; lined with grasses, moss, twigs, sod, forbs. Same nest used year after year; may have 2 nests used alternate years. Nests added to each year; may eventually topple of own weight. Old nests may be 8–10 ft. (2.4–3.1 m) in diam. **Eggs:** 2, sometimes 1, rarely 3, probably laid at intervals of 3–4 days; southern race, av. 70.5 x 54.2 mm; northern race, 74.4 x 57.1 mm; small for size of bird. Short-oval to oval. Shell rough or coarsely granulated. Dull white, unmarked. Both sexes incubate; about 35 days, 34–35 days (Maestrelli and Wiemeyer). **Notes:** Endangered species in 43 states, threatened species in 5: Michigan, Wisconsin, Minnesota, Oregon, Washington.

MARSH HAWK *Circus cyaneus*   Pl. 6
(Northern Harrier)

Breeding range: Washington to Minnesota, south to Mexico, n. Texas, Missouri (rare).
Habitat: Freshwater or saltwater marshes, wet meadows, sloughs; may nest in dry fields, prairies, close to water.
Nest: On or near ground, sometimes built over shallow water. Flimsy to well-made structure of sticks, straw, and grasses. Built mostly by female; male often gathers material for mate. Outside diam. 15–30 in. (38.1–76.2 cm); inside diam. 8–9 in. (20.3–22.9 cm).
Eggs: 5, frequently 4 or 6; occasionally 7–9; there may be more than 1 day between layings; av. 46.6 x 36.4 mm. Oval to short-oval. Shell smooth, little or no gloss. Dull white or pale bluish white; generally unmarked, occasionally sparsely spotted. Incubation mostly or entirely by female, often beginning with laying of 1st egg; incubation variously given as 21–31 days, probably 29 or 30, 29–33 days (Breckenridge).
Notes: Polygyny reported occasionally (1 male defending nests of 2 females in same area).

OSPREY *Pandion haliaetus*   Pl. 6

Breeding range: Throughout western states; rare, casual, or absent in Nebraska, Iowa, Kansas, Missouri, Oklahoma, Arkansas, and Louisiana.
Habitat: Normally near fresh or salt water.
Nest: Tends to be in small loose colonies. On ground to 60 ft. (18.3 m) above ground on dead snags, living trees, cliffs, utility poles, aerials, duck blinds, fishing shacks, storage tanks, cranes, billboards, chimneys, windmills, fences, channel buoys, and wooden platforms on poles erected by man. Foundation of small to huge sticks, lined with inner bark, sod, grasses, vines, and a great

variety of odd objects (see **Notes**). Often used successive years.
Eggs: 3–4, occasionally 2, rarely 5; av. 61.0 x 45.6 mm. Oval, short-oval, elliptical, or long-oval. Shell fairly smooth, finely granulated. White, pinkish white, pale pinkish cinnamon; heavily spotted or blotched with reddish brown. Incubation by female, about 35 days. 1 brood.

Notes: Objects found in Ospreys' nests include shorts, bath towels, garden rake, rope, broom, barrel staves, hoops, fishnet, toy boat, old shoes, fishlines, straw hat, rag doll, bottles, tin cans, shells, and sponges.

CARACARA *Caracara cheriway*
(Audubon's or Crested Caracara)

Breeding range: Uncommon or rare in s. Arizona, s. and cen. New Mexico (prob.), s. Texas, Louisiana (prob. in Cameron Parish).

Habitat: Open pasturelands and prairies with creeks and arroyos bordered by trees.

Nest: 8–50 ft. (2.4–15.3 m) above ground in variety of trees; bulky, loosely constructed of brush, vines, and briars, piled in a heap and trampled to make a hollow for eggs.

Eggs: 2–3; av. 59.4 x 46.5 mm. Oval. Whitish, heavily brown-blotched. Incubation by both sexes; about 28 days.

OSPREY

PRAIRIE FALCON   *Falco mexicanus*   **Pl. 6**

Breeding range: Washington to Montana, south to Mexico. Rare east of Rockies.

Habitat: Dry plains, prairies, mountains, typically with cliffs and rocky outcrops.

Nest: On cliffs, usually perpendicular, 23 ft. to over 400 ft. (7–122 m) high, and generally inaccessible to man. When possible, recesses or cavities in cliffs chosen. Where there are no cliffs, nests placed in variety of situations, including dirt banks and in abandoned nests of Red-tailed Hawks or Common Ravens. No nest built; eggs laid in scrapes on bare ground or gravel.

Eggs: 4–5, sometimes 3, rarely 2 or 6; av. 52.3 x 40.5 mm. Oval. Finely granulated to smooth, often pimpled. White or creamy white, heavily spotted or splashed with brown, often concealing the ground color. Markings tend to be *lighter* than those of Peregrine Falcon eggs. Incubation mostly by female; 29–33 days (Enderson; Webster).

Notes: At 36 nest sites studied in s. Wyoming and n. Colorado, all but 1 were on ledges directly overhung by portion of cliff. Prairie Falcons and Common Ravens nest on same cliffs at same time without apparent conflict.

PEREGRINE FALCON   *Falco peregrinus*   **opp. p. 35**

Breeding range: Rare throughout limited range, Washington to Montana, south to Mexico. Endangered species; probably extirpated east of Rockies.

Habitat: Inaccessible mountain cliffs, prairie escarpments, canyon walls.

PRAIRIE FALCON

Nest: Almost always on inaccessible ledges in rocky cliffs; rarely in trees. No nest built; eggs laid in scrape in ground or on accumulated trash on ledge, in recess, or in old nests of other raptors. Same site may be used annually.

Eggs: 4, sometimes 3, occasionally 5; typically laid every other day; av. 52 x 41 mm. Short-oval to long-oval. Shell smooth or finely granulated. Creamy white or whitish pink, almost concealed by blotches and spots of brilliant rich browns; often overlaid. Markings tend to be *darker* and *brighter* than those of Prairie Falcon eggs. Incubation mostly by female; 32–35 days. 1 brood.

Notes: Concentration of DDT in food chain, leading to production of thin-shelled or infertile eggs, has caused serious decline in Peregrine population in the U.S. Started in 1973, propagation of Peregrines at Cornell University has resulted in introduction of 133 young falcons to the wild in 12 states including California, Idaho, New Mexico, and mainly Colorado. Biologists aim for 100 breeding pairs in Rocky Mts. and sw. U.S. by 1995. Cost estimated at $60,000 per breeding pair.

APLOMADO FALCON   *Falco femoralis*

Breeding range: Casual in sw. New Mexico; formerly se. Arizona to s. Texas.

Nest: The few nests observed in U.S. have been 10–14 ft. (3.1–4.3 m) above ground in Spanish Bayonet or mesquite. Platform of twigs lined with grass.

Eggs: 2–4; av. 44.5 x 34.5. Creamy white; dotted, splashed, or blotched with reddish brown.

MERLIN   *Falco columbarius*

Breeding range: Uncommon or rare Washington to ne. and n.-cen. Minnesota, south to Oregon, s. Idaho, Wyoming.

Habitat: Open woods, heavy timberlands, cliffs, in wilderness.

Nest: 35–60 ft. (10.7–18.3 m) above ground in trees, on cliff ledges; in natural cavities of trees, on old nests of other birds, rarely on ground, or under roofs of deserted buildings. Sticks interwoven with moss; sparingly lined with fine twigs, lichens, conifer needles.

Eggs: 4–5, occasionally 3, rarely 6; av. 40.2 x 31.3 mm. Short-oval, oval, elliptical. Shell smooth, no gloss. Whitish, almost covered with fine dots or bold blotches of browns; sometimes wreathed. *Like small Peregrine Falcon eggs.* Incubation mostly by female; about 30 days, 28–32 days (Campbell and Nelson).

Notes: When an intruder is near nest, adults scream excitedly and fly about nervously. Two nests in Idaho (Butte and Blaine Cos.) were in Black-billed Magpie nests.

AMERICAN KESTREL   *Falco sparverius*   Pl. 6

Breeding range: All western states.

Habitat: Open woods, orchards, deserts, mountains, farms.

Nest: Natural tree cavities, old woodpecker holes, man-made nest boxes, crannies in eaves of buildings; rarely in open in old nests of other birds. Little or no nesting material added to cavity.

Eggs: 3–5, commonly 4–5, laid on alternate days; av. 35 x 29 mm. Oval, short-oval. Shell smooth, no gloss. White, pinkish white, or light cinnamon, rather evenly covered with small dots and spots of various shades of brown; markings sometimes concentrated at one end or in ring around egg. Incubation mostly by female; 29–31 days.

Notes: Author has been successful in attracting Kestrels to man-made boxes and nail kegs; roofed, with 3-in. (7.6 cm) opening in side, placed 20–30 ft. (6.1–9.2 m) above ground on trees and utility poles. In Nevada, author found Kestrel incubating 4 eggs in pile of litter and trash in open cupboard inside an abandoned trailer (see Plate 6).

CHACHALACA *Ortalis vetula* opp. p. 147

Breeding range: Lower Rio Grande Valley of Texas, mainly Santa Ana National Wildlife Refuge.

Habitat: Thorny thickets.

Nest: In Cedar Elm, hackberry, mesquite, ebony, or similar native trees. Of sticks, plant fiber, Spanish Moss, leaves (green or dead). Small and frail for large bird.

Eggs: Normally 3; av. 58.4 x 40.9 mm. Shell thick, roughly granulated. Creamy white. Incubation by female, 25 days.

Notes: With constant protection from human molestation, Santa Ana birds, a population of about 2000, have become quite tame, almost chickenlike.

BLUE GROUSE *Dendragapus obscurus*
(including Dusky Grouse and Sooty Grouse)

Breeding range: E. and n. Washington along coast to n. California; in mountains of Idaho, w. Montana, Wyoming, Colorado, Utah to s. California, n. and e. Arizona, w.-cen. New Mexico.

Habitat: Mountainous forest country, semi-open to open mixed conifer-aspen shrub areas, mule ears–sagebrush flats.

Nest: Under or adjacent to old logs, roots of fallen trees, rocks, shrubs. Shallow — 1–2 in. (2.5–5.1 cm) — depression in ground about 6 in. (15.2 cm) in diameter slightly lined with dried grass, pine needles, occasionally feathers.

Eggs: 6–9, commonly 7, laid irregularly every 1–2 days; av. 49.7 x 34.9 mm. Oval to long-oval. Shell smooth with little or no gloss. Buff, quite thickly and evenly covered with small cinnamon-brown spots or minute dots. Incubation by female, beginning with laying of last egg; 26 days (Johnsgard). Male promiscuous; no pair bond formed.

Notes: Females on nests hold tightly before flushing.

RUFFED GROUSE

SPRUCE GROUSE *Canachites canadensis*
(including Franklin's Grouse)

Breeding range: N. and w. Washington, ne. Oregon, cen. Idaho, w. Montana, extreme nw. Wyoming, ne. and n.-cen. Minnesota.
Habitat: Coniferous forests of Rocky and Cascade Mts.
Nest: On ground under low coniferous branches, in brush, in deep moss in or near spruce thickets. Slight depression lined with pine needles, forbs, mosses, ferns, other adjacent materials, and a few feathers. Inside diam. about 7 in. (17.8 cm), depth 3 in. (7.6 cm).
Eggs: 6–10, usually 6–7; laid 2 every 3 days; av. 43.5 x 31.7 mm. Oval to long-oval. Shell smooth with slight gloss. Buff, well marked with large spots and blotches of rich browns. Female incubates; 23–24 days. Male promiscuous; no pair bond made.

RUFFED GROUSE *Bonasa umbellus*   Pl. 6

Breeding range: Washington, w. and ne. Oregon, nw. California, n. and e. Idaho, n.-cen. Utah, w. and cen. Montana, nw. Wyoming, ne. N. Dakota, w. S. Dakota, Minnesota, ne. Iowa (unc.), Missouri (cas.). Recently introduced into Nevada.
Habitat: Coniferous, deciduous, or mixed forests.
Nest: In thick woods and dense cover, female hollows nest at base of tree, adjacent to log, rock, or root, or in dense brush in dry situations. Lined with leaves, pine needles, available material, mixed with a few grouse feathers.
Eggs: 9–12, occasionally less, sometimes to 14; laid 2 every 3 days;

av. 38.9 x 29.6 mm. Short-oval to long-oval. Shell smooth, slight gloss. Buffy; a few eggs speckled with brownish spots. Incubation by female alone; 24–25 days (affected by cold wet weather or by interruptions). Male promiscuous; no pair bond formed.

Notes: A Minnesota study of 12 females equipped with radio transmitters indicated that after incubation began hens spent 95.7 percent of time on nests, left nests only to feed, and most left only 2 or 3 times per day. Transmittered birds averaged 18–24 minutes per absence for a total of 57–70 minutes off nest per day.

WHITE-TAILED PTARMIGAN *Lagopus leucurus*   Pl. 6

Breeding range: Discontinuous from Cascade Mts., Washington, and from Montana along Rocky Mts. south to n. New Mexico. Introduced into Wallowa Mts., Oregon; Sierra Nevada (Tioga Pass), California; and Uinta Mts., Utah.

Habitat: Alpine tundra in or above Krummholz (stunted) areas of willows and Engelmann Spruce. Hillsides or ridges to 13,100 ft. (3996 m).

Nest: In dry location, protected from wind, with easy escape route. On ground in or near Krummholz or near rock. Shallow scrape or bowl lined with vegetation gathered at nest site. Female adds to nest by picking up surrounding leaves and grasses as she lays or incubates. Nest may contain white feathers dislodged from female during nest molding, not intentionally plucked. Av. of 20 Colorado nests: inside diam. $4\frac{2}{3}$ x $5\frac{1}{2}$ in. (11.9 x 14.0 cm); depth 0 (no bowl) to $2\frac{3}{4}$ in. (7.1 cm), av. $1\frac{5}{8}$ in. (4.1 cm).

Eggs: 5–7, rarely 8–9 (re-nests 2–5); laid about 2 every 3 days; av. 43.7 x 29.7 mm (192 eggs, Giesen and Braun). Oval to long-oval. Little or no gloss. Buff, more or less evenly covered with brown spots or dots. Incubation by female only; 22–23 days. If 1st clutch destroyed, 25–50 percent of hens attempt to re-nest.

Notes: White-tailed Ptarmigan normally monogamous; some males attract 2 females. Time of breeding controlled by weather. Amount of snow cover in May and early June appears most important factor. Strongly protective coloration makes it very difficult to see incubating birds which sit very tight.

GREATER PRAIRIE CHICKEN   Pl. 6
Tympanuchus cupido

Breeding range: Uncommon and local from N. Dakota and nw. Minnesota south to ne. Colorado, ne. Oklahoma, sw. Missouri. Attwater's Prairie Chicken (*T. c. attwateri*), an endangered race, occurs in Texas coastal prairies.

Habitat: Ungrazed and undisturbed tall-grass prairies; also in adjacent croplands such as alfalfa and hayfields.

Nest: On ground among grasses, forbs, low bushes. Natural cavity or hollow scraped by female, concealed by heavy vegetation;

WHITE-TAILED PTARMIGAN

Tundra habitat

sparsely lined with grass, sedges, twigs, feathers. No canopy built but often naturally arched. Inside diam. about 7 in. (17.8 cm); depth 2–3 in. (5.1–7.6 cm).

Eggs: 5–17, av. 12; laid at irregular intervals; av. 44.86 x 33.59 mm. Oval. Shell smooth, slight gloss. Olive-buff or grayish olive, dotted with fine, or a few large, sepia spots. Incubation by female alone; 23–24 days. 1 brood.

Notes: Males promiscuous. In early spring females attracted to booming grounds (leks) where mating occurs. A national wildlife refuge, ultimately to cover 10,000 acres (4047 ha), has been established in Texas as part of survival plan for Attwater's Prairie Chicken. Total population of 2400 birds in 12 Texas counties was estimated in 1975.

LESSER PRAIRIE CHICKEN *Tympanuchus pallidicinctus*

Breeding range: Se. Colorado, sw. Kansas (east to Pratt Co.), nw. Oklahoma, e. New Mexico, and nw. Texas.

Habitat: Short- and mid-grass prairie intermixed with low shrubby vegetation such as Sand Sage and Shinnery Oak.

Nest: Shallow depression under bush or in tuft of grass.

Eggs: 8–13, usually 10–12; av. 41.9 x 32.0 mm. Buff or yellowish; unmarked or with fine dots of pale brown. Incubation by female alone; 23–24 days. Nest and incubating female blend well with surroundings. Males are promiscuous.

Notes: Breeding displays similar to those of Greater Prairie Chicken. Males display on gobbling grounds (leks) in early spring to attract females for mating.

SHARP-TAILED GROUSE *Pedioecetes phasianellus* **Pl. 6**

Breeding range: E. Washington, extreme e. Oregon, cen. and s. Idaho, n. Utah, Wyoming, nw. and e.-cen. Colorado, N. Dakota, S. Dakota, w. Nebraska, n. Minnesota.

Habitat: Prairie brushlands, woodland clearings, open woodland with brushy growth, often in or near marshy areas.
Nest: Under thick tufts of grass, forbs, bushes. Hollow in ground; scantily lined with grass, leaves, ferns. Inside diam. 7–8 in. (17.8–20.3 cm), depth $2\frac{1}{2}$–4 in. (6.4–10.2 cm).
Eggs: 9–17, typically 12; av. 42.6 x 32.0 mm. Oval. Shell smooth with slight gloss. Light brown to olive-buff, often with dark brown speckles, small spots, or dots. Incubation by female; about 23–24 days.
Notes: As with Prairie Chickens, courtship is social — dancing on display grounds (leks) by promiscuous males.

SAGE GROUSE *Centrocercus urophasianus*   Pl. 7

Breeding range: Cen. Washington, s. Idaho, e. and s. Montana, sw. N. Dakota south to e. California, Nevada, Utah, w. Colorado, w. S. Dakota.
Habitat: Sagebrush ranges and associated hay meadows. Throughout its range, in high valleys, mesas, and mountain slopes, this species is associated with sagebrush.
Nest: On ground, in slight depression under a sagebrush, thinly lined with vegetation gathered nearby.
Eggs: 7–13, typically 8; av. 55 x 38 mm. Oval to long-oval. Shell smooth with little or no gloss. Olive or olive-buff, quite evenly marked with small spots and dots in shades of brown. Eggs in a clutch may not be uniform. Incubation by female, 22 days (Bendire), 25–27 days (Johnsgard).
Notes: Males congregate on strutting grounds (leks) where polygamous mating occurs. Apart from this brief contact with females, males are not involved in nesting biology.

BOBWHITE *Colinus virginianus*   Pl. 7

Breeding range: Se. Wyoming, s. S. Dakota, s. and cen. Minnesota, south to e. New Mexico, Texas, Louisiana. Introduced with mixed success in Washington, Oregon, sw. Idaho, nw. Wyoming, s. Arizona.
Habitat: Grassy cover for nesting, bushy cover for escape, cultivated or natural plants for food. In a report of nests studied by Stoddard (1931), 97 were in woodlands, 336 in brown-sedge fields, 88 in fallow fields, and 24 in cultivated fields.
Nest: Scrape or hollow in tussock of dead grass or among growing grasses; plants often woven into arch over nest completely concealing it; lined with dead or growing grass or other nearby material; built by both sexes, mostly female.
Eggs: 12–20, typically 14–16, as few as 7–8, laid about 1 per day; av. 30 x 24 mm. Short-pyriform, sometimes quite pointed. Shell smooth, hard, tough, slightly glossy. Dull or cream-white, unmarked. Incubation by both sexes; 23–24 days. 1 brood in North but probably 2 in South.

Notes: Nest seldom found except by accident; close-sitting bird will not flush until almost stepped upon.

SCALED QUAIL *Callipepla squamata*

Breeding range: S. Arizona, New Mexico, se. Colorado, sw. Kansas, sw. Oklahoma, s. and w. Texas. Introduced into cen. Washington, e. Nevada.

Habitat: Desert grasslands, brush-covered mesas and valleys, dry washes, arroyos.

Nest: Under tuft of grass sheltered by sagebrush, Creosote Bush, mesquite, catclaw, cactus, or yucca. Hollow in ground arched over with grass, lined with dry grass.

Eggs; 9–16, commonly 12–14; av. 32.6 x 25.2 mm. Oval or short-oval, usually quite pointed. Shell thick, smooth, little or no gloss. Dull white or cream-white, sparingly or well marked with small spots or dots of brown or buff. Some eggs may be immaculate or nearly so. Incubation probably by female alone; 21–23 days. Commonly 2 broods.

Notes: Nests have been found in meadows, grainfields, gardens, and haystacks, but these are atypical.

CALIFORNIA QUAIL *Lophortyx californicus* Pl. 7

Breeding range: S. Oregon, w. Nevada, south to Baja. Introduced into Washington, Idaho, n. Oregon, n. and cen. Utah.

Habitat: Woodland-brush areas interspersed with grassy areas.

Nest: Under bush, brushpile, beside rock or log, in grass clump, cactus, under haystack, or in rock cranny. Slight hollow or scrape in ground lined with grass or leaves. Nests have been found in vines and even on rooftops.

Eggs: 10–15, commonly 13–14; laid about 5 a week; av. 31 x 24 mm. Short-oval, often rather pointed. Shell thick, hard, little or no gloss. Cream-buff or dull white, variously blotched or dotted with shades of brown. *Less heavily marked* than eggs of Gambel's Quail; Mountain Quail eggs unmarked. Incubation by female, 21–23 days. Possibly 2 broods.

Notes: Although male does not normally incubate, he may assume this duty at the loss of his mate.

GAMBEL'S QUAIL *Lophortyx gambelii*

Breeding range: S. California, s. Nevada, s. Utah, e. Colorado, south to Mexico. Introduced in Lemhi Co., Idaho.

Habitat: Desert scrub and grassland, usually in bottomland; sagebrush country, especially near cultivated areas. Conditions may be extremely dry.

Nest: In grasses, forbs; under desert trees or shrubs.

Eggs: 10–15, typically 10–12, laid 1 a day; av. 31.5 x 24.0 mm.

Short-oval, often somewhat pointed. Smooth, slightly glossy. Dull white or pale buff irregularly spotted and blotched with browns. *More heavily marked* than eggs of California Quail. Incubation by female; 21–24 days.

Notes: Frequently 2 or more females lay in same nest. Occasionally nests are placed above ground in woodpile, rotted stump, or abandoned nest of thrasher, Roadrunner, or Cactus Wren.

MOUNTAIN QUAIL *Oreortyx pictus* Pl. 7

Breeding range: Resident in e. Washington, Oregon, sw. Idaho, Nevada, and California to Baja.
Habitat: Brushy clearings in forested mountains; often in sprout areas after burns; also coniferous forests.
Nest: Under bush, log, rock, or clump of grass. A shallow depression or scrape on ground, lined with leaves, pine needles, feathers, and grass.
Eggs: 8–12, commonly 9–10; av. 34.7 x 27.0 mm. Oval to short-oval, some quite pointed. Shell smooth, glossy. Pale cream to light buff, *entirely unspotted* (unlike California or Gambel's Quail eggs which are well marked). Incubation by female, about 24 days. 2 broods atypical.

MONTEZUMA (HARLEQUIN) QUAIL
Cyrtonyx montezumae

Breeding range: Se. and cen. Arizona, cen. New Mexico, w. Texas.
Habitat: Grassy pine-oak canyons and hillsides.
Nest: On ground. Built of grasses, domed; well lined with dry grass, bits of down. Chamber 4–6 in. (10.2–15.2 cm) high.
Eggs: 8–14, commonly 10–12; av. 31.9 x 24.7 mm. Usually longer than Bobwhite eggs. White, glossy, often nest-stained. Male's part in incubation uncertain; 25–26 days.

RING-NECKED PHEASANT *Phasianus colchicus* Pl. 7

Breeding range: Throughout western states except lower Mississippi Valley and e. Texas.
Habitat: Grain-growing farmlands, bushy pastures, hedgerows; rarely in woods or at any great distance from water. Optimum conditions supplied by diversified farming in eastern portions of northern Great Plains.
Nest: On ground in open weedy fields, bushy pastures, hayfields. In natural hollow or one scraped by female; lined with forbs, grasses, leaves, feathers; concealed by surrounding vegetation.
Eggs: 6–15, commonly 10–12; av. 41.85 x 33.50 mm. Oval to short-oval. Shell smooth with slight gloss. Rich brownish olive or

olive-buff, unmarked. Incubation by female alone; 23–25 days. Incubating female more protectively marked than exposed eggs; will not leave nest until almost stepped upon. Males polygamous; pair bonds tenuous.

Notes: Large clutches or dump nests resulting from laying of more than 1 female not uncommon.

CHUKAR *Alectoris chukar*   Pl. 7

Breeding range: E. Washington, Oregon, and California to Baja; east through Nevada, Idaho, Utah, w. Colorado, Wyoming, Montana; small populations introduced into Arizona, New Mexico, w. S. Dakota, Minnesota.

Habitat: Typically sagebrush grassland or saltbush grassland; dry, rocky slopes.

Nest: On ground, usually under bush or rock; well formed, lined with small twigs, dry grass, and feathers.

Eggs: 7–16, av. 9; av. 43.0 x 31.4 mm. Short-oval. Smooth, and glossy. Pale yellowish, buff, or brown, heavily dotted with reddish brown. Incubation by female; 22–23 days.

Notes: Male's role in incubation and brood care not completely known. Some observers believe male incubates first clutch while female begins second.

GRAY (HUNGARIAN) PARTRIDGE *Perdix perdix*

Breeding range: Introduced stock now well established from Washington, Oregon, ne. California to Minnesota and n. Iowa, south to n. Nevada, n.-cen. Wyoming, S. Dakota.

Habitat: Natural, open, dry grasslands, particularly near cropland; irrigated land in desert scrub regions.

Nest: Often in alfalfa, wheat, and other grain fields. Shallow scrape on ground lined with dry forbs.

Eggs: 8–15 or 20, probably 10–12 typical; laid at 1–2-day intervals; av. 36.8 x 27.4 mm. Short-oval to short-pyriform. Smooth, glossy. Uniform shades of buff, brown, or olive. Incubation by female; 23–25 days. 1 brood.

BLACK FRANCOLIN *Francolinus francolinus*

Notes: Successfully introduced in Louisiana; imported from Pakistan in 1961 and 1962 and released in Morehead and Cameron Parishes. Seems to be flourishing in latter parish but has not succeeded in former. Reproductive biology is similar to that of other partridges.

TURKEY *Meleagris gallopavo*   Pl. 7

Breeding range: Native range extends from Arizona, Colorado, s. Kansas, Missouri, to Mexico and the Gulf Coast. Introduced or re-introduced into California, Iowa, Kansas, Montana, Nebraska, N. Dakota, S. Dakota, Oregon, Utah, Washington, Wyoming.

Habitat: Wooded southern swamps, sparsely wooded flatlands and river bottoms of Great Plains, coniferous and pine-oak forests of western mountains, dry brushlands of Southwest.

Nest: On dry ground, usually near strutting ground of male; a depression in dry leaves, often under log or bush or at base of tree; lining almost entirely of leaves.

Eggs: 8–15, often 11–13; av. 62.6 x 44.6 mm. Short-oval to long-oval, sometimes quite pointed. Shell smooth, little or no gloss. Pale buff or buffy white; rather evenly marked with reddish brown or pinkish buff spots or fine dots. Incubation by female alone; 28 days. 1 brood. Male polygamous, each gobbler with harem of several hens.

Notes: As hen sits on nest, she covers her back with leaves. Upon departing, she slides out from under leaves which then form a protective cover for her eggs.

SANDHILL CRANE *Grus canadensis*   Pl. 7

Breeding range: S.-cen. and se. Oregon, ne. California, cen. and se. Idaho, ne. Nevada, ne. Utah (Rich Co., poss.), w. Montana, nw. Wyoming, nw. Colorado (rare), N. Dakota (McHenry Co., 1973), nw. and cen. Minnesota.

Habitat: In isolated river valleys, marshes, and meadows.

Nest: In or close to shallow water in undisturbed marshes, bogs, prairie ponds. Mound of sticks, mosses, dead reeds, rushes, tufts of grass, built 6–8 in. (15.2–20.3 cm) above surrounding water; sometimes in drier situation at edge of marsh. Outside diam. 3–5 ft. (0.9–1.5 m) or more.

Eggs: 2, sometimes 1, rarely 3; laid about every other day; av. 96.2 x 61.4 mm. Oval to long-oval. Shell smooth, little or no gloss. Drab buff or olive with lavender spots overlaid with brown and olive spots. Incubation by both sexes; 28–31 days.

Notes: After Sandhill Cranes mature at 4 years, they mate for life. Pairs may defend same territory year after year and may use same nest site. Except in protected places (state and national parks and sanctuaries), wilderness demanded by this shy bird is rapidly disappearing.

KING RAIL *Rallus elegans*

Breeding range: N. Dakota and Minnesota south to Gulf.

Habitat: Inland freshwater marshes, ponds, sloughs, marshy edges of lakes, sluggish streams, roadside ditches. Not known to nest in coastal saltmarshes.

Nest: 6–18 in. (15.2–45.7 cm) above water in hummock, clump of cattails, among marsh grasses, rushes, other aquatic vegetation. Basketlike structure of dead rushes, grasses, cattails, generally with natural canopy. Built mostly by male. Outside diam. about 8 in. (20.3 cm).

Eggs: 6–15, typically 10–12; laid 1 a day; av. 41 x 30 mm. Oval. Shell smooth, very slight gloss. Pale buff, sparingly and irregularly spotted with shades of brown; overlaid appearance. Incubation by both sexes; 21–23 days. Eggs may be laid before nest complete. 1, possibly 2, broods.

Notes: Incubating birds seldom flush until intruder is 10 ft. (3.1 m) or less from nest.

CLAPPER RAIL   *Rallus longirostris*

Breeding range: Coastal Louisiana and e. Texas saltwater marshes — Louisiana Clapper Rail (*R. l. saturatus*); s. California tidal marshes — 2 endangered races, California Clapper Rail (*R. l. obsoletus*) and Light-footed Clapper Rail (*R. l. levipes*); freshwater marshes along Colorado R. between Arizona and California — endangered race Yuma Clapper Rail (*R. l. yumanensis*).

Nest: Elevated and arched over in marsh vegetation.

Eggs: 4–12, generally 8–11; laid 1 a day; av. 42.0 x 29.3 mm (*R. l. saturatus*). Buff with brown spots. Incubation by both sexes; 18–22 days, av. 20. 1, possibly 2, broods.

VIRGINIA RAIL   *Rallus limicola*   Pl. 8

Breeding range: Local, common to rare, in all states.

Habitat: Mostly freshwater marshes, principally sedge borders and cattail belts; upper reaches of saltmarshes.

Nest: In marsh vegetation in drier areas or over water, usually

CLAPPER RAIL

2–5 in. (5.1–12.7 cm) above water level. Built of cattails, coarse grass stems, or other available plant material; may use only rushes. Usually has canopy of live sedges and rushes. Outside diam. 6¾ in. (17.1 cm), height 3 in. (7.6 cm); inside diam. 4¼ in. (10.8 cm), depth 1½ in. (3.8 cm).

Eggs: 6–13, commonly 8–10; laid 1 a day; av. 32.0 x 24.5 mm. Oval to long-oval. Shell smooth, little or no gloss. Pale buff or nearly white, sparingly and irregularly spotted with browns, often concentrated at larger end. Virginia eggs *lighter colored, less heavily marked, less glossy* than Sora's. Incubation by both sexes; 18–20 days, av. 19, starting when last or next to last egg laid. 2 broods have been reported.

Notes: Virginia Rails and Soras nest in same habitat; Virginias generally nest in drier areas.

SORA *Porzana carolina*   Pl. 8

Breeding range: Washington to Minnesota, south to Baja; Nevada, Utah, Colorado, Kansas (unc.), n. Missouri.

Habitat: Soggy freshwater marshes, swamps, slough borders, grassy meadows. Sedges or cattails where mud and water are quite deep are preferred.

Nest: Basket built about 6 in. (15.2 cm) above water level, supported and arched over by surrounding growing vegetation, commonly cattails or bulrushes. Constructed of dead cattail blades, bulrushes, grasses; finely lined. Sometimes a runway, made of nest material, leads to nest. Av. outside diam. 6 in. (15.2 cm), height 5 in. (12.7 cm); inside diam. 3 in. (7.6 cm), depth 2 in. (5.1 cm). **Eggs:** 6–18, av. 10–12, laid 1 a day; av. 31.5 x 22.5 mm. Oval. Shell smooth, glossy. Rich buff, irregularly spotted with shades of brown. *Eggs more richly colored, more heavily spotted, glossier than those of Virginia Rail.* Incubation by both sexes; 18–19 days, starting after laying of first few eggs. At one time nest may contain young just hatched, eggs unhatched and hatching. While one bird incubates, other cares for precocial young. 1 brood, possibly 2.

Notes: Empty nest indistinguishable from nest of Virginia Rail; Sora's more likely over deep water.

YELLOW RAIL *Coturnicops noveboracensis*

Breeding range: Northern N. Dakota and n. Minnesota; a few nesting records for e.-cen California (Mono Co.).

Habitat: Marsh edges, grassy or sedge meadows.

Nest: Under mass of dead rushes or grasses; or hidden by natural canopy of growing vegetation.

Eggs: 7–10; av. 28.3 x 20.7 mm. Creamy buff; capped with large reddish brown spots. *Paler* than Sora eggs; *darker* than Virginia Rail eggs. Incubation probably 16–20 days.

BLACK RAIL *Laterallus jamaicensis*

Breeding range: Rare, casual, or uncommon in Kansas, Nebraska, Missouri; also California, south from San Francisco area to Baja, including 20 miles (32.2 km) of disjunct localities along lower Colorado R. Colorado R. race (*L. j. coturniculus*) considered endangered; survey of area indicated only about 116 territories established by breeding pairs.

Habitat: Wet meadows and marshes.

Nest: Deep cup of loosely woven fine grasses in depression under arch of matted dead marsh grasses with entrance at side. *Resembles nest of Meadowlark.*

Eggs: 6–10; av. 25.6 x 19.8 mm. Oval. Buffy white or pinkish white, marked with evenly distributed fine brown dots. Incubated by both sexes, probably 16–20 days. 1 brood, possibly 2.

PURPLE GALLINULE *Porphyrula martinica*

Breeding range: Se. Oklahoma, Arkansas, s. Texas, and Louisiana.

Habitat: Freshwater marshes; borders of ponds, lakes, lagoons; rice plantations.

Nest: Floating mass of dead flags, green or decaying leaves, plant stalks; interwoven with and held up by surrounding vegetation.

Eggs: 5-15, commonly 6-8; av. 39.2 x 28.8 mm. Pale pinkish buff; a few unevenly scattered brown spots or dots. Eggs smaller, paler, with spots smaller and more regular in size and distribution than those of Common Gallinule. Incubation probably by both sexes; about 22 days.

COMMON GALLINULE *Gallinula chloropus* Pl. 8

Breeding range: California, Arizona, New Mexico, se. Nebraska (rare), Kansas (Barton, Stafford Cos.), Oklahoma, Texas; and s. Minnesota south to Louisiana.
Habitat: Freshwater marshes, canals, ponds, reservoirs.
Nest: Typically over water that is often covered with duckweed, anchored in clump of vegetation; occasionally in shrub (willow, alder, wild rose) in or near water. Well-made cup of dead cattails, rushes, stems of aquatic plants; often has ramp from water to nest. Nestlike platforms often nearby (roosting, loafing, brooding areas). Size of 1 nest: outside diam. 15 in. (38.1 cm), height 8 in. (20.3 cm); inside diam. 8 in. (20.3 cm), depth 3 in. (7.6 cm).
Eggs: 6-17, typically 10-12; laid 1 a day; av. 44 x 31 mm. Oval. Shell smooth, little or no gloss. Cinnamon to buff, irregularly marked with brownish spots, fine dots. Differ from Purple Gallinule's in being larger, with ground color slightly darker; spots larger, more irregular, less evenly distributed. Incubation by both sexes; 19-22 days, beginning about time 5th egg laid.
Notes: Nests in same habitat as Purple Gallinule but generally in shallower water and lower nest site.

AMERICAN COOT *Fulica americana* Pl. 8

Breeding range: Throughout western states; highest densities in prairie pothole region of n.-cen. U.S., particularly in Dakotas; coastal wetlands of Louisiana and Texas.
Habitat: Freshwater marshes, ponds, lakes, wet meadows.
Nest: Typically floating in $11\frac{3}{4}$-$39\frac{3}{8}$ in. (30-100 cm) of water, attached to surrounding dead or growing plants. Cupped platform of dead bulrushes, cattails, sedges, preferably dry, placed several inches above surface of water. Both sexes build. Av. outside diam. 14-18 in. (35.6-45.7 cm); inside diam. 7 in. (17.8 cm).
Eggs: 2-16, typically 6-11, av. about 8; laid at intervals of slightly more than 24 hours; av. 49.0 x 33.5 mm. Oval, sometimes quite pointed. Shell smooth, has slight gloss. Buff with dense covering of evenly distributed dark brown spots. Incubation by both sexes; 23-24 days; generally starts after laying of 3rd or 4th egg. Usually 1 brood, but 2 broods have been noted (California, Utah).
Notes: In Colorado study of 211 nests, Gorenzel reports 68 percent in bulrushes, 28 percent cattails, 3 percent mixture of both, and 1 percent sedge. Average distance from nest to open water or

channel 18 ft. (5.5 m). Additional platforms built unless Muskrat houses or other structures available for resting, copulating, brooding young.

JACANA *Jacana spinosa*

Breeding range: S. and se. Texas (Kleberg Co. in 1968 and Manor Lake near Angleton, Brazoria Co., in 1971).
Habitat: Freshwater marshes.
Nest: Frail raft of water plants and rubbish floating on or among marsh vegetation including water lilies.
Eggs: 3–5, commonly 4; av. 30.1 x 23.0 mm. Unique; very glossy brown with black scrawls and tangled fine penlike lines. Only male incubates.
Notes: Male alone cares for young. Female maintains pair bonds with 1–4 males.

AMERICAN OYSTERCATCHER *Haematopus palliatus*

Breeding range: Texas and Louisiana Gulf coasts (rare).
Habitat: Higher parts of sandy beaches.
Nest: Hollow in sand or shell.
Eggs: 2–3, sometimes 4; av. 55.7 x 38.7 mm. Buff or olive-buff; irregularly marked and overlaid with spots and blotches of light and dark brown. Incubation by both sexes; about 27 days.

AMERICAN OYSTERCATCHER

BLACK OYSTERCATCHER   *Haematopus bachmani*   Pl. 8

Breeding range: Pacific coast from Washington to Baja.
Habitat: Rocky shores of mainland and offshore islands.
Nest: Depression in beach gravel or weedy turf; hollow of bare rock. Sparsely lined with bits of shell or broken stone; typically 5–21 ft. (1.5–6.4 m) above mean high tide.
Eggs: 2–3, occasionally 1, rarely 4, laid at intervals of 1–3 days; av. 56.2 x 39.5 mm. Oval. Very slight gloss. Cream-buff to olive-buff; usually quite evenly covered with small black or dark brown spots, scrawls. Incubation by both sexes; about 27 days.
Notes: Reports of more than 4 eggs probably indicate more than 1 female laying in same nest. In one nest where eggs were chilled by prolonged exposure, adults sat for 55 days before abandoning clutch. Ravens are important predators on eggs. Black Oyster-catchers may remain mated for life.

SEMIPALMATED PLOVER   *Charadrius semipalmatus*

Notes: In July 1973, 2 mated pairs, each with 1 downy young, were observed at Ocean Shores, Gray's Harbor Co., Washington. This appears to be the only nesting record of this species in U.S.

PIPING PLOVER   *Charadrius melodus*

Breeding range: Uncommon, local, or casual in ne. Montana, N. Dakota, S. Dakota, n. Minnesota, e. Nebraska, w. Iowa.
Habitat: Exposed, sparsely vegetated shores and islands of shallow lakes, ponds, impoundments; undisturbed beaches.
Nest: Solitary. Slight hollow in sand or gravel; rimmed or lined with pebbles, broken shell, bits of driftwood.
Eggs: Almost always 4, laid every other day; may be 3 in second nesting attempt; av. 31.4 x 24.2 mm. Oval to pyriform. Shell smooth; no gloss. Light buff, evenly and lightly marked with fine spots of dark brown. Incubation by both sexes; 27–28 days; may start with 3rd egg. 1 brood.
Notes: Banded adults often return annually to same nesting area. Some have same mates in consecutive years.

SNOWY PLOVER   *Charadrius alexandrinus*

Breeding range: W. Washington, Oregon, California, s.-cen. Montana (prob.), cen. Utah, Colorado (rare), New Mexico, s.-cen. Kansas, Oklahoma, coastal Texas.
Habitat: Sandy shores, alkali flats, dry lake beds.
Nest: May be in loose colonies where habitat is suitable, but single nests not uncommon; sometimes near tern colony. Slight hollow in ground lined with, and often surrounded by, pieces of shell, pebbles, or debris.
Eggs: 3, sometimes 2 (record of 44 clutches: 3 eggs in 32; 2 in 11);

PIPING PLOVER

av. 30.4 x 22.3 mm. Oval to pyriform. Shell smooth, has no gloss. Light buff (sand-colored), more or less evenly covered with small spots, dots, little scrawls of black. Incubation by both sexes; 24 days. 1 brood.

Notes: As with similar Piping Plover, color and markings of eggs, young, and adult birds provide excellent camouflage with sand and shell surroundings.

WILSON'S PLOVER *Charadrius wilsonia*

Breeding range: Texas and Louisiana coasts.
Habitat: Open areas on sandy islands and shell beaches with scattered vegetation; near salt or brackish water.
Nest: Simple hollow in sand or shell, generally lined with bits of broken shell, sometimes concealed by beach plants.
Eggs: 3, sometimes 2, rarely 4; av. 35.7 x 26.2 mm. Buff; quite evenly blotched, spotted, and scrawled with black or dark brown. Incubation by both sexes; 24 days. 1 brood.

KILLDEER *Charadrius vociferus* Pl. 8

Breeding range: All western states.
Habitat: Often near human habitation, far from water — lawns, airports, cemeteries, driveways, roadsides, parking lots, cultivated fields — with ground cover (gravel, cinders, stones, rubble) that affords camouflage.
Nest: In open where incubating bird has extended view. Male makes various scrapes in ground; one is later accepted by female as nest site. Depression in ground may be unlined or lined with pebbles, wood chips, grass, assorted debris. Outside diam. 5–7 in.

KILLDEER incubating　　　　　　　**KILLDEER** feigning injury

(12.7–17.8 cm.); depth $1–1\frac{1}{2}$ in. (2.5–3.8 cm).
Eggs: 4, rarely 3 or 5; av. 36.3 x 26.6 mm. Oval to pyriform, typically quite pointed. Shell smooth, has no gloss. Shades of buff with bold black or brown spots, scrawls, blotches; sometimes wreathed or capped. Incubation by both sexes; 24–26 days. Sometimes 2 broods.
Notes: Killdeer use "broken-wing" ruse to draw intruder away from nest. Nests have been found on gravel roofs, some as high as 50 ft. (15.3 m) above ground; in heaps of broken glass; between ties of railroad tracks in use.

MOUNTAIN PLOVER　*Charadrius montanus*　　Pl. 8

Breeding range: E. Montana, e. Wyoming, sw. Nebraska (rare), e. Colorado, nw. New Mexico (loc., unc.), nw. Oklahoma (Cimarron Co., unc.), nw. Texas (loc., unc.). Greatest density in Pawnee National Grassland, Weld Co., Colorado.
Habitat: Large flats of short-grass prairie, especially those covered mainly by Blue Grama Grass (*Bouteloua gracilis*) and/or Buffalo Grass (*Buchloe dactyloides*). Tall vegetation avoided; level areas preferred, on hilltops or in valleys.
Nest: Scrape in ground with no nest material when 1st egg is laid; attending adult adds nest material throughout egg-laying and incubation period. Tendency to place nest near old, gray cow manure piles. Nest material includes manure chips, grass rootlets, leaves, seedpods.
Eggs: 3, sometimes 2, rarely 1 or 4 (in 154 Colorado nests: 2 of 1, 17 of 2, 134 of 3, 1 of 4), normally laid at 1–2 day intervals; av. 37.3 x 28.3 mm. Oval to short-oval. No gloss. Dark olive-buff; irregularly marked, chiefly near larger end, with black spots and scrawls. Female typically lays 2 clutches, 1 incubated by male, the other by female. While both sexes incubate simultaneously, the

male attends only the 1st nest; the female attends the 2nd one alone (Graul).

Notes: Misnamed; not a bird of mountains but of tablelands and prairies. Pair bonds are short-lived. Male may fertilize 2nd clutch for original female or for another; female may lay 2nd clutch for original male or for new mate.

MOUNTAIN PLOVER habitat

AMERICAN WOODCOCK *Philohela minor*

Breeding range: Minnesota to Louisiana; very locally westward to extreme e. N. Dakota and e. S. Dakota, Nebraska (Missouri R.), Kansas (poss.), Oklahoma, ne. Texas.

Habitat: Generally in young forests with scattered openings. Includes areas for singing grounds, nesting, and moist soil where birds can probe for earthworms.

Nest: Near male's singing grounds and within a few yards of brushy field edge. Cup on ground, sometimes at base of shrub or small tree; often rimmed with twigs, lined with leaves or pine needles; built by female.

Eggs: 4 (late nests 3); laid 1 a day; av. 38 x 29 mm; large for so small a bird. Oval. Shell smooth, has slight gloss. Pinkish buff to cinnamon, covered with light brown spots or blotches overlaid with darker brown markings. Male promiscuous, probably polygamous. Female disturbed during early stages of incubation may abandon nest. 1 brood.

Notes: Female attracted to singing ground, site of male's court-ship performance, where mating occurs. Most crepuscular and nocturnal of North American shorebirds. Solitary nester, but may share feeding grounds with other woodcocks. Close sitting of bird and cryptic plumage make nests hard to find. Incubating bird sometimes permits stroking by hand.

COMMON SNIPE *Capella gallinago* Pl. 8

Breeding range: Washington to Minnesota, south to n. California, Nevada, Utah, Colorado, and locally to Nebraska, Kansas, Oklahoma, Iowa.
Habitat: Freshwater marshes, wet meadows, bogs; sometimes in dry brushy margins of clearings.
Nest: In or at edge of marsh or bog, in tussock of grass; sometimes buried in sphagnum. Neat, well-cupped, generally built of grasses; sometimes with overstory of living plants woven into protective canopy. Outside diam. 5–6 in. (12.7–15.2 cm), height 2¼ in. (5.7 cm); inside diam. 3–4 in. (7.6–10.2 cm), depth 1¼ in. (3.2 cm).
Eggs: 4, rarely 5; av. 38.6 x 28.1 mm. Pyriform. Shell smooth, has slight gloss. 2 color types: light buff or dark brown. Both types spotted, heavily blotched, scrawled, overlaid with deep brown. Incubation by female; 18–20 days, av. 19. Male monogamous, helps care for young. 1 brood.
Notes: Male "winnows" in spectacular aerial performance until territory established. Display attracts female; pair bond is formed. Incubating bird is close sitter; stroking back of bird or even lifting her from nest not uncommon.

AMERICAN WOODCOCK

LONG-BILLED CURLEW *Numenius americanus*   **Pl. 9**

Breeding range: Washington to N. Dakota, south to ne. California, Nevada, Utah, New Mexico, extreme nw. Texas.
Habitat: Both upland and aquatic; moist meadows to very dry prairies.
Nest: May be close to each other in favorable habitat. Slight hollow in ground, usually thinly lined with forbs, grasses. Rim may be elevated above surroundings. Typical nest: inside diam. 8 in. (20.3 cm), depth 2 in. (5.1 cm).
Eggs: 4, occasionally 5; av. 65.0 x 45.8 mm. Oval, short-oval. Slight gloss. Olive-buff, quite evenly spotted with various shades of brown and olive. Incubation by both sexes; probably about 30 days.
Notes: Incubating bird conspicuous on nest; typically allows close approach before flushing.

UPLAND SANDPIPER *Bartramia longicauda*   **Pl. 9**

Breeding range: E. Washington to Minnesota, south to Oregon, e. Wyoming, e. Colorado, n. Oklahoma, Missouri.
Habitat: Prairies, open grassy fields, hayfields.
Nest: In loosely spaced colonies; density varies, $1\frac{1}{2}$–15 acres (0.6–6.1 ha) per nest. In depression in thick clump of grass arched over top; invisible from above. Grass twisted in circle to form nest cup. Outside diam. 4–5 in. (10.2–12.7 cm); depth 2–3 in. (5.1–7.6 cm).
Eggs: 4, rarely 5; av. 45.0 x 32.5 mm. Oval to pyriform. Shell smooth, slight gloss. Creamy or pinkish buff; speckled, spotted, overlaid with light reddish brown. Incubation by both sexes; 21 days. 1 brood.
Notes: Each incubating bird has its own flushing distance. Some flush when intruder is 6 ft. (1.8 m) away, others permit back-stroking on nest. Flushing does not cause desertion. Like Prairie Horned Lark, this species took advantage of man's openings in forests to increase its range.

SPOTTED SANDPIPER *Actitis macularia*   **Pl. 9**

Breeding range: Most western states; nesting evidence sparse in Oklahoma, Missouri, Arkansas, Texas, Louisiana.
Habitat: Prairies, pastures, edges of freshwater ponds, sloughs, lakes; weed-choked shoulders of roads.
Nest: Solitary or in loose colonies. Grass-lined depression in ground under rank forbs, bushes, or in grass 6 in. (15.2 cm) or higher. Often remote from water. Both sexes build. Diam. $4\frac{1}{2}$–5 in. (11.4–12.7 cm).
Eggs: 4, occasionally 3, rarely 5 (of 37 nests, 33 had 4 eggs, 3 had 3, 1 had 5); av. 32 x 23 mm. Oval to pyriform. Shell smooth, slight

SPOTTED SANDPIPER

gloss. Buff, heavily spotted and blotched with brown shades. Incubation principally by *male;* 20–22 days, usually 21.

Notes: Females often polyandrous. One observer watched 5 females initiate 12 nests: 2 were monogamous, 2 had 2 mates, 1 had 4 mates. Females shared incubation only in final clutches. Elsewhere, 12 females were observed with 19 clutches for 14 males. Variant behavior of females seems to indicate that polyandry is in process of evolving.

SOLITARY SANDPIPER *Tringa solitaria*

Notes: One breeding record for the U.S.: On July 11, 1973, a pair and 1 young bird were found along the Mississippi R. in Verdon Township, Aikin Co., Minnesota.

WILLET *Catoptrophorus semipalmatus*   Pl. 9

Breeding range: Oregon to Minnesota (cas.), south to ne. California, n. and cen. Utah, n.-cen. Colorado, Nebraska (Sandhills); Gulf Coast of Texas and Louisiana.

Habitat: Open areas (prairies inland) in salt and brackish marshes, saline flats, intertidal zones, lakes.

Nest: In colonies, usually 200 ft. (61 m) or farther apart. On ground in short, thick grass; sometimes on open beach or flat. Grass blades bent to form thin base in natural hollow; lined with fine grass. Female selects site. Outside diam. 6–7 in. (15.2–17.8 cm).

Eggs: 4, rarely 5, laid at intervals of 1 or more days; av.

WILLET nest, eggs

WILLET incubating

54.1 x 37.6 mm (western race). Oval to pyriform. Shell smooth, has slight gloss. Grayish, greenish, or olive-buff, boldly marked with an overlay of small to large spots and blotches of brown shades. Incubation by female (possibly male at night); 22–29 days, probably starting before clutch complete. 1 brood.

MARBLED GODWIT *Limosa fedoa*

Breeding range: Unc. to rare in Montana, N. Dakota, S. Dakota, nw. Minnesota.
Habitat: Grassy prairies.
Nest: In small colonies in short grass. A slight hollow lined with dry grass. No attempt at concealment.
Eggs: 4, rarely 3 or 5; av. 57.0 x 39.6 mm. Olive-buff; sparingly, unevenly marked with brown spots, blotches.
Notes: Bird commonly tame in vicinity of nest but shy elsewhere (incubating birds have been lifted from nests). In N. Dakota, 4 nests found in native prairie, 4 in cropland, 1 in hayland.

AMERICAN AVOCET *Recurvirostra americana* Pl. 9

Breeding range: E. and cen. Washington to N. Dakota, south to Mexico and Texas coast; Minnesota (poss.).
Habitat: Borders of muddy, saline, alkaline, and freshwater ponds, lakes, marshes.
Nest: In colonies, on ground on dry, sun-baked mud flats or on low, gravelly or sandy islands with scant vegetation. Nests vary from almost nothing to elevated piles of debris. No attempt at concealment; eggs blend well with surroundings. Nest hollows 3–7 in. (7.6–17.8 cm) in diameter.
Eggs: 4, often 3, sometimes 5; av. 49.8 x 34.0 mm. Oval to oval-pyriform, usually elongated. Smooth, not glossy. Olive-buff covered with irregular brown or black spots, blotches in various sizes.

Very similar to eggs of Black-necked Stilt, but *larger* and *less heavily marked*. Incubation by both sexes; about 25 days.

Notes: When nests approached, all Avocets in area dart at intruder, issuing harsh, shrill cries; some land to continue alarm cries as they run about with half-open wings. Much like Black-necked Stilts in this behavior.

BLACK-NECKED STILT   *Himantopus mexicanus*   **Pl. 9**

Breeding range: S. Oregon, n. Utah, s. Colorado, Kansas (Barton Co., rare), south to Mexico and along Gulf Coast to Louisiana.

Habitat: Ponds, sloughs, canals, fresh or brackish marshes, wet meadows, mud flats, rice plantations, shores of drainage ditches.

Nest: In small loose colonies from a few to several dozen pairs. Dry site near water or mound built up above shallow water level. No nest (eggs on bare ground) or a scrape in ground lined with bits of shells; or elaborate mound of mud, sticks, shells, debris, hollowed in center. Outside diam. 6–10 in. (15.2–25.4 cm); inside diam. 4 in. (10.2 cm).

Eggs: 4, occasionally 3, rarely 5; av. 44.0 x 30.5 mm. Oval to pyriform, typically quite pointed. Shell smooth, little or no gloss. Buffy or sandy; blotched with dark brown or black, sometimes with dots and spots; often badly stained with mud. Very similar to eggs of American Avocet, but *smaller* and *more heavily marked*. Incubation by both sexes, probably about 25 days.

Notes: Nesting birds in colony join forces to distract intruder; fly overhead in sweeping circles uttering loud, harsh, shrill cries. Assumed to be single-brooded, but fresh eggs are found from April through July.

BLACK-NECKED STILT

WILSON'S PHALAROPE *Steganopus tricolor*   Pl. 9

Breeding range: Washington to w. and cen. Minnesota, south to California, Nevada, Utah, Colorado, nw. Iowa (prob.).
Habitat: Inland marshes, prairie sloughs, wet or moist meadows bordering lakes, marshy islands.
Nest: Loosely colonial in favorable habitat. Hollow in small hummock in damp ground, often surrounded by shallow water; either scantily or well lined with grass. Male alone builds. Typical inside diam. 2¾-3½ in. (7.1-8.9 cm).
Eggs: Commonly 4, sometimes 3; av. 33.0 x 23.4 mm. Oval to pyriform. Slight gloss. Buff; covered with brown spots, dots, mixed with irregular blotches. Incubation by *male* alone, 20-21 days.
Notes: Although female takes no part in nest activity except to lay eggs, she remains in adjacent area and shows considerable anxiety when nest is approached. Incubating male usually leaves nest well in advance of approaching intruder. Birds very noisy when disturbed.

GLAUCOUS-WINGED GULL *Larus glaucescens*

Breeding range: Washington coast, Oregon coast (loc.).
Habitat: Ledges of steep cliffs or grassy or sandy flats on small coastal islands.
Nest: Bulky, well made of grass and seaweed, especially kelp.
Eggs: 2-3; av. 72.8 x 50.8 mm. Buff to pale olive, spotted or blotched with darker browns. *Not distinguishable from eggs of other species of gulls of similar size.*
Notes: Known to hybridize with Western Gulls.

WESTERN GULL *Larus occidentalis*   Pl. 9

Breeding range: Pacific coast from Washington to Baja. Only gull nesting along California coast.
Habitat: Offshore islands; in California thousands nest on Farallon Is., 28 miles (45 km) west of San Francisco.
Nest: In colonies with other seabirds on grassy hillsides or exposed ledges of cliffs on rocky offshore islands, headlands, islets, dikes; rarely on bridges, boats, roofs. A low mound of forbs and grasses; often repaired, used in succeeding years. Inside diam. 9-14 in. (22.9-35.6 cm), av. 11 in. (27.9 cm); depth 2-4 in. (5.1-10.2 cm), av. 2½ in. (6.4 cm).
Eggs: 1-4, typically 3, probably laid every other day; av. 72.4 x 50.4 mm. Oval, short-oval, and long-oval. Shell thin, finely granulated; slight luster. Buffy to cinnamon-brown and gray; vary within as well as between clutches. Incubation 25-29 days, typically 26; mostly by female usually beginning when clutch complete. 1 brood.

Notes: Recent study by ornithologists found that in 8 to 14 percent of 1200 pairs on Santa Barbara I., California, both birds were females. The twosome went through all motions of heterosexual pair but laid sterile eggs. Nests often contained 4 to 6 eggs. No similar union noted among male gulls.

HERRING GULL   *Larus argentatus*

Notes: A rare breeder in Montana; also in Lake Superior and a few smaller lakes in Minnesota. Recently nests have been found in a Ring-billed Gull colony on Hennepin I., Mille Lacs Lake, cen. Minnesota. For details of breeding biology see *A Field Guide to Birds' Nests East of the Mississippi River.*

CALIFORNIA GULL   *Larus californicus*   Pl. 10

Breeding range: Washington to N. Dakota (local, unc.) south to ne. California, Nevada, n. Utah, cen. Colorado (Weld, Park Cos.).
Habitat: Interior freshwater lakes and marshes, commonly on islands.
Nest: In colonies, some huge, with nests as close as 2 ft. (0.6 m) apart. Usually a depression in the ground, lined sparingly or heavily with forbs, grasses, sticks, bones, rubbish, feathers. Eggs sometimes laid on bare ground in natural depression. Outside diam. 10–12 in. (25.4–30.5 cm); inside diam. about 7 in. (17.8 cm), depth av. 2 in. (5.1 cm).
Eggs: 1–3, usually 2; av. 67.5 x 45.5 mm. Short to long-oval; may be more pointed than other gull eggs. Shell thin and lusterless. Dark brown to light drab, gray, or buff; spotted or blotched with brown or gray. Sometimes decorated with scrawls and irregular lines. Incubation by both sexes; 23–27 days, av. 25. 1 brood.
Notes: In colony in Utah, 13 foreign eggs were found in gull nests: 8 Ring-necked Pheasant, 3 American Coot, 1 Cinnamon Teal, and 1 Northern Shoveler. In Idaho, eggs found in gull's nests included Cinnamon Teal, Ring-necked Pheasant, American Coot, Black-necked Stilt, Eared Grebe. None of these nested near colonies; inference is that gulls carried eggs to their nests.

RING-BILLED GULL   *Larus delawarensis*   Pl. 10

Breeding range: Washington to Minnesota (unc.), south to ne. California, s. Idaho, S. Dakota.
Habitat: Islands in inland lakes.
Nest: In colonies sometimes mixed with California Gulls; also adjacent to nests of terns, ducks, cormorants. In open situations on ground on matted vegetation or at upper edges of beaches among rocks. Made of dried grasses, mosses, forbs, rubbish; lined with finer grasses, some feathers. Outside diam. 10–12 in. (25.4–30.5 cm), height 3–4 in. (7.6–10.2 cm); inside diam. 6–9 in. (15.2–22.9 cm), depth 2 in. (5.1 cm).

LAUGHING GULL

Eggs: 3, often 2, rarely 4; av. 59.3 x 42.3 mm. Oval or short-oval.
Shell smooth, lusterless. Buffy to whitish with spots, dots, irregular scrawls, splashes, blotches in shades of brown; markings appear
overlaid. Incubation by both sexes; 21 days. 1 brood.
Notes: Colonies not always permanent; from year to year may
shift from one island to another.

LAUGHING GULL   *Larus atricilla*

Notes: Abundant permanent resident in Louisiana (only gull that
breeds in that state), locally along Texas Gulf Coast. Formerly
bred in small numbers at south end of California's Salton Sea
where it still occurs as postbreeding visitor. Nests in compact
colonies in salt meadows interspersed with tidal creeks; also grassy
islands. For details of breeding biology see *A Field Guide to Birds'
Nests East of the Mississippi River.*

FRANKLIN'S GULL   *Larus pipixcan*

Breeding range: Oregon (Malheur National Wildlife Refuge), s.
Idaho, Utah, n.-cen. and ne. Montana, Wyoming, N. Dakota, w.
Minnesota, se. S. Dakota, nw. Iowa.
Habitat: Prairie marshes, sloughs, marshy lakes.
Nest: In large colonies; sometimes in water waist-deep or deeper.
Large floating masses of dead reeds, well secured, often among
standing green reeds. Vary greatly in size and construction. Outside diam. 12–30 in. (30.5–76.2 cm); height above water 4–8 in.
(10.2–20.3 cm); inner cavity, slightly hollowed, about 5 in.
(12.7 cm) in diam.

Eggs: Generally 3, sometimes 2, rarely 4 (product of 2 females?); av. 52 x 36 mm. Oval to long-oval. Shell thin, almost lusterless. Great variety of buff and greenish buff shades, sparingly or heavily marked with large and small spots, blotches, irregular scrawls of brown. Incubation probably by both sexes; about 20 days.

Notes: Formerly in immense colonies of 10,000–20,000 nests; 15–20 nests in an area of 10 yds. square (83.6 m²).

GULL-BILLED TERN *Gelochelidon nilotica*

Breeding range: Texas and Louisiana coasts; colony at south end of California's Salton Sea (mouth of New R.).

Habitat: Spoil banks, flats, shores, and grassy areas of islands or mainland along seacoast; marshes.

Nest: In colonies. In depression in grass or hollow in sand. May or may not be sparingly to heavily lined.

Eggs: 2–3, occasionally 4; av. 47 x 34 mm. Light buff, spotted, blotched with shades of brown. Incubation by both sexes; 22–23 days. 1 brood.

GULL-BILLED TERN

FORSTER'S TERN *Sterna forsteri*   Pl. 10

Breeding range: Washington to w. Minnesota, south to California, Nevada, Utah, Colorado, Kansas (Barton Co.), nw. Iowa; also resident along Louisiana and Texas coasts.

Habitat: Extensive inland marshes and marshy borders of lakes, large ponds. Coastal saltmarshes behind beaches.

Nest: In colonies, close together. Inland nests often on muskrat houses, feeding platforms, floating material. Placed higher and

COMMON TERN

drier than Black Tern nests often found in same marshes; 107 nests averaged 8 ½ in. (21.6 cm) above water. Cupped depressions with a few pieces of emergent vegetation added. Coastal nests large, elaborate; well built piles of dead grasses, sedges; lined with fine grass, reeds. Outside diam. 20–30 in. (50.8–76.2 cm); inside diam. 7–8 in. (17.8–20.3 cm), depth 1–1 ½ in. (2.5–3.8 cm).

Eggs: 3, sometimes 2 or 4, rarely 5; av. 43 x 31 mm. Oval, short-oval, long-oval. Shell smooth, no luster. Olive or grayish or pinkish buff marked and overlaid with small brownish spots; often wreathed near large end; sometimes boldly marked with large brownish blotches or irregular scrawls. *Eggs indistinguishable from those of Common Tern.* Incubation by both sexes; 23–24 days. 1 brood.

COMMON TERN *Sterna hirundo*

Breeding range: N. Montana, N. Dakota, S. Dakota (local), n.-cen. and ne. Minnesota; also rare breeder on Louisiana Gulf Coast; w. Washington (1977, prob.).

Habitat: Typically, isolated sparsely vegetated islands in large lakes; marshes, ponds, coastal beaches.

Nest: May be slight hollow in sand, shells, or pebbles; depression in windrows of trash and seaweed.

Eggs: 2–4, generally 3; av. 41.5 x 30.0 mm. Pale buff generally spotted with shades of dark brown. *Eggs indistinguishable from those of Forster's Tern.* Incubation by both sexes; 24–26 days. 1 brood.

SOOTY TERN *Sterna fuscata*

Notes: Nest sparingly but regularly in Chandeleur Is., Louisiana, and locally and sparingly along Gulf Coast of Texas. Normally nest in large colonies on tropical islands but are confined to small groups in U.S. except in Dry Tortugas, Florida, where they gather in one of largest concentrations of nesting birds in North America (estimated up to 100,000 birds). For details of breeding biology see *A Field Guide to Birds' Nests East of the Mississippi River.*

LEAST TERN *Sterna albifrons*

Notes: California Least Tern (*S. a. browni*), in 1977 confined to 775 pairs in 29 breeding colonies from San Francisco Bay to Baja, is an endangered species. The Interior Least Tern (*S. a. athalassos*), which west of the Mississippi R. is restricted to a few colonies in Kansas, Oklahoma, Texas, Missouri, S. Dakota, and New Mexico, is considered a threatened species. The latter nests on large sandbars of major rivers of the plains and on a few extensive bare salt flats. Population threatened by floods, both natural and those proposed by Corps of Engineers. The Eastern Least Tern (*S. a. antillarum*) is the commonest nesting tern in Louisiana, a local breeder in Texas along the Gulf, and nests intermittently on sandbars of Red R. in n. Texas.

For details of breeding biology see *A Field Guide to Birds' Nests East of the Mississippi River.*

LEAST TERN

ROYAL TERN *Sterna maxima*

Notes: Permanent resident on Louisiana and Texas coasts. In colonies, often large, on sandy islands and isolated strands of beach. Nests, or has nested (1959–60) in California at southern end of San Diego Bay. For details of breeding biology see *A Field Guide to Birds' Nests East of the Mississippi River.*

ELEGANT TERN *Sterna elegans*

Breeding range: In 1959 a colony of this Mexican species was discovered in Caspian Tern nesting area on dikes between salt ponds in San Diego Bay, California, and has bred there intermittently ever since. Has exhibited range and population expansion in recent years and may be expected to nest farther north in future.
Habitat: Seacoast, offshore islands, mud flats.
Nest: Strongly gregarious when nesting. Nest is slight depression in sand.
Eggs: 1, rarely 2; av. 53.5 x 38.0 mm. Oval to long-oval. Pinkish buff to white; some boldly and heavily marked with blotches of shades of dark brown; others spotted.
Notes: Eggs of this species have been likened to eggs of both Royal and Sandwich Terns.

SANDWICH TERN *Sterna sandvicensis*

Notes: Uncommon to locally abundant along Gulf coasts of Texas and Louisiana, where it nests in colonies on sandy islands, often in association with Royal Terns. For details of breeding biology see *A Field Guide to Birds' Nests East of the Mississippi River.*

CASPIAN TERN *Sterna caspia*   **Pl. 10**

Breeding range: Uncommon and local: Washington, Oregon, s. California, s. Idaho, Utah (Bear River Refuge), Wyoming, Minnesota (poss.); Louisiana and Texas coasts.
Habitat: Low, flat marine and lake islands; marshes, mainland beaches.
Nest: In compact colonies, generally near nests of other terns and gulls, but typically in segregated groups. May also nest singly. Shallow hollows in ground, sparingly lined, with little material added; or large deep hollows, lined with sticks, straws, rubbish, shells, with rim generally built up more like gull nest than usual tern nest.
Eggs: 1–4, typically 2–3; av. 64.5 x 45.0 mm. Oval or long-oval. Shell somewhat rough, lusterless. Buffy, sparingly marked and overlaid with small or large brown spots, irregular blotches, occasional scrawls. Look more like gull eggs than typical tern eggs.

BLACK TERN

Similar to Royal Tern eggs. Incubation by both sexes; 20–22 days. 1 brood.
Notes: Unlike most terns, Caspians do not normally attack human intruders who enter nesting colonies.

BLACK TERN *Chlidonias niger* Pl. 10

Breeding range: Washington to Minnesota, south to e. Oregon, California (e. of Cascade Mts.), cen. Nevada, Utah, Colorado, cen. Kansas, Iowa.
Habitat: Inland marshes, prairie sloughs, wet meadows.
Nest: In very loose colonies. Typically on low, thin, wet islands of dead floating vegetation. In N. Dakota, water depths at 41 nest sites ranged 4–34 in. (10.2–86.4 cm), av. 17 in. (43.2 cm). May be elaborately built; more often a few pieces of forbs, dead reeds, cane, cattails; loosely cup-shaped. Sometimes eggs laid in slight depression in floating rubbish with no attempt at nest building; eggs often wet. 197 nests av. 1⅓ in. (3.4 cm) above water.
Eggs: 3, occasionally 2, rarely 4–5 (av. clutch in 151 nests, 2.6 eggs; 63 percent contained 3 eggs); av. 34 x 24 mm. Oval to pyriform. Shell smooth, dull luster. Deep olive or buff; heavily spotted, blotched, overlaid with black or dark brown; frequently wreathed. Incubation by both sexes; 21–24 days. 1 brood, possibly 2.
Notes: Hordes of Black Terns and Forster's Terns may breed in same marsh; Forster's favor higher, drier areas (muskrat houses typical); Blacks prefer lower, wetter sites.

BLACK SKIMMER *Rynchops niger*

Notes: Texas and Louisiana coasts; also sporadic nesting in s. California, principally at southern end of Salton Sea. Typically, Skimmers nest in large colonies on coastal islands. For details of breeding biology see *A Field Guide to Birds' Nests East of the Mississippi River.*

COMMON MURRE *Uria aalge*   Pl. 10

Breeding range: Coastal Washington to cen. California.
Habitat: Rocky ledges, cliffs of coast and offshore islands.
Nest: Often in huge colonies (Farallon Is., California; Three Arch Rocks, Oregon) where in compact groups on bare rocky ledges the birds deposit their single eggs, frequently on loose soil formed by disintegrating rock.
Eggs: 1 egg; av. 81.0 x 50.5 mm. Pyriform to long-oval, with a tendency toward the more pointed shape. Shell thick, rough; no gloss; tough, not easily broken. White to light blues and greens, sometimes without spots but usually beautifully dotted, scrawled or blotched with shades of brown, black. Incubation by both sexes; 30 days.
Notes: Birds incubate by sitting horizontally upon egg as other birds do, not standing up or straddling it as some observers have stated. Eggs usually so covered with excrement that beautiful markings cannot be seen. Hundreds of eggs have been counted in space of 100 sq. ft. (9.3 m²). Pyriform shape allows egg to roll in circle if disturbed instead of rolling off ledges. Before 1900 commercial egg collectors robbed nests of murres for San Francisco markets; over 7600 dozen known to have been taken in 1896 alone.

COMMON MURRE egg *(left);* BARRED OWL egg *(right)*

PIGEON GUILLEMOT *Cepphus columba*

Breeding range: Pacific coast, Washington to s. California.
Habitat: Precipitous sea cliffs, rocky headlands, rocky offshore islands.
Nest: In colonies. No nest built; eggs usually laid on bed of chips or pebbles. May be on bare rocks or in cranny or crevice among rocks; sometimes in burrow.
Eggs: 2, laid several days apart; av. 60.5 x 41.0 mm. Pointed-oval to long-oval. Shell smooth, lusterless. Pale greenish white, bluish white, or pure white; typically heavily spotted or boldly blotched with dark brown or black; some less boldly marked or finely dotted. Both sexes incubate; about 21 days.

MARBLED MURRELET *Brachyramphus marmoratus*

Notes: First nest discovered on August 7, 1974, by tree surgeon working in Big Basin Redwoods State Park, Santa Cruz Co., California. The nest, $137\frac{1}{3}$ ft. (41.9 m) above ground on the branch of a Douglas Fir $2\frac{2}{3}$ in. (6.9 cm) out from trunk, contained a single chick. It was little more than a depression or "bowl" in bark incompletely ringed by droppings held together by the underlying meshwork of living moss. During nest recovery, 165 fragments of eggshell were removed from the ring of droppings, representing perhaps a 3rd of a shell. Fragments were "pale glass green with spots of lavender-gray, deep madder blue, sepia, bone brown and black" (*Wilson Bulletin,* Vol. 87, No. 3). Clutch size is indicated as 1 egg. A close relative of the Marbled Murrelet, the Kittlitz's Murrelet (*B. brevirostris*) nests on ground amid lichen-covered rocks on the coasts of the Bering Sea and se. Alaska.

XANTUS' MURRELET *Endomychura hypoleuca*

Breeding range: Anacapa, Santa Barbara, Los Coronados, and San Clemente Is. off s. California coast.
Habitat: High, rugged, rocky, sparsely vegetated islands.
Nest: In colonies. Dark niche or crevice among rocks; sometimes hollow at base of plant.
Eggs: 1, sometimes 2 often with 1 infertile; av. 53.5 x 36.0 mm. In sets of 2 eggs, colors frequently different: dark chocolate to plain sky-blue with a few spots (perhaps this indicates 2 females); typically, greenish with a variety of brown and lavender markings. Incubation probably by both sexes. 2 broods often indicated.

ANCIENT MURRELET *Synthliboramphus antiquus*

Breeding range: Irregular and casual in nw. Washington.
Habitat: Offshore islands.
Nest: In burrows under fallen trees or roots of standing trees; on

grass-covered rocky slopes. Lined with dry grass, leaves.
Eggs: Usually 2, occasionally 1. In 19 clutches, an average of 7 days between laying of eggs. Av. 61.1 x 38.6 mm. Deep buff, spotted and marked with light brown and lavender. Incubation shared equally by both sexes; about 35 days. Duration of each shift invariably 72 hours, with changeover always taking place at night.
Notes: In 151 burrows, 147 had 2 eggs, 4 had 1.

CASSIN'S AUKLET *Ptychoramphus aleuticus*

Breeding range: Pacific coast, Washington to Baja.
Habitat: Rocky offshore islands.
Nest: Burrow from 1 ft. (0.3 m) to several ft. long; or natural cavity or crevice in rocks. Burrow opening generally in roots of trees, under partly buried log or rock. Egg chamber at end of burrow may contain a few twigs, fragments of moss, or pieces of cones. Both sexes dig burrow.
Eggs: 1; av. 46.9 x 34.3 mm. Oval to long-oval. Shell smooth, no gloss. Dull white, milk-white, creamy white; unmarked, but often badly nest-stained. Both sexes incubate, changing at night; about 30 days. 1 brood; 2 possible.
Notes: Cassin's Auklets come and go from their nesting islands only during darkness, as do petrels.

RHINOCEROS AUKLET *Cerorhinca monocerata*

Breeding range: Pacific coast from Washington south to Farallon Is., California.
Habitat: Offshore rocky islands.
Nest: In chamber at end of burrow dug by both sexes; burrow typically 5-8 ft. (1.5-2.4 m) long, sometimes 20 ft. (6.1 m) long. Of twigs, moss, ferns.
Eggs: 1; av. 68.5 x 46.2 mm. Dull white, sometimes spotless, but usually with faint spots of lavender, gray, or light brown. Incubation by both sexes; about 3 weeks. Changing at nest occurs only at dusk or during darkness.

TUFTED PUFFIN *Lunda cirrhata*

Breeding range: Pacific coast, Washington to s. California.
Habitat: Coastal headlands, rocky islands with cliffs and turf-covered slopes.
Nest: In colonies numbering a few individuals to hundreds. In crevices in rocks or in burrows on sloping turf-covered sides of islands, sometimes on ground under bushes or in grass tufts. Using feet and bill, both sexes dig burrow. Sometimes crude nest of forbs, grasses, and feathers at end of burrow; often no nest. Burrows 2-6½ ft. (0.6-2.0 m) long; 4-6 in. (10.2-15.2 cm) diam.
Eggs: 1; av. 72.0 x 49.2 mm. Oval to oval-pyriform. Shell thick,

no gloss. Pale bluish white, or dull dirty white; some with numerous brown or gray spots, scrawls. Both sexes incubate; probably about 41 days (as with Common Puffin of Atlantic coast). Apparently 2 broods in southern range. Do not normally breed before 5th year.

BAND-TAILED PIGEON *Columba fasciata*

Breeding range: Washington south to Baja; Nevada (Clark Co.), cen. Utah, Colorado, south to Mexico and w. Texas.
Habitat: In mountains in spruce-fir, pine, oak forests, woodlands, canyons.
Nest: May be loosely colonial. In conifers or broad-leaved trees from 8–180 ft. (2.4–54.9 m) above ground, typically 15–40 ft. (4.6–12.2 m) high on horizontal limb or fork close to trunk. Loose, bulky platform of twigs with very little shaping, *similar to nest of Mourning Dove.* Male probably selects nest tree; female builds in 2–6 days with material brought by male.
Eggs: Typically 1 in coastal populations, 2 in 8 percent of interior populations; av. 39.7 x 27.9 mm. Elliptical, generally somewhat pointed. Shell smooth, slightly glossy. Pure white. Incubation by male from midmorning until late afternoon, female throughout night; 19 days. 1–3 broods.
Notes: Reported nomadic behavior unlikely. Studies indicate birds tend to nest in same area year after year.

RED-BILLED PIGEON *Columba flavirostris*

Breeding range: Rio Grande Valley, Texas.
Habitat: Heavily wooded bottomland.
Nest: In thickets of trees, tangles of vines and shrubs 8–30 ft. (2.4–9.2 m) above ground. Of sticks, twigs; lined with grass stems. Outside diam. about 8 in. (20.3 cm).
Eggs: 1, possibly 2 (rare); av. 38.6 x 27.3 mm. Oval or long-oval. Shell smooth, slightly glossy. Pure white. Both sexes incubate; probably several broods.

ROCK DOVE (DOMESTIC PIGEON)   Pl. 10
Columba livia

Breeding range: Resident in all western states.
Habitat: Wild birds typically on cliffs, in caves, generally near water; feral birds generally in populated areas, farms, suburbs, cities.
Nest: In colonies or singly. On window ledges, crevices in buildings, under bridges, in barns, and similar situations; on remote sea cliffs. Shallow, flimsy platform of carelessly arranged grasses, straw, feathers, debris.
Eggs: 1–2, normally 2; av. 38.1 x 27.9 mm. Oval to elliptical.

Shell smooth, glossy. White, unmarked. Incubation by both sexes; 17–19 days. Several broods annually; breeding season extends most of year.

Notes: Thousands of Domestic Pigeons, introduced from Europe, have escaped and live as wild birds. The A.O.U. recognizes this species and lists it under its ancestral name from Old World.

WHITE-WINGED DOVE *Zenaida asiatica* Pl. 10

Breeding range: Se. California, s. Nevada, sw. Utah (Beaver Dam Wash), s. Arizona, sw. New Mexico, s. Texas, Louisiana (Delta National Wildlife Refuge, 1971).

Habitat: In Texas, woodlands with densely foliaged trees and open ground cover. In arid West, chaparral, oak woodlands, desert mesquite, often desert washes.

Nest: Colonial in suitable nesting locations, often in same tree. Usually on horizontal branch, crotch, or in thick shrub. Male carries nesting material, mostly twigs; female builds, in 2–10 days, a flat platform with depression merely large enough to hold eggs.

Eggs: Almost invariably 2, rarely 1 or 3; av. 31.1 x 23.3 mm. Oval to long-oval. Shell smooth, not glossy. *Creamy buff,* varies to pale creamy white or nearly pure white. Incubation by both sexes, male during most of day, female from late afternoon until morning; 14 days. Eggs hatch about 24 hours apart. Multiple broods typical; desert birds may have only 1.

Notes: Land reclamation, dropping water tables, flood-control projects, burning, and clearing have reduced habitat for colonial nesting to a fraction of its former acreage.

MOURNING DOVE *Zenaida macroura* Pl. 11

Breeding range: All western states.

Habitat: Species adapts to many ecological types. Wood edges, shelterbelts, cities, farmlands, orchards. Absent from high mountain forests and alpine areas.

Nest: Solitary. Usually on horizontal branch of tree or in high shrub; may be 10–100 ft. (3.1–30.5 m) above ground or on ground often under protective vegetation. A loose, often bulky, platform of sticks, unlined or scantily lined with grass, forbs, rootlets. Both sexes build.

Eggs: 2, occasionally 3, rarely 4; av. 28.0 x 20.9 mm (western race). Oval to elliptical. Shell smooth, has slight gloss. White, unmarked. Incubation by both sexes, 14 days. Female normally incubates from dusk to dawn, when male replaces her. 2 to 4 broods.

Notes: Nest platform often so frail that eggs may be viewed from ground. Sometimes uses nests of American Robin, Gray Catbird, Common Grackle, or other species as foundation for platform of twigs. In some southern states, Mourning Doves reported nesting throughout year.

SPOTTED DOVE   *Streptopelia chinensis*

Breeding range: Released or escaped from Los Angeles aviary about 1914, and has spread north to Santa Barbara and Kern Cos., east in Los Angeles Co. to Lancaster, and south to Palm Springs and San Diego areas.
Habitat: Wooded urban or residential regions, city parks.
Nest: Flimsy platform of twigs, 5–35 ft. (1.5–10.7 m) above ground in tree.
Eggs: 2, white. Both incubate, 14–15 days. 2-4 broods.

SPOTTED DOVE

RINGED TURTLE DOVE   *Streptopelia risoria*

Notes: This native of southern Europe through southern Asia was first seen around Pershing Square, Los Angeles, about 1926. It now ranges east to San Bernardino and Redlands in San Bernardino Co. and most of San Fernando Valley in Los Angeles Co. Like its close relative, the Spotted Dove, its habitat is mostly urban. 2 white eggs laid in flimsy stick platform in tree.

GROUND DOVE *Columbina passerina* **Pl. 11**

Breeding range: S. California to s. Texas; nests first found in Louisiana in 1950s.

Habitat: Dooryard bird in small villages; ranches, gardens, barnyards, cultivated fields, woodland river bottoms, along irrigation ditches.

Nest: Of twigs, grass, palm fibers; on ground, on palm fronds, in bushes, or in trees up to 25 ft. (7.6 m) above ground. Nest well matted and material in cup typically twisted to make a circular form. Nests of other species frequently used as foundation. With renovation, same nest may be used for subsequent broods. Outside diam. 2½–3 in. (6.4–7.6 cm); very little depression (eggs show over rim).

Eggs: 2, rarely 3; av. 21.9 x 16.2 mm. Oval to elliptical. Shell smooth, little or no gloss. White, unmarked. *Indistinguishable from eggs of Inca Dove.* Incubation by both sexes, 12–14 days. Breeding season prolonged — 2, 3, or more broods.

Notes: Of 45 nests examined by author, none was on ground and none contained more or less than 2 eggs or 2 young.

INCA DOVE *Scardafella inca*

Breeding range: Se. California, s. Arizona, s. New Mexico, s. Texas.

Habitat: In villages, towns, near houses, barns. Prefers to nest in populated areas, especially in shade trees.

Nest: On horizontal fork or flattened limb of tree or in bush 4–25 ft. (1.2–7.6 m) above ground, typically 10–12 ft. (3.1–3.7 m). A small, compact, firmly matted, almost flat platform of plant stems, tiny twigs, dried grass, rootlets, a few straws and feathers; occasionally nests contain string, horsehair, strips of bark. Sometimes built on nests of other species: Mourning Dove, Mockingbird, Cactus Wren. About 5 in. (12.7 cm) in diam.

Eggs: Almost invariably 2; av. 22.3 x 16.8 mm. Elliptical, oval. Smooth with very little gloss. White. *Indistinguishable from eggs of Ground Dove.* Incubation by both sexes; about 2 weeks. At least 2 broods, probably more.

Notes: In Austin, Texas, Inca Doves built nest on trolley wire at switch where every 7 minutes streetcars raised it from 6 to 12 in. (15.2–30.5 cm) above normal position.

WHITE-FRONTED DOVE *Leptotila verreauxi*

Breeding range: Uncommon and local along Mexican border of southernmost Texas.

Habitat: Dense, moist woodlands and thickets.

Nest: Frail or substantially built of twigs, straw, forbs. In tree or bush up to 10–12 ft. (3.1–3.7 m) above ground.

Eggs: 2; av. 30.6 x 22.9 mm. Long-oval. Slight gloss. Creamy buff to white. Similar to eggs of White-winged Dove.

YELLOW-BILLED CUCKOO *Coccyzus americanus* **Pl. 11**

Breeding range: Common to rare in all western states; absent from Rocky Mt. region.

Habitat: Deciduous woodlands, moist thickets, orchards, overgrown pastures.

Nest: In trees, vines, shrubs as high as 35 ft. (10.7 m) above ground, av. 4–10 ft. (1.2–3.1 m); thick bushes overgrown with wild grapes and other vines favored. Small, shallow, frail platform of sticks, vines, twigs, rootlets; thinly lined with bits of moss, grass, pine needles, catkins. Very little depression to hold eggs. Both sexes build; male carries twigs, female arranges in nest. Outside diam. about 5 in. (12.7 cm); depth about 1½ in. (3.8 cm).

Eggs: 3–4, sometimes 1–2, rarely 5; av. 30.4 x 23.0 mm; *larger than eggs of Black-billed Cuckoo.* Elliptical to cylindrical. Shell smooth, no gloss, unmarked. Pale greenish blue, fading to greenish yellow during incubation, *lighter, greener than eggs of Black-billed.* Incubation by both sexes, mostly by female, "said to be about 14 days" (Bent). Eggs laid at irregular intervals; incubation may start before clutch complete.

Notes: Yellow-billed and Black-billed often lay in each other's nests. Yellow-billed's eggs have been found in nests of American Robin, Gray Catbird, Dickcissel, Cedar Waxwing, Cardinal, Wood Thrush, Mourning Dove, Red-winged Blackbird.

YELLOW-BILLED CUCKOO nest parasitized by Black-billed Cuckoo (small egg, *left*).

BLACK-BILLED CUCKOO   Pl. 11
Coccyzus erythropthalmus

Breeding range: East of Rocky Mts.; e. and cen. Montana to Minnesota, south to n.-cen. Colorado (prob.), Texas, Iowa. Rare in Missouri, Arkansas; absent from Louisiana.
Habitat: Groves of trees, forest edges, moist thickets, overgrown pastures.
Nest: In deciduous or evergreen trees, 2–20 ft. (0.6–6.1 m) — av. about 6 ft. (1.8 m) — above ground. Platform of small twigs loosely interwoven; lined with catkins, cottony fibers, dry leaves, pine needles; generally *more substantially lined* than nest of Yellow-billed. Outside diam. 8 in. (20.3 cm); inside diam. 3–3½ in. (7.6–8.9 cm), depth ¾–1 in. (1.9–2.5 cm).
Eggs: 2–4, occasionally 5; av. 27.18 x 20.57; *smaller than eggs of Yellow-billed.* Elliptical. Shell smooth, no gloss. Greenish blue, *darker, bluer, than eggs of Yellow-billed;* occasionally marbled. Laid at intervals of 1–3 days. Incubation by both sexes; reported as 14 days, also 10–11 days. Incubation starts with 1st egg.
Notes: Black-billed and Yellow-billed lay eggs in each other's nests. Black-billed has laid in nests of Yellow Warbler, Chipping Sparrow, Eastern Wood Pewee, Cardinal, Cedar Waxwing, Gray Catbird, Wood Thrush. Characteristic of species to leave eggshells in nest after young hatch.

ROADRUNNER   *Geococcyx californianus*   Pl. 11

Breeding range: California, s. Nevada, sw. Utah (unc.), se. Colorado (unc.), s. and sw. Kansas (unc.), sw. Missouri (rare), south to Mexico, Texas, Louisiana (unc.).
Habitat: Open, dry country with thickets of mesquite, chaparral, cactus, low trees, thick shrubs.
Nest: In low tree or bush; rarely on ground. Foundation of sticks, lined with leaves, grass, roots, feathers, occasionally snakeskins, dry bits of cow or horse manure. Outside diam. about 1 ft. (30.5 cm), height 6–8 in. (15.2–20.3 cm).
Eggs: 3–6; laid at irregular intervals; av. 39.2 x 30.1 mm. Oval or elliptical. White with chalky overlay which may turn yellowish. Incubation probably by female, beginning before clutch complete; 18 days. Possibly 2 broods.

GROOVE-BILLED ANI   *Crotophaga sulcirostris*

Breeding range: Texas, lower Rio Grande Valley; Louisiana, delta region south of New Orleans (cas. or rare).
Habitat: Open country, bushy pastures, marshes, orchards; not heavily forested country.
Nest: In trees, often citrus. Bulky, usually shallow, bowl-shaped, open above; lining of small, fresh, green leaves gathered even

during incubation. Built by both sexes of single pair or by community of several individuals in cooperative nesting effort.

Eggs: 3–15, depending upon number of females laying in 1 nest; probably 3–5 laid by single female; av. 30.93 x 24.06 mm. Both sexes incubate, bringing fresh leaves or twigs at each changeover; about 13 days. Monogamy, polyandry, or polygyny may exist in 1 flock.

BARN OWL   *Tyto alba*   Pl. 11

Breeding range: Casual to rare in all western states; nowhere common, usually very local in distribution.

Habitat: Open country in farmland; rodent-infested grasslands, forest edges, villages, cities.

Nest: In barns, church steeples, silos, natural cavities in trees, duck blinds, chalk cliffs, shale bluffs, sides of old wells, abandoned mine shafts, artificial nesting sites (boxes, barrels, baskets). No nest built. Owl castings (disgorged pellets) generally form base for eggs.

Eggs: 3–11, generally 5–9, laid at intervals of 2–3 days; av. 43.1 x 33.0 mm. Mostly elliptical, not as round as typical owl eggs. Shell finely granulated, little or no gloss. Pure white, becoming yellow-stained. Incubation by female (fed regularly by male); reported as 32–34 days or 21–24 days, starting with 1st egg. Shorter period presumably indicates hatching time of single egg; longer period, time required to incubate full clutch. 1st owlet may be 2 weeks old when last egg hatches. 2 broods probable.

Notes: Known to nest throughout year. When food is scarce, this owl is said to lay fewer eggs or not to nest at all.

SCREECH OWL   *Otus asio*   Pl. 11

Breeding range: Resident in all western states.

Habitat: Open deciduous woods, orchards, farm woodlots, urban shade trees, typically in foothills, valleys, deserts.

Nest: In natural cavities in many kinds of trees; abandoned nesting holes of large woodpeckers; crevices in buildings; birdhouses (see Plate 11); av. 5–30 ft. (1.5–9.2 m) above ground. No nest built, no material carried. Eggs laid in rotted chips, leaves, rubble contained in cavity; often includes owl feathers or fur and feathers of prey.

Eggs: 2–7, generally 3–5, laid at intervals of 2–3 days; av. 35.5 x 30.0 mm. Elliptical to nearly spherical. Shell very finely granulated, moderately glossy. White; *indistinguishable from eggs of Whiskered Owl, larger than eggs of Flammulated Owl.* Incubation entirely or mostly by female; reported 21–30 days, av. probably about 26; may start with 1st, 2nd, or 3rd egg.

Notes: Not uncommon to find pair together in nest cavity during day. Throughout incubation male feeds female at night. Female usually sits tight on eggs when disturbed.

SCREECH OWL in birdbox

WHISKERED OWL *Otus trichopsis*

Breeding range: Se. Arizona.
Habitat: Dense woods of sycamores, oaks, or oaks and pines, at altitudes of 5000–6500 ft. (1525–1982.5 m).
Nest: In natural cavity or old woodpecker hole. Eggs laid in chips and rubble already in cavity.
Eggs: 3, sometimes 4; av. 33.0 x 27.6 mm. White. *Indistinguishable from eggs of Screech Owl, larger than eggs of Flammulated Owl.*
Notes: Nesting biology similar to that of other *Otus* owls. Most easily distinguished by habitat and voice.

FLAMMULATED OWL *Otus flammeolus*

Breeding range: Rocky Mt. and Pacific states (inland).
Habitat: Coniferous forests, commonly Ponderosa Pine, or mixture of oak-pine, typically at high altitudes up to 10,000 ft. (3050 m).
Nest: At bottom of woodpecker hole (often Common Flicker). No material added; eggs laid on chips and debris in cavity.
Eggs: 3–4; av. 29.1 x 25.5 mm. Oval. Finely granulated, slightly glossy. White; *smaller than eggs of Whiskered and Screech Owls.* Incubation by female, fed by male; probably about 26 days.

GREAT HORNED OWL *Bubo virginianus*   Pl. 11

Breeding range: All western states.
Habitat: Heavy forests; large farms, ranch woodlots; swamps; deserts; usually remote wilderness, sometimes city park.

Nest: Generally in old nests of large birds: hawks, eagles, herons, ravens, crows; squirrels' nests. Also in tree cavities, stumps, on rocky ledges, in caves; rarely on ground in logs, among rocks. Little if any material added except feathers and down from breast.
Eggs: 1-4, rarely 5; av. 54.7 x 46.5 mm (western race). Elliptical to nearly spherical. Shell coarsely granulated (feels rough to touch), has little or no gloss. Dull white, unmarked. Incubation mostly by female; variously reported at 28, 30, 35 days; begins with 1st egg. 1 brood.
Notes: Breeding pair often will attack person climbing to nest. Of 29 nests: 13 in Red-tailed Hawk nests, 8 in Common Crow nests, 3 in hollow trees, 2 in unidentified nests, 2 in rocky crevices, 1 in Fox Squirrel nest.

GREAT HORNED OWL incubating in cliff nest

HAWK OWL *Surnia ulula*

Breeding range: After major winter invasions from the North a few pairs have remained in Minnesota to nest in Norman, Roseau, and St. Louis Cos. (rare and cas.).
Habitat: Coniferous forests.
Nest: In cavities in trees or in abandoned nests of other birds (often crows), or in ends of broken-off stubs.
Eggs: 3-7; av. 40.1 x 31.9 mm. Pure white.

PYGMY OWL *Glaucidium gnoma*

Breeding range: Washington to w. Montana, south to Mexico, New Mexico.
Habitat: Open coniferous or mixed woods (often aspen, oak); wooded canyons. Typically 5000–10,000 ft. (1525–3050 m).
Nest: In abandoned woodpecker hole (Hairy or Acorn Woodpecker, Common Flicker), preferably 8–20 ft. (2.4–6.1 m) above ground. Eggs laid upon bare bottom of cavity.
Eggs: Normally 3–4, occasionally more or less; av. 26.6 x 23.2 mm (*G. g. pinicola*), 29.6 x 24.3 mm (*G. g. californicum*). Short-oval to spherical. Incubation by female, probably starting with 1st egg. 1 brood.

FERRUGINOUS OWL *Glaucidium brasilianum*

Breeding range: Rare and local in s. Arizona and Texas in lower Rio Grande Valley.
Habitat: In Arizona — desert Saguaros and riparian forests of cottonwood, mesquite. In Texas — mesquite, ebony, cane.
Nest: In abandoned woodpecker holes. No material added.
Eggs: 3–4, occasionally 5; av. 28.5 x 23.2 mm. Pure white.

ELF OWL *Microthene whitneyi*   Pl. 12

Breeding range: S. California to s. Texas.
Habitat: Deserts, forested river bottoms, mountain foothills, in oak-pine-sycamore associations.
Nest: In abandoned woodpecker holes. Often, in Arizona, in Saguaro cacti, 15–30 ft. (4.6–9.2 m) above ground; also in other suitable locations. No material added.
Eggs: 2–5, commonly 3; av. 26.8 x 23.2 mm. Oval. Shell finely granulated, glossy or slightly glossy. White. Incubation by female, probably assisted by male.

ELF OWL habitat

Notes: Author observed nesting pairs in abandoned woodpecker holes in utility poles in Madera Canyon, Santa Rita Mts., Arizona, where tourists gathered nightly with flashlights to watch these smallest of all owls.

BURROWING OWL   Nest cavity

BURROWING OWL   *Athene cunicularia*   Pl. 12

Breeding range: E. Washington to w. Minnesota, south to Mexico, Texas. Absent from nw. Iowa south through Mississippi Valley states.

Habitat: Prairies, deserts, sagebrush flats, canal dikes, airports, large vacant urban lots.

Nest: In burrows, single or well separated in scattered colonies. Burrows dug by owls; or use of abandoned rodent tunnels common. Often in prairie dog towns, colonies of ground squirrels, badger holes. Tunnels vary greatly in length and depth, up to 10 ft. (3.1 m) or more. Nest chamber at end of burrow, 12–18 in. (30.5–45.7 cm) in diam. Typically lined with dry chips of horse or cow manure, sometimes with grasses, plant stalks, assortment of trash. Entrance to tunnel often paved with manure chips.

Eggs: 6–11, commonly 7–9; av. 31.0 x 25.5 mm (western race). Elliptical to short-oval. Shell smooth, quite glossy. Pure white when laid but soon badly nest-stained. Incubation by both sexes, about 3 weeks. 1 brood.

Notes: Fantastic stories about rattlesnakes and Burrowing Owls occupying same burrow are untrue. Prairie Dog tunnels are used as convenient nest sites but not when occupied by the rodents.

BARRED OWL   *Strix varia*

Breeding range: N. Dakota, Minnesota, south to Texas and Gulf Coast. In West extending southward from British Columbia to nw. Washington; possibly or probably to ne. Oregon, n. Idaho, nw. Montana.

BARRED OWL

Habitat: Forests, mainly swampy woodlands.
Nest: Typically a tree cavity; hollow in top of a broken tree stub; abandoned nest of squirrel, crow, hawk (often Red-shouldered Hawk); rarely on ground. No lining in cavity nests except debris already present; open nests may be sparingly lined with green sprigs of pine.
Eggs: 2–3, rarely 4; av. 49 x 42 mm. Oval or elliptical. Shell granulated (slightly rough to touch), no gloss. Pure white; *indistinguishable from eggs of Spotted Owl.* Incubation possibly by both sexes, mostly by female, begins with 1st egg; 28–33 days. 1 brood.
Notes: Pair shows strong attachment to same nest area from year to year. In alternate years may use same nest as Red-shouldered Hawks. 2 nests found in different years contained incubated eggs of both species at same time; in 1 nest, owl incubating; hawk incubating in other. In one wooded area, nests of 2 species found 24 yds. (21.9 m) apart. Of 38 nests, 18 in old hawk nests, 15 in hollow trees, 5 in squirrel nests.

SPOTTED OWL *Strix occidentalis*

Breeding range: Uncommon to rare resident in w. Washington, w. Oregon, w. California, s. Arizona, New Mexico, Texas (Guadalupe Mts., prob.).
Habitat: Spruce- or fir-covered mountainsides, canyons.
Nest: In natural cavities in trees, hollows in cliffs, abandoned nests of ravens, hawks, magpies. Nest of rubbish, feathers, bones, pellets.

Eggs: Commonly 2, sometimes 3, rarely 4; av. 49.9 x 41.3 mm. Oval. Shell slightly granulated, not glossy. White. *Indistinguishable from eggs of Barred Owl.*
Notes: Northern Spotted Owl (*S. o. caurina*) is candidate for U.S. Endangered Species status. In Oregon, in 3 years, 64 of 123 occupied territorial sites have been or will be timbered. Each pair requires several hundred acres of territory as habitat, and the Douglas Fir timber on such land is worth at least $1,600,000 per hundred acres. In nw. Washington, range overlaps that of Barred Owl. Breeding biology is so similar continued coexistence seems unlikely.

GREAT GRAY OWL   *Strix nebulosa*

Breeding range: Rare resident Washington south to cen. California, e. Idaho, w. Montana, nw. Wyoming (Yellowstone); rare and casual in Minnesota (Roseau Co.).
Habitat: Boreal coniferous forests, muskeg bogs.
Nest: On old hawk nests from 13–50 ft. (4.0–15.3 m) above ground. Lining of twigs, moss, feathers; bark may be added.
Eggs: 2–5, usually 3, laid at variable intervals; av. 54.2 x 43.4 mm, small for size of bird. Oval to elliptical, *not as round as eggs of most other owls.* Shell roughly granulated, not glossy. Dull white. Incubation by female, beginning with 1st egg. 1 brood.

LONG-EARED OWL eggs in old Common Crow nest

LONG-EARED OWL *Asio otus*   Pl. 12

Breeding range: Washington to Minnesota, south to Mexico, Texas; absent from lower Mississippi Valley, rare or casual in Missouri, Iowa.
Habitat: Deciduous and evergreen forests; wooded parks, orchards, farm woodlots.
Nest: Typically in old nests of crows; also of hawks, squirrels, magpies; occasionally in tree cavities, tops of broken tree stubs; rarely on ground. Nest unlined or lined sparingly with grass, green twigs, leaves, feathers. Rarely constructs own nest. May evict owner of occupied nest (broken eggs of crow found beneath incubating owl).
Eggs: 3–8, normally 4–5, laid every other day; av. 40.0 x 32.5 mm. Oval. Shell smooth, glossy. Pure white. Incubation by female, starting with 1st egg; 21 days. Oldest owlet may be 8–10 days old when last egg hatches.
Notes: Female sits very tight on nest; generally will not flush when tree is tapped. Male roosts near nest tree, carries food at night to incubating mate.

SHORT-EARED OWL *Asio flammeus*   Pl. 12

Breeding range: Washington to Minnesota, south to California, Arizona, Colorado, Kansas.
Habitat: Marshes, prairies, open country with short vegetation; thicket and forest clearings.
Nest: On ground, generally in slight depression sparsely lined with grasses, forbs, stubble, feathers. Occasionally flattened vegetation; exposed, or hidden by grass, plant clumps, low shrubs. Outside diam. 9–12 in. (22.9–30.5 cm), height 1½–2 in. (3.8–5.1 cm).
Eggs: 4–9, typically 5–7; av. 39 x 31 mm. Oval to elliptical. Shell smooth or finely granulated, little or no gloss. White or faintly creamy white; becomes nest soiled. Incubation entirely or mostly by female; about 21 days.
Notes: One of few owls that constructs own nest — such as it is. Some ornithologists believe that clutch size varies according to abundance of food. Frequently nests near Marsh Hawk, apparently without friction.

BOREAL OWL *Aegolius funereus*

Breeding range: N. Minnesota (Cook Co., 1978), nw. Montana (prob.).
Habitat: Boreal coniferous forests and muskeg bogs.
Nest: In old woodpecker holes or natural cavities.
Eggs: 3–6, laid in 8–12 days; av. 32.3 x 26.9 mm. Oval. Pure white.

SAW-WHET OWL   *Aegolius acadicus*

Breeding range: Washington to w. and cen. Montana, south in mountains to w. Texas (rare); also n. Minnesota.
Habitat: Coniferous or deciduous forests, woodlots, swamps, occasionally shade trees.
Nest: In tree cavity, 14–60 ft. (4.3–18.3 m) above ground, usually abandoned hole of Common Flicker or Pileated Woodpecker; birdhouses. No material added except breast feathers.
Eggs: 4–7, generally 5–6, laid at intervals of 1–3 days; av. 29.9 x 25.0 mm. Oval to nearly spherical. Shell smooth, little or no gloss. White. Incubation mostly by female, probably 21–28 days, beginning with 1st egg.
Notes: Unlike Screech Owl, this species usually appears at cavity opening when tree is tapped. Disturbed while incubating, will not leave cavity unless lifted out.

CHUCK-WILL'S-WIDOW   *Caprimulgus carolinensis*

Breeding range: E. Kansas, se. Iowa (rare) south to e. and cen. Texas and Gulf Coast.
Habitat: Oak, pine woodlands, edges of clearings and forest roads.
Nest: None; eggs laid on ground on dead leaves (often oak) or pine needles. Incubating bird very well camouflaged. Eggs conspicuous when exposed.
Eggs: 2, laid on succeeding days; av. 35.56 x 25.57 mm. Oval to elliptical. Shell smooth, glossy. Creamy white, profusely blotched, marbled, spotted with shades of brown, overlaid on and mixed with lavender and gray. Incubation by both sexes; 20 days, starting with 1st egg.

CHUCK-WILL'S-WIDOW

Notes: Audubon's account of disturbed Chuck-will's-widow carrying eggs in mouth to new location is doubted by reputable ornithologists. Although transfer not observed, there have been instances in which clutches of eggs were found moved several feet from original nest site. Further study needed. Evidently depending upon camouflage, incubating bird usually permits close approach before flushing.

WHIP-POOR-WILL eggs   Incubating

WHIP-POOR-WILL *Caprimulgus vociferus*

Breeding range: Minnesota south through Mississippi Valley to Arkansas; e. Nebraska (Missouri R.), e. Kansas, e. Oklahoma (prob.); se. and cen. Arizona, s. New Mexico.

Habitat: Oak, pine woodlands, canyons; younger drier hardwood areas preferred to mature forests.

Nest: None; eggs laid on ground on dead leaves, typically where light and shadows filter through trees, blending incubating bird with surroundings. As incubation progresses, a depression is formed around eggs by female's body.

Eggs: 2, laid on alternate days; av. 29.0 x 21.3 mm. Oval to elliptical, typically equal-ended. Shell smooth, somewhat glossy. White, irregularly spotted, blotched with gray, overlaid with brown. Incubation by female (possibly some assistance from male); probably 19 days or more, starting with laying of 1st egg. 1 brood.

Notes: Reports that Whip-poor-wills remove eggs or young from nesting site when disturbed need further study and verification. Pair attached to a nesting locality will return year after year. Incubating bird sits close; when flushed, flies silently away like a moth. Occasionally will try to decoy intruder by feigning broken wing. Eggs usually discovered by accident rather than by search.

BUFF-COLLARED NIGHTJAR   *Caprimulgus ridgwayi*

Notes: This Mexican species, known also as Ridgway's Whip-poor-will, probably nests uncommonly or casually in Guadalupe Canyon, Hidalgo Co., extreme sw. New Mexico. Breeding habitats are rocky hillsides with fairly open stands of juniper and mesquite and rocky canyon floors. Although no nests have been found, birds on territory have been observed regularly in Guadalupe Canyon.

POOR-WILL   *Phalaenoptilus nuttallii*   **Pl. 12**

Breeding range: Washington to sw. N. Dakota (Slope Co., prob.), south to w. and cen. Texas.
Habitat: Barren, arid regions; open prairies, deserts, chaparral.
Nest: None; a slight hollow may be scraped in bare earth or eggs may be laid on gravelly ground or on flat rock. May be partially shaded or in open.
Eggs: 2; av. 26.3 x 19.9 mm. Oval to long-oval. Shell moderately glossy. White; may have faint pinkish tint; typically unmarked, but may have faint spots at larger end. Both sexes said to incubate.
Notes: Discovered hibernating in California desert, surviving severe cold weather in torpid condition with body temperature lowered almost to that of surroundings.

PAURAQUE   *Nyctidromus albicollis*

Notes: One of several Mexican species whose breeding range barely reaches the U.S. in s. Texas, principally the lower Rio Grande Valley. Its 2 pinkish buff eggs are laid on ground, usually in open woodland with leaf-covered floor. Author has found this species a common nesting bird in Santa Ana National Wildlife Refuge, Texas.

PAURAQUE eggs   GREEN JAY stealing egg

COMMON NIGHTHAWK   *Chordeiles minor*   Pl. 12

Breeding range: All western states.
Habitat: Prairies, dikes, open woodlands, burned-over areas, plowed fields, railroad right-of-ways, cities.
Nest: None. Eggs laid on ground, often gravelly, sparsely vegetated; on gravel roofs of city buildings.
Eggs: 2, laid successive days; av. 29.97 x 21.84 mm. Oval or elliptical. Shell close-grained, moderately glossy. Cream to pale gray, dotted with brown and gray, so densely on some eggs that ground color is almost obscured. *Darker and larger than eggs of Lesser Nighthawk.* Incubation by female; 19 days, beginning with 2nd egg. 1 brood.
Notes: Banded female returned 2 successive years to same gravel roof, although mates were different. Adequate nesting sites, not gregariousness, believed to explain occasional loose colonies. Incubating bird keeps sun at back all day; has no orientation on cloudy days. 1 egg, purposely moved by observer 3 in. (7.6 cm) from nest site, was retrieved by female by pushing with bill, feet, breast feathers. An egg moved 36 in. (91.4 cm) from nest site ignored and single egg incubated until other egg was returned to within 12 in. (30.5 cm), when female brought it back in same way and continued to incubate both eggs.

LESSER NIGHTHAWK   *Chordeiles acutipennis*   Pl. 12

Breeding range: S. California to w. and s. Texas, including s. Nevada, sw. Utah.
Habitat: Arid deserts, river bottoms, dry washes, canyons, rocky hills.
Nest: None. Eggs laid on ground in open sandy or gravelly spot often near a bush; flat roofs of adobe houses.
Eggs: 2; av. 27.05 x 19.53 mm. Oval to long-oval. Shell close-grained, glossy. Pale gray to pale cream-white, minutely marbled, speckled, peppered with fine dots of gray, lilac. *Paler and smaller than eggs of Common Nighthawk.* Incubation mostly or all by female; 18–19 days.
Notes: Observer reports eggs moved on hot day to partial shade of nearby shrub; restored to original position later. Eggs hard to see due to similarity in color to general surroundings. Female sits close; when flushed, flies nearby and returns quickly to eggs when intruder leaves.

BLACK SWIFT   *Cypseloides niger*

Breeding range: Washington, California, nw. Montana, w. Colorado, ne. Utah (Wasatch Mts.).
Habitat: Mountain and coastal cliffs, canyon walls, typically very close to water, often near or behind waterfalls.

Nest: In colonies where habitat suitable; usually on inaccessible ledge or hollow on perpendicular wall of rocky cliff. When close to waterfall constantly wet from spray. Cone-shaped mud and moss nest (moss may continue to grow). Outside diam. 3–8 in. (7.6–20.3 cm), height 3 in. (7.6 cm).

Eggs: 1; av. 28.6 x 19.0 mm. Long-oval. Shell smooth, no gloss. Pure white; usually nest-stained. Incubation probably mostly or entirely by female; 24–27 days.

Notes: Requirements for nesting appear to include presence of water, inaccessibility, darkness (little or no sun strikes nest), absence of obstructions in vicinity of nest. Waterfalls are not obstructions in approaching nest as birds fly through water with ease. In 10 counties in Colorado Rockies, investigators found 80 nests in 27 colonies.

CHIMNEY SWIFT   *Chaetura pelagica*   Pl. 12

Breeding range: E. Montana to Minnesota, south to e. and cen. Colorado, Texas; several nests found near Davis, California, in 1975.

Habitat: Cities, towns, villages, farms; formerly hollow trees and caves.

Nest: In chimneys, air shafts, silos, barns, attics, old wells, garages; very rarely in hollow trees. Frail, thin, half-saucer platform of twigs attached to inside of chimney by adults' glutinous saliva, which hardens and binds material. In flight, birds break twigs from ends of dead tree limbs with feet; transfer them to bill before

CHIMNEY SWIFT

reaching nest. Building by both sexes, requires 3–6 days. Nest 4 in. (10.2 cm) wide, 3 in. (7.6 cm) from front edge to wall.

Eggs: 3–6, generally 4–5, laid every other day; av. 20.10 x 13.24 mm. Long-oval to cylindrical. Shell smooth, moderately glossy. Pure white. Incubation by both sexes (may both occasionally occupy nest at same time); 18–21 days; may start with laying of next to last egg. 1 brood.

Notes: One of few North American birds favorably affected by white man's arrival. Hazards of chimney nesting include use of fireplaces on cold days and loosening of nests from chimney walls by rain. In 85 nests, average distance from top of chimney was 20¾ ft. (6.3 m).

VAUX'S SWIFT   *Chaetura vauxi*

Breeding range: Pacific Coast states, n. Idaho, nw. Montana; uncommon to rare throughout range.

Habitat: River bottoms or burned or cutover areas with hollow stubs available; occasionally chimneys.

Nest: Unlike Chimney Swift, has not commonly accepted chimneys in place of hollow trees. Nest is small, saucer-shaped, *attached to inner wall of hollow tree;* made of twigs or pine needles glued together with bird's saliva.

Eggs: 3–7, typically 4–6; av. 18.5 x 12.4 mm. Pure white. Incubation by both sexes; 19 days.

WHITE-THROATED SWIFT   *Aeronautes saxatalis*

Breeding range: Washington to w. and s. Montana, south to sw. Texas; also w. S. Dakota, nw. Nebraska.

Habitat: Precipitous mountain cliffs up to about 13,000 ft. (4000 m); steep canyons; rocky seacoasts, offshore islands.

Nest: In cracks, crevices in mostly inaccessible rocky cliffs. Far back in narrow crevice, often beyond reach and out of sight; forbs, grasses, glued together with birds' saliva into basket-shaped structure; lined with feathers.

Eggs: 3–6, commonly 4–5; av. 21.24 x 13.74 mm. Long-oval to cylindrical. No gloss. Pure white, creamy white.

Notes: Nests have been found in cracks in wall of old mission building at San Juan Capistrano, California.

LUCIFER HUMMINGBIRD   *Calothorax lucifer*

Breeding range: Observed in Arizona but found nesting in U.S. only in Chisos Mts., Big Bend National Park, Texas.

Habitat: Arid slopes and open deserts.

Nest: In agave or shrub, typically close to ground.

Eggs: 2; white; *indistinguishable from eggs of other hummingbirds of similar size.*

RUBY-THROATED HUMMINGBIRD

RUBY-THROATED HUMMINGBIRD   *Archilochus colubris*

Breeding range: N.-cen. and e. N. Dakota, e. S. Dakota (unc.), e. Nebraska, e. Kansas, Oklahoma, e. and cen. Texas, south from Minnesota throughout Mississippi Valley; also ne. Montana (rare).
Habitat: Woodlands, orchards, shade trees, gardens, parks.
Nest: Solitary; in variety of trees, 6–50 ft. (1.8–15.3 m), av. 10–20 ft. (3.1–6.1 m), above ground, attached to twig or small branch that slants downward from tree, usually sheltered by leafy branches, open to ground. Of plant down, fibers, bud scales, attached to limb with spider silk; lined with plant down; covered with greenish gray lichens. Viewed from ground, nest looks like mossy knot on limb. Building entirely by female, requires about 5 days; some construction continues throughout life of nest. Outside diam. 1–1¾ in. (2.5–4.5 cm), height 1–2 in. (2.5–5.1 cm); inside diam. ¾–1 in. (1.9–2.5 cm), depth ¾ in. (1.9 cm).
Eggs: 2; av. 12.9 x 8.5 mm. Elliptical, one end slightly more pointed. Shell smooth, no gloss. Pure white.
Notes: Males take no part in nesting activity; suspected of polygamy. Female observed alternately feeding 1 young in nest, incubating 2 eggs in 2nd nest 4 ft. (1.2 m) away. Both nests successfully fledged young.

BLACK-CHINNED HUMMINGBIRD   Pl. 13
Archilochus alexandri

Breeding range: E. Washington to nw. Montana, south (except in Oregon) to Mexico and w. and cen. Texas.
Habitat: Semiarid country near water in semiwooded canyons, slopes, chaparral, orchards, parks.
Nest: Typically 4–8 ft. (1.2–2.4 m) above ground in tree or shrub; has been found as high as 30 ft. (9.2 m). Dry white or buff plant down collected from sycamores, willows, milkweed, thistles;

tightly worked together; thickly coated with spider silk. Outer wall may have dry leaf, flower, feather, hair, lichens. Elastic, spongy, bound to supporting twigs with spider silk. Rim of deeply hollowed cup curved inward at top. New nest may be built on old.

Eggs: Typically 2; 1 and 3 have been found; av. 12.51 x 8.30 mm. Long-oval. No gloss. Pure white. Incubation by female; about 16 days. 2 or possibly 3 broods.

Notes: May build 2nd nest, lay eggs, and even start incubating while still feeding nestlings in 1st nest.

COSTA'S HUMMINGBIRD
Calypte costae

Pl. 13 and
next page

Breeding range: S. California, s. Nevada, sw. Utah, Arizona. Not known to nest in New Mexico.

Habitat: Dry deserts of ocotillas, yuccas, cacti, often far from water; chaparral in s. California; dry washes.

Nest: Usually 2–9 ft. (0.6–2.8 m), av. near 4 ft. (1.2 m), above ground in variety of bushes, small trees, weedy plants; typically near outside of limb positioned to give bird unobstructed view. Dense leafy trees avoided. Shallow exterior of fine plant fibers held together with spider silk. Loosely made. Rim and interior commonly of small dark feathers. Female continues to build up sides during incubation. General gray appearance of nest distinctive. Outside diam. $1\frac{1}{4}$–2 in. (3.2–5.1 cm), av. about $1\frac{1}{2}$ (3.8 cm); height $1\frac{1}{4}$–$1\frac{1}{2}$ in. (3.2–3.8 cm).

Eggs: Invariably 2, laid about 2 days apart; av. 12.4 x 8.2 mm. Long-oval. No gloss. White. *Indistinguishable from eggs of other hummingbirds of similar size.* Incubation by female alone, starting with laying of 1st egg; 15–18 days, av. 16. Probably only 1 brood.

Notes: Female very tame; will return to nest if observer stands motionless nearby. Colonize in favored locations; as many as 6 pairs found within 100-ft. (30.5 m) radius. In s. Arizona author found female Black-chins and Costas indistinguishable away from nest but noted difference in nests each builds.

ANNA'S HUMMINGBIRD   *Calypte anna*   Pl. 13

Breeding range: Both resident and migratory in s. Oregon to Baja, mostly coastal foothills; also s. Arizona.

Habitat: Chaparral, mixed woodlands, parks, gardens.

Nest: From insulated electric light wires in Los Angeles to dense oak groves in remote wooded canyons. Of 52 nests in California heights ranged from 17 in. (43.2 cm) to 30 ft. (9.2 m) above ground. Nests comparatively large, well made of plant down held together with spider silk; lined with fine down and feathers. Mere platform devoid of camouflage when eggs laid; built up and decorated with lichens during incubation. Early nests may require month to

COSTA'S HUMMINGBIRD with incubation of 2 eggs started (May 12).

Same nest (May 23) built higher during incubation.

build; later nests have been built in 2 days.

Eggs: 2; av. 13.31 x 8.65 mm. Long-oval. No gloss. Dead white. *Indistinguishable from eggs of other hummingbirds of similar size.* Incubation by female alone; av. 16 days. 2 broods, possibly 3. May build new nest, lay eggs, and start to incubate while still feeding nestlings in 1st nest.

Notes: Nesting season begins as early as December in California, before arrival of any migrant hummingbirds; extends through spring and sporadically throughout summer.

ANNA'S HUMMINGBIRD

BROAD-TAILED HUMMINGBIRD Pl. 13
Selasphorus platycercus

Breeding range: California to Wyoming, south to Mexico, w. Texas; also Idaho (unc.), w. Montana (prob.), w. Oklahoma (Cimarron Co., rare). Common breeding hummer of Rockies.
Habitat: Pinyon-juniper forests, mixed forests, canyons, mountain glades.
Nest: On low, horizontal branches of willows, alders, cottonwoods, junipers, oaks, sycamores; usually 3–20 ft. (0.9–6.1 m) above ground. Outer walls made of willow, cottonwood down, decorated with lichens, shreds of bark, fine leaves, plant fibers. Inner lining of soft down.

BROAD-TAILED HUMMINGBIRD

Eggs: 2; av. 13.0 x 8.8 mm. Long-oval. No gloss. White. *Indistinguishable from eggs of other hummingbirds of similar size.* Incubation by female; 14–16 days.
Notes: Often returns to same nest site annually. Av. height above ground of 14 nests found by author in Arizona 14½ ft. (4.4 m).

RUFOUS HUMMINGBIRD   *Selasphorus rufus*   Pl. 13

Breeding range: Washington, Oregon, nw. California, n. Idaho, nw. Montana. Common breeding hummingbird of w. Washington and Oregon.
Habitat: Forest edges, chaparral, thickets, streamsides.
Nest: In low-drooping branches of conifers, in vines, roots of upturned trees. Of plant fibers, spider silk, mosses, lichens; often decorated on outside with leaf or bud scales, shreds of bark, lichens; bound together with spider silk. Very often nests in colonies; as many as 20 nests in a small area. New nest sometimes built over last year's.
Eggs: 2; av. 13.1 x 8.8 mm. Oval to long-oval. Pure white. *Indistinguishable from eggs of other hummingbirds of similar size.* Incubation by female; probably about 14 days.
Notes: This species is very pugnacious on its nesting territory, driving away much larger birds.

ALLEN'S HUMMINGBIRD   *Selasphorus sasin*   Pl. 13

Breeding range: Pacific coast, s. Oregon to s. California.
Habitat: Coastal chaparral; woody or brushy ravines, canyons; forest edges; parks.
Nest: In various types of trees, shrubs; sometimes in hedges, plant stalks, 10 in. (25.4 cm) to 90 ft. (27.5 m) above ground. Nests close together — within 50 ft. (15.3 m) of each other — in desirable habitat. Attached to limbs, twigs; built of green tree mosses, lichens; securely fastened with spider silk; lined with plant down.
Eggs: 2; av. 12.7 x 8.6 mm. Oval to long-oval. No gloss. White. *Indistinguishable from eggs of other hummingbirds of similar size.* Incubation by female; 15–16 days.
Notes: Nest of Allen's resembles nest of Anna's more than that of Rufous. Nest that author photographed in Averill Park, San Pedro, California, was decorated with chips of green paint peeled from nearby picnic tables. (See Plate 13.)

CALLIOPE HUMMINGBIRD   *Stellula calliope*   Pl. 13

Breeding range: Washington, e. Oregon, Idaho, w. and s.-cen. Montana, south through California, Nevada, Utah (unc.), Colorado (poss.).
Habitat: In southern mountains at 4000–8000 ft. (1220–2440 m) above sea level; occasionally at lower levels northward. Open coniferous forests, mountain slopes, aspen woods.

Nest: In tree or bush; sometimes on pine cone; 22 in. (55.9 cm) to 75 ft. (22.9 m) above ground. Almost invariably built on branch or twig directly under larger branch, or under canopy of foliage which protects nest from overhead. Small cup of shredded bark, mosses, plant fiber, lichens; fastened with spider silk.

Eggs: Typically 2; av. 12.1 x 8.3 mm. Oval to long-oval. No gloss. White. *Indistinguishable from eggs of other hummingbirds of similar size.* Female incubates; 15 days.

Notes: Nests resemble cones when attached to cones or limbs of conifers. A series of 2, 3, or even 4 nests, built one on top of another in succeeding years have been observed. Sometimes old nest is repaired from year to year.

RIVOLI'S HUMMINGBIRD   *Eugenes fulgens*

Breeding range: Se. Arizona; sw. New Mexico (poss.), Texas (Chisos Mts.).

Habitat: Mountain glades, pine-oak woods, canyons, at altitudes of 5000–8000 ft. (1525–2440 m).

Nest: High above ground in trees. Saddled on horizontal branch; of silky plant fibers, mosses; lined with fine down, soft feathers; decorated with lichens bound by spider silk. Similar to nest of Ruby-throat of East but larger.

Eggs: 2; av. 15.4 x 10.0 mm. White. *Indistinguishable from eggs of Blue-throated Hummingbird* but larger than those of most other North American species. Incubation by female; probably about 16 days.

Notes: Of 7 nests of this largest North American hummingbird found in s. Arizona, 5 were in maple 20–55 ft. (6.1–16.8 m) above ground.

BLUE-THROATED HUMMINGBIRD
Lampornis clemenciae

Breeding range: S. Arizona; New Mexico (Hidalgo Co., poss.); Texas (Chisos Mts., prob.).

Habitat: Forested mountain canyons.

Nest: Natural site is vertical plant stalk, but bird has propensity for attaching nest to electric wires inside or outside cabins. Variety of plant materials used, bound together with spider silk.

Eggs: 2, sometimes 1; av. 15.1 x 10.0 mm. White. *Indistinguishable from eggs of Rivoli's Hummingbird* but larger than eggs of most other North American species. Incubation by female; 17–18 days (in Mexico).

BUFF-BELLIED HUMMINGBIRD   *Amazilia yucatanensis*

Breeding range: Known to nest in U.S. only in Texas, Rio Grande Valley (Cameron and Hidalgo Cos.).

Habitat: Open woods, edges of thickets.

Nest: In tree or bush 3–8 ft. (0.9–2.4 m) above ground. Saddled on small drooping limb or horizontal fork.
Eggs: 2; av. 13.24 x 8.65 mm. White. *Indistinguishable from eggs of other hummingbirds of similar size.*

VIOLET-CROWNED HUMMINGBIRD   *Amazilia verticalis*

Notes: This common breeding species of Mexico is uncommon or casual in Guadalupe Canyon, se. Arizona (Cochise Co.) and sw. New Mexico (Hidalgo Co.). Nests saddled to horizontal limbs of sycamores 25–40 ft. (7.6–12.2 m) above ground. First nests found in U.S. in 1959.

BERYLLINE HUMMINGBIRD   *Amazilia beryllina*

Notes: This species, unknown within the U.S. before 1967, was found nesting on July 13, 1976, at the Southwestern Research Station in Chiricahua Mts., se. Arizona. At time of discovery, female was incubating 2 eggs.

BROAD-BILLED HUMMINGBIRD   Pl. 13
Cynanthus latirostris

Breeding range: S. Arizona, sw. New Mexico (Hidalgo Co., rare), Texas (Brewster Co., rare).
Habitat: Thickets in arid country, desert canyons, streamside bushes.
Nest: Decorated with brown bark, dried leaves, bits of grasses; lined with soft plant down.
Eggs: 2; av. 12.6 x 8.5 mm. White. *Indistinguishable from eggs of other hummingbirds of similar size.*
Notes: 6 nests found by author in Arizona appeared much rougher and more loosely constructed than nests of other hummers in area (Costa's and Black-chinned). In 1 nest, plant material dangled underneath for about $3\frac{1}{2}$ in. (9 cm).

COPPERY-TAILED TROGON   *Trogon elegans*

Breeding range: Se. Arizona.
Habitat: Wooded canyons.
Nest: In sycamore trees in natural cavities or large, deserted woodpecker holes.
Eggs: 3–4, av. 28.50 x 23.18 mm. Oval. Smooth, not glossy. Dull white or pale bluish white.

BELTED KINGFISHER   *Megaceryle alcyon*   Pl. 14

Breeding range: All western states, with probable exception of Arizona; rare or casual in New Mexico.

BROAD-BILLED HUMMINGBIRD nesting on clothesline (*left*), horse bit (*right*).

Habitat: Fresh- and salt-water sandbanks, river bluffs, road and railroad cuts, sand and gravel pits.

Nest: Burrow in bank excavated by birds, preferably near water. Generally 1–3 ft. (0.3–0.9 m) from top of bank, extending inward, curved or uncurved, sloping slightly upward, 3–6 ft. (0.9–1.8 m), rarely 10–15 ft. (3.1–4.6 m). Sexes take turns digging. Excavation time depends upon nature of soil, 2–3 weeks or less. Same burrow may be used succeeding years. Nest cavity enlarged, domed chamber at end of tunnel; diam. 10–12 in. (25.4–30.5 cm), height 6–7 in. (15.2–17.8 cm). Tunnel entrance width 3½–4 in. (8.9–10.2 cm); height 3–3½ in. (7.6–8.9 cm).

Eggs: 5–8, commonly 6–7; av. 33.9 x 26.7 mm. Short-oval to elliptical. Shell smooth, rather glossy. Pure white. Incubation by both sexes; 23–24 days. 1 brood.

Notes: In new burrow eggs are laid on bare ground. Succeeding years, eggs laid on base of fish scales, residue from feeding young in previous years. Male may excavate roosting burrow for himself near burrow where female incubates during night. Bird arriving to relieve mate calls from nearby perch; bird on eggs leaves before mate enters tunnel.

RINGED KINGFISHER *Megaceryle torquata*

Breeding range: Texas, lower Rio Grande Valley.

Habitat: Banks of rivers and arroyos.

Nest: At end of tunnel in bank.

Eggs: 2–6, usually 4–5; av. 43.72 x 34.52 mm. Oval to short-oval. Smooth, quite glossy. White.

Notes: First U.S. nest found April 8, 1970, in bank of arroyo 2 mi. (3.2 km) below Falcon Dam on Rio Grande R. Both adults were feeding young at end of tunnel 8⅓ ft. (2.5 m) long; 4 ft. (1.2 m) below top of bank.

GREEN KINGFISHER   *Chloroceryle americana*

Breeding range: S. Texas.
Habitat: High banks of rivers, woodland streams, sloughs.
Nest: In burrow about 3 ft. (0.9 m) long. Entrance, diam. 2–
2¼ in. (5.1–5.6 cm), often concealed by vines or dead vegetation
draping top of bank.
Eggs: 3–6, usually 5; av. 24.36 x 19.23 mm. Oval to long-oval.
Glossy white.

COMMON FLICKER

COMMON FLICKER   *Colaptes auratus*   **Pl. 14**
(Including Red-shafted, Yellow-shafted, and Gilded Flickers)

Breeding range: All western states.
Habitat: Deciduous, coniferous, and mixed woods, parks, gardens,
orchards, roadsides; desert cacti (Gilded Flicker).
Nest: In cavity in tree, cactus; fencepost, utility pole, side of
building; 2–60 ft. (0.6–18.3 m) above ground. Dug by both sexes,
no material added. Building time 1–2 weeks. Old cavity may be
repaired. Entrance width 2–4 in. (5.1–10.2 cm), av. 3 in. (7.6 cm);
depth of cavity 10–36 in. (25.4–91.4 cm). Birdhouses used if
proper size.
Eggs: 3–10, typically 6–8 (Gilded Flicker averages fewer), laid 1 a
day; av. 28.18 x 21.85 mm (Red-shafted), 26.85 x 20.58 mm (Yellow-shafted), 27.86 x 21.34 mm (Gilded). Oval to short-oval.
Smooth, brilliant gloss. Pure white. Incubation by both sexes,
mostly by male at night, shared during day; 11–12 days.

Notes: The Red-shafted and Yellow-shafted forms freely inter-breed on Great Plains where the 2 races meet, but Gilded Flicker is isolated in desert habitat.

PILEATED WOODPECKER *Dryocopus pileatus*

Breeding range: Washington to cen. California, Minnesota to Louisiana; rare or absent in Rocky Mt. states, e. N. Dakota, e. Kansas, e. Oklahoma, e. Texas.

Habitat: Dense forests of conifers or mixed woodlands.

Nest: New hole dug annually in same nest area; often in dead stub (hole typically faces east or south), may be in live tree; 15–70 ft. (4.6–21.4 m) above ground; av. 45 ft. (13.7 m). Both sexes excavate; no nest material brought in. Entrance sometimes circular, but tends to be oval or triangular, peaked above, leveled below. Inner chamber conical, tapering from domed top to bowl-like bottom. Entrance 3¼ in. (8.3 cm) horizontally, 3½ in. (8.9 cm) vertically; depth of cavity from bottom of entrance 10–24 in. (25.4–61.0 cm), av. 19 in. (48.3 cm).

Eggs: 3–4, av. 33.16 x 25.21 mm (northern race); 3–5, av. 32.90 x 24.72 mm (southern race). Oval or elliptical, some quite pointed. Shell smooth, decidedly glossy. China-white. Incubation by both sexes, male probably at night, alternating by day; 18 days. May start before clutch complete. 1 brood.

Notes: Requires large territory. As forests dwindle, especially in agricultural areas, it disappears. Fortunately it has adapted to some extent and nests occasionally in less remote areas.

PILEATED WOOD-PECKER nesting holes in dead tree

RED-BELLIED WOODPECKER

RED-BELLIED WOODPECKER   Pl. 14
Melanerpes carolinus

Breeding range: Se. S. Dakota and se. Minnesota, south to Texas and Louisiana.
Habitat: Coniferous, deciduous forests; orchards, yards.
Nest: Hole dug in live or dead tree, stump, utility pole, wooden building; 5–70 ft. (1.5–21.4 m) above ground, usually under 40 ft. (12.2 m). May be in deserted nesting hole of other woodpecker or frequently in birdhouse. Both sexes excavate, mostly male. Entrance diam. $1\frac{3}{4}$–$2\frac{1}{4}$ in. (4.5–5.7 cm); depth 12 in. (30.5 cm).
Eggs: 3–8, generally 4–5, laid 1 a day; av. 25.06 x 18.78 mm. Mostly oval. Shell fine-grained, has no gloss when laid but becomes moderately glossy during incubation. Pure white. Incubation by both sexes; said to be 14 days. Probably 1 brood in North, 2 broods in South.
Notes: European Starlings are aggressive competitors of Red-bellied Woodpeckers, often forcing them to abandon excavations after completion.

GOLDEN-FRONTED WOODPECKER
Melanerpes aurifrons

Breeding range: Sw. Oklahoma, Texas.
Habitat: Mesquite forests, flats; river bottomlands.

Nest: In holes in trees (live or dead), poles, posts, usually 6–25 ft. (1.8–7.6 m) above ground; often in utility pole. Excavation by both sexes, requires 6–10 days. Cavities rarely over 12 in. (30.5 cm) deep.
Eggs: 4–7, usually 4–5; av. 25.82 x 19.50 mm. Incubation by both sexes; about 14 days.

GILA WOODPECKER *Melanerpes uropygialis*

Breeding range: Resident in se. California, s. tip of Nevada, s. Arizona, sw. New Mexico.
Habitat: Desert scrub, cacti, mesquite, thorny brush, canyon foothills. Common in Saguaros.
Nest: Cavity excavated in cactus (often Saguaro), mesquite, cottonwood, willow. Diam. of entrance in 18 Arizona nesting cavities 1⅞–2¼ in. (4.8–5.8 cm), av. just under 2 in. (4.9 cm); depth of cavity 9–16 in. (22.9–40.6 cm), av. 12 in. (30.5 cm). Entrance holes not always round. Both sexes excavate; no material added; eggs laid on bare floor. Nest holes used succeeding years.
Eggs: 3–4, sometimes 5; av. 25.14 x 18.56 mm. Oval to long-oval, sometimes quite pointed. Not glossy when laid, but quite glossy when heavily incubated. Pure white. Incubation by both sexes; about 2 weeks. 2 or 3 broods.
Notes: Cavities excavated by Gila Woodpeckers provide nesting sites for many other species of hole-nesting birds: Elf Owl, Ferruginous Owl, Screech Owl, Ash-throated Flycatcher, Great Crested Flycatcher, Purple Martin. Also homes for snakes, lizards, rats, mice.

RED-HEADED WOODPECKER   Pl. 14
Melanerpes erythrocephalus

Breeding range: E. and cen. Montana to Minnesota, south to s. New Mexico and Gulf; rare in ne. Utah.
Habitat: Open country (typically not a forest nester), groves, old burns, farm woodlots, roadside trees, parks.
Nest: Hole dug in live tree, dead stub, utility pole, fencepost, 8–80 ft. (2.4–24.4 m) above ground; no material added. Both sexes excavate. Diam. of entrance 1¾ in. (4.5 cm); depth of cavity 8–24 in. (20.3–61.0 cm).
Eggs: 4–7, commonly 5, laid 1 a day; av. 25.14 x19.17 mm. Oval to short-oval. Shell smooth, glossy when incubated. White. Incubation by both sexes, about 14 days; may start before clutch complete. 1 brood, possibly 2 in South.
Notes: Six sets of eggs, 28 in all, were collected from same nest in 1 season, after which pair drilled new hole in same tree and raised 4 young (total 32 eggs). Shun birdhouses as nesting sites. Utility poles treated with creosote have been lethal to eggs and young.

ACORN WOODPECKER   *Melanerpes formicivorus*   **Pl. 14**

Breeding range: Sw. Oregon south to Mexico and east through Arizona, New Mexico, w. Texas.
Habitat: Valleys, foothills, canyons of oak or pine-oak.
Nest: In colonies, mostly in dead or live oaks, typically 6–25 ft. (1.8–7.6 m) above ground. Isolated pairs nesting singly are exceptions. Members of colony may share in excavating nest cavities. No material added. Entrance hole perfectly round; diam. about 1½ in. (3.8 cm); inner cavity 8–24 in. (20.3–61.0 cm) deep.
Eggs: 4–5, sometimes 6; av. 25.98 x 19.78 mm. Short- to long-oval. Little or no gloss. Pure white. Incubation by both sexes; about 14 days. 2 or possibly 3 broods.
Notes: Segregated into nesting groups containing up to 10 individuals with at least 2 older birds and some 1st-year birds. A pair is assisted by others in excavating, feeding, and possibly brooding or even incubating. Polyandry suggested but not proved. In s. Arizona, author found Acorn Woodpeckers nesting in same Mexican Blue Oak with Hooded Oriole, Western Kingbird, Olivaceous Flycatcher.

LEWIS' WOODPECKER   *Melanerpes lewis*

Breeding range: Washington to Montana, south to cen. Arizona, s. New Mexico; also sw. S. Dakota (Black Hills), nw. Nebraska, nw. Oklahoma.
Habitat: Openness is prerequisite for aerial foraging for insects: logged or burned coniferous forests, streamside woodlands, open oak forests.
Nest: In loose colonies where food supply is abundant. In cavities 4⅞–169¾ ft. (1.5–51.8 m) above ground in dead or live trees; sometimes utility poles. In 64 nesting sites, 47 in dead stubs, 17 in live trees. Male selects nest site, may do most of excavating. Depth of cavity 9–30 in. (22.8–76.2 cm); diam. of entrance hole 2–2⅞ in. (5.1–7.4 cm).
Eggs: 5–9, typically 6–7; av. 26.22 x 19.99 mm. Mostly oval to short-oval, but vary. Shell close-grained, no gloss when laid. White. Both sexes incubate; about 2 weeks. Male incubates at night; birds alternate during day. Pairs may mate for life; fidelity is quite evident.
Notes: Lewis' Woodpecker tends to use old nest sites rather than dig new ones and tends to nest in natural cavities or dead stubs; probably less well-adapted for digging than more forest-dwelling species of woodpeckers.

YELLOW-BELLIED SAPSUCKER   **Pl. 14**
Sphyrapicus varius
(includes Red-naped Sapsucker, Red-breasted Sapsucker)

Breeding range: Washington to n. Minnesota, south to Mexico,

w. Texas; also S. Dakota (Black Hills).
Habitat: Aspen groves, edges of coniferous forests, mountain gulches, sheltered hillsides.
Nest: Typically in deciduous trees, mostly aspen; sometimes in conifer, 5–30 ft. (1.5–9.2 m) above ground. Entrance hole quite small, $1\frac{1}{4}$–$1\frac{1}{2}$ in. (3.2–3.8 cm), perfectly round; cavity 5–10 in. (12.7–25.4 cm) deep. No material added. May use same tree annually, digging new cavities for 5–6 years; rarely use old nest hole.
Eggs: 3–6, typically 5; av. 22.44 x 16.92 (Yellow-bellied race); av. 22.89 x 17.28 mm (Red-naped race); av. 23.61 x 17.51 mm (Red-breasted race). Oval to elliptical. Shell smooth, has little or no gloss. Pure white. Incubation by both sexes; 12–13 days.
Notes: Nests easily found since adults become very vocal when alarmed. Aspen and a few other trees affected with tinder fungus (*Fomes igniarius*) are favored as nest trees. Fungus attacks heartwood; creates a center of soft decay that can be excavated readily. Outer surface, unaffected, is tough living shell, a deterrent to predators.

WILLIAMSON'S SAPSUCKER   Pl. 14
Sphyrapicus thyroideus
(includes Natalie's Sapsucker)

Breeding range: Washington to w. Montana, south through cen. Colorado and New Mexico to Mexico.
Habitat: Aspen groves, high coniferous forests.
Nest: In cavity in tree. Often in same tree for many years, a new cavity dug for each nesting (1 California tree had 38 holes), 5–60 ft. (1.5–18.3 m) above ground. Cavity opening about $1\frac{1}{2}$ in. (3.8 cm) in diam.
Eggs: 3–7, usually 5–6; av. 23.54 x 17.23 mm. Oval to long-oval, a few sometimes pyriform. Shell close-grained, slightly glossy. White. Both incubate; 14 days.
Notes: Despite this species' supposed affinity for conifers as nesting sites, all nests observed by author in Colorado Rockies were in aspen; all within 10 ft. (3.1 m) of ground.

HAIRY WOODPECKER *Picoides villosus*   Pl. 14

Breeding range: Permanent resident in all western states.
Habitat: Deciduous and coniferous forests, wooded swamps.
Nest: Hole dug in live or dead tree or stub, 5–40 ft. (1.5–12.2 m) or more above ground. Both sexes excavate, mostly male, taking 2–3 weeks depending upon hardness of wood. Aspens or other trees with decayed centers favored. Normally a new nesting cavity dug annually; may also dig roosting cavity. No material carried in; eggs laid on chips. Typical entrance hole somewhat elongated: $2\frac{1}{2}$ in. (6.4 cm) high, 2 in. (5.1 cm) wide; cavity 10–12 in. (25.4–30.5 cm) or more deep; base inside $4\frac{1}{2}$ in. (11.4 cm) in diam.
Eggs: 3–6, commonly 4; av. 24.49 x 18.38 mm (Rocky Mt. race).

Oval to elliptical. Shell smooth, quite glossy. Pure white. Both sexes incubate; male at night, alternately during day; 11–12 days. 1 brood.

Notes: Female spends entire year in breeding territory; male joins her at start of breeding season in late winter. Pair formation, courtship, occurs as much as 3 months before start of actual nesting. Either male or female may initiate cavity excavation and do large part of work.

DOWNY WOODPECKER   *Picoides pubescens*   Pl. 15

Breeding range: Permanent resident in all western states.
Habitat: Open forests of mixed growth, swamps, orchards, parks, gardens.
Nest: Hole in live or dead tree, stump, stub, fencepost, often in rotting wood, 3–50 ft. (0.9–15.3 m) above ground. Both birds excavate but mostly male. Common for entrance hole to be on *underside* of exposed limb. Cavity opening a perfect circle, about 1¼ in. (3.2 cm) in diam.; goes straight-in for several inches before turning downward 8–10 in. (20.3–25.4 cm); cavity narrows from 3 in. (7.6 cm) at top to 2 in. (5.1 cm) at bottom.
Eggs: 3–6, generally 4–5; av. 19.35 x 15.05 mm (northern race). Oval to short-oval. Shell smooth, little or no gloss. White. Incubation by both sexes alternately during day, male at night; 12 days. 1 brood; may be 2 in South.
Notes: Pair formation and courtship occur in late winter, often several months before nesting. Each bird excavates a winter roost hole. Birdhouses may be used as winter roosts but rarely as nest sites.

LADDER-BACKED WOODPECKER   *Picoides scalaris*

Breeding range: S. California, s. Nevada, Arizona, New Mexico, se. Colorado (Baca Co., unc.), nw. and sw. Oklahoma, w. and cen. Texas.
Habitat: Mostly deserts and other arid regions, mesquite, scrub oak, pinyon-juniper forests, thickets.
Nest: Excavated cavity 4–25 ft. (1.2–7.6 m), av. 12 ft. (3.7 m), above ground in rotted stub, dead or dying branch of oak, mesquite, hackberry, willow, often along waterway. May nest in fencepost, utility pole, desert cactus, agave, yucca. Entrance hole 1½ in. (3.8 cm) in diam.; cavity 7–10 in. (17.8–25.4 cm) deep.
Eggs: 2–6, generally 4 or 5; av. 21.48 x 16.18 mm (*P. s. cactophilus*). Oval or short-oval, sometimes long-oval. More or less glossy. White. Both incubate, about 13 days.

NUTTALL'S WOODPECKER   *Picoides nuttallii*

Breeding range: California west of Sierra Nevada.
Habitat: Typically sycamore canyons, hillsides of oak and chap-

RED-COCKADED WOODPECKER
Resin flowing at and around nest hole

arral, woodlands along small streams.

Nest: In cavity about 1 ft. (30.5 cm) deep, excavated 2½–60 ft. (0.8–18.3 m) above ground, typically in dead stub.

Eggs: 3–6, commonly 4–5; av. 21.75 x 16.27 mm. White. Incubation by both sexes; 14 days.

Notes: Breeding biology similar to that of Ladder-backed.

ARIZONA WOODPECKER   *Picoides arizonae*

Breeding range: Se. Arizona and sw. New Mexico.

Habitat: Mountain canyons.

Nest: Excavated cavity in trunk or branch of deciduous tree, 20–50 ft. (6.1–15.3 m) above ground.

Eggs: 3–4; av. 22.82 x 17.33 mm. White. Incubation by both sexes; 14 days.

RED-COCKADED WOODPECKER   *Picoides borealis*

Breeding range: E. Texas, Louisiana, Arkansas, se. Oklahoma (McCurtain, Pushmataha Cos.).

Habitat: Pine woods.

Nest: Cavity dug 8–12 in. (20.3–30.5 cm) deep, 4–100 ft. (1.2–30.5 m), mostly 10–40 ft. (3.1–12.2 m), above ground in pine. Tree usually infected with fungal disease called red heart (*Fomes pini*) which attacks heart of tree and causes it to become soft and pithy.

Eggs: 3–5; av. 24.04 x 17.86 mm. White, but sticky from pine gum carried on breast of incubating bird.

Notes: Birds chip holes through bark into sapwood for several feet above and below nest entrance, causing resin to flow freely. This may deter predators.

WHITE-HEADED WOODPECKER   Pl. 15
Picoides albolarvatus

Breeding range: E. Washington, w. Idaho, Oregon, California, w. Nevada. Absent from Pacific Coast rain forest.
Habitat: Montane forests of pine and fir, typically at altitudes of 4000–9000 ft. (1220–2745 m).
Nest: Usually in hole excavated by both sexes in dead stub of pine or fir; may be in live tree (oak, aspen). Entrance hole seldom over 15 ft. (4.6 m) above ground, often lower; is perfectly circular, about 1½ in. (3.8 cm) in diam.; inner cavity 8–15 in. (20.3–38.1 cm) deep.
Eggs: 3–7, usually 4–5; av. 24.26 x 18.11 mm. Oval to short-oval. Moderately or quite glossy. Pure white. Incubation by both sexes; 14 days.
Notes: Of 10 nests found in Yosemite region of California, the lowest was 58 in. (147.3 cm) and highest 15 ft. (4.6 m) above ground. None in living conifer. 1 stub had 5 holes.

BLACK-BACKED THREE-TOED WOODPECKER
Picoides arcticus

Breeding range: Washington, n. and e. Idaho, w. Montana, n. Minnesota, cen. California (high Sierras), Nevada, ne. Wyoming, S. Dakota (Black Hills).
Habitat: Fir and spruce forests; lodgepole pine or fir burns.
Nest: Hole chiseled in live (generally with dead heart) or dead tree, stump, fencepost, utility pole, at low height atypical for woodpecker: 26 nest holes 2–15 ft. (0.6–4.6 m) above ground. Both sexes excavate, usually a new cavity each year. Entrance about 1½ in. (3.8 cm) high, 1¾ in. (4.5 cm) wide; *strongly beveled* at lower edge, forming "doorstep." Cavity 9–11 in. (22.9–27.9 cm) deep.
Eggs: 2–6, commonly 4; av. 21.32 x 18.94 mm. Oval to elliptical. Shell smooth, dull, or slightly glossy. White. *Indistinguishable from eggs of Northern Three-toed Woodpecker.* Incubation by both sexes; about 14 days. 1 brood.
Notes: Although Hairy Woodpecker sometimes bevels bottom of nest entrance, this characteristic plus the fact that nest site is usually lower are helpful in identifying Three-toed cavity. Birds tame at nest site; frequently visit nest while observer is near.

NORTHERN THREE-TOED WOODPECKER
Picoides tridactylus

Breeding range: Washington, Oregon, e. Nevada, cen. Arizona, east to w. Montana, Wyoming (unc.), cen. Colorado, cen. New Mexico; also S. Dakota (Black Hills).

Habitat: Coniferous forests, high aspen groves.
Nest: Hole 5–12 ft. (1.5–3.7 m) above ground, rarely as high as 40 ft. (12.2 m), dug by both sexes in live or dead tree (commonly conifer or aspen) or in utility pole. Entrance hole has lower edge chiseled to a slope resulting in irregular-shaped opening 1¾ in. (4.5 cm) wide, 2 in. (5.1 cm) high. Inward ½ in. (1.3 cm) from trunk surface, hole becomes round, diam. 1½ in. (3.8 cm). Interior depth 10–12 in. (25.4–30.5 cm).
Eggs: 4, rarely 5; av. 23.32 x 18.01 mm. Oval. Shell smooth, moderately glossy. Pure white. *Eggs indistinguishable from eggs of Black-backed Three-toed Woodpecker.* Incubation by both sexes; about 14 days. 1 brood.
Notes: Loosely colonial where nesting habitat is particularly suitable and food supply abundant. Where ranges overlap, similar Black-backed species is more common. At nest, birds are unsuspicious and quite tame; usually will enter or leave nest cavity while intruder is close by.

ROSE-THROATED BECARD   opp. p. 121
Platypsaris aglaiae

Breeding range: Se. Arizona, Texas (Rio Grande Valley), sw. New Mexico (poss. in Guadalupe Mts.).
Habitat: Riparian deciduous woodland; open brushy woods.
Nest: Suspended from end of tree branch, often a sycamore, as high as 50 ft. (15.3 m) or more above ground. Large, globular structure of grasses, plant stems, lichens, wool, fibrous bark, vines, spider cocoons, and a wide variety of similar items; interior of cavity lined with soft materials. Entrance hole well hidden below middle of "bushel basket of vegetable miscellany." Both sexes build; may continue after incubation starts. Completed nest 12–14 in. (30.5–35.6 cm) high, 9–12 in. (22.9–30.5 cm) in diam.; walls 1½–2½ in. (3.8–6.4 cm) thick.
Eggs: 4–6; av. 23.2 x 16.9 mm. Dull white to buff, thickly marked with brown spots, blotches. Female incubates.

EASTERN KINGBIRD   *Tyrannus tyrannus*   Pl. 15

Breeding range: E. Washington to Minnesota, south to n. California (poss.), n. Nevada (cas.), n. Utah, ne. New Mexico, n.-cen. and e. Texas, Gulf of Mexico.
Habitat: Open woods, orchards, shade trees, rangeland, forest edges, fencerows, swamps, marshes, stream banks.
Nest: On tree limb well out from trunk, 2–60 ft. (0.6–18.3 m), av. 10–20 ft. (3.1–6.1 m), above ground; sometimes in crotch of dead stub, often over water. Bulky cup (large for size of bird), rough unkempt exterior of forbs, grasses, mosses; lined with fine grasses, plant down. Both build. Outside diam. 5½ in. (14 cm), height 3¼ in. (8.3 cm); inside diam. 3 in. (7.6 cm), depth 1¾ in. (4.5 cm).
Eggs: 3–5; av. 24.2 x 17.7 mm. Vary from short-oval to long-oval.

ROSE-THROATED BECARD

SULPHUR-BELLIED FLYCATCHER

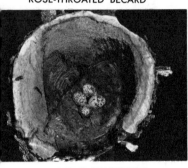

OLIVACEOUS FLYCATCHER

LUCY'S WARBLER

BROWN-THROATED WREN

RED-FACED WARBLER

PAINTED REDSTART

YELLOW-EYED JUNCO

Shell smooth, slightly glossy. Creamy white, heavily and irregularly spotted with brown, black, lavender; sometimes wreathed. *Indistinguishable from eggs of Western Kingbird and Scissortailed Flycatcher.* Incubation by female; 12–13 days, perhaps longer. 1 brood.

Notes: Sometimes nests in tree with other species, often Northern Oriole. Many reports of strange nest sites including inside gourd in Purple Martin colony, in reflector of electric street light, inside confiscated Northern Oriole nest, on top of 4-ft. (1.2 m) fencepost.

TROPICAL KINGBIRD *Tyrannus melancholicus*

Breeding range: Texas (lower Rio Grande Valley), s. Arizona.
Habitat: Forests of mesquite, ebony, retama, granjena; open cottonwood areas.
Nest: On branch or in fork of tree 8–20 ft. (2.4–6.1 m) or more above ground. Of Spanish Moss, strips of bark, plant down; lined with rootlets, hairlike moss.
Eggs: Commonly 3–4, sometimes 5; av. 24.8 x 18.4 mm. Creamy pink or rich buff; blotched, spotted with brown, purples, lavenders. *Ground color diagnostic;* distinguishes eggs from those of other kingbirds.

WESTERN KINGBIRD *Tyrannus verticalis*   **Pl. 15**

Breeding range: Most or all western states, but rare or absent in many parts of Mississippi Valley.
Habitat: Open country with scattered trees; farms, roadsides, parks, yards.
Nest: Almost anywhere but on ground; apparently trees preferred. Placed against trunk, in crotch, or commonly on horizontal branch, 8–40 ft. (2.4–12.2 m), oftener 15–30 ft. (4.6–9.2 m), above ground. Both build using forb stems, twigs, plant fibers, rootlets, intermixed with wool, hair, feathers, cocoons, string, milkweed, pieces of paper; lined with finer material of same kind. (Nest found by author in Arizona contained cigarette butts.) Typical nest: outside diam. 6 in. (15.2 cm), height 3 in. (7.6 cm); inside diam. 3 in. (7.6 cm), depth 1¾ in. (4.5 cm).
Eggs: 3–5, commonly 4; av. 23.5 x 17.7 mm. Oval to short-oval. Shell smooth, slightly glossy. Creamy white, heavily and irregularly spotted with brown, black, lavender; sometimes wreathed. *Indistinguishable from eggs of Eastern Kingbird and Scissortailed Flycatcher.* Incubation entirely or mostly by female, 12–14 days. 1 brood.
Notes: Unusual nesting sites include towers, parts of buildings, fenceposts, windmills, utility poles, oil derricks, in barns, on rocky cliff ledges, in abandoned nests of American Robin and Northern Oriole. Author found nest near Tucson in same tree (Mexican Oak) with nests of Olivaceous Flycatcher, Acorn Woodpecker, and Hooded Oriole.

Opposite: Southern Arizona Birds

CASSIN'S KINGBIRD   *Tyrannus vociferans*   **Pl. 15**

Breeding range: Se. Montana, e. Wyoming, s. Utah, Colorado, south to Mexico; also s. California (west of desert), w. Oklahoma, w. Texas.

Habitat: Foothills, mountains, sycamore canyons; coastal savannahs (California).

Nests: In pines, oaks, cottonwoods, hackberries, sycamores, well out from trunk on horizontal limb, usually 20–40 ft. (6.1–12.2 m) above ground. Large bulky structure, slightly larger than nest of Western Kingbird, but composed of similar materials. Average nest: outside diam. 8 in. (20.3 cm), height 3 in. (7.6 cm); inside diam. 3½ in. (8.9 cm), depth 1¾ in. (4.5 cm).

Eggs: 3–4, rarely 2 or 5; av. 23.5 x 17.4 mm. Oval. Slightly glossy. White or creamy white with brown spots, dots, often grouped at large end. Typically *less spotted* than eggs of other kingbirds. Female incubates, 12–14 days.

Notes: Author observed bird building in giant sycamore along Sonoita Creek, Pima Co., Arizona, at 100 ft. (30.5 m) above ground, near outer end of long stout limb. Most others in same area were built 25–50 ft. (7.6–15.3 m) above ground; all were well out from trunk.

THICK-BILLED KINGBIRD   *Tyrannus crassirostris*

Notes: Casual or uncommon in Guadalupe Canyon in se. Arizona and sw. New Mexico; also in Sonoita Creek region near Patagonia, Arizona. This Mexican species builds a frail, thin nest of twigs and grass high in large sycamore or cottonwood. Both incubate 3–4 eggs spotted with brown.

SCISSOR-TAILED FLYCATCHER   **Pl. 15**
Muscivora forficata

Breeding range: Se. Colorado (cas.), e. New Mexico, east to sw. Missouri (rare), w. Arkansas, Louisiana; rare in s. Nebraska and nw. Kansas.

Habitat: Open country, ranches, roadsides, coastal prairies, towns.

Nest: In tree 7–30 ft. (2.1–9.2 m) above ground, generally on horizontal limb or fork, sometimes in crotch; also on utility poles, windmills, towers, bridge frameworks. Nest roughly built of forbs, twigs, rootlets, cotton, wool, sometimes rags, corn husks, twine; lined with cotton, Indian tobacco, rootlets, horsehair. Outside diam. 4½–6 in. (11.4–15.2 cm), height about 3 in. (7.6 cm); inside diam. 2¾–3 x 3½ in. (7.0–7.6 x 8.9 cm), depth 1¾–2¼ in. (4.5–5.7 cm).

Eggs: 3–6, commonly 4–5, laid 1 a day; av. 22.5 x 17.0 mm. Oval. Slightly glossy. White or creamy white, more or less spotted or blotched with dark browns with underlying markings of gray or drab brown. *Indistinguishable from eggs of Eastern and Western Kingbirds.* Female incubates; 12–13 days.

Notes: Author found 16 nests in 1 day in Runnels, Taylor, Callahan Cos., Texas, all in roadside mesquite trees, all 7–13 ft. (2.1–4.0 m) above ground, most 7–8 ft. (2.1–2.4 m). Of 9 nests that could be examined, 1 had 3 eggs, 5 had 4, 3 had 5.

KISKADEE FLYCATCHER   *Pitangus sulphuratus*

Breeding range: Texas (lower Rio Grande Valley), Louisiana (2 nests found).

Habitat: Borders of ponds, lakes, small streams, resacas.

Nest: In tree or tall shrub. Bulky football-shaped structure of grass, moss, small twigs, pieces of vines; lined with similar but finer material. Entrance on side, generally directed slightly downward. Outside measurements: about 10 x 14 in. (25.4 x 35.6 cm).

Eggs: 2–5, commonly 4; av. 28.5 x 21.0 mm. Mostly oval. Shell smooth, slightly glossy. Pale creamy white, sparingly marked with brown spots and dots.

SULPHUR-BELLIED FLYCATCHER   opp. p. 121
Myiodynastes luteiventris

Breeding range: Se. Arizona, especially Santa Rita, Huachuca, and Chiricahua Mts.; Texas (Starr Co., 1977).

Habitat: Sycamore canyons.

Nest: Female builds in natural cavity of large sycamore, often in rotted-out knothole, generally 20–50 ft. (6.1–15.3 m) above ground. Cavity is filled with trash to within an inch or two of opening. Top of nest finished almost entirely of leaf petioles and midribs, pine needles, or plant stems, arranged in circle. Diam. of inner cup 3–4 in. (7.6–10.2 cm). Incubating female has view of surroundings.

Eggs: 3–4; av. 25.9 x 19.0 mm. White to creamy buff, profusely spotted and blotched usually over entire surface with rich red-dish browns. Female incubates, 15–16 days.

GREAT CRESTED FLYCATCHER   Pl. 15
Myiarchus crinitus

Breeding range: E. and cen. N. Dakota, Minnesota south to cen. and e. Texas and Gulf Coast; ne. Colorado (prob.).

Habitat: Woodlands, old orchards, swamps, parks, edges of clearings.

Nest: In natural cavity or abandoned woodpecker hole in live or dead tree 3–75 ft. (0.9–22.9 m) above ground, av. 10–20 ft. (3.1–6.1 m). Often in birdhouses. A bulky mass of twigs, leaves, hair, feathers, bark fibers, rope, other trash. Almost always includes cast-off snakeskin or piece of cellophane (see Plate 15).

Small cup for eggs formed in trashy surroundings; lined with finer material, feathers. Both build, for as long as 2 weeks. Cup diam. $2\frac{3}{4}$–$3\frac{1}{2}$ in. (7.1–8.9 cm), depth $1\frac{1}{2}$–2 in. (3.8–5.1 cm).

Eggs: 4–6, generally 5; av. 22.6 x 17.2 mm. Oval to short-oval. Shell smooth, slightly glossy. Yellowish or pinkish white; scratched, lined, streaked, blotched with dark brown, purple. Markings often so dense that ground color almost obliterated. Incubation by female; 13–15 days.

Notes: It is likely that use of snakeskins in nest building is instinctive rather than a conscious act aimed at frightening away predators. As nest-building evolved, it is likely that those who used snakeskins produced more viable offspring than those who did not. Other species, such as Tufted Titmouse, also add snakeskins to their nests.

GREAT CRESTED FLYCATCHER nest in mailbox; note cast-off snakeskins.

WIED'S CRESTED FLYCATCHER   *Myiarchus tyrannulus*

Breeding range: Se. California (rare), Nevada (Colorado R. valley), Arizona, sw. New Mexico, s. Texas.

Habitat: Sycamore canyons, cactus deserts (Saguaros); in Texas, river groves and woodlands.

Nest: Deserted woodpecker holes in cactus, cavities in sycamores, cottonwoods, mesquites. Nest holes filled with hair, fur, feathers; lined with variety of soft materials; usually 1 or more cast-off snakeskins included.

Eggs: 3–5; av. 24.1 x 18.2 mm. Oval to short-oval. Slightly glossy. Creamy buff; elongated blotches, spots, and scrawls of brown, purple, lavender. *Indistinguishable from eggs of Ash-throated Flycatcher.* Similar to eggs of Great Crested Flycatcher; less heavily marked.

Notes: Although breeding ranges of Wied's and Great Crested Flycatchers overlap, Wied's is the form typical of deserts and more arid lands.

ASH-THROATED FLYCATCHER   Pl. 15
Myiarchus cinerascens

Breeding range: E. Washington, s. Idaho, sw. Wyoming (rare), south to Baja and s. and w. Texas; also sw. Oklahoma.

Habitat: Groves, mesquite thickets, canyons, desert washes.

Nest: In knotholes or abandoned woodpecker holes in mesquite, oak, sycamore, juniper, cottonwood, usually 20 ft. (6.1 m) or less above ground. Cavity filled with forbs, rootlets, grass, bits of manure; cup is felted mass of hair and fur.

Eggs: Generally 4–5; av. 22.4 x 16.5 mm. Oval to long-oval. Very little gloss. Creamy white to pinkish; streaked, splashed, spotted, or blotched with browns and purples. *Indistinguishable from eggs of Wied's Crested Flycatcher.* Similar to eggs of Great Crested Flycatcher; more sparingly marked. Incubation by female; 15 days.

Notes: This species may choose unusual nesting sites: drain pipe on eaves of house, abandoned nest of Cactus Wren, old tin can or pot, hole in fencepost, empty mailbox, birdhouse, exhaust pipe of an abandoned oil engine.

OLIVACEOUS FLYCATCHER   opp. p. 121
Myiarchus tuberculifer

Breeding range: Se. Arizona, sw. New Mexico.

Habitat: Live oak and streamside forests in mountains.

Nest: In natural cavities or abandoned woodpecker holes high above ground.

Eggs: 4–5; av. 19.6 x 15.2 mm. Oval. Slightly glossy. Creamy white, marked with browns, purples, olive drab. Similar to eggs of Ash-throated and Wied's Crested Flycatchers but *markings are finer and generally paler.*

Notes: 5 nests found by author were 11 ft. (3.4 m), 18 ft. (5.5 m), 45 ft. (13.7 m), 50 ft. (15.3 m), and 50 ft. (15.3 m) above ground; 2 in oaks, 2 in sycamores, 1 in dead stub.

EASTERN PHOEBE

EASTERN PHOEBE *Sayornis phoebe*

Breeding range: East of Rockies to Minnesota, south to ne. New Mexico (rare), cen. and ne. Texas, nw. Louisiana; uncommon in Colorado.

Habitat: Farms, open woodlands, cliffs, bridges, buildings.

Nest: On shelflike projections: windows, rafters of farm buildings, girders under bridges, trestles; plastered to rocky ledges, concrete and wooden walls. Large, well constructed of forbs, grasses, fibers, mud; covered with mosses, lined with finer grasses and hair. Semi-circular when attached to wall, circular when flat on beam or rafter — less mud used when circular. Female builds in 3–13 days. Outside diam. 4½ in. (11.4 cm), height 4 in. (10.2 cm); inside diam. 2½ in. (6.4 cm), depth 1¾ in. (4.5 cm).

Eggs: 3–6, commonly 5, rarely more; av. 19.0 x 14.7 mm. Oval. Shell smooth, little or no gloss. White, except 1 or 2 eggs (the last laid) sparsely dotted. *Indistinguishable from eggs of other phoebes.* Incubation by female alone; 15–16 days. Usually 2 broods.

Notes: Author found long periods (as much as 3 weeks) between completion of nest and egg-laying. Lack of orientation may cause female to build many nests side by side on long beam or girder. Author found 6 complete, 22 partly built nests on a bridge beam; 3 eggs in 1 nest, 1 egg in another.

126

Color Plates

Photographs of nests of 256 species
arranged in systematic order

Plate 1
LOON, GREBES, STORM-PETREL, PELICAN

COMMON LOON *Gavia immer*   p. 1
Nests close to water on edges and islands of wilderness freshwater
lakes along northern border of U.S. Commonly 2 large spotted,
blotched greenish or brownish olive eggs. (*Photograph by William
A. Dyer.*)

RED-NECKED GREBE *Podiceps grisegena*   p. 1
Range confined to northernmost states. Usually solitary but
sometimes in loose colonies on larger ponds, lakes. Nests floating
but anchored to emergent vegetation. 3–5 eggs, slightly chalky.
Among grebes, only Western eggs larger.

EARED GREBE *Podiceps nigricollis*   p. 2
Nests in *dense colonies* on lakes, ponds, river impoundments,
backwaters; floating rafts of matted wet plant material in extensive bed of submerged vegetation, often close together. Ordinarily
little effort made to conceal nests. 3–5 eggs, chalky, bluish or
greenish white, nest-stained buff or brown. *Indistinguishable from
eggs of Pied-billed and Horned Grebes.*

LEAST GREBE *Podiceps dominicus*   p. 3
Only in s. Texas. Single nest in roadside ditch, canal, intermittent
pond. Cone-shaped mass of decayed vegetation anchored to
plants. Typically 4–5 eggs; *smallest grebe eggs.*

WESTERN GREBE *Aechmophorus occidentalis*   p. 3
In colonies on large freshwater lakes bordered by tules, rushes;
nests closely spaced. 3–4 eggs; *largest grebe eggs.*

PIED-BILLED GREBE *Podilymbus podiceps*   p. 4
Commonest grebe — in all western states in freshwater ponds,
marshes, sloughs. Sodden, floating mass of decaying aquatic
plants holds 4–8 nest-stained eggs. *Indistinguishable from eggs of
Eared and Horned Grebes.*

LEACH'S STORM-PETREL *Oceanodroma leucorhoa*   p. 6
On islands off Pacific coast. In burrows in open field. *1 unmarked*
or faintly spotted white egg. *Musky petrel odor* strong in nest
area. Incubating birds change places only at night. One of 4
petrels on West Coast with similar nesting habits. Fork-tailed egg
is spotted; Ashy egg may be spotted. Black Storm-petrel rare.

WHITE PELICAN *Pelecanus erythrorhynchos*   p. 7
Locally common in about 12 western states. In colonies of a few to
several hundred nests — mounds of debris and earth. 1–3 large
white eggs, *streaked with blood.*

COMMON LOON

RED-NECKED GREBE

EARED GREBE

LEAST GREBE

WESTERN GREBE

PIED-BILLED GREBE

LEACH'S STORM-PETREL

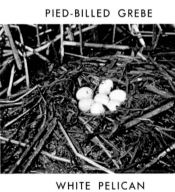

WHITE PELICAN

Plate 2
CORMORANTS, HERONS, EGRETS

DOUBLE-CRESTED CORMORANT p. 8
Phalacrocorax auritus
Mostly in colonies; on ground or in trees by freshwater lakes, ponds, swamps; also coastal islands, cliffs, bays. Only cormorant nest in freshwater areas except Olivaceous Cormorant nest in Louisiana and Texas which tends to be smaller.

BRANDT'S CORMORANT p. 9
Phalacrocorax penicillatus
Only on islands and headlands of Pacific coast. Seaweed, moss (*no sticks*); colonial nests on grassy slopes, flat island tops; less likely on cliffs (Pelagic uses inaccessible cliffs). Should see bird for positive identification of nest of Brandt's, Pelagic, or Double-crested Cormorants. (*Photograph by Raymond J. Quigley.*)

GREAT BLUE HERON *Ardea herodias* p. 10
Generally in colonies, commonly with nests of other herons. Platform of large sticks; outside diam. 25–40 in. (63.5–101.6 cm). Usually in highest parts of trees in mixed colony. (*Photograph by Ted and Lois Matthews.*)

GREEN HERON *Butorides striatus* p. 11
Commonly solitary; usually shallow, flimsy platform of twigs, may not be lined. Mostly in bushes or trees up to 30 ft. (9.2 m) above ground or water. Often far from water. Pale bluish green unmarked eggs smaller than Snowy Egret eggs.

CATTLE EGRET *Bubulcus ibis* p. 12
In colonies with other herons. Bluish white eggs are obviously *palest* of heron eggs.

GREAT EGRET *Casmerodius albus* p. 13
In colonies. Larger and more substantial than small herons' nests but not as bulky as Great Blue's. Great Blue lays larger eggs; night heron eggs slightly smaller.

SNOWY EGRET *Egretta thula* p. 13
In colonies with other herons. 12–24-in. (30.5–61.0 cm) loose platform of sticks, twigs; 4–5 bluish green eggs. *Indistinguishable from nests and eggs of Little Blue and Louisiana Herons.*

BLACK-CROWNED NIGHT HERON p. 14
Nycticorax nycticorax
In colonies; on ground to 160 ft. (48.8 m) up in trees. Flimsy to substantial platform. 3–5 bluish green eggs smaller than Great Egret eggs, larger than Snowy eggs. *Indistinguishable from nest and eggs of Yellow-crowned Night Heron.*

UBLE-CRESTED CORMORANT

BRANDT'S CORMORANT

GREAT BLUE HERON

GREEN HERON

CATTLE EGRET

GREAT EGRET

SNOWY EGRET

BLACK-CROWNED NIGHT HERON

Plate 3
BITTERNS, CANADA GOOSE, DUCKS

LEAST BITTERN   *Ixobrychus exilis*   p. 15
Solitary nest; mainly in freshwater marshes; often in cattails, tall grass, low bushes; typically less than 3 ft. (0.9 m) above water or ground. 3–6 unmarked bluish green eggs, *smallest of heron eggs.* Rail eggs are marked. When approached at nest, bird "freezes," bill pointed upward.

AMERICAN BITTERN   *Botaurus lentiginosus*   p. 16
Solitary. Scanty platform or mound on dry ground or over shallow water; among tall plants. Commonly 4–5 buffy brown to olive-buff eggs. Ducks lay larger clutches, generally paler eggs. Female "freezes" when approached.

CANADA GOOSE   *Branta canadensis*   p. 18
Only native goose breeding in U.S. Nest usually on ground near water; heavily lined with gray downy breast feathers after incubation begins. 5–6 unmarked eggs; creamy white or dirty white until nest-stained. *Larger than duck eggs.*

MALLARD   *Anas platyrhynchos*   p. 20
Unmarked light greenish buff to light grayish buff eggs. *Almost indistinguishable from eggs of Common Pintail and Northern Shoveler* but average larger. Nest concealed in dense vegetation; may not be close to water.

GADWALL   *Anas strepera*   p. 22
Less likely than most duck nests to be over water; tall dense vegetation in fields, on dikes, and islands favored. Unmarked dull creamy white eggs, *indistinguishable from eggs of American Wigeon, but Gadwall's nest down somewhat darker.*

GREEN-WINGED TEAL   *Anas crecca*   p. 23
Nest in tall grass, forbs, brush; lined with *dark brown down.* Creamy white or pale olive-buff eggs, *indistinguishable from eggs of other teal.* Smallest duck eggs.

CINNAMON TEAL   *Anas cyanoptera*   p. 24
Eggs indistinguishable from eggs of other teal; identification of female Cinnamon and female Blue-winged difficult, but pair bond in former maintained throughout most of incubation; flushed female known by male that joins her.

NORTHERN SHOVELER   *Anas clypeata*   p. 25
Upland nester in grass usually under 12 in. (30.5 cm) high. *Eggs almost indistinguishable from eggs of Mallard and Pintail,* but average smaller.

LEAST BITTERN

AMERICAN BITTERN

CANADA GOOSE

MALLARD

GADWALL

GREEN-WINGED TEAL

CINNAMON TEAL

NORTHERN SHOVELER

Plate 4

DUCKS, VULTURE, KITE

WOOD DUCK *Aix sponsa*   p. 26
One of several cavity-nesting ducks. American and Barrow's Goldeneyes and Buffleheads breed almost entirely in Northwest. Hooded Merganser eggs white and larger. Common Merganser eggs much larger. (*Photograph by Kenneth Vierling.*)

REDHEAD *Aythya americana*   p. 26
Usually over water in emergent vegetation. Basketlike, lined with bits of dead cattail blades and *much white down.* Eggs similar to eggs of Mallard but larger, more glossy.

CANVASBACK *Aythya valisineria*   p. 27
Resembles nest of Redhead but down is *pearly gray.* Often parasitized by Redhead. Redhead eggs pale olive-buff; Canvasback eggs olive-gray or olive-brown; same in size.

LESSER SCAUP *Aythya affinis*   p. 28
Nests concentrated in marshes of Hardstem Bulrush (*Scirpus acutus*) bordering lakes. Similar Ring-necked Duck prefers sedge, sweetgale, leatherleaf habitat. *Eggs of 2 species alike.*

RUDDY DUCK *Oxyura jamaicensis*   p. 30
Woven, basketlike nest in tall cattails, bulrushes, reeds. Eggs surprisingly large for size of bird (av. 62.3 x 45.6 mm); shell *thick, rough, granular,* white or creamy white. "Dump" nests common; up to 80 eggs have been found in 1 nest.

HOODED MERGANSER *Lophodytes cucullatus*   p. 31
In tree cavities near water similar to those used by Wood Duck. Eggs *pure white* (resemble domestic chicken eggs); larger than buffy eggs of Wood Duck; smaller than pale buff eggs of cavity-nesting Common Merganser.

TURKEY VULTURE *Cathartes aura*   p. 32
No nest. Eggs on ground in dense shrub, hollow log or stump, cave. Off-white with dark brown markings overlaid on paler markings. Ground color of Black Vulture eggs commonly gray-green. Eggs *smaller* than eggs of Black; generally *more profusely marked.*

WHITE-TAILED KITE *Elanus leucurus*   p. 33
Range limited to California, s. Texas, Louisiana. Bulky nest of twigs in crotch of deciduous tree. Eggs white, *profusely marked* with rich brown; Mississippi Kite eggs unmarked. (*Photograph by Raymond J. Quigley.*)

WOOD DUCK

REDHEAD

CANVASBACK

LESSER SCAUP

RUDDY DUCK

HOODED MERGANSER

TURKEY VULTURE

WHITE-TAILED KITE

Plate 5

HAWKS, GOLDEN EAGLE

GOSHAWK *Accipiter gentilis* p. 36
Usually in tall tree in remote forest. More decorated with greenery than nest of Cooper's Hawk. Unmarked, pale bluish white eggs *similar to Cooper's eggs but larger.* Buteo hawk eggs commonly well marked. (*Photograph by Ted and Lois Matthews.*)

COOPER'S HAWK *Accipiter cooperii* p. 36
Nest substantial; of sticks, twigs, typically *lined with chips or flakes of outer bark;* not decorated with greenery as often as buteo nests. Eggs similar to but *smaller than eggs of Goshawk.* Eggs of Sharp-shinned Hawk heavily marked.

RED-TAILED HAWK *Buteo jamaicensis* p. 37
Habitat varied — deserts to mountaintops. Large nest decorated with green leaves in tree or tall shrub. Nest and eggs *larger* than those of Red-shouldered Hawk. Eggs *more heavily marked* than eggs of Swainson's and less heavily marked than Red-shouldered.

RED-SHOULDERED HAWK *Buteo lineatus* p. 38
Prefers river-bottom woodlands, swamp borders. Nest and eggs smaller than those of Red-tailed, larger than those of Broad-winged. (*Photograph by Ed. N. Harrison.*)

SWAINSON'S HAWK *Buteo swainsoni* p. 39
Nests in trees on wide open prairies, plains, deserts; avoids dense timber. A bulky, *disorderly, sprawling* mass of sticks, sagebrush, Russian thistle, brambles. Eggs less heavily marked than those of Red-tailed and Red-shouldered Hawks. Ferruginous Hawk nest more sturdy.

FERRUGINOUS HAWK *Buteo regalis* p. 40
In same habitat as Swainson's Hawk nest but usually recognizable. Large solid accumulation of sticks, rubbish, bark, sod, *large chunks of cow or horse dung.* May be *large as eagle's nest.* Nest site averages lower than Swainson's nests; sometimes built on ground. (*Photograph by Ed N. Harrison.*)

HARRIS' HAWK *Parabuteo unicinctus* p. 41
Breeding range confined to s. Arizona, se. New Mexico, s. and cen. Texas, typically in deserts and mesquite forests. Eggs *dull white, usually unmarked.* (*Photograph by William J. Mader.*)

GOLDEN EAGLE *Aquila chrysaetos* p. 42
Golden and Bald Eagles build largest nests of all hawks. In trees or on rocky, often inaccessible, cliffs. Bald Eagle eggs white, unmarked; Golden Eagle eggs have variety of *heavy markings;* sometimes 1 egg unmarked. (*Photograph by Ronald K. Quigley.*)

GOSHAWK

COOPER'S HAWK

RED-TAILED HAWK

RED-SHOULDERED HAWK

SWAINSON'S HAWK

FERRUGINOUS HAWK

HARRIS' HAWK

GOLDEN EAGLE

Plate 6

HAWKS, GALLINACEOUS BIRDS

MARSH HAWK *Circus cyaneus*   p. 44
Nest on or near ground, sometimes over shallow water. Eggs unmarked or sparsely spotted. Nest of Short-eared Owl is flimsier, eggs pure white. Hawk's eggs *larger,* often *bluish white.* American Bittern eggs brown or olive-buff.

OSPREY *Pandion haliaetus*   p. 44
Normally near fresh or salt water, often in loose colonies; on ground to 60 ft. (18.3 m) above ground on natural or man-made sites: trees, snags, billboards, duck blinds, utility poles, aerials. Large, *highly visible* nest of sticks lined with bark and grasses; may include odd objects: bath towel, rake, toy boat, hat, rag doll. 3–4 heavily marked eggs.

PRAIRIE FALCON *Falco mexicanus*   p. 46
Typically on cliffs; eggs on bare ground in hollow. Eggs same size as Peregrine Falcon eggs but *paler, duller;* clutch larger. (*Photograph by Ronald K. Quigley.*)

AMERICAN KESTREL *Falco sparverius*   p. 47
Only cavity-nesting falcon except Merlin; latter limited to northern wilderness. Adds little or no nest material to cavity. Eggs covered with fine spots of brown; *smaller* than Merlin eggs.

RUFFED GROUSE *Bonasa umbellus*   p. 49
Unmarked or very lightly dotted buffy eggs.

WHITE-TAILED PTARMIGAN *Lagopus leucurus*   p. 50
Only grouse breeding in alpine tundra. Shallow scrape in ground sparsely lined with vegetation gathered at nest site. Cryptic coloring makes it difficult to see incubating bird, which sits very tight.

GREATER PRAIRIE CHICKEN   p. 50
Tympanuchus cupido
On ground in undisturbed tall-grass prairies. More eastern breeding range eliminates confusion with nests of Sage and Sharp-tailed Grouse except in Dakotas and Nebraska. Lesser Prairie Chicken more southern. 5–17 olive-buff or grayish olive eggs with sepia spots. (*Photograph by George H. Harrison.*)

SHARP-TAILED GROUSE *Pedioecetes phasianellus*   p. 51
Range overlaps that of Greater Prairie Chicken and Sage Grouse in Dakotas and Nebraska. Sharp-tailed prefers brushy, rolling hills. Eggs smaller, shorter, paler than eggs of Sage Grouse; similar to but generally more distinctly spotted than eggs of Prairie Chicken. (*Photograph by George H. Harrison.*)

MARSH HAWK

OSPREY

PRAIRIE FALCON

AMERICAN KESTREL

RUFFED GROUSE

WHITE-TAILED PTARMIGAN

GREATER PRAIRIE CHICKEN

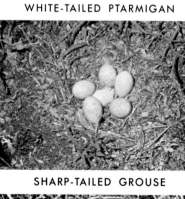

SHARP-TAILED GROUSE

Plate 7

GALLINACEOUS BIRDS,
SANDHILL CRANE

SAGE GROUSE *Centrocercus urophasianus* p. 52
Throughout range *associated with sagebrush* and adjacent hay meadows. Nest on ground under sagebrush. Eggs larger, longer, greener than eggs of Prairie Chicken. (*Photograph by David A. Weber.*)

BOBWHITE *Colinus virginianus* p. 52
A grass-lined hollow in tussock of grass, av. 12–14 eggs. White, *short-pyriform,* slightly glossy eggs diagnostic. Eggs of rare Montezuma Quail of Arizona, New Mexico, and w. Texas white but usually more elongated than eggs of Bobwhite.

CALIFORNIA QUAIL *Lophortyx californicus* p. 53
On ground; in woodland brush interspersed with grassy areas. Eggs buffy, *spotted* (less heavily than Gambel's eggs). Gambel's and Scaled Quail are desert scrub and grassland birds; both lay pale eggs marked with brown. (*Photograph by Raymond J. Quigley.*)

MOUNTAIN QUAIL *Oreortyx pictus* p. 54
Habitat and nests of Mountain and California Quail similar, but Mountain Quail breeds at higher altitudes and eggs are buffy, *unmarked.*

RING-NECKED PHEASANT *Phasianus colchicus* p. 54
On ground in open weedy fields, brushy pastures, hayfields. Eggs slightly glossy, rich brownish olive or olive-buff, *unmarked.* Gray Partridge eggs similar but smaller. Incubating female protectively marked.

CHUKAR *Alectoris chukar* p. 55
In sagebrush-grassland or on dry, rocky slopes. Well-formed nest, on ground, usually under bush or rock. Eggs buff or brown with find reddish brown dots.

TURKEY *Meleagris gallopavo* p. 55
Simple depression in dry leaves on dry ground, usually near strutting grounds of polygamous male. 11–13 buffy eggs evenly marked with brown or buff spots or fine dots. *Largest eggs among gallinaceous birds.*

SANDHILL CRANE *Grus canadensis* p. 56
In or close to shallow water in marshes and prairie ponds. Mound of sticks, mosses, reeds, rushes; *outside diam. 3–5 ft.* (0.9–1.5 m) or more. Commonly 2 buff or olive eggs with lavender spots overlaid with brown and olive spots. (*Photograph by George H. Harrison.*)

SAGE GROUSE

BOBWHITE

CALIFORNIA QUAIL

MOUNTAIN QUAIL

RING-NECKED PHEASANT

CHUKAR

TURKEY

SANDHILL CRANE

Plate 8

RAILS, GALLINULE, COOT,
PLOVERS, SNIPE

VIRGINIA RAIL *Rallus limicola*   p. 57
Nest similar to nest of Sora which often shares marshy habitat.
Virginia's eggs are *paler, less heavily marked,* and *less glossy.*
Eggs of King and Clapper Rails considerably larger. Yellow Rail
eggs darker, smaller, distinctively capped.

SORA *Porzana carolina*   p. 58
In freshwater marsh, supported a few inches above water by marsh
vegetation. Sora eggs more *richly colored* (olive-buff), more *heavily spotted,* glossier than those of Virginia. Tends to nest over
deeper water than Virginia. Yellow Rail eggs smaller, paler.

COMMON GALLINULE *Gallinula chloropus*   p. 60
Range overlaps that of Purple Gallinule; habitats similar. Common nests in shallower water. Eggs of Common *larger, darker,*
with spots larger and more irregular in size and distribution.

AMERICAN COOT *Fulica americana*   p. 60
Cupped platform of dead bulrushes, cattails, sedges; attached to
surrounding vegetation above water in freshwater marsh, lake.
Eggs densely covered with evenly distributed spots and dots.
Common Gallinule eggs irregularly spotted; duck eggs unmarked.

BLACK OYSTERCATCHER *Haematopus bachmani*   p. 62
Only oystercatcher breeding on Pacific coast. Nest is depression in
beach gravel on rocky shores of mainland or offshore islands;
sparsely lined with bits of shell or broken stone. 2–3 large, pale
buffy eggs evenly marked with small spots, scrawls. (*Photograph
by Raymond J. Quigley.*)

KILLDEER *Charadrius vociferus*   p. 63
Often nests near human habitation far from water. In open, often
gravelly areas where incubating bird has extended view. Nest is
shallow scrape unlined or lined with debris. Almost always 4 buff
eggs boldly spotted and blotched, typically quite pointed.

MOUNTAIN PLOVER *Charadrius montanus*   p. 64
Nests on ground in *short-grass* prairies of Midwest. Tends to nest
near old, gray cow manure piles. Manure chips in thinly lined
nest. Almost always 3 eggs, dark olive-buff marked with black.

COMMON SNIPE *Capella gallinago*   p. 66
Well-cupped nest in tussock of grass in marsh, wet meadow, bog. 4
pyriform eggs may be either of 2 types: light buff or dark brown;
spotted, heavily blotched, scrawled with deep brown. Nest may
have canopy woven of living plants.

VIRGINIA RAIL

SORA

COMMON GALLINULE

AMERICAN COOT

BLACK OYSTERCATCHER

KILLDEER

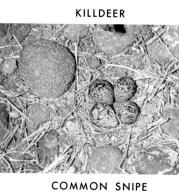

MOUNTAIN PLOVER

COMMON SNIPE

Plate 9

SANDPIPERS, AVOCET,
STILT, PHALAROPE, GULL

LONG-BILLED CURLEW *Numenius americanus* p. 67
Habitat includes moist meadows to very dry prairies. Nest is shallow hollow in ground thinly lined with grasses. Incubating bird conspicuous on nest. Eggs olive-buff, spotted, large.

UPLAND SANDPIPER *Bartramia longicauda* p. 67
On broad flat prairies, in depression in thick clump of grass arched over top; invisible from above. 4 slightly glossy eggs; light buff, speckled and spotted with reddish brown.

SPOTTED SANDPIPER *Actitis macularia* p. 67
Solitary or in loose colonies in prairies, pastures, sloughs, shoulders of roads. Grass-lined depression in ground, sometimes remote from water. Females often polyandrous. Usually 4 eggs, grayish buff, spotted and blotched with brown.

WILLET *Catoptrophorus semipalmatus* p. 68
Nests in colonies in salt and brackish marshes, saline flats, in short thick grass. Nests usually 200 ft. (61 m) or farther apart. Commonly 4 eggs, dark buff, boldly marked.

AMERICAN AVOCET *Recurvirostra americana* p. 69
Nest on ground on dry mud flat or sparsely vegetated gravelly island. May be scanty or an elevated pile of debris. Usually 4 eggs, olive-buff, evenly marked with spots and blotches of brown or black. Nest and eggs similar to those of Black-necked Stilt but eggs *larger, less heavily marked.*

BLACK-NECKED STILT *Himantopus mexicanus* p. 70
Near or built up above shallow water. Nest and eggs *similar to* those of American Avocet, but eggs are smaller, more heavily marked. Usually 4 eggs, buffy or sandy, marked with dark brown or black. Markings tend to be somewhat lengthened and mostly running lengthwise on the shell. Often badly stained with mud.

WILSON'S PHALAROPE *Steganopus tricolor* p. 71
Nest of grass in tuft of grass in marsh or *wet meadow.* Incubation by *male* alone. Eggs brownish or greenish buff with brown markings.

WESTERN GULL *Larus occidentalis* p. 71
Only gull nesting along California coast. Color of markings varies within as well as between clutches. Low mound of forbs and grass in colonies with other seabirds on grassy hillside or exposed ledge. (*Photograph by Raymond J. Quigley.*)

LONG-BILLED CURLEW

UPLAND SANDPIPER

SPOTTED SANDPIPER

AMERICAN AVOCET

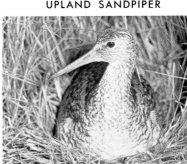

WILLET

BLACK-NECKED STILT

WILSON'S PHALAROPE

WESTERN GULL

Plate 10
GULLS, TERNS, MURRE, DOVES

CALIFORNIA GULL *Larus californicus* p. 72
In colonies in interior freshwater lakes, marshes, sometimes mixed with Ring-billed Gulls. 1–3, usually 2, eggs variable in color and markings; may be more pointed than eggs of other gulls. Slightly *larger* than eggs of Ring-billed Gull.

RING-BILLED GULL *Larus delawarensis* p. 72
Slight hollow, perhaps skimpily lined with grass. Nests and eggs similar to those of California Gulls with which they often nest. 3, often 2, eggs; somewhat smaller than California eggs.

FORSTER'S TERN *Sterna forsteri* p. 74
In colonies in salt marshes and inland marshes. Usually 3 eggs, buffy, spotted with dark brown. Inland nest a shallow depression, scantily lined. Higher and drier than nests of Black Tern, eggs larger, not as heavily marked. Coastal nests more elaborate piles of grass and sedges. Eggs *indistinguishable from eggs of Common Tern.*

CASPIAN TERN *Sterna caspia* p. 77
Hollow in sand unlined or well-lined. Eggs *resemble gull eggs.* Similar to eggs of Royal Tern; ranges overlap along Gulf Coast. (*Photograph by Ronald K. Quigley.*)

BLACK TERN *Chlidonias niger* p. 78
Often breeds in same inland marshes as Forster's Terns but nests in lower, wetter sites. Black Tern eggs smaller, more heavily spotted, have darker ground color.

COMMON MURRE *Uria aalge* p. 79
1 pointed, pear-shaped egg laid on bare, rocky ledge (no nest) on coastal cliff in crowded colony. Eggs highly variable in color. (*Photograph by Ed N. Harrison.*)

ROCK DOVE (DOMESTIC PIGEON) p. 82
Columba livia
Nests on window ledges, under bridges, in barns and crevices in buildings; wild birds sometimes nest on cliffs and in caves. Normally 2 white eggs on carelessly made platform of straw and debris. (*Photograph by George H. Harrison.*)

WHITE-WINGED DOVE *Zenaida asiatica* p. 83
In tree; platform of twigs similar to that of Mourning Dove. Usually 2 eggs, *creamy buff* or *creamy white;* Mourning Dove eggs white. Ranges overlap only in extreme southern areas.

CALIFORNIA GULL

RING-BILLED GULL

FORSTER'S TERN

CASPIAN TERN

BLACK TERN

COMMON MURRE

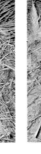

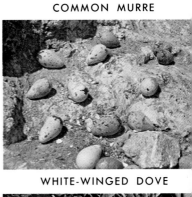

ROCK DOVE

WHITE-WINGED DOVE

Plate 11

DOVES, CUCKOOS, OWLS

MOURNING DOVE   *Zenaida macroura*   p. 83
A loose platform of twigs on ground or in bush or tree. 2 white eggs. Spotted and Ringed Turtle Doves in limited California urban areas have similar nests and eggs. Ground Dove nest smaller and more substantial; eggs much smaller.

GROUND DOVE   *Columbina passerina*   p. 85
Nest well matted; material in cup typically *twisted* to make circular form; more substantial than nest of Mourning Dove. On ground, in bush, tree, cactus. 2 white eggs *smaller* than Mourning Dove eggs; *indistinguishable from eggs of Inca Dove.*

YELLOW-BILLED CUCKOO   *Coccyzus americanus*   p. 86
Shallow frail platform thinly lined, very little cup. Pale bluish green eggs similar to eggs of Black-billed Cuckoo but *greener, paler,* and *larger.* (*Photograph by Kenneth Vierling.*)

BLACK-BILLED CUCKOO   p. 87
Coccyzus erythropthalmus
Generally *more substantially lined* than nest of Yellow-billed Cuckoo; eggs *smaller, bluer, darker,* sometimes have marbled appearance. Both cuckoos lay eggs in each other's nests.

ROADRUNNER   *Geococcyx californianus*   p. 87
In open, dry country throughout southern states. Nest built in thicket in low bush or tree; has solid foundation of sticks. 3–6 eggs, unique: white with overlay of chalky film which may turn yellow during incubation.

BARN OWL   *Tyto alba*   p. 88
In barns, church steeples, silos, hollow trees, ledges of cliffs. No nest built; owl castings form base for 5–9 white eggs which are not as round as typical owl eggs.

SCREECH OWL   *Otus asio*   p. 88
In cavity; no nest material added, but rubble in cavity may include owl feathers, and fur and feathers of prey. Usually 3–5 almost spherical eggs, *indistinguishable from eggs of Whiskered Owl* (se. Arizona) and larger than eggs of Flammulated Owl (Rocky Mts. and Pacific states). Screech Owl usually nests at lower altitudes.

GREAT HORNED OWL   *Bubo virginianus*   p. 89
May be in old nests of large birds, natural tree cavities, on rocky ledges, caves. 1–4 white eggs, *largest* of all owl eggs (av. 54.7 x 46.5 mm) except those of rare Great Gray Owl.

MOURNING DOVE

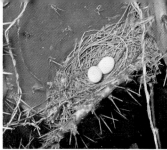

GROUND DOVE

YELLOW-BILLED CUCKOO

BLACK-BILLED CUCKOO

ROADRUNNER

BARN OWL

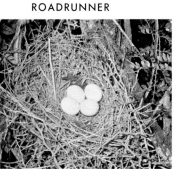

SCREECH OWL

GREAT HORNED OWL

Plate 12

OWLS, NIGHTJARS, CHIMNEY SWIFT

ELF OWL *Micrathene whitneyi*   p. 91
In abandoned woodpecker holes, often in Saguaro cacti. 2–5 white
eggs, *smallest of owl eggs* (av. 26.8 x 23.2 mm). Eggs of rare and
local Ferruginous Owl similar but slightly larger. (*Photograph by
Lewis Wayne Walker.*)

BURROWING OWL *Athene cunicularia*   p. 92
Only owl that nests in burrow in ground. Burrow may be dug by
owls or be abandoned tunnel-home of rodent (often prairie dog).
Nest chamber lined with trash, usually including dry chips of
manure. 6–11 white elliptical eggs.

LONG-EARED OWL *Asio otus*   p. 95
Usually in old nest of crow, hawk, squirrel; seldom in tree cavity.
Range overlaps that of Barred Owl mostly in eastern areas; white
eggs similar but *smaller* and normally in larger clutch (4–5).
(*Photograph by Ed N. Harrison.*)

SHORT-EARED OWL *Asio flammeus*   p. 95
Habitually nests *on ground* (Burrowing Owls nest *in* ground, Barn
and Great Horned Owls occasionally on ground); constructs own
nest. Eggs white. Marsh Hawks use same habitat but have pale
bluish white eggs. (*Photograph by George H. Harrison.*)

POOR-WILL *Phalaenoptilus nuttallii*   p. 98
Only nightjar that lays *white unmarked eggs.* No nest; 2 eggs laid
on ground in slight hollow in barren arid regions.

COMMON NIGHTHAWK *Chordeiles minor*   p. 99
2 eggs laid on ground in flat open area or on gravel roof of city
building; no nest. Eggs cream to pale gray densely dotted with
brown and gray; *darker* and *larger* than eggs of Lesser Nighthawk. Poor-will eggs white.

LESSER NIGHTHAWK *Chordeiles acutipennis*   p. 99
Eggs on ground in open sandy or gravelly place. 2 eggs, pale gray
to pale cream white with gray and lilac markings; *lighter* and
smaller than eggs of Common Nighthawk; ranges overlap only in
southern states. Poor-will eggs white.

CHIMNEY SWIFT *Chaetura pelagica*   p. 100
Frail platform of twigs attached to side of chimney with adults'
glutinous saliva. Other swifts nest in hollow trees, cliffs, caves. All
swifts lay 4–5 white eggs except Black Swift which lays only 1.

ELF OWL

BURROWING OWL

LONG-EARED OWL

SHORT-EARED OWL

POOR-WILL

COMMON NIGHTHAWK

LESSER NIGHTHAWK

CHIMNEY SWIFT

Plate 13

HUMMINGBIRDS

BLACK-CHINNED HUMMINGBIRD   p. 102
Archilochus alexandri
Elastic spongy structure of *white* or *buff* plant down tightly worked together, coated with spider silk on outside. Rim of deeply hollowed cup *curved inward.*

COSTA'S HUMMINGBIRD   *Calypte costae*   p. 103
Nest positioned near outside of limb of bush or small tree to give unobstructed view. General *gray* appearance of *shallow* nest distinctive; rim and interior commonly of small dark feathers.

ANNA'S HUMMINGBIRD   *Calypte anna*   p. 103
Range confined to Pacific coastal area (s. Oregon to Baja) and s. Arizona. Nest *large* for hummer, well made of plant down, decorated with lichens. Eggs *indistinguishable from eggs of other hummingbirds of similar size.*

BROAD-TAILED HUMMINGBIRD   p. 105
Selasphorus platycercus
Common breeding hummingbird of Rockies. In pinyon-juniper and mixed forests, especially in canyons and mountain glades. Outer walls of nest made of willow and cottonwood down, decorated with lichens, shreds of bark. *No feathers* in inner lining.

RUFOUS HUMMINGBIRD   *Selasphorus rufus*   p. 106
Nest and eggs similar to those of hummingbirds of similar size, but breeding range in Pacific Northwest remote from range of most other western species. Often in colonies in forest edges, chaparral, thickets. (*Photograph by Robert Burr Smith.*)

ALLEN'S HUMMINGBIRD   *Selasphorus sasin*   p. 106
Resembles nest of Anna's more than nest of Rufous Hummingbird; *eggs indistinguishable from either.* Compactly built of green mosses, lichens; lined with vegetable down. Nests close together in desirable habitat.

CALLIOPE HUMMINGBIRD   *Stellula calliope*   p. 106
Position of nest unique: almost invariably on branch or twig *directly under larger branch,* or under canopy of foliage which protects nest from above. Sometimes attached to pine cones or limbs of conifers where nests resemble cones.

BROAD-BILLED HUMMINGBIRD   p. 108
Cynanthus latirostris
Breeds most commonly in arid s. Arizona thickets. *Rougher,* more *loosely constructed* than nests of most hummingbirds. Generally brown bark, dried leaves, bits of grass, rather than lichens, decorate nest.

ACK-CHINNED HUMMINGBIRD

COSTA'S HUMMINGBIRD

ANNA'S HUMMINGBIRD

BROAD-TAILED HUMMINGBIRD

RUFOUS HUMMINGBIRD

ALLEN'S HUMMINGBIRD

CALLIOPE HUMMINGBIRD

BROAD-BILLED HUMMINGBIRD

Plate 14

KINGFISHER, WOODPECKERS

BELTED KINGFISHER *Megaceryle alcyon* p. 108
Single pair excavates burrow in sand or clay bank; nest chamber at end of tunnel. Green and Ringed Kingfishers of Rio Grande Valley have similar burrows. 5–8 white eggs; Green's eggs smaller, Ringed eggs larger than Belted's eggs.

COMMON FLICKER *Colaptes auratus* p. 110
All western states in many habitats. Cavity entrance 2–4 in. (5.1–10.2 cm). 6–8 white eggs (Gilded averages fewer), largest woodpecker eggs except Pileated's. (Photograph of ♂ Red-shafted.)

RED-BELLIED WOODPECKER p. 112
Melanerpes carolinus
In forests, orchards, yards. Range overlaps that of Red-headed Woodpecker, which prefers open country. 4–5 glossy white eggs *indistinguishable from eggs of Red-headed Woodpecker.* Often nests in birdhouses.

RED-HEADED WOODPECKER p. 113
Melanerpes erythrocephalus
Tends to seek *open country* (usually not a forest nester), but often found near habitation. Unlike Red-bellied, *shuns birdhouses.* Commonly 5 white eggs, *indistinguishable from Red-bellied eggs.*

ACORN WOODPECKER *Melanerpes formicivorus* p. 114
In colonies, segregated into nesting groups containing up to 10 individuals, an older pair assisted by others in excavating and feeding. Pairs nesting singly are exceptions. In pine-oak forests usually in dead or live oaks. Nest hole perfectly round, diam. about 1½ in. (3.8 cm). Cavity may be reused.

YELLOW-BELLIED SAPSUCKER p. 114
Sphyrapicus varius
Range, habitat, nest hole similar to those of Williamson's Sapsucker. Aspen trees favored. Entrance to cavity round, 1¼–1½ in. (3.2–3.8 cm). Typically 5 white eggs *indistinguishable from eggs of Williamson's.* Birds should be seen for nest identification. (*Photograph of ♂ by Ted and Lois Matthews.*)

WILLIAMSON'S SAPSUCKER p. 115
Sphyrapicus thyroideus
Breeding biology similar to that of Yellow-bellied Sapsucker. Prefers conifers. 5–6 white eggs *indistinguishable from Yellow-bellied eggs.* (*Photograph of ♀ by Ted and Lois Matthews.*)

HAIRY WOODPECKER *Picoides villosus* p. 115
In all western states in variety of habitats. Overlaps ranges of all other woodpeckers; must see bird for positive nest identification. Typical nest hole elongated: 2½ in. (6.4 cm) high, 2 in. (5.1 cm) wide. Pure white eggs.

BELTED KINGFISHER

COMMON FLICKER

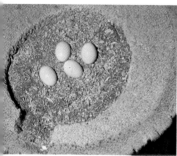

ED-BELLIED WOODPECKER

RED-HEADED WOODPECKER

ACORN WOODPECKER

YELLOW-BELLIED SAPSUCKER

'ILLIAMSON'S SAPSUCKER

HAIRY WOODPECKER

Plate 15
WOODPECKERS, KINGBIRDS, FLYCATCHERS

DOWNY WOODPECKER *Picoides pubescens* p. 116
Range, habitat, nesting biology similar to that of Hairy Woodpecker. Often but not always places entrance hole on underside of exposed limb. Entrance a perfect circle about $1\frac{1}{4}$ in. (3.2 cm) in diam. (*Photograph of ♂ by George H. Harrison.*)

WHITE-HEADED WOODPECKER p. 118
Picoides albolarvatus
West of Rockies in forests up to 9,000 ft. (2745 m); absent from rain forests. *Prefers dead stubs.* Entrance about $1\frac{1}{2}$ in. (3.8 cm) in diam., *seldom over 15 ft.* (4.6 m) above ground, often lower. (*Photograph of ♂ by Lynn Fuller.*)

EASTERN KINGBIRD *Tyrannus tyrannus* p. 119
Builds bulky cup (large for size of bird) with rough, unkempt exterior, on limb well out from trunk; sometimes in crotch of dead stub over water. 3–5 eggs, creamy white, heavily spotted; *indistinguishable from Western Kingbird and Scissor-tailed Flycatcher.*

WESTERN KINGBIRD *Tyrannus verticalis* p. 121
In great variety of situations; almost anywhere but on ground. Variety of materials used. Eggs *indistinguishable from eggs of Eastern Kingbird and Scissor-tailed Flycatcher.*

CASSIN'S KINGBIRD *Tyrannus vociferans* p. 122
Generally in *higher country* than Western Kingbird. Bulky nest slightly larger than Western's; composed of similar materials. Eggs typically *less spotted* than eggs of other kingbirds.

SCISSOR-TAILED FLYCATCHER p. 122
Muscivora forficata
Breeding range confined to se. part of western states. In roadside trees in open country; may be on utility pole, windmill, tower, bridge. Roughly built of trashy materials but neatly lined with soft cottony substances, rootlets, horsehair. Eggs *indistinguishable from eggs of Eastern and Western Kingbirds.*

GREAT CRESTED FLYCATCHER p. 123
Myiarchus crinitus
In natural cavity or abandoned woodpecker hole; often birdhouse. Nest is bulky mass of trash filling cavity; usually includes cast-off snakeskin or cellophane. Eggs off-white *streaked* with brown.

ASH-THROATED FLYCATCHER p. 125
Myiarchus cinerascens
Nest and eggs similar to Great Crested Flycatcher; range generally more western. Less a desert bird than Wied's Crested Flycatcher. Eggs white, streaked; *indistinguishable from eggs of Wied's Crested,* more sparingly marked than eggs of Great Crested, markings heavier and darker than on eggs of Olivaceous Flycatcher.

DOWNY WOODPECKER

WHITE-HEADED WOODPECKER

EASTERN KINGBIRD

WESTERN KINGBIRD

CASSIN'S KINGBIRD

SCISSOR-TAILED FLYCATCHER

REAT CRESTED FLYCATCHER

ASH-THROATED FLYCATCHER

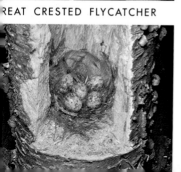

Plate 16

PHOEBES, EMPIDONAX FLYCATCHERS

BLACK PHOEBE *Sayornis nigricans* p. 127
Nest plastered on cliff face, concrete wall, bridge. *Principally of
mud;* looks somewhat like Barn Swallow's nest. 4–6 white eggs
indistinguishable from eggs of other phoebes. Barn Swallow eggs
spotted.

SAY'S PHOEBE *Sayornis saya* p. 127
Distinguishable from nests of other phoebes because it usually
lacks mud. Prefers abandoned buildings as nest sites. Eggs *indistinguishable from eggs of other phoebes.*

WILLOW FLYCATCHER *Empidonax traillii* p. 129
Nest and eggs difficult to distinguish from those of Alder Flycatcher, but range is *more western and southern* than range of
Alder. Nest *similar to nest of Yellow Warbler* but often has
material dangling from bottom. Eggs often *buffy* with brown
markings; eggs of Alder Flycatcher have *white* background.

LEAST FLYCATCHER *Empidonax minimus* p. 130
Resembles nests of Yellow Warbler and American Redstart, but
eggs are *white, unmarked;* latter 2 species lay spotted eggs. Nests
commonly 10–20 ft. (3.1–6.1 m) above ground.

HAMMOND'S FLYCATCHER p. 130
Empidonax hammondii
Typically much higher above ground than nest of Dusky Flycatcher—25–40 ft. (7.6–12.2 m) or more above ground. Resembles
nest of Western Wood Pewee but eggs of Hammond's are *white,
unmarked.* Eggs *indistinguishable from eggs of Dusky Flycatcher.*

DUSKY FLYCATCHER *Empidonax oberholseri* p. 131
Nest in shrub or small tree typically 4–7 ft. (1.2–2.1 m) above
ground, *much lower* than nest of Hammond's. Gray Flycatcher
prefers sagebrush habitat; builds bulkier, less tidy nest. *Eggs
indistinguishable from eggs of Hammond's or Gray Flycatcher.*

GRAY FLYCATCHER *Empidonax wrightii* p. 131
Commonly in loose colonies on *sagebrush plains.* Nest low in
bark-filled crotch of bush. White eggs *indistinguishable from eggs
of Dusky Flycatcher.*

WESTERN FLYCATCHER *Empidonax difficilis* p. 132
Usually near or on ground; may be up to 30 ft. (9.2 m) above. Of
green and dry moss, lichens, bark; blends with surroundings; lined
with myriad materials taken from inhabited areas. 3–4 creamy
white eggs *spotted* and *blotched* with brown.

BLACK PHOEBE

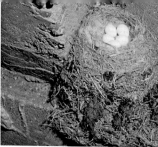
SAY'S PHOEBE

WILLOW FLYCATCHER

HAMMOND'S FLYCATCHER

LEAST FLYCATCHER

DUSKY FLYCATCHER

GRAY FLYCATCHER

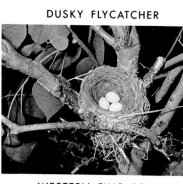
WESTERN FLYCATCHER

Plate 17

FLYCATCHERS, HORNED
LARK, SWALLOWS

WESTERN WOOD PEWEE *Contopus sordidulus*   p. 134
Little if any range overlap with Eastern Wood Pewee. Nest saddled
to horizontal fork of dead or live limb 15–40 ft. (4.6–12.2 m) above
ground. From below looks like lichen-covered knot. Similar to
Vermilion Flycatcher nest but eggs *not as heavily marked.*

OLIVE-SIDED FLYCATCHER *Nuttallornis borealis*   p. 135
Breeds in cool, coniferous forests, boreal bogs, muskeg. Nest shallow, twiggy, on horizontal branch of conifer in cluster of needles
7–50 ft. (2.1–15.3 m) above ground. Deciduous trees used occasionally.

VERMILION FLYCATCHER *Pyrocephalus rubinus*   p. 135
Range overlaps that of Western Wood Pewee in extreme southern
regions. Nest similar to Pewee's but eggs typically *more heavily
marked.* (*Photograph by Raymond J. Quigley.*)

HORNED LARK *Eremophila alpestris*   p. 136
Grassy nest in hollow in ground in open grasslands, tundra, golf
course, airport (short grass). Often one side of rim paved with
small pebbles or clods. Rarely concealed from above. Nest similar
to nests of longspurs but egg markings differ; site is less protected.

TREE SWALLOW *Iridoprocne bicolor*   p. 137
In cavity in dead or live tree, birdhouse. Nest of grass lined with
feathers. Commonly in aspen groves. 5–7 white eggs. Breeding
biology similar to that of Violet-green Swallow. *Birds must be
seen* for positive identification of nest.

BANK SWALLOW *Riparia riparia*   p. 138
In dense colonies in self-made burrows in banks of rivers, gravel
pits, road cuts. Grass and *feathers used* in nest chamber. Commonly 5 *oval* white eggs similar to Rough-winged eggs.

ROUGH-WINGED SWALLOW   p. 139
Stelgidopteryx ruficollis
Solitary nesters in tunnels in banks, often old Belted Kingfisher
holes. *Does not use feathers* in lining. Commonly 5–7 *long-oval*
white eggs. Eggs half the size of Belted Kingfisher eggs.

BARN SWALLOW *Hirundo rustica*   p. 140
Usually built on man-made structure—barn or bridge. Nest is
bowl, open at top; built of mud pellets, lined with feathers. 4–5
eggs *indistinguishable from eggs of Cliff Swallow.* Cliff Swallow
nest *gourd-shaped.*

WESTERN WOOD PEWEE

OLIVE-SIDED FLYCATCHER

VERMILION FLYCATCHER

HORNED LARK

TREE SWALLOW

BANK SWALLOW

ROUGH-WINGED SWALLOW

BARN SWALLOW

Plate 18

SWALLOWS, JAYS, MAGPIE, RAVEN

CLIFF SWALLOW *Petrochelidon pyrrhonota* p. 141
In colonies; gourd-shaped nests made of *mud pellets,* plastered to sides of buildings, bridges, cliffs. *Eggs indistinguishable from eggs of Barn Swallow;* nests differ. (*Photograph by George H. Harrison.*)

PURPLE MARTIN *Progne subis* p. 142
Nests colonial or single; more likely to be in natural cavity in West than in East, where birdhouses are favored. *Bulky* nest of leaves, trash. Often mud and fresh green leaves in lining. 4–5 white eggs.

BLUE JAY *Cyanocitta cristata* p. 143
Only jay nesting in Mississippi Valley and neighboring states. Bulky nest in crotch or outer branch of coniferous or deciduous tree. Eggs have 2 distinct ground colors: greenish or buff. Marked with dark brown and gray dots and spots.

STELLER'S JAY *Cyanocitta stelleri* p. 144
Nests single in trees 15–25 ft. (4.6–7.6 m) above ground. Rough-looking, built of leaves, moss, sticks, trash, often with base of paper; lining has mud base. Eggs bluer, less densely spotted than finely dotted Pinyon Jay eggs. Pinyon is colonial.

SCRUB JAY *Aphelocoma coerulescens* p. 144
Fairly low in bush or tree; compactly built, well-made platform of twigs, moss, grass; lined with hair, fine roots (*no mud*). *Two types of eggs:* green background with olive markings; grayish white to green with reddish brown markings.

MEXICAN JAY *Aphelocoma ultramarina* p. 145
Breeding range limited to s. Arizona, sw. New Mexico, w. Texas. Birds live in loose colonies on communal basis. Greenish blue eggs spotted and dotted with brown; eggs of Arizona race unmarked. Nest commonly in live oak.

BLACK-BILLED MAGPIE *Pica pica* p. 147
Nest unmistakable: *huge sphere* of interlacing sticks with base of inner lining of mud or cow dung; may be as much as 4 ft. (1.2 m) high. Yellow-billed Magpie of central California builds similar nest. (*Photograph by Lynn Fuller.*)

COMMON RAVEN *Corvus corax* p. 148
Nest is large structure warmly lined with animal hair; mostly on cliff ledges or in coniferous trees. Eggs *similar to eggs of Common Crow* but considerably *larger.* (*Photograph by Lynn Fuller.*)

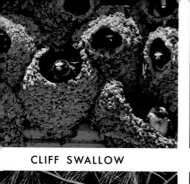

CLIFF SWALLOW

PURPLE MARTIN

BLUE JAY

STELLER'S JAY

SCRUB JAY

MEXICAN JAY

BLACK-BILLED MAGPIE

COMMON RAVEN

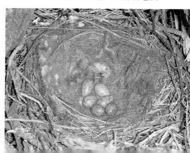

Plate 19

RAVEN, CROW, JAYS,
CHICKADEES, TITMICE

WHITE-NECKED RAVEN *Corvus cryptoleucus* p. 148
Limited to deserts, open plains, arid farmlands. Trashy nest, usually filthy from excrement. Eggs generally *paler* than eggs of other Corvidae. (*Photograph by Suzanne Arguello.*)

COMMON CROW *Corvus brachyrhynchos* p. 150
Substantial basket of sticks in crotch of tree. Range overlaps that of Fish Crow and Northwestern Crow. *Nests and eggs* (bluish or grayish green irregularly marked with browns) *indistinguishable except for larger size* of Common Crow nest and eggs. Northwestern Crow may nest on ground.

PINYON JAY *Gymnorhinus cyanocephalus* p. 151
Colonial in pinyon-juniper woodlands; mixed pine and oak. Nests rather large, somewhat trashy. Eggs whitish, more finely dotted, densely marked, than spotted eggs of Steller's Jay.

CLARK'S NUTCRACKER *Nucifraga columbiana* p. 152
In mountains near timberline, early in year, often snow on ground. 11–12 in. (27.9–30.5 cm) in diam., 8–45 ft. (2.4–13.7 m) above ground in conifer. Eggs pale green, brown spots. Gray Jay nests early, generally at lower altitudes; 6–8 ft. (1.8–2.4 m) above ground; nest smaller, lined with hair, fur; eggs pale gray with gray or olive-buff spots. (*Photograph by Raymond J. Quigley.*)

BLACK-CAPPED CHICKADEE *Parus atricapillus* p. 152
Birds dig hole in soft stub or use woodpecker hole or other cavity. 6–8 white eggs; reddish brown spots. Nest of soft downy material and twigs. Breeding range overlaps that of Mountain Chickadee more than any other. Generally eggs of Black-capped more heavily marked.

MOUNTAIN CHICKADEE *Parus gambeli* p. 153
Prefers natural cavity or abandoned woodpecker hole; commonly 7–9 eggs. Confined mostly to coniferous forests, foothills to timberline. Chestnut-backed Chickadee more coastal in humid Pacific Northwest. Boreal Chickadee rare.

TUFTED TITMOUSE *Parus bicolor* p. 155
Does not excavate cavity. Generally lays *fewer eggs* (5–6) than chickadees; *eggs larger*. Often uses shed snakeskin in nest. (Photograph of Black-crested race, *P. b. atricristatus*).

PLAIN TITMOUSE *Parus inornatus* p. 156
Almost no overlap with range of Tufted Titmouse. Lays unmarked or faintly dotted eggs. Rarely excavates own cavity.

WHITE-NECKED RAVEN

COMMON CROW

PINYON JAY

CLARK'S NUTCRACKER

BLACK-CAPPED CHICKADEE

MOUNTAIN CHICKADEE

TUFTED TITMOUSE

PLAIN TITMOUSE

Plate 20

VERDIN, BUSHTIT,
NUTHATCHES, CREEPER, DIPPER

VERDIN *Auriparus flaviceps*   p. 156
Oval-shaped ball of interlaced thorny twigs in desert shrub or
cactus. Entrance near bottom. Old nests endure for years.

BUSHTIT *Psaltriparus minimus*   p. 157
Unique; a gourd-shaped hanging pocket, 8–9 in. (20.3–22.9 cm)
long, woven into and supported by small twigs and branches of
tree or bush. Kinglet's hanging nest much shorter, found only in
coniferous forest. Entrance hole in side near top. 5–7 white *unmarked eggs;* kinglet eggs spotted.

WHITE-BREASTED NUTHATCH *Sitta carolinensis* p. 157
In natural cavity or woodpecker hole; rarely excavates own cavity. Eggs similar to eggs of Red-breasted and Pygmy Nuthatches
but somewhat *larger.* Nest material less soft and downy than
chickadees'; less twiggy than House Wren's.

RED-BREASTED NUTHATCH *Sitta canadensis*   p. 158
Generally excavates own cavity in soft dead stub. Globules of
pitch are smeared around entrance hole by adults. (*Photograph
by Ted and Lois Matthews.*)

PYGMY NUTHATCH *Sitta pygmaea*   p. 159
Nesting cavities laboriously dug by birds. Cracks in interior
caulked with nest material, "weatherproofing" the cavity. Eggs
similar to eggs of Red-breasted Nuthatch but smaller than eggs of
White-breasted Nuthatch.

BROWN CREEPER *Certhia familiaris*   p. 159
Nest unique. *Behind loose slab of bark* still attached to living or
dead tree; crescent shape conforms with space in which placed.
Eggs similar to eggs of Black-capped Chickadee.

WRENTIT *Chamaea fasciata*   p. 160
Limited generally to coastal Oregon and California. Nest commonly in chaparral, 18–24 in. (45.7–61.0 cm) above ground. Eggs
pale greenish blue; no markings.

DIPPER *Cinclus mexicanus*   p. 161
On rock or ledge along swift-flowing mountain stream where spray
keeps nest moist or even wet. A *domed structure* of mosses, a few
leaves and grasses, with entrance on side. Sometimes placed under
bridges over streams. White eggs are unmarked. (*Photograph by
Ted and Lois Matthews.*)

VERDIN

BUSHTIT

HITE-BREASTED NUTHATCH

RED-BREASTED NUTHATCH

PYGMY NUTHATCH

BROWN CREEPER

WRENTIT

DIPPER

Plate 21

WRENS, MOCKINGBIRD, GRAY CATBIRD

HOUSE WREN *Troglodytes aedon* p. 162
Best known wren; nests in cavity in myriad places, often close to human habitation. Cup of grasses, rootlets, feathers, hair, placed on thick *base of twigs.* Eggs *heavily speckled* with reddish brown dots. (*Photograph by George H. Harrison.*)

BEWICK'S WREN *Thryomanes bewickii* p. 163
Likely to use natural cavity, but sometimes nests in birdhouse. Eggs much more *sparingly marked* than eggs of House Wren.

CACTUS WREN *Campylorhynchus brunneicapillus* p. 164
Nest in cactus unmistakable; *football-shaped* structure of *straw-colored* plant stems, grasses, placed horizontally with entrance to globular nest chamber at one end. Salmon-buff eggs heavily covered with spots, dots; larger than eggs of other wrens. (*Photograph by Raymond J. Quigley*).

LONG-BILLED MARSH WREN p. 165
Cistothorus palustris
Breeds in marshes. Nest is an *upright oblong* with side opening, woven of wet cattails, reeds, lashed to standing aquatic vegetation. 3–6 eggs heavily marked with brown. Short-billed Marsh Wren builds round nest; lays pure white eggs.

CANYON WREN *Catherpes mexicanus* p. 166
Nest on shelf or in cranny in rock wall, crevice in building. Stick nest substantially lined with wool, fur, feathers, down; somewhat like nest of Eastern Phoebe. Eggs very similar to eggs of Rock Wren but not as heavily marked as eggs of other wrens.

ROCK WREN *Salpinctes obsoletus* p. 167
Nest in crevice on rocky hillside, under overhanging rock, with entrance generally *paved with bits of rock.* Eggs very similar to eggs of Canyon Wren but not as heavily marked as eggs of other wrens.

MOCKINGBIRD *Mimus polyglottos* p. 168
Partial to site near house—porch vines, foundation and garden plantings. Bulky twig nest with lining of rootlets, grasses, sometimes horsehair, plant down. Blue or greenish eggs *heavily blotched* and *spotted* with brown; similar to eggs of Sage Thrasher but ground color of Mockingbird eggs paler.

GRAY CATBIRD *Dumetella carolinensis* p. 169
Nest thrasherlike but eggs *unmarked;* similar to eggs of American Robin but smaller, darker (*deep greenish blue*).

HOUSE WREN

BEWICK'S WREN

CACTUS WREN

LONG-BILLED MARSH WREN

CANYON WREN

ROCK WREN

MOCKINGBIRD

GRAY CATBIRD

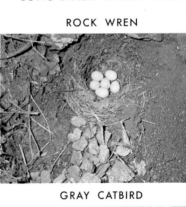

Plate 22

THRASHERS, ROBIN

BROWN THRASHER *Toxostoma rufum* p. 169
Breeding range east of Rockies eliminates confusion with most
other thrashers. Eggs bluish white; faintly, evenly covered with
fine brown dots. Sage Thrasher eggs deep greenish blue, heavily
marked; Mockingbird nest smaller, eggs heavily marked.

BENDIRE'S THRASHER *Toxostoma bendirei* p. 170
Shy bird of Southwest desert scrub. Nest generally smaller, more
compact, of *finer material* than nests of most other thrashers.
(*Photograph by Raymond J. Quigley.*)

CURVE-BILLED THRASHER p. 171
Toxostoma curvirostre
Bulky loose bowl of coarse thorny twigs most often in cactus,
desert thorn, or mesquite. Nest and eggs similar to those of Mockingbird but eggs are *finely marked;* Mockingbird's are heavily
spotted and blotched.

CALIFORNIA THRASHER *Toxostoma redivivum* p. 172
Breeds only in California. Nest in shrub resembles Mockingbird's
but is larger. Eggs larger and generally not as heavily marked as
eggs of Mockingbird.

LE CONTE'S THRASHER *Toxostoma lecontei* p. 172
Breeding range restricted to low, hot, barren deserts and valleys of
extreme Southwest. Eggs *smaller* than eggs of California
Thrasher; same size as eggs of Curve-billed Thrasher; usually less
heavily spotted than either. (*Photograph by Raymond J. Quigley.*)

CRISSAL THRASHER *Toxostoma dorsale* p. 172
Only thrasher that lays *unmarked eggs;* much like eggs of American Robin.

SAGE THRASHER *Oreoscoptes montanus* p. 173
Range generally *more northern* than desert thrashers; favors
sagebrush and saltbush plains. Eggs similar to eggs of Mockingbird but are deeper, richer color.

AMERICAN ROBIN *Turdus migratorius* p. 173
Dooryard bird, but may nest in woods and mountains to timberline. Use of *ample mud* in construction is diagnostic. Nest of
Wood Thrush similar but smaller, invariably with leaves in foundation and rootlets instead of grass in lining. Eggs "Robin's-egg-
blue," unmarked; Wood Thrush eggs smaller, paler.

BROWN THRASHER

BENDIRE'S THRASHER

CURVE-BILLED THRASHER

CALIFORNIA THRASHER

LE CONTE'S THRASHER

CRISSAL THRASHER

SAGE THRASHER

AMERICAN ROBIN

Plate 23

THRUSHES, BLUEBIRDS,
SOLITAIRE, GNATCATCHER

HERMIT THRUSH *Catharus guttatus* p. 175
Range mostly Rockies and west in coniferous forests, typically in high mountains to timberline. Unlike eastern race, usually nests in low bushes or trees. Eggs similar to Veery's eggs but *paler blue*.

SWAINSON'S THRUSH *Catharus ustulatus* p. 175
Range overlaps that of Hermit Thrush and Veery, but blue eggs of Swainson's Thrush are *spotted, blotched;* others unmarked. Nests in trees or bushes.

VEERY *Catharus fuscescens* p. 176
Nests on or near ground in moist deciduous woodlands. Nest large for size of bird. Eggs resemble eggs of Hermit Thrush but are *darker blue.* Wood Thrush nests in trees, lays larger eggs.

EASTERN BLUEBIRD *Sialia sialis* p. 177
Breeding range generally east of both Western and Mountain Bluebirds. Cavity nest made mostly of *grasses.* Unmarked blue eggs *indistinguishable from eggs of Western Bluebird; darker* than eggs of Mountain Bluebird.

WESTERN BLUEBIRD *Sialia mexicana* p. 177
Breeding range overlaps that of Mountain Bluebird but is mostly west of Eastern Bluebird's range. Eggs *indistinguishable from eggs of Eastern Bluebird* but *darker* than eggs of Mountain Bluebird.

MOUNTAIN BLUEBIRD *Sialia currucoides* p. 178
Breeding biology similar to that of Western Bluebird. Eggs paler. *Bird should be seen* for positive identification of bluebird nests. (*Photograph of ♂ by George H. Harrison.*)

TOWNSEND'S SOLITAIRE *Myadestes townsendi* p. 178
Nests on or near ground often beneath rock or under stump in coniferous forest in mountains. Eggs entirely different from eggs of other North American thrushes. Ground color *dull white* or *pale blue,* evenly covered with brown spots, scrawls.

BLUE-GRAY GNATCATCHER *Polioptila caerulea* p. 179
Delicate nest saddled to limb or in small crotch; comparable to nest of hummingbird but larger. Eggs *indistinguishable from eggs of Black-tailed Gnatcatcher,* but Black-tailed generally nests low, 2–4 ft. (0.6–1.2 m) above ground, and does not use much lichen on exterior.

HERMIT THRUSH

SWAINSON'S THRUSH

VEERY

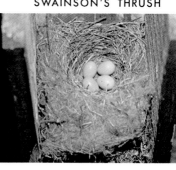

EASTERN BLUEBIRD

WESTERN BLUEBIRD

MOUNTAIN BLUEBIRD

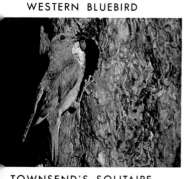

TOWNSEND'S SOLITAIRE

BLUE-GRAY GNATCATCHER

Plate 24

KINGLET, PIPIT, WAXWING, PHAINOPEPLA, SHRIKE, STARLING, VIREOS

RUBY-CROWNED KINGLET *Regulus calendula* p. 181
Small pendent globe of moss; 7–9 eggs, off-white with reddish brown dots. *Nest and eggs indistinguishable from those of Golden-crowned Kinglet;* must see bird for positive identification of nest. Bushtit nest much more elongated; eggs white.

WATER PIPIT *Anthus spinoletta* p. 181
In hollow in ground on tundra, invariably sheltered from above. Chocolate brown markings on eggs so thick *ground color often obliterated.* Nest of Horned Lark more open; eggs pale gray with salt-and-pepper spots.

CEDAR WAXWING *Bombycilla cedrorum* p. 183
Generally avoids dense woods. Bohemian Waxwing commonly found in northern coniferous forests and muskeg bogs. Eggs of 2 species pale bluish gray with dark brown spots; Bohemian eggs larger.

PHAINOPEPLA *Phainopepla nitens* p. 183
Limited to southwestern states. *Male* builds shallow (*small for size of bird*), compact, thinly lined nest in tree or shrub, often in clump of mistletoe. Eggs pale gray with black dots.

LOGGERHEAD SHRIKE *Lanius ludovicianus* p. 184
In open country where lookout perches are available. Bulky, well-made, deep cup, a dense concentration of fine trashy material; lined with hair, rootlets, feathers, cottony fibers. Hidden by dense foliage in tree, shrub, mistletoe clump.

STARLING *Sturnus vulgaris* p. 184
Solitary or in colonies. In cavity or hole almost anywhere; filled with mass of material. 4–5 pale bluish or greenish white eggs, unmarked, rather glossy.

WHITE-EYED VIREO *Vireo griseus* p. 185
Range overlaps that of Bell's Vireo in eastern section; *nest and eggs indistinguishable.* Distinguished from round, cup-shaped nest of Red-eyed Vireo by exterior *conelike pointed bottom.*

HUTTON'S VIREO *Vireo huttoni* p. 185
From ground, white nest looks like *baseball* hanging from horizontal twigs of tree (most often oak), 7–25 ft. (2.1–7.6 m) above ground. Warbling Vireo nest generally lacks white appearance of Hutton's nest; eggs are similar.

RUBY-CROWNED KINGLET

WATER PIPIT

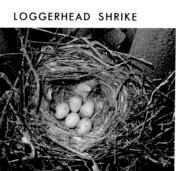

CEDAR WAXWING

PHAINOPEPLA

LOGGERHEAD SHRIKE

STARLING

WHITE-EYED VIREO

HUTTON'S VIREO

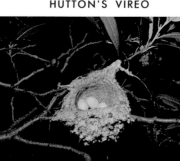

Plate 25
VIREOS, WOOD WARBLERS

BELL'S VIREO   *Vireo bellii*   p. 186
Nest and eggs indistinguishable from those of White-eyed Vireo
which also nests within 6 ft. (1.8 m) of ground in shrub or tree.
Exterior *conelike pointed bottom* of Bell's distinct from cup-
shaped nest of Red-eyed Vireo. Warbling Vireo nests high. Solitary Vireo nest bulkier.

SOLITARY VIREO   *Vireo solitarius*   p. 188
Bulkier and *more loosely constructed* than nests of other vireos.
Often *decorated externally* with paper, spider egg cases, bits of old
hornet nests. Male *sings while incubating.*

RED-EYED VIREO   *Vireo olivaceus*   p. 189
Does not breed in much of range of Hutton's, Gray, and Solitary
Vireos. *Cup-shaped* nest differs from conelike pointed nests of
White-eyed and Bell's Vireos. *Walls thinner* than in nests of most
vireos.

WARBLING VIREO   *Vireo gilvus*   p. 189
Male *sings while incubating.* Commonly placed higher than nest
of Solitary and Red-eyed Vireos. Usually *well out from trunk*
often in aspen or poplar. Yellow-throated Vireo ordinarily builds
nest closer to tree trunk.

BLACK-AND-WHITE WARBLER   *Mniotilta varia*   p. 191
Breeding range more eastern than many other ground-nesting
warblers (Orange-crowned, Nashville, Virginia's, Wilson's). Nest
in deciduous woodland, usually *hidden from above,* often in drift
of leaves under log or at base of tree.

NASHVILLE WARBLER   *Vermivora ruficapilla*   p. 195
Invariably *on ground* in depression in moss, often with overhanging low plant cover. Nest and eggs similar to those of Virginia's
and Orange-crowned Warblers.

YELLOW WARBLER   *Dendroica petechia*   p. 197
Nests in shrub or tree, *lower* than some warblers with similar nests
(Yellow-rumped, Black-throated Gray). Nest walls silvery, thick,
less neatly built than in American Redstart nest. Neater and more
compact than nest of Willow Flycatcher.

YELLOW-RUMPED WARBLER   p. 200
Dendroica coronata
Arrangement of feathers in lining is identifying factor—woven or
imbedded into lining so that *tips bend inward* over cup, hiding
eggs. Nest typically on horizontal branch of conifer, often near
trunk. Ground color of eggs has greenish tinge. (Photograph of
nest of Audubon's Warbler, *D. c. auduboni.*)

BELL'S VIREO

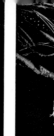

SOLITARY VIREO

RED-EYED VIREO

WARBLING VIREO

BLACK-AND-WHITE WARBLER

NASHVILLE WARBLER

YELLOW WARBLER

YELLOW-RUMPED WARBLER

Plate 26

WOOD WARBLERS

BLACK-THROATED GRAY WARBLER p. 200
Dendroica nigrescens
Nests on horizontal branch of conifer, well out from trunk. Many feathers woven into lining, but not arranged as in Yellow-rumped Warbler nest. Eggs slightly *smaller, whiter,* and generally more finely marked than eggs of Yellow-rumped.

OVENBIRD *Seiurus aurocapillus* p. 206
Prefers deciduous woods with carpet of dry leaves. Ground nest unique in shape: *like an old-fashioned oven,* domed on top with opening at ground level. Well hidden; flushing the bird is usual method of discovery.

NORTHERN WATERTHRUSH p. 207
Seiurus noveboracensis
In swamps and bogs *in upturned roots or mossy banks.* Eggs similar to eggs of Louisiana Waterthrush, which nests in banks of flowing streams. Habitats rarely overlap even where ranges do.

MacGILLIVRAY'S WARBLER *Oporornis tolmiei* p. 209
Nest in thick shrub 1–5 ft. (0.3–1.5 m) above ground. Loosely built; supported by several stalks. Commonly 4 eggs, white with light brownish drab markings overlaid with darker browns.

COMMON YELLOWTHROAT *Geothlypis trichas* p. 210
In low cover usually in moist areas. Nest is *bulky* (large for small bird), built of dry grasses, reed shreds, leaves, hair; securely lodged in surrounding vegetation, on or near ground.

YELLOW-BREASTED CHAT *Icteria virens* p. 210
Bulky nest of leaves, vines, grasses, commonly placed in briar tangle 2–6 ft. (0.6–1.8 m) above ground. Eggs similar to eggs of Ovenbird, but nests and habitat differ.

WILSON'S WARBLER *Wilsonia pusilla* p. 211
Nest compact, on or near ground often at base of small shrub. Commonly 5 white, spotted eggs *smaller than eggs of most warblers.* Incubating bird sits tight; difficult to flush.

AMERICAN REDSTART *Setophaga ruticilla* p. 212
Similar to Yellow Warbler's nest but has *neater construction, thinner walls.* American Goldfinch nest wider than high; American Redstart nest higher than wide. Goldfinch eggs unmarked.

CK-THROATED GRAY WARBLER

OVENBIRD

NORTHERN WATERTHRUSH

MacGILLIVRAY'S WARBLER

COMMON YELLOWTHROAT

YELLOW-BREASTED CHAT

WILSON'S WARBLER

AMERICAN REDSTART

Plate 27

HOUSE SPARROW, BLACKBIRDS, ORIOLES

HOUSE SPARROW *Passer domesticus*   p. 213
Usually in cavity, often around man-made structures; ancestral
Weaver Finch type of nest (huge ball of grasses, trash) sometimes
built in fork of tree branch. Eggs are white with grayish markings.
Starlings lay blue eggs in cavities.

BOBOLINK *Dolichonyx oryzivorus*   p. 214
Nests in open meadows, prairies, hayfields, often with meadowlarks. Bobolink nest is *open grass cup;* Meadowlark nest is
domed. Bobolink eggs *heavily spotted, blotched* with browns;
ground color sometimes hidden. Eggs more heavily marked than
eggs of Meadowlark or grassland sparrows.

WESTERN MEADOWLARK *Sturnella neglecta*   p. 215
Nest and eggs indistinguishable from Eastern Meadowlark. Song
of male in whose territory nest is found must be identified. Eggs
much larger than eggs of Bobolink or grassland sparrows.

YELLOW-HEADED BLACKBIRD   p. 216
Xanthocephalus xanthocephalus
Yellow-headed Blackbirds and Red-winged Blackbirds in same
marshes tend to separate into distinct colonies. Yellow-headed
eggs are grayish or greenish white dotted with browns, grays;
Red-winged eggs are bluish green with dark spots, blotches,
scrawls.

RED-WINGED BLACKBIRD *Agelaius phoeniceus*   p. 216
In California and s. Oregon range overlaps that of Tricolored
Blackbird. *Nest and eggs indistinguishable.* Nest material se-
curely interwoven with upright stalks of supporting vegetation.

ORCHARD ORIOLE *Icterus spurius*   p. 217
Invariable *use of grasses,* sometimes for entire structure, is diagnostic. Range overlaps that of Northern Oriole. Orchard nest not
as pendulous as Northern's.

HOODED ORIOLE *Icterus cucullatus*   p. 219
A pouch of grass or shredded palm fibers attached to underside of
leaves, especially palm, 12–45 ft. (3.7–13.7 m) above ground. Lines
and tracings so evident in most oriole eggs generally absent from
Hooded eggs. (*Photograph by Stephen I. Rothstein.*)

SCOTT'S ORIOLE *Icterus parisorum*   p. 219
Basketlike nest of grasses, fibers, often lashed to leaves of yucca,
palm, or sometimes in mistletoe clump; typically 8–20 ft. (2.4–
6.1 m) above ground. Eggs have *zigzag markings;* differ from
blotched, spotted eggs of Hooded Oriole. (Photo of ♂).

HOUSE SPARROW

BOBOLINK

WESTERN MEADOWLARK

YELLOW-HEADED BLACKBIRD

RED-WINGED BLACKBIRD

ORCHARD ORIOLE

HOODED ORIOLE

SCOTT'S ORIOLE

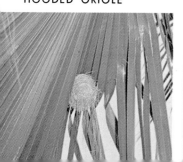

Plate 28

ORIOLE, BLACKBIRD, GRACKLE, COWBIRDS, TANAGERS, CARDINAL

NORTHERN ORIOLE *Icterus galbula* p. 220
May be confused with nest of Orchard Oriole. Has *deeper pouch* than Orchard nest; uses *greater variety of materials;* use of grass restricted in Northern nest, abundant in Orchard nest.

BREWER'S BLACKBIRD *Euphagus cyanocephalus* p. 221
Breeding range generally more western than that of Common Grackle. Nests of 2 species very similar; both include mud beneath lining. Markings on eggs of Brewer's often *almost obliterate ground color.*

COMMON GRACKLE *Quiscalus quiscula* p. 223
Breeds east of Rockies; overlaps ranges of Great-tailed and Boat-tailed Grackles. Common Grackle nests and eggs are smaller. Eggs marked with blotches and scrawls of dark brown; much less heavily marked than Brewer's Blackbird eggs.

BROWN-HEADED COWBIRD *Molothrus ater* p. 224
Photograph shows 3 Brown-headed Cowbird eggs in Eastern Phoebe's nest with 5 Phoebe eggs. Shape of Cowbird eggs varies greatly but markings are typically dots and streaks of brown.

BRONZED COWBIRD *Molothrus aeneus* p. 225
Parasitizes other passerines in extreme southern regions. Pale bluish green (also white) eggs are unmarked. Photograph shows 4 eggs of Bronzed Cowbird in nest of Long-billed Thrasher.

WESTERN TANAGER *Piranga ludoviciana* p. 225
Breeding range west of that of Scarlet Tanager, overlaps that of Summer Tanager and Hepatic Tanager in Southwest; habitats vary. Tanager nests similar—shallow saucers of twigs; but eggs of Western Tanager tend to be more heavily marked than eggs of Hepatic Tanager. Nest and eggs similar to but smaller than those of Black-headed Grosbeak.

SUMMER TANAGER *Piranga rubra* p. 227
In eastern part of range nesting habitat overlaps that of Scarlet Tanager. Nests similar; eggs of Summer Tanager are *more boldly marked* than those of Scarlet and Hepatic Tanagers.

CARDINAL *Cardinalis cardinalis* p. 228
In Southwest, range overlaps that of Pyrrhuloxia; *nests similar, eggs indistinguishable.* Gray Catbird nest similar but has foundation of leaves, lining of rootlets. Cardinal nest has *few* or *no leaves,* lining of *grasses.* Eggs entirely different.

NORTHERN ORIOLE

BREWER'S BLACKBIRD

COMMON GRACKLE

BROWN-HEADED COWBIRD

BRONZED COWBIRD

WESTERN TANAGER

SUMMER TANAGER

CARDINAL

Plate 29
PYRRHULOXIA, GROSBEAKS, FINCHES

PYRRHULOXIA *Cardinalis sinuatus* p. 228
Nest similar to and eggs indistinguishable from those of Cardinal; Pyrrhuloxia tends to nest in *denser woods.* Material used often gives Pyrrhuloxia nest a *gray* appearance.

BLACK-HEADED GROSBEAK p. 230
Pheucticus melanocephalus
Breeding range overlaps that of Rose-breasted Grosbeak east of Rockies; *nests and eggs indistinguishable.* Hybridization between the 2 species is frequent. Nest an open cup of twigs in fork of shrub or tree; eggs pale bluish green marked with brown. Similar to tanager eggs but larger and usually more heavily marked.

BLUE GROSBEAK *Guiraca caerulea* p. 230
Compact deep cup low in bush or tangle; often includes cast-off snakeskin. Habitat similar to that of Indigo, Lazuli, and Varied Buntings; pale bluish-white eggs also similar to but *larger* than bunting eggs; *unlike all other grosbeak eggs.*

LAZULI BUNTING *Passerina amoena* p. 232
Range generally more westward than that of Indigo Bunting. Varied Bunting range overlaps in extreme South and Southwest. *Bluish white eggs of 3 species indistinguishable;* smaller than eggs of Blue Grosbeak.

DICKCISSEL *Spiza americana* p. 233
Nest on ground or a few inches above ground in rank growth of grass, alfalfa. Pale blue eggs *indistinguishable from eggs of Lark Bunting.* Bunting nest is in depression in ground. Ranges overlap on Great Plains.

PURPLE FINCH *Carpodacus purpureus* p. 234
Neat shallow cup in conifer. Nest and eggs *indistinguishable from those of Cassin's Finch;* where ranges overlap, birds should be seen for positive identification. Tanager eggs similar but larger, nest frailer. House Finch eggs paler.

HOUSE FINCH *Carpodacus mexicanus* p. 235
Common in farms, cities, suburbs; nest is well-made cup, placed in great variety of situations. Nests of other species often appropriated. 4–5 pale bluish green eggs are sparingly marked.

AMERICAN GOLDFINCH *Carduelis tristis* p. 237
Neat cup of vegetable fibers, wider than deep, with 4–6 pale blue unmarked eggs; in tree. Nest similar to and eggs *indistinguishable from those of Lesser Goldfinch.* Thick rim of excrement around edge of nest, deposited by young, is diagnostic of all goldfinches. Wrentit eggs similar; nest low in dense chaparral.

PYRRHULOXIA

BLACK-HEADED GROSBEAK

BLUE GROSBEAK

LAZULI BUNTING

DICKCISSEL

PURPLE FINCH

HOUSE FINCH

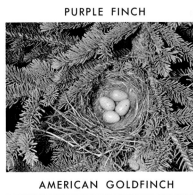

AMERICAN GOLDFINCH

Plate 30

GOLDFINCHES, TOWHEES, SPARROWS

LESSER GOLDFINCH *Carduelis psaltria* p. 238
Nest similar to and *eggs indistinguishable from those of American Goldfinch.*

LAWRENCE'S GOLDFINCH *Carduelis lawrencei* p. 238
Confusion with other goldfinch nests possible only in Lawrence's limited breeding range in cen. and s. California. *White* or *very pale bluish white* eggs of Lawrence's Goldfinch diagnostic.

GREEN-TAILED TOWHEE *Pipilo chlorurus* p. 240
In montane and high plateau chaparral, alpine meadow thickets to over 10,000 ft. (3050 m); avoids forests. Bulky nest on or near ground in low bush; similar to nest of Rufous-sided Towhee, but latter normally nests at lower altitudes.

RUFOUS-SIDED TOWHEE *Pipilo erythrophthalmus* p. 240
Typically a *ground nester.* Brown and Abert's Towhees place nests in low bushes, vines, small trees, sometimes mistletoe.

BROWN TOWHEE *Pipilo fuscus* p. 241
Similar to nest of Abert's Towhee; above ground in shrub or low tree. Eggs of Pacific Coast race of Brown Towhee (*P. f. senicula*) *indistinguishable from eggs of Abert's Towhee.*

LARK BUNTING *Calamospiza melanocorys* p. 242
Range overlaps that of Dickcissel on Great Plains; unmarked pale blue eggs are *indistinguishable,* but Lark Bunting nest usually in depression in ground in short-grass prairie with scattered low shrubs. Dickcissel nest on or near ground in low, rank vegetation. Unmarked pale blue eggs distinguish Lark Bunting nest from those of other ground nesters on short-grass prairie.

SAVANNAH SPARROW *Passerculus sandwichensis* p. 242
In hollow in ground usually concealed under straw layer of last year's plant growth; deep cup of grass stems lined with grass, rootlets, hair; feathers used in coastal areas. Eggs have variety of markings; *similar to but smaller than eggs of Vesper and Baird's Sparrows.* (*Photograph by Raymond J. Quigley.*)

GRASSHOPPER SPARROW p. 243
Ammodramus savannarum
Nest in ground concealed by canopy of grass, forbs; often domed at back. Eggs creamy white, not greenish blue or heavily spotted like eggs of Savannah. Meadowlark eggs larger; Bobolink eggs very heavily marked.

LESSER GOLDFINCH

LAWRENCE'S GOLDFINCH

GREEN-TAILED TOWHEE

RUFOUS-SIDED TOWHEE

BROWN TOWHEE

LARK BUNTING

SAVANNAH SPARROW

GRASSHOPPER SPARROW

Plate 31

SPARROWS, JUNCOS

VESPER SPARROW *Pooecetes gramineus* p. 245
Nest similar to nests of Baird's, Savannah, Henslow's, Grasshopper Sparrows, which are also on ground in open grasslands. Vesper nest *bulky, thick-rimmed, well-cupped, loosely woven.* Eggs slightly larger than eggs of Baird's and Savannah Sparrows.

LARK SPARROW *Chondestes grammacus* p. 245
Prefers grasslands with scattered trees. Commonly (but not always) on ground. Scrawl markings on eggs similar to those of Northern Oriole.

BLACK-THROATED SPARROW p. 248
Amphispiza bilineata
A desert sparrow that lays bluish white unmarked eggs. Nest close to ground in low vegetation. Whitish lining in nest typical. Eggs of Brewer's and Sage Sparrows marked.

SAGE SPARROW *Amphispiza belli* p. 248
In sagebrush, chaparral, 3–40 in. (7.6–101.6 cm) above ground; commonly lined with wool, hair, fur. Bluish eggs are *speckled* and *spotted;* larger and paler than eggs of Brewer's Sparrow. Black-chinned Sparrow eggs usually unmarked. (*Photograph by Raymond J. Quigley.*)

DARK-EYED JUNCO *Junco hyemalis* p. 249
Nests in coniferous and mixed forest edges and openings; usually on ground; occasionally in trees. Eggs bluish white heavily marked with browns; capped. Similar to nest of Gray-headed Junco; Gray-headed eggs more sparingly spotted.

GRAY-HEADED JUNCO *Junco caniceps* p. 250
Nests in same habitat as Dark-eyed Junco, often at higher altitudes up to 12,000 ft. (3660 m). Almost always on ground hidden by overhanging tufts of grass. Eggs *indistinguishable from eggs of Yellow-eyed Junco; less heavily marked* than eggs of Dark-eyed Junco.

CHIPPING SPARROW *Spizella passerina* p. 250
Small neat cup of fine grasslike materials, often in conifer; *more compact* than nest of Clay-colored Sparrow. Resembles nest of Brewer's Sparrow, but latter commonly in sagebrush or saltbush. Eggs light bluish green marked with dark brown; *indistinguishable from eggs of Clay-colored and Brewer's Sparrows.*

BREWER'S SPARROW *Spizella breweri* p. 252
Habitat typically sagebrush or saltbush. Nest similar to and eggs *indistinguishable from those of Clay-colored and Chipping Sparrows;* habitats differ.

VESPER SPARROW

LARK SPARROW

LACK-THROATED SPARROW

SAGE SPARROW

DARK-EYED JUNCO

GRAY-HEADED JUNCO

CHIPPING SPARROW

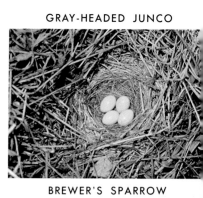

BREWER'S SPARROW

Plate 32

SPARROWS, LONGSPURS

FIELD SPARROW *Spizella pusilla* p. 252
Breeding range east of Rockies. Early nests on ground, later nests
up to 4 ft. (1.2 m) above ground in bush or low tree in brushy field.
Small compact nest mostly of grass. Eggs cream or pale bluish
white; marked with reddish brown.

BLACK-CHINNED SPARROW *Spizella atrogularis* p. 253
In arid chaparral, sage brushlands. Grass cup in sage or other
shrub. Eggs pale blue, unmarked or marked with small scattered
dark brown spots.

WHITE-CROWNED SPARROW p. 253
Zonotrichia leucophrys
In mountain clearings, forest edges, alpine meadows on ground or
a few feet above in dense vegetation. Much variation in egg markings, but often so dense that *ground color obscured.*

FOX SPARROW *Passerella iliaca* p. 254
In mountain chaparral, thickets, edges of forests, logged areas,
burns. Nest well constructed on ground or in bush or low tree.
Pale bluish green eggs, *boldly marked* with spots, blotches.

LINCOLN'S SPARROW *Melospiza lincolnii* p. 254
From Rockies west, range overlaps that of Song Sparrow. Commonly nests on ground in mountain meadows with willow or alder
thickets, brushy bogs, marshes. Eggs *indistinguishable from eggs
of Song Sparrow.* (*Photograph by Ted and Lois Matthews*).

SONG SPARROW *Melospiza melodia* p. 256
Grass nest on ground under tuft of grass, brush, or in low bush or
tree. Greenish or bluish white eggs with markings usually over
entire egg, often *obscuring ground color; indistinguishable from
eggs of Swamp and Lincoln's Sparrows.*

McCOWN'S LONGSPUR *Calcarius mccownii* p. 257
On short-grass prairies. Nest of Horned Lark similar. Longspur
eggs marked with lines, scrawls, spots, speckles; Lark's eggs have
salt-and-pepper markings over entire surface. Lark Bunting eggs
unmarked blue.

CHESTNUT-COLLARED LONGSPUR p. 258
Calcarius ornatus
On short-grass prairies. Chestnut-collared typically prefers *taller
grass* than McCown's Longspur or Horned Lark. Ground color of
Chestnut-collared eggs is *white;* McCown's are more gray or olive.

FIELD SPARROW

BLACK-CHINNED SPARROW

HITE-CROWNED SPARROW

FOX SPARROW

LINCOLN'S SPARROW

SONG SPARROW

McCOWN'S LONGSPUR

CHESTNUT-COLLARED LONGSPU

BLACK PHOEBE   *Sayornis nigricans*   **Pl. 16**

Breeding range: Oregon (unc.), s. Nevada (prob.), California, sw. Utah (unc.), Arizona, s. New Mexico, w. and cen. Texas.
Habitat: Lowland ponds; sycamore-bordered streams; farms, parks, gardens in vicinity of water.
Nest: Mud nests plastered to rocky cliff faces, concrete walls, wooden buildings, bridges, old wells, often beneath overhead projection. Proximity of water assures mud, which, mixed with hair, grasses, and forbs, makes up nest shell. Lined with wool, hair, grass tops, fine roots, strips of bark, plant fibers, occasionally feathers. Location like that of nest of Eastern Phoebe; outside like Barn Swallow's nest. Outside diam. 5 in. (12.7 cm), height 3½ in. (8.9 cm); inside diam. 2¾ in. (7.1 cm), depth 1¼ in. (3.2 cm).
Eggs: 3–6, normally 4; av. 18.7 x 14.4 mm. Oval. Shell smooth, little or no gloss. White, except 1 or 2 eggs (the last laid) with tiny dustlike spots. *Indistinguishable from eggs of other phoebes.* Incubation by female, 15–17 days. 2 broods, possibly 3.
Notes: Seems undisturbed by activity near its nest, which may be in a place of heavy human traffic. Habitually returns to same nesting site from year to year.

SAY'S PHOEBE   *Sayornis saya*   **Pl. 16**

Breeding range: East of Cascades and Sierras in Pacific states east to w. and s.-cen. N. Dakota, S. Dakota (west of Missouri R.), w. Nebraska, w. Iowa (rare), w. Kansas, w. Oklahoma, w. Texas.
Habitat: Open country, ranches, sagebrush flats, badlands, foothills, desert borders, arroyos, cliffs, caves.
Nest: Birds show decided preference for abandoned buildings, entering through cracks, broken windows, knotholes; also build in

BLACK PHOEBE

caves, crevices in arroyo banks, cliff pockets, under bridges, on window- and door-sills, in abandoned mine shafts and other sheltered nooks. Unlike other phoebes, *ordinarily does not use mud.* Nest is flat structure of forbs, dry grasses, moss, wool, empty cocoons, and hair, with inner lining of wool and cattle hair. Outside diam. 5½ in. (14 cm), height 2¼ in. (5.7 cm); inside diam. 2½ in. (6.4 cm), depth 1¼ in. (3.2 cm).

Eggs: 4–5, sometimes 3, rarely more; av. 19.5 x 15.1 mm. Oval to short-oval. Little or no gloss. White; 1 or 2 eggs may have small brown dots. *Indistinguishable from eggs of other phoebes.* Incubation by female; about 2 weeks. 2 broods.

Notes: Odd nest locations: old mailbox, lard pail inserted in chimney stovepipe hole, crevice of old well 15 ft. (4.6 m) below surface, old nest of Cliff Swallow, Bank Swallow burrow, old American Robin's nest.

YELLOW-BELLIED FLYCATCHER   *Empidonax flaviventris*

Notes: Summer resident in coniferous forests and boreal bogs of ne. and n.-cen. Minnesota with breeding records from n. Lake Co. For details of breeding biology see *A Field Guide to Birds' Nests East of the Mississippi River.*

FLYCATCHER

ACADIAN FLYCATCHER *Empidonax virescens*

Breeding range: Minnesota (Houston Co.), Iowa (rare), south to Louisiana; e. Nebraska (rare), e. Kansas (unc.), e. Oklahoma, e. and cen. Texas.

Habitat: Deciduous woodlands, shaded ravines, heavily wooded bottomlands, river swamps.

Nest: On lower branch of large tree, far out from trunk; usually shaded by leafy branches; 8–20 ft. (2.4–6.1 m) above ground; av. for 44 nests 10½ ft. (3.2 m). Frail, saucer-shaped, shallow basket swung hammocklike between horizontal twigs of a slender limb. Built of fine, dry plant stems, plant fibers, tendrils, catkins, by female alone. Slight lining of grass stems, fine rootlets, plant down, and spider webs. Invariably *long streamers* of dried grass, grapevine, and other fibrous material *hang below nest* 1–2 ft. (0.3–0.6 m), giving it misleading trashy appearance from below. Outside diam. 3½ in. (8.9 cm); inside diam. 1½ in. (3.8 cm), depth ⅞ in. (2.2 cm).

Eggs: 2–4, generally 3; av. 18.4 x 13.8 mm. Oval to long-oval. Shell smooth, very little gloss. Creamy to buffy white, sparingly marked with small brown spots or dots, mainly near large end. Female incubates; 13–14 days. 1 brood.

Notes: Unique — cannot be mistaken for any other nest.

WILLOW FLYCATCHER *Empidonax traillii*   **Pl. 16**

Breeding range: Pacific coast east to s. and w. Minnesota, south to w. Texas, Arkansas. More western and southern than range of Alder Flycatcher (*Empidonax alnorum*).

Habitat: Dry brushy fields, willow thickets, margins of mixed deciduous woods with water or low damp ground nearby.

Nest: In fork or on horizontal limb of shrub; 3½–15 ft. (1.1–4.6 m) above ground (usually higher than Alder Flycatcher). Tends to be compact cup of plant bark and fiber and bleached grass; lined with thin layer of fine grass, cottony and silky plant materials; has silvery appearance; typically with feathers in rim. *Similar to Yellow Warbler nest.* May have plant material dangling from bottom.

Eggs: 3–4; av. 17.91 x 13.70 mm. Oval. Shell smooth, dull or slightly glossy. Often *buffy* (Alder Flycatcher eggs are white) or sometimes creamy white; blotched, spotted with shades of brown, markings mostly at large end. Incubation by female; 12–15 days.

Notes: Male's song (*fitz-bew*) diagnostic.

ALDER FLYCATCHER *Empidonax alnorum*

Breeding range: N. Minnesota and possibly areas to south and west. Western extreme uncertain, but generally more eastern than range of Willow Flycatcher (*Empidonax traillii*).

Habitat: Edges of boreal bogs, alder thickets, brushy swamp and marsh borders.
Nest: In shrubs; under 6 ft. (1.8 m), av. 22⅜ in. (56.9 cm) above ground. Tends to be loosely built like nest of Song Sparrow or Indigo Bunting. Of coarse grass, moss, cattail down, rootlets, bark, twiglets; a small amount of cottony or silky material; untidy, regularly has plant strips dangling from bottom.
Eggs: 3–4; av. 18.51 x 14.06 mm. Oval. Shell smooth, dull or slightly glossy. *White* (Willow Flycatcher eggs usually buff); speckled and dotted with shades of brown, densest around large end. Incubation by female; 12–14 days.
Notes: Speciation not as evident in nest and eggs as in song (*fee-bee'-o*).

LEAST FLYCATCHER   *Empidonax minimus*   Pl. 16

Breeding range: Montana to Minnesota, south to s. Idaho (unc.).
Habitat: Open woodlands, old orchards, city parks, suburban gardens, roadside shade trees.
Nest: In crotch or fastened to limb of deciduous or coniferous tree 2–60 ft. (0.6–18.3 m) above ground, commonly 10–20 ft. (3.1–6.1 m). Compact, deep cup; well made of bark, forb stems, grasses; lined with plant down, feathers, hair. Built by female in 6–8 days. *Resembles nests of American Redstart and Yellow Warbler.* Outside diam. 2½–3 in. (6.4–7.6 cm), height 1¾–2½ in. (4.5–6.4 cm); inside diam. 1¾–2 in. (4.5–5.1 cm), depth 1¼–1½ in. (3.2–3.8 cm).
Eggs: 3–6, commonly 4; av. 16.1 x 12.9 mm. Oval to short-oval. Shell smooth, no gloss. *Creamy white, unmarked.* Incubation by female; about 14 days. 1 brood, possibly 2 at times.

HAMMOND'S FLYCATCHER   Pl. 16
Empidonax hammondii

Breeding range: Washington to w. Montana, south to Mexico and New Mexico; absent from Arizona; rare in Nevada.
Habitat: Open coniferous forests, mixed conifer-deciduous forests, bush-clad hillsides, generally at high altitudes.
Nest: Saddled 25–40 ft. (7.6–12.2 m) or higher above ground on horizontal branch of large tree. Of plant fibers, dark strips of bark, rootlets, grass stems, feathers, cocoons; lined with hair, fine grass, dry moss, feathers. Shape and position of nest more like that of Western Wood Pewee than of other flycatchers (*Empidonaces*). Outside diam. 3½ in. (8.9 cm), height about 2¾ in. (7.1 cm); inside diam. 2⅜ in. (6.1 cm), depth 1¼ in. (3.2 cm).
Eggs: 2–4, commonly 3; av. 16.8 x 12.9 mm. Oval. Little or no gloss. Dull white to creamy white, mostly unmarked; occasionally some marked with small brown dots. Generally *indistinguishable from eggs of Dusky Flycatcher*. Incubation by female; "about 12

GRAY FLYCATCHER

days" (Bent); "15 days from laying last egg" (Davis).
Notes: Nests of Hammond's Flycatcher and Dusky Flycatcher confusing, but latter typically in bushes not over 5–6 ft. (1.5–1.8 m) above ground.

DUSKY FLYCATCHER *Empidonax oberholseri* Pl. 16

Breeding range: Washington to w. and cen. Montana, south to Mexico; also S. Dakota (Black Hills).
Habitat: Foothills and slopes of mountains, chaparral, open brushy coniferous and mixed forests.
Nest: Typically 4–7 ft. (1.2–2.1 m) above ground in upright crotch of willows, alders, aspens, low shrubs. Firm compact cup well built of forb stems, grasses, vegetable fiber, plant down; lined with fine bark, bits of vegetable down, cattle hair, often bound together with spider silk. Outside diam. 2¾ in. (7.1 cm), height 3½ in. (8.9 cm); inside diam. 1¾ in. (4.5 cm), depth 2 in. (5.1 cm).
Eggs: 3–4, rarely 2; av. 17.3 x 13.2 mm. Oval to short-oval; some said to be shaped like Bobwhite eggs (short-pyriform). Dull white, very rarely spotted. Generally *indistinguishable from eggs of Hammond's and Gray Flycatchers.* Incubation by female; 12–15 days.
Notes: Nests of Dusky Flycatcher and those of Hammond's Flycatcher sometimes confused. Dusky typically nests low in crotch of bush; Hammond's on horizontal branch of tree, usually high. Gray Flycatcher is bird of sagebrush plains that builds a bulkier, less tidy nest than Dusky.

GRAY FLYCATCHER *Empidonax wrightii* Pl. 16

Breeding range: S.-cen. Washington, e. Oregon (unc.), ne. California, s. Idaho, sw. Wyoming, south to Nevada, Utah, w. and cen. Colorado, n. Arizona (unc.), w. New Mexico.
Habitat: Predominately sagebrush plains; semiarid flats overgrown with desert underbrush or junipers.

Nest: In loose colonies in favorable habitat (sagebrush and winter-killed thornbush). Low in bark-filled crotches of bushes; blend with surroundings. Of sloughed-off strips of bark; lined with wool, animal hair, feathers. Outside diam. $3\frac{2}{3}$ in. (9.4 cm), height 4 in. (10.2 cm); inside diam. 2 in. (5.1 cm), depth $1\frac{1}{2}$ in. (3.8 cm).
Eggs: 3–4; av. 17.7 x 13.4 mm. Oval or short-oval. Creamy white. *Indistinguishable from eggs of Dusky Flycatcher.* Incubation by female; 14 days. 2 broods.
Notes: Author found nests in loose colony on Mono Lake flats, California, all built in lower branches of sagebrush. Into body and lining of 1 nest were built 36 small white cocoons and several hundred tiny feathers.

WESTERN FLYCATCHER *Empidonax difficilis* Pl. 16

Breeding range: Washington to w. and cen. Montana, south through mountains to Mexico, w. Texas; also S. Dakota (Black Hills).
Habitat: Moist, shaded deciduous forests preferred; also coniferous and mixed woods. Common near settlements.
Nest: Typically near or on ground (bank) or up to 30 ft. (9.2 m) above. Nesting sites include roots of upturned tree, top of low stump, crotch of small tree, behind slab of loose bark, side of oak tree trunk, beams in unoccupied buildings. Female builds with green and dry moss, lichens, strips of bark, dry and green leaves, grass stems; lining of fine strips of shredded bark, dry grass, hair, feathers, trash. Same site often used in successive years. Outside diam. 4 in. (10.2 cm), height 2 in. (5.1 cm); inside diam. $2\frac{1}{4}$ in. (5.7 cm), depth $1\frac{3}{4}$ in. (4.5 cm).
Eggs: 3–4, rarely 5; av. 16.8 x 13.1 mm. Oval to short-oval. No gloss. Dull white or creamy white; spotted and blotched with

WESTERN FLYCATCHER

browns, usually concentrated about large end. Incubation by female; 14-15 days. 2 broods.

Notes: In building, birds use whatever material readily available: thread, string, burlap, paper, human hair, yarn, horsehair, straw, wood chips, onion skin.

BUFF-BREASTED FLYCATCHER   *Empidonax fulvifrons*

Breeding range: Mexican and Central American species that breeds in U.S. only in se. Arizona, sw. New Mexico.

Habitat: Lower elevations of mountains in open stands of pine, oak, sycamore; riparian groves.

Nest: Deeply hollowed cup of lichenlike leaves, forbs, held together with spider silk; lined with fine grasses, rootlets, hair, feathers. Saddled on horizontal live limb or stub against tree trunk often with protecting branch directly overhead. Similar to nest of Blue-gray Gnatcatcher.

Eggs: 2-4, generally 3; av. 15.5 x 11.9 mm. Unmarked, creamy white. Female builds and incubates alone.

COUES' FLYCATCHER   *Contopus pertinax*

Breeding range: S. Arizona and s. New Mexico.

Habitat: Sycamore canyons, pine and pine-oak forests as high as 10,000 ft. (3050 m).

Nest: Firmly plastered to horizontal fork high in pine, sycamore, or other tall tree. Compactly made of fine grasses, forb stems, bits of dry leaves; decorated with lichens often selected to match those naturally growing on nest limb; deep interior lined with fine yellow grasses.

Eggs: 3-4; av. 21.1 x 15.8 mm. Oval. No gloss. White, sparingly marked with small brown spots or dots.

EASTERN WOOD PEWEE   *Contopus virens*

Breeding range: Mississippi Valley from Minnesota to Louisiana; also N. Dakota, e. S. Dakota (unc.), e. Nebraska, Kansas, e. and cen. Oklahoma.

Habitat: Mature forests, farm woodlots, orchards, parks, borders of fields, clearings, roadsides.

Nest: On horizontal tree limb, live or dead, typically far out from trunk, 15-65 ft. (4.6-19.8 m) above ground. Dainty, shallow, thick-walled cup of grasses, forb stems, plant fibers, spider webs, hair; lined with finer pieces of same materials, covered on outside with lichens. From below looks like lichen-covered knot or piece of fungus on limb; small for size of bird. Built entirely by female. Outside diam. 2¾ in. (7.1 cm), height 1¾ in. (4.5 cm); inside diam. 1¾ in. (4.5 cm), depth 1¼ in. (3.2 cm).

Eggs: 3, occasionally 2, rarely 4; av. 18.24 x 13.65 mm. Oval to

EASTERN WOOD PEWEE

short-oval. Shell smooth, no gloss. Creamy white, with brown blotches, spots. Female incubates; 12–13 days.
Notes: Of 18 nests found by author, 14 in oak. All but 1 inaccessible for study or photography; all far from trunk.

WESTERN WOOD PEWEE *Contopus sordidulus* Pl. 17

Breeding range: Washington south to Baja, east to Montana and south to Arizona and New Mexico; also sw. N. Dakota (prob.), w. S. Dakota, nw. Nebraska, w. Kansas (prob.), Oklahoma (Cimarron Co.), Minnesota (Roseau Co., 1977).
Habitat: Coniferous, deciduous, mixed forests; orchards, towns, cultivated valleys, canyons.
Nest: Saddled to horizontal limb or fork, dead or live, in great variety of trees (aspens often chosen) generally 15–40 ft. (4.6–12.2 m) above ground. Shallow cup of small bits of plant fiber, cottonwood or other down, fine dry grass, bud scales, neatly woven and decorated outside with bits of gray moss; lined with dry grass. Larger, more compact, more deeply hollowed than nest of Eastern Wood Pewee. Outside diam. $3\frac{1}{3}$ in. (8.5 cm), height $2\frac{5}{8}$ in. (6.6 cm); inside diam. $1\frac{7}{8}$ in. (4.8 cm), depth $1\frac{1}{3}$ in. (3.4 cm).
Eggs: 3, sometimes 2, rarely 4; av. 18.3 x 13.6 mm. Oval to short-oval. Shell smooth, no gloss. Creamy white, wreathed with brown blotches, spots. Similar to eggs of Vermilion Flycatcher but typically less heavily marked. Incubation by female, probably about 12 days. Polygyny has been observed (Colorado) in this species.
Notes: Of 9 nests found by author in Arizona, only 2 were under

30 ft. (9.1 m) above ground; of 4 nests found in Lassen Co., California, 3 were in pines only about 8 ft. (2.4 m) from ground. All contained 3 eggs.

OLIVE-SIDED FLYCATCHER *Nuttallornis borealis* Pl. 17

Breeding range: Washington to w. Montana, south to Mexico and Texas (Guadalupe Mts., cas.); also S. Dakota (Black Hills, poss.).

Habitat: Cool coniferous forests, open woodlands, forest burns, boreal bogs, muskeg.

Nest: On horizontal branch of conifer (usually well out from trunk), hidden among needles in cluster of upright twigs, 7–50 ft. (2.1–15.3 m) above ground. In some regions deciduous trees favored, especially birches, aspens, and maples, and eucalyptus in California. Flat saucer-shaped platform of twigs, rootlets, lichens; lined with pine needles, fine rootlets, and mosses. Outside diam. 5–6 in. (12.7–15.2 cm), height 2⅛ in. (5.4 cm); inside diam. 2½ in. (6.4 cm), depth 1 in. (2.5 cm).

Eggs: 3, rarely 2 or 4; av. 21.7 x 16.1 mm. Oval, occasionally short-oval. Shell smooth, lusterless. Creamy white to light buff, wreathed at larger end with blotches, spots of brown. Incubation by female; 16–17 days. 1 brood.

Notes: Author found nest with 3 eggs which was destroyed on June 28; 12 days later female had new nest and was incubating 3 eggs. This nest was destroyed. 16 days later same female incubating 3 eggs in new nest, which was successful.

VERMILION FLYCATCHER *Pyrocephalus rubinus* Pl. 17

Breeding range: Arizona, New Mexico, s. and w. Texas; also California (San Bernardino Co.), s. Nevada, s. Utah (unc.), w. Oklahoma (poss.).

Habitat: River bottoms, roadsides, deserts, willow and cottonwood thickets, dry washes.

Nest: On horizontal crotches or forks 8–60 ft. (2.4–18.3 m) above ground in willow, sycamore, mesquite, cottonwood, oak, paloverde, hackberry, or others. Flat, well made of dead twigs, forb stalks, fine grasses, rootlets, dry leaves, lichens, bark, cocoons, spider silk; lined with similar material, plant down, hair, fur, feathers. Usually deep in tree fork; very inconspicuous. Outside diam. 2½–3 in. (6.4–7.6 cm), height 2 in. (5.1 cm); inside diam. 1¾–2 in. (4.5–5.1 cm), depth 1 in. (2.5 cm).

Eggs: Typically 3, sometimes 2, rarely 4; av. 17.4 x 13.1 mm. Oval or short-oval, sometimes elliptical. No gloss. White to creamy white; heavily marked, chiefly near larger end, with dark brown and underlying lavender blotches or spots. Similar to eggs of Western Wood Pewee; more heavily marked. Female incubates; 12 days. Possibly 2 broods.

BEARDLESS FLYCATCHER   *Camptostoma imberbe*

Breeding range: S. Arizona, sw. New Mexico (Hidalgo Co.), extreme s. Texas (Rio Grande delta, cas.).
Habitat: Mesquite thickets, dry washes, cottonwoods, willows.
Nest: Typically far out on horizontal limb, up to 50 ft. (15.3 m) above ground. Often in mistletoe. Domed, thick-walled, of grasses and fine forbs; lined with plant down, fur, feathers. Height of globe about 4 in. (10.2 cm).
Eggs: Commonly 3; av. 16.5 x 12.2 mm. Oval. No gloss. White, finely sprinkled with brown spots or dots.
Notes: This species has been observed nesting in willow that contained tent caterpillar webs. Attached to a triangular web, nest is almost invisible.

SKYLARK   *Alauda arvensis*

Notes: Introduced onto Vancouver I., British Columbia, Canada, in 1903 and 1913. Two nests, 1 with 3 eggs and 1 with 4 young, were discovered on San Juan I., Washington, on May 17, 1970, marking the 1st nesting in continental U.S. About 12 pairs of Skylarks were in the area. Vancouver I. is approximately 15 miles (24.1 km) from San Juan I.

HORNED LARK   *Eremophila alpestris*   Pl. 17

Breeding range: All western states.
Habitat: Open grasslands, farmlands, prairies, tundras, airports, beaches, golf courses, cemeteries, parklands.
Nest: In hollow in ground, typically beside or partially under grass tuft or clod of dry manure (western grasslands and prairies). Shallow cup of coarse stems, leaves; lined with fine grasses. One side of nest rim often lined with "paving" of small pebbles or clods forming patio or doorstep. Female alone builds; 2–4 days. Outside diam. 3¼ x 4 in. (8.3 x 10.2 cm), height 2 in. (5.1 cm); inside diam. 2 x 2½ in. (5.1 x 6.4 cm), depth 1½ in. (3.8 cm).
Eggs: 3–5, usually 4 (fewer in early nests); av. 21.6 x 15.7 mm. Commonly oval. Shell smooth, little or no gloss. Pale gray or grayish white, occasionally with greenish tinge; blotched and spotted with browns (salt-and-pepper appearance). Incubation by female alone; 11 days. 2 or 3 broods.
Notes: Often nests in Feb., March; many nestings destroyed by heavy snows and freezing weather. Nest rarely well-concealed from above but fits into environment so closely that search for nest without observing birds' behavior is usually fruitless. Incubating female leaves nest when intruder 25–100 yds. (22.9–91.4 m) or more away.

VIOLET-GREEN SWALLOW *Tachycineta thalassina*

Breeding range: Washington to Montana, south to Mexico, sw. Texas; also S. Dakota (Black Hills).
Habitat: Open deciduous and coniferous forests, farms, parks, towns, cliffs.
Nest: Sometimes in colonies, often singly, in variety of places: natural cavities or old woodpecker holes in live or dead trees, holes in cliffs, crannies in houses, birdhouses. Built of straws, dry grasses; lined with abundance of feathers. *Indistinguishable from nest of Tree Swallow.*
Eggs: 4–5, sometimes 6; av. 18.7 x 13.1 mm. Oval. White, no markings. *Indistinguishable from eggs of Tree Swallow.* Incubation by female; 13–14 days. 1 brood.
Notes: Violet-greens often nest near Tree Swallows, sometimes competing for nest holes. May occupy same tree with bluebirds, nuthatches, woodpeckers, wrens. In a number of colonial situations it appeared to author that Violet-greens chose highest of available cavities.

TREE SWALLOW *Iridoprocne bicolor*   Pl. 17

Breeding range: Washington to Minnesota, south to Baja, Arizona (Coconino Co., cas.), New Mexico (unc.), Texas (cas.); recent record for Barton Co., Kansas; probably does *not* breed in Oklahoma, Arkansas, Louisiana.
Habitat: Typically near water in marshes, mountain meadows, parks, lakeshores, river bottomlands, wooded swamps.
Nest: Commonly solitary, also in colonies where suitable tree

TREE SWALLOW

cavities or birdhouses are available; in old woodpecker holes, fenceposts, rural mailboxes, holes in buildings, holes in rocky cliffs. Material is accumulation of dry grass, hollowed in center or in corner; lined with feathers, often placed so tips curve over eggs. Female builds, taking a few days to 2 weeks. *Indistinguishable from nest of Violet-green Swallow.*

Eggs: 3–8, commonly 5–7; av. 18.7 x 13.2 mm. Oval to long-oval. Shell smooth, without gloss. Pure white. *Indistinguishable from eggs of Violet-green Swallow.*

Notes: Eggs in 115 California nests: 4 sets of 3; 10 of 4; 28 of 5; 52 of 6; 20 of 7; 1 of 8. Apartment houses for Purple Martins and Wood Duck boxes attract nesting pairs.

BANK SWALLOW *Riparia riparia* Pl. 17

Breeding range: Almost all western states. Apparently *not* in Arkansas, Oklahoma, Louisiana, s. Missouri, w. S. Dakota; deserts, and rain forests of Northwest.

Habitat: Banks of rivers, lakes, creeks; gravel pits, road cuts.

Nest: Dense colonies (as many as several hundred nests). In burrows dug by both sexes, using feet and bill, at rate of about 5 in. (12.7 cm) per day. Floor of chamber flat, ceiling arched. Straw and grass stalks gathered by both sexes. Feathers added after incubation begun. Burrows 15–47 in. (38.1–119.4 cm) deep, av. 28 in. (71.1 cm); 4–12 in. (10.2–30.5 cm) apart; outside opening 1½ x 2¼ in. (3.8 x 5.7 cm).

BANK SWALLOW nesting colony

Eggs: 4–6, commonly 5 (*av. clutch smaller* than that of Rough-winged Swallow); av. 17.9 x 12.7 mm. Oval to short-oval; *shorter* than Rough-winged eggs. Shell smooth, no gloss. Pure white. Incubation by both sexes; 15 days, begun before clutch complete.
Notes: More burrows dug in colony than actually occupied. Obstacles (rocks) often halt 1st efforts. Unmated or young birds start, never finish tunnels. Colonies have been reported in sawdust piles and in dry well walls.

ROUGH-WINGED SWALLOW

ROUGH-WINGED SWALLOW   Pl. 17
Stelgidopteryx ruficollis

Breeding range: All western states.
Habitat: Banks of creeks and rivers, highway cuts, steep escarpments, often in colony of Bank Swallows.
Nest: Generally solitary; *do not colonize* like Bank Swallows although favorable nest site may attract several pairs. Typically a burrow in bank. May be in crevice in side of building, cave, quarry; cranny under bridge, culvert, wharf; in drainpipe or gutter. Bulky nest at end of tunnel; of twigs, bark, roots, and forbs; lined with finer grasses. No feathers in lining.
Eggs: 4–8, commonly 5–7 (*av. clutch larger* than that of Bank Swallow); av. 18.3 x 13.2 mm. Long-oval (*longer* than Bank Swallow eggs). Shell smooth, slightly glossy. Pure white. Incubation by both sexes; 16 days. 1 brood.

BARN SWALLOW

Notes: Rough-wings capable of excavating own nesting cavity but prefer tunnels already available. No nest site found by author was excavated by birds themselves; most in abandoned Belted Kingfisher holes.

BARN SWALLOW *Hirundo rustica*   Pl. 17

Breeding range: All western states.
Habitat: Farmlands, rural or suburban areas, villages.
Nest: Often in colonies around many kinds of structures, especially barns and other farm outbuildings; also under bridges, wharves, boathouses, culverts. Formerly, now rarely, on cliffs, in caves, and niches in rocks. Of mud and straw plastered to beams, upright walls, eaves; profusely lined with poultry feathers, usually white. Nest has semicircular top, tapers downward in cone shape. Both birds build, carrying mud pellets in beaks. Female more active in lining. Building requires 6–8 days. Egg-laying may be delayed after nest complete. Old nests often repaired for new brood.
Eggs: 4–5, sometimes 6; av. 18.8 x 13.5 mm. Oval to long-oval. Shell smooth, has no gloss. White, spotted and dotted with browns. *Indistinguishable from eggs of Cliff Swallow.* Both sexes incubate, about 15 days, changing about every 15 minutes during day; female at night with male perched nearby. Starts before clutch complete. 1 and 2 broods reported.
Notes: As many as 55 nests reported in 1 barn; 6–8 common. Several instances of nesting on moving boats reported.

CLIFF SWALLOW *Petrochelidon pyrrhonota* **Pl. 18**

Breeding range: All western states.
Habitat: Farmlands, villages, cliffs, fresh- or salt-water areas, typically in open country.
Nest: In dense colonies; hundreds of nests may occupy site (approximately 800 reported in 1 colony). Plastered to sides of buildings, bridges; under eaves of barns, houses, public buildings; to cliff faces. Gourd-shaped, of pellets of mud and clay; narrows from globular chamber outward to entrance tunnel with opening downward. Tunnel may be 5–6 in. (12.7–15.2 cm) long, may be absent. Chamber lined sparsely with grass, hair, feathers. Both sexes build, gathering mud in mouth at puddles shared with other pairs. Typical nest contains 900–1200 mud pellets. Building requires 1–2 weeks. Av. for 15 nests: overall length 7¾ in. (19.7 cm); width at base 6⅓ in. (16 cm); opening 1¾ in. (4.4 cm) high, 2 in. (5.1 cm) wide.
Eggs: 2–6, commonly 3–5; av. 20.3 x 13.9 mm. Oval to long-oval. Shell smooth, without gloss. White, spotted and dotted with shades of brown. *Indistinguishable from eggs of Barn Swallow.* Incubation by both sexes; about 15 days. 1 brood, perhaps 2 occasionally.
Notes: Known to add mud front to old Bank Swallow tunnel to use as nest. Have converted Robin, phoebe, and Barn Swallow nests for use. May attach nest to tree trunk.

CAVE SWALLOW *Petrochelidon fulva*

Breeding range: Cen., s., and w. Texas in at least 29 colonies in several counties; locally in se. New Mexico.
Habitat: Twilight zone of limestone caves; sinkholes, culverts.
Nest: In colonies at various heights above ground, typically on walls of caves in isolated crevices, pockets, overhanging ledges; also on walls of culverts. An unroofed half-cup shell of pellets of mud and/or guano, lined with feathers and plant fibers. Used year after year, becoming progressively larger as more pellets are added. Usually well screened in all directions from neighboring nests.
Eggs: 2–5, commonly 4; av. 19.5 x 14.0 mm. Oval to long-oval. Shell smooth, without gloss. White; spotted and dotted with shades of brown. *Indistinguishable from eggs of Cliff and Barn Swallows.*
Notes: Although in U.S. known to nest almost exclusively in caves and sinkholes, has recently been discovered nesting with Barn Swallows and, to lesser extent, Cliff Swallows in Texas highway culverts. In Mexico, Cave Swallows commonly nest with other swallows. Cave-nesting may be way of meeting competition with Cliff Swallows for nesting sites. Cave Swallows do not enter caves beyond twilight zone, and are incapable of special acoustic orientation like that of Oilbirds (*Steatornis*) of South America.

PURPLE MARTIN *Progne subis*   **Pl. 18**

Breeding range: Washington to Baja mainly west of Cascade-Sierra divide (unc.); locally in Rockies and Great Plains from Wyoming south to s. Arizona, s. New Mexico, Texas; also cen. and e. N. Dakota and Minnesota south to Gulf Coast.

Habitat: Open or lumbered forests, towns, farms, Saguaro deserts.

Nest: In colonies or often single. More likely in West than East to be in natural site such as old woodpecker hole, less common in birdhouses. Also in eaves, cornices, drainpipes, holes in outdoor signs, roofs of picnic shelters. Of leaves, grass, trash, some mud; commonly lined with small green leaves. Old nests often renovated. Males arrive first, establish territory. Both sexes build. Nest usually started 1 month before eggs laid.

Eggs: 5, sometimes 4, rarely 6; av. 24.5 x 17.5 mm. Oval to long-oval. Shell smooth, has slight gloss. Pure white. Incubation by female; probably 15–16 days. 1 brood, rarely 2. Polygamy observed (in each case, 1 male mated with 2 females).

Notes: Ground nests rare, but colony has nested among large boulders on islets in Lake Mille Lacs, Minnesota.

PURPLE MARTIN
nesting gourds

BLUE JAY

GRAY JAY *Perisoreus canadensis*

Breeding range: Washington to w. Montana, south to Baja, Arizona, New Mexico (cas.); also S. Dakota (Black Hills), ne. and n.-cen. Minnesota.

Habitat: Coniferous forests, tamarack swamps, wilderness areas.

Nest: On branch near trunk or in upright crotch of conifer 4–30 ft. (1.2–9.2 m) above ground, commonly 6–8 ft. (1.8–2.4 m). Bulky, compact; of strips of bark, sticks, twigs, grasses, spider web, cocoons, catkins; thick insulating lining of bark, fine grasses, feathers (grouse), hair, fur. Outside diam. 7–8 in. (17.8–20.3 cm), height 3–5 in. (7.6–12.7 cm); inside diam. 3–3½ in. (7.6–8.9 cm), depth 2–2½ in. (5.1–6.4 cm).

Eggs: 2–5, typically 3–4; av. 29.4 x 21.3 mm. Oval, rarely short-oval. Shell smooth, glossy. Pale gray to pale greenish, evenly spotted or peppered with gray or olive-buff. Incubation by female; 16–18 days. 1 brood.

Notes: Birds nest so early that snow is often deep on ground. Good insulation needed to protect eggs and young. Suspected of storing material (deer hair) before use in nesting.

BLUE JAY *Cyanocitta cristata*   Pl. 18

Breeding range: East of Rockies — se. Montana to Minnesota south to e. and cen. Texas and Gulf Coast.

Habitat: Oak woods, pine plantings, farms, parks, cities.

Nest: Bulky, in crotch or outer branch of coniferous or deciduous tree, 5–50 ft. (1.5–15.3 m) above ground, commonly 10–25 ft. (3.1–7.6 m). Built by both sexes. Of thorny twigs, bark, mosses, string, leaves; lined with rootlets. Outside diam. 7–8 in. (17.8–20.3 cm), height 4–4½ in. (10.2–11.4 cm); inside diam. 3½–4 in. (8.9–10.2 cm), depth 2½ in. (6.4 cm).

Eggs: 3–6, commonly 4–5; av. 28.02 x 20.44 mm. Uniformly oval. Shell smooth, slightly glossy. 2 distinct ground colors: greenish (usual) or buff, rarely a bluish type; marked with dark brown, grayish dots and spots. Incubation by both sexes, probably mostly by female; 17–18 days. 1 or 2 broods.

Notes: Hybrids between Blue and Steller's Jays observed in Colorado. For a typically noisy bird, is remarkably quiet around its nest. Some incubating birds flush quickly, others have been lifted from nest. Frequently nest near houses, sometimes on porch vines or trellises.

STELLER'S JAY *Cyanocitta stelleri*   Pl. 18

Breeding range: Washington to Montana south to Mexico and w. Texas (Guadalupe Mts.).

Habitat: Coniferous forests, mixed woods of pine and oak.

Nest: In trees, usually conifers, sometimes in shrubs or bushes, 8–40 ft. (2.4–12.2 m) above ground, av. 15–25 ft. (4.6–7.6 m). Both sexes build large rough-looking structure of plant fibers, dry leaves, moss, sticks, trash, mixed with mud; lined with coarse rootlets and pine needles inside mud base. Nest often contains paper in base. Outside diam. 10–17 in. (25.4–43.2 cm), height 6–7 in. (15.2–17.8 cm); inside diam. 4¼–5 in. (10.8–12.7 cm), depth 2¼–3½ in. (5.7–8.9 cm).

Eggs: 3–5, usually 4; av. 31.4 x 22.5 mm. Oval. Slightly glossy. Pale greenish blue or bluish green, marked with fine brown or olive dots and spots. Incubation entirely or mostly by female; probably 17–18 days.

Notes: Hybrids between Steller's and Blue Jays observed in Colorado. 1 nest found by author in California contained newspaper, facial tissue, a piece of Japanese rice paper 12 in. (30.5 cm) long dangling beneath. Birds quiet in vicinity of nest but make great outcry when nest discovered.

SCRUB JAY *Aphelocoma coerulescens*   Pl. 18

Breeding range: Sw. Washington south to Baja; s. Idaho, sw. Wyoming (rare) south to Texas (Trans-Pecos); also Oklahoma (Cimarron Co.).

Habitat: Woodlands with scrub cover, mesquite, deserts, canyons, foothills, stream bottomlands.

Nest: In trees, bushes, shrubs, usually fairly low, 3–30 ft. (0.9–9.2 m) above ground. Compactly built, well-constructed platform of twigs, mixed with moss and dry grass, lined with hair and fine roots (no mud). Sizes of 4 California nests measured by author: outside diam. 13–23 in. (33.0–58.4 cm), height 5–7 in. (12.7–

17.8 cm); inside diam. 4–5 in. (10.2–12.7 cm), depth 2½–3¼ in. (6.4–8.3 cm). Both sexes build, one guards as other carries material.

Eggs: 4–6, commonly 3–4; av. 27.6 x 20.5 mm. Oval, rarely long-oval. Two recognized types: more common green type is pale- to lichen-green, marked with spots, dots, and blotches of deep olive; red type is grayish white to green, dotted and spotted with shades of reddish brown. Incubation by female (possibly male); about 16 days.

MEXICAN JAY   *Aphelocoma ultramarina*   Pl. 18

Breeding range: S. Arizona, sw. New Mexico, w. Texas (Chisos Mts.).

Habitat: Oak forests, wooded canyons.

Nest: In tree, commonly live oak, 6–49 ft. (1.8–15.0 m) above ground. Loosely built bulky nest of sticks and twigs broken from trees, not picked up from ground; lined with closely woven rootlets, fine grass, animal hair. Birds live in loose colonies on communal basis; often several birds assist in building nest. Pilfering of nest material within colony common. Typical nest: outside diam. 18 in. (45.7 cm), height 7½ in. (19.1 cm); inside diam. 4⅔ in. (11.8 cm), depth 3⅛ in. (7.9 cm).

Eggs: 4–5, sometimes 3; av. 30.28 x 22.26 mm. Oval to long-oval. Glossy. Arizona race (*A. u. arizonae*) lays *unmarked* greenish eggs (unique among jays); similar to Crissal Thrasher eggs but *greener, larger,* and *glossier.* Eggs of other races spotted and dotted with brown. Both sexes may incubate; about 16 days.

Notes: This species lives in flocks of as many as 20 birds that join in defending territory in which at least 2 pairs build nests. Non-breeders assist in nest building and later in feeding young. Most nest helpers are males.

GREEN JAY   *Cyanocorax yncas*   opp. p. 147

Breeding range: Rio Grande delta, southernmost Texas.

Habitat: Thickets and open forests with thick undergrowth.

Nest: Usually 5–15 ft. (1.5–4.6 m) above ground in small tree or shrub. Deeply cupped but thin-walled structure of thorny twigs; sparingly lined with fine rootlets, bits of vine, moss, dry grass, occasionally leaves.

Eggs: 3–5, commonly 4; av. 27.31 x 20.43 mm. Oval, sometimes short-oval. Shell close-grained, little or no gloss. Grayish white, occasionally pale greenish white, profusely spotted and blotched with shades of brown, gray, and lavender. Incubation by female, who is fed by male and possibly other members of flock; 17 days.

Notes: Flocks do not dissolve when nesting. Nest built mainly by single pair; other flock members may assist.

CHACHALACA

GREEN JAY

LICHTENSTEIN'S ORIOLE

BLACK-BELLIED WHISTLING-DUCK

LONG-BILLED THRASHER

OLIVE SPARROW

BROWN JAY *Psilorhinus morio*

Notes: First U.S. nesting of this species was recorded in 1974 near the Rio Grande R. west of Roma, Starr Co., Texas. In 1976 an estimated population of 40–50 birds was scattered along the river from below Falcon Dam to Fronton. Brown Jays apparently breed annually now in the area.

BLACK-BILLED MAGPIE *Pica pica* Pl. 18

Breeding range: Washington to w. and cen. N. Dakota and Minnesota (cas.) south through nw. California, Nevada, Utah, n. New Mexico, nw. Oklahoma, w. and cen. Kansas.
Habitat: Rangeland, open woodlands, thickets, brush-covered country.
Nest: In small colonies with scattered nests, typically in tall thorny bushes, sometimes in trees. A huge canopy of interlacing twigs and sticks over an inner bowl with base of mud or cow dung 8–10 in. (20.3–25.4 cm) in diam., 1–2 in. (2.5–5.1 cm) thick, and matted lining of fine rootlets or pine needles. Obscure entrance on one side of sphere; escape exit on opposite side. Both sexes build, requiring as much as 6 weeks. May use same nest in succeeding years, but new nest on top of old more likely. Entire structure ordinarily about 3 ft. (0.9 m) in diam. 1 Montana nest 4 ft. (1.2 m) across, 4 ft. (1.2 m) high; another in Washington 7 ft. (2.1 m) from top to bottom.
Eggs: 6–9, commonly 7, laid 1 a day; av. 32.54 x 22.86 mm. Short-oval, spherical, elliptical, or long-oval. Close-grained, little or no gloss. Greenish gray profusely spotted, flecked, and blotched with shades of brown. Incubation by female when clutch complete; about 18 days. 1 brood.
Notes: Kestrels, Long-eared owls, and Great Horned Owls use magpie spheres as nests; Black-crowned Night Herons, Sharp-shinned Hawks, and Mourning Doves use them as bases for nests.

YELLOW-BILLED MAGPIE

BLACK-BILLED MAGPIE nest

Opposite: Texas (Rio Grande Valley) Birds

YELLOW-BILLED MAGPIE   *Pica nuttalli*

Breeding range: Only in California, centered in Sacramento and San Joaquin valleys and adjacent foothills. Range does not overlap that of Black-billed Magpie.
Habitat: River-bottom cottonwoods, foothill oaks, parklike groves, mixed cover of oaks, ceanothus, pines.
Nest: In scattered colonies. 40–60 ft. (12.2–18.3 m) above ground, often in mistletoe clumps or in trees with clumps of mistletoe. (From ground, nest resembles clump.) Much like nests of closely related Black-billed Magpie: twigs and long sticks, sometimes bound together with mud. Both sexes build, requiring several weeks. Typically, outside diam. 2½ ft. (0.8 m); height about 3 ft. (0.9 m).
Eggs: 5–8, usually 7; av. 31.54 x 22.54 mm. Spherical to cylindrical. Olive-green or olive-buff; finely, evenly dotted and spotted with brown or olive. Laid about 10 days after nest completed. Incubation by female probably about 18 days ("21 days," Dawson).
Notes: Female close sitter. Leaves nest via hidden exit when disturbed. Pairs said to mate for life.

COMMON RAVEN   *Corvus corax*   **Pl. 18**

Breeding range: Washington to w. and s.-cen. Montana, south to Baja, Oklahoma (Cimarron Co.), sw. and cen. Texas; also ne. and n.-cen. Minnesota.
Habitat: Mountains, forests, canyons, deserts, rocky coasts; greatly varied and mostly inaccessible.
Nest: Mostly on cliff ledges or in coniferous trees. Large structure built of tree branches, sticks, twigs, vines; deeply hollowed, thickly lined with animal hair, mosses, grasses, bark shreds. Often built on top of nest of previous year. Outside diam. 2–4 ft. (0.6–1.2 m); inside diam. 1 ft. (30.5 cm), depth 6 in. (15.2 cm).
Eggs: 4–7, commonly 5–6; av. 49.53 x 32.76 (western race, *C. c. sinuatus*). Oval to long-oval. Shell slightly rough, little or no gloss. Greenish with brown or olive markings, variously patterned (*large version of American Crow eggs*). Incubation entirely or mostly by female; about 3 weeks.
Notes: Often a huge pile of sticks at base of cliff which have fallen as birds build above. This material untouched; other material brought in. Area around nest often "whitewashed" with excrement. In Oregon, an adult raven threw 8 stones at 2 students descending a cliff after inspecting nest containing 6 young. Bird picked stones up in bill and cast them in direction of intruders.

WHITE-NECKED RAVEN   *Corvus cryptoleucus*   **Pl. 19**

Breeding range: Se. Arizona, s. and e. New Mexico, se. Colorado, sw. Kansas, w. Oklahoma, w. Texas.

Comparative egg size: COMMON RAVEN (*left*); COMMON CROW (*right*)

WHITE-NECKED RAVEN nest in farm machine

Habitat: Deserts, open plains, arid farmlands, extending into foothills (New Mexico).

Nest: In solitary trees, shrubs (mesquite), on old buildings, windmills, abandoned farm machinery, utility poles. Sometimes colonial where there is a concentration of suitable nest sites. Loosely built by female of sticks, thorny twigs, sometimes interlaced with trash (rags, rope, newspapers); inner cup deeply hollowed, smoothly lined with cattle- or horse-hair, fur, grass, inner bark, and bits of trash. Generally filthy and foul-smelling from excrement. Nests made entirely of wire strands not uncommon. Old nests often repaired from year to year, some several layers high. Typical nest: outside diam. 20 in. (50.8 cm); inside diam. 8 in. (20.3 cm), depth 5 in. (12.7 cm).

Eggs: 3–8, usually 5; av. 44.20 x 30.22 mm. Mostly oval. Pale green to grayish green; spotted, blotched, streaked with brown and lavender. Generally *paler* than eggs of other Corvidae. Both sexes said to incubate (Bendire in Bent); probably 18–19 days. 1 brood.

Notes: Nests unusually late for *Corvus*. Most nests built in June; may be tied to rainy season in arid country, when food is normally more abundant after rains commence.

COMMON CROW *Corvus brachyrhynchos*   Pl. 19

Breeding range: All western states.

Habitat: Many types of open country; deciduous, coniferous woods; farmlands, parks, suburbs. Generally avoids deserts and dense coniferous forests.

Nest: Single or rarely in small colonies. In trees, shrubs, on utility poles. Generally placed in crotch or near tree trunk on supporting limbs, 10–70 ft. (3.1–21.4 m) above ground, av. over 25 ft. (7.6 m). Large substantial basket of sticks, twigs, bark, and vines with some mud; lined with shredded bark fibers, moss, grass, feathers, fur, hair, roots, leaves. Built by both sexes; takes about 12 days. Outside diam. 22 x 26 in. (55.9 x 66.0 cm), height 9 in. (22.9 cm); inside diam. 6 x 7 in. (15.2 x 17.8 cm), depth 4½ in. (11.4 cm).

Eggs: 4–7, commonly 5–6; av. 41.1 x 28.8 mm (western race, *C. b. hesperis*). Typically oval. Shell slightly rough, has some gloss. Bluish or grayish green, irregularly blotched, spotted with browns and grays. Incubation said to be by both sexes (Bent); 18 days. 1 or 2 broods. Eggs vary considerably in shape, size, color, markings.

Notes: Breeding ranges of Common Crow, Fish Crow, and Northwestern Crow overlap only in limited areas. Eggs are *indistinguishable* except for slightly larger size of Common Crow eggs. Calls of the 3 species differ.

NORTHWESTERN CROW *Corvus caurinus*

Breeding range: Coastal Washington only.

Habitat: Wooded shores, beaches, islands, villages.

Nest: Sometimes in small loose-knit colonies, or in scattered pairs. Exterior of sticks, twigs, mud; lined with cedar bark, grass, hair; placed in tree, shrub, in recesses of rocks, on ground under overhanging boulders, beneath bushes and windfalls. Smaller than nest of Common Crow.

Eggs: 4–5; av. 40.4 x 28.2 mm. Oval. Shell slightly rough, with some gloss. Bluish or grayish green, irregularly blotched and spotted with browns and grays. *Indistinguishable from eggs of Common Crow except for smaller size.*

Notes: Restricted to saltwater beaches, seldom straying more than a mile from tidal waters. Call differs from that of Common Crow.

FISH CROW   *Corvus ossifragus*

Breeding range: Se. Missouri (cas.), Arkansas, Oklahoma (Arkansas and Red rivers), s. Louisiana, Texas (Orange Co., rare).

Habitat: Wooded marine shorelines; brackish shores, islands, bays, rivers. Inland lakes, marshes, rivers.

Nest: Often in loose colonies, 2–4 pairs in same area; also solitary nests. In tops of tall trees, 20–80 ft. (6.1–24.4 m) above ground. Sticks, twigs, bark fibers; lined with bark strips, grasses, roots, paper, hair, feathers. Both sexes build. Outside diam. 14–18 in. (35.6–45.7 cm), height 10–14 in. (25.4–35.6 cm); inside diam. $6\frac{1}{2}$–$7\frac{1}{2}$ in. (16.5–19.1 cm), depth 5–6 in. (12.7–15.2 cm).

Eggs: 4–5, rarely more; av. 37.17 x 26.97 mm. Oval. Shell slightly rough, with some gloss. Bluish or grayish green, irregularly blotched and spotted with browns and grays. *Indistinguishable from eggs of Common Crow except for smaller size.* Both sexes said to incubate; 17–18 days. 1 brood.

Notes: Call differs from that of Common Crow.

MEXICAN CROW   *Corvus imparatus*

Notes: Although this species has not been found nesting in the U.S. at this time, the continuing appearance of a large flock at the Brownsville, Texas, dump is encouraging. Little is known of its breeding biology, but the habitat in extreme s. Texas appears favorable for breeding.

PINYON JAY   *Gymnorhinus cyanocephalus*   Pl. 19

Breeding range: Oregon to se. and s.-cen. Montana, south to Baja, cen. Arizona, s. New Mexico, sw. Texas; also S. Dakota (Black Hills), nw. Nebraska, Oklahoma (Cimarron Co.).

Habitat: Pinyon-juniper woodlands; pine-oak forests.

Nest: Single flocks that forage together throughout year nest colonially in areas with adequate food supply, often using same territory in succeeding years. Nest in pinyon-juniper placed 3–18 ft. (0.9–5.5 m) above ground; in Ponderosa Pine, $5\frac{1}{2}$–78 ft.

(1.7–23.8 m). Fairly bulky; outer platform usually of twigs; inner cup of shredded grass, paper, rootlets, pine needles, cloth, horsehair. Sexes participate equally in building. Pilfering material from nearby unattended nests common.

Eggs: 3–6, generally 3–4; av. 29.2 x 21.7 mm. Short-oval to long-oval. Slightly glossy. Pale bluish white, greenish white, grayish white, evenly covered with minute dots and spots of browns. Incubation by females alone (males form feeding flocks during this period; regularly feed females at nest); 16 days. 1 brood.

Notes: Pinyon Jays wander freely throughout colony's nesting area without much conflict, but each pair protects only its own nest and eggs.

CLARK'S NUTCRACKER   *Nucifraga columbiana*   Pl. 19

Breeding range: Washington to w. and cen. Montana, south to Baja, e. Arizona, w. New Mexico.

Habitat: High mountain ranges in Canadian and Hudsonian life zones in stands of juniper, Ponderosa Pine, larch.

Nest: Built early in season, often while snow is deep on ground; in conifer 8–45 ft. (2.4–13.7 m) above ground, usually well out on horizontal limb. Both sexes build platform of dry twigs, often juniper, matted together and reinforced by bark strips; inner cup deep and thick-walled, of fine bark strips quilted together with grasses and pine straw but apparently without fur or feathers. Outside diam. 11–12 in. (27.9–30.5 cm), height 7 in. (17.8 cm); inside diam. 4–5 in. (10.2–12.7 cm), depth 3 in. (7.6 cm); walls about 1½ in. (3.8 cm) thick.

Eggs: 2–3, often 4, rarely more; av. 32.4 x 23.4 mm. Oval to long-oval. Slightly glossy. Pale tints of green, spotted and dotted thinly and evenly with browns or grays. Incubation by both sexes; 16–18 days. 1 brood.

Notes: Incubating bird well hidden in deep cup; sits very close, sometimes refusing to leave until picked up.

BLACK-CAPPED CHICKADEE   *Parus atricapillus*   Pl. 19

Breeding range: Washington to Minnesota, south to nw. California (unc.), n. Nevada, Utah, n. New Mexico, Kansas, n. Missouri.

Habitat: Deciduous and coniferous forests, woodlands.

Nest: In holes made by birds themselves in soft, rotting wood of dead stump or stub, typically 4–10 ft. (1.2–3.1 m) above ground; also in natural cavities, abandoned woodpecker holes, birdhouses. Both sexes excavate, scattering chips away from immediate area. Cavity lined by female with wool, hair, fur (rabbit), moss, feathers, insect cocoons, cottony fibers. Excavation requires 7–10 days, building 3–4 days. Entrance hole diam. 1⅜ in. (3.5 cm); diam. of cavity at rim of nest cup 2⅜ in. (6 cm), depth of cup 1 in. (2.5 cm).

Eggs: 5–10, commonly 6–8; av. 15.2 x 12.2 mm. Oval to short-oval. Shell smooth, very thin, little or no gloss. White; spotted and dotted with reddish brown, concentrated at larger end. *Indistinguishable from eggs of Carolina Chickadee.* More heavily marked than eggs of Mountain Chickadee. Incubation by female; 12–13 days. Before clutch complete, eggs kept covered with soft nest lining.

Notes: The distinctive call notes of Black-capped and Carolina Chickadees can be helpful in identifying a nest.

CAROLINA CHICKADEE   *Parus carolinensis*

Breeding range: S. Kansas, s. Missouri, south to e. Texas, Louisiana.

Habitat: Deciduous and coniferous forests, woodlands.

Nest: Both sexes excavate, 5–6 in. (12.7–15.2 cm) deep, in soft wood of rotting tree stub or stump, 5–6 ft. (1.5–1.8 m) above ground. Excavation requires up to 2 weeks. Loosened chips discarded away from vicinity of cavity. May also nest in natural cavity, abandoned woodpecker hole, birdhouse. Bottom of cavity thickly lined with moss, animal hair, fur, feathers, down. Entrance diam. 1½ in. (3.8 cm).

Eggs: 5–8, commonly 6; av. 14.8 x 11.5 mm. Oval to short-oval. Shell smooth, very thin, little or no gloss. White; rather evenly spotted and dotted with reddish brown, concentrated at larger end. *Indistinguishable from eggs of Black-capped Chickadee.* Incubation by female, 13 days.

MEXICAN CHICKADEE   *Parus sclateri*

Breeding range: Se. Arizona (Chiricahua Mts.), sw. New Mexico (Hidalgo Co.). Only chickadee in this range.

Habitat: Pine and spruce-fir forests, pine-oak woods at high altitudes.

Nest: Cavity excavated by birds in dead stub, lined mostly or entirely with fur and hair firmly felted together.

Eggs: Commonly 6; av. 14.3 x 11.1 mm. White, faintly marked with fine dots, spots of reddish brown; occasionally unmarked.

Notes: Brandt attracted this uncommon breeder in Arizona to 5 birdhouses in one season in Chiricahuas.

MOUNTAIN CHICKADEE   *Parus gambeli*   Pl. 19

Breeding range: Washington to w. and cen. Montana, south to Baja and w. Texas (Guadalupe Mts.).

Habitat: Coniferous forests from foothills to timberline.

Nest: May be in cavity excavated by birds, but natural cavity or abandoned woodpecker hole preferred. 1–80 ft. (0.3–24.4 m) above ground, typically 6–15 ft. (1.8–4.6 m), many less than 6 ft. (1.8 m). Cavity lined with mosses, fur, hair.

Eggs: Commonly 7–9 (sets of 10, 11, 12 have been seen); av.

15.6 x 12.3 mm. Oval to round-oval. Shell smooth, little or no gloss. White with much variety in extent of reddish brown markings; some unmarked. Less heavily marked than eggs of Black-capped.

Notes: Author found 8 nests in Lassen National Forest, California, in area where old logging operations and fires had left rotting stumps. Nests in cavities in soft wood from 18 in. (45.7 cm) to 4 ft. (1.2 m) above ground.

BOREAL CHICKADEE   *Parus hudsonicus*

Breeding range: Washington (Okanogan Co., prob.), nw. Montana, ne. and n.-cen. Minnesota.

Habitat: Coniferous and mixed forests, muskeg bogs.

Nest: In cavity, dug by both birds, in rotting stub or stump, 1–12 ft. (0.3–3.7 m) above ground, but usually below 3 ft. (0.9 cm). Also in natural tree cavities, abandoned woodpecker holes. Bottom lined with fur, hair, cottony plant down, bark strips, moss, feathers.

Eggs: 4–9, commonly 5–7; av. 15.3 x 12.3 mm (*P. h. hudsonicus*). Oval to short-oval. Shell smooth, little or no gloss. White; sparingly and unevenly sprinkled with reddish brown dots and small spots, often concentrated at larger end. Incubation probably by female; 12–13 days. 1 brood.

Notes: Nests difficult to find. Female sits tight while incubating; generally will not flush when stub is tapped.

BOREAL CHICKADEE

CHESTNUT-BACKED CHICKADEE *Parus rufescens*

Breeding range: Washington, Oregon, nw. California (coastal), n. Idaho, nw. Montana (unc.).

Habitat: Humid coastal belt, moist coniferous forests.

Nest: In cavity, usually less than 10 ft. (3.1 m) above ground, rarely to 80 ft. (24.4 m), dug by birds themselves in rotting stump or stub; also in natural cavity or abandoned woodpecker hole. Lined with mosses, hair, fur, small feathers, some trash.

Eggs: 5–8, commonly 6–7; av. 15.3 x 12.0 mm. Oval to short-oval, some slightly pointed. White; sparingly sprinkled with reddish brown dots, irregularly distributed or concentrated at larger end; occasionally unmarked.

Notes: May nest in loose colonies. 7 nests found within small area, some not more than 50 yds. (45.7 m) apart.

TUFTED TITMOUSE *Parus bicolor*　　　　**Pl. 19**
(including Black-crested Titmouse)

Breeding range: Se. S. Dakota (Union Co.) and se. Minnesota, south through Mississippi Valley to Gulf; also Nebraska (Missouri R.), e. Kansas, sw. Oklahoma, Texas.

Habitat: Moist woodlands, groves, deciduous and coniferous forests, suburban shade trees.

Nest: In natural tree cavity, abandoned woodpecker hole, 2–87 ft. (0.6–26.5 m) above ground; occasionally in birdhouse. Is not be-

TUFTED TITMOUSE

lieved to excavate own nest hole. Cavity lined with bark strips, dead leaves, moss, grass; nest cupped, padded with hair, fur, bits of string, cloth.

Eggs: 4–8, commonly 5–6; av. 18.4 x 14.1 mm. Oval to long-oval. Shell smooth, little or no gloss. White or creamy white; evenly speckled with small spots, dots, often concentrated at larger end. Eggs covered with nest material when unattended. Incubation by female only; 13–14 days. Male feeds incubating female after calling her from nest. Pair bonds appear to be permanent.

Notes: Female observed pulling hair for nest from a live squirrel's tail, a woodchuck's back, a man's head and beard. Like Great Crested Flycatcher, this species commonly uses shed snakeskins as nest material. Female sits tight.

PLAIN TITMOUSE *Parus inornatus*   Pl. 19

Breeding range: S. Oregon, s. Idaho, sw. Wyoming, south to Baja, Arizona, New Mexico, w. Texas (Guadalupe Mts., rare); also Oklahoma (Cimarron Co.).

Habitat: Deciduous woodlands, especially oaks; cottonwoods, forest edges, towns, parks, suburban gardens.

Nest: Up to 32 ft. (9.8 m) above ground in natural cavities in trees, old woodpecker holes, fenceposts, crevices in buildings; birdhouses. Naturally rotted cavities may be further excavated by birds. Nest hole filled with moss, grass, forb stems, fibers; lined with feathers and fur.

Eggs: 6–8, commonly 7; av. 17.4 x 13.4 mm. Mostly oval. No gloss. White; usually unmarked but occasionally with minute dots of pale reddish brown. Incubation probably by female alone; 14 days.

Notes: Female sits closely and may have to be removed from nest by hand to examine eggs. In California, of 14 pairs recaptured, 11 were mated together for at least 2 years; only 3 were not. Where birdhouses available, birds nested within 43–90 yds. (39.3–82.3 m) of each other.

BRIDLED TITMOUSE *Parus wollweberi*

Breeding range: S. Arizona and sw. New Mexico.

Habitat: Oak, pine-oak, and riparian woodlands.

Nest: Natural cavities or abandoned woodpecker holes, 4–20 ft. (1.2–6.1 m) above ground; also in birdhouses. Cavities lined on bottom and well up sides with mat of cottonwood down, shreds of grass, hair, fur, cottony materials.

Eggs: 5–7; av. 16.1 x 12.6 mm. Oval. White; no markings.

VERDIN *Auriparus flaviceps*   Pl. 20

Breeding range: Se. California, Nevada, sw. Utah, Arizona, New Mexico to w. and s. Texas.

Habitat: Low brushy deserts, mesquite thickets.
Nest: Oval-shaped ball of interlaced thorny twigs, firmly constructed, 6–8 in. (15.2–20.3 cm) in diam., placed conspicuously 2½–10 ft. (0.8–3.1 m) above ground in desert shrub or cactus (mesquite, hackberry, catclaw, cholla, Creosote Bush). Large for small bird. Entrance, near bottom, leads to interior cup made of grasses, leaves, and an abundance of feathers all bound together with spider silk. Well-insulated nests protect eggs and young from desert heat.
Eggs: 3–6, normally 4; av. 15.3 x 11.0 mm. Oval. No gloss. Pale greenish blue or green, dotted with reddish brown, chiefly around larger end. Probably 2 broods.
Notes: Abundance of nests found gives false impression of number of birds in area. Birds also build roosting nests and old nests are so firmly anchored they endure year after year, resulting in many unoccupied structures.

BUSHTIT *Psaltriparus minimus*   Pl. 20

Breeding range: Washington to Baja, s. Idaho to Arizona, s. Colorado (unc.), New Mexico, Oklahoma (Cimarron Co.), w. and cen. Texas.
Habitat: Deciduous and coniferous forests, forest edges, streamsides, thickets (alder), oak woodlands, chaparral, canyons.
Nest: Gourd-shaped hanging pocket 6–12 in. (15.2–30.5 cm) long, typically 8–9 in. (20.3–22.9 cm), woven into and supported by twigs and branches of tree or bush 6–35 ft. (1.8–10.7 m) above ground. Of mosses, lichens, leaves, cocoons, grasses, woven with spider silk; lined with plant down, wool, hair, feathers. Entrance hole in side near top. Both sexes build; 13–51 days. Material added during egg-laying and incubation.
Eggs: Commonly 5–7; av. 13.7 x 10.1 mm. Mostly oval. Little or no gloss. White, unmarked. Both sexes incubate; 12–13 days. Both birds spend night in nest. Probably 2 broods.
Notes: Pairs disturbed during nest-building, egg-laying, or incubation frequently desert and build 2nd nests, often with new mates. After nest is completed, birds may leave it for a while before laying eggs. 1 completed nest left unused for almost 30 days before eggs laid.

WHITE-BREASTED NUTHATCH *Sitta carolinensis* Pl. 20

Breeding range: All western states.
Habitat: Deciduous, coniferous, and mixed forests, orchards, village trees.
Nest: In natural cavity (sometimes surprisingly large) in tree, 15–50 ft. (4.6–15.3 m) above ground; in old woodpecker hole, birdhouse. Cavity lined by female with bark shreds, twigs, grasses, rootlets, fur, hair. Reported sometimes to excavate own cavity.
Eggs: 5–10, commonly 8; av. 18.9 x 14.2 mm (*S. c. nelsoni*). Oval

to short-oval. Shell smooth, very little gloss. White; usually heavily marked with light brown and lavender spots, often densest at larger end. *Similar to eggs of Red-breasted Nuthatch but larger.* Incubation by female, fed by male; reported to be 12 days. 1 brood. Pair bond may extend beyond 1 nesting season; may even be permanent.

RED-BREASTED NUTHATCH *Sitta canadensis*   Pl. 20

Breeding range: Washington to Montana, south to Mexico; also S. Dakota (Black Hills), Kansas (Riley Co.), ne. and n.-cen. Minnesota.
Habitat: Coniferous forests, mixed woodlands.
Nest: Generally in excavated cavity in rotted stub such as the branch of a dead tree, 5–40 ft. (1.5–12.2 m) above ground, av. 15 ft. (4.6 m); old woodpecker holes, rarely birdhouses. Cavity lined with bark shreds, grass, moss, feathers. Entrance hole diam. 1½ in. (3.8 cm); hole slants for 3–4 in. (7.6–10.2 cm) then goes straight down for about 4 in. (10.2 cm). Both birds smear pitch (resin) heavily around entrance to cavity, continuing to do so during nesting period.
Eggs: 4–7, commonly 5–6; av. 15.2 x 11.9 mm. Oval to short-oval or long-oval. Shell smooth, little or no gloss. White; heavily or sparingly spotted and dotted with reddish brown. *Similar to eggs of White-breasted Nuthatch but smaller.* Incubation by female; said to be 12 days. 1 brood.
Notes: Pitch around entrance may prevent insects, small mammals, or other birds from entering. To avoid pitch, female entering cavity generally flies straight in. Dead body of nuthatch has been found stuck to entrance hole.

BROWN-HEADED NUTHATCH *Sitta pusilla*

Breeding range: Se. Oklahoma, e.-cen. Texas, Arkansas, Louisiana.
Habitat: Open pine woods.
Nest: In old woodpecker hole in tree stump or stub, fencepost; sometimes both sexes dig cavity, usually less than 10 ft. (3.1 m) above ground. Cavity lined with pine-seed husks (occasionally make up entire nest), inner bark strips, wood chips, grasses, cotton, feathers.
Eggs: 3–9, commonly 5–6; av. 15.5 x 12.3 mm. Oval or short-oval. Shell smooth, practically no gloss. White; *profusely marked* (more than any other nuthatch eggs) with evenly distributed fine reddish brown dots, small spots, blotches. Incubation by female; said to be 14 days. 1 brood.
Notes: Birds usually caulk or "weather-strip" with pieces of cottony plant down any cracks, holes, crevices in cavity that might expose the nest to conditions outside.

PYGMY NUTHATCH *Sitta pygmaea* Pl. 20

Breeding range: Washington to w. and s. Montana, south to Mexico, Texas (Guadalupe Mts.); also S. Dakota (Black Hills, prob.).

Habitat: Pine forests, especially Ponderosa and Yellow Pine; also forests of fir and larch.

Nest: Cavity in rotted pine stub or dead limb excavated by birds themselves, typically 8–60 ft. (2.4–18.3 m) above ground; lined with shreds of bark, bits of cocoons, wool, plant down, feathers. Cavity commonly extends downward 8–10 in. (20.3–25.4 cm) from irregularly-shaped entrance hole.

Eggs: 4–9, usually 6–8; av. 15.3 x 11.9 mm. Oval to short-oval. No gloss. White; unevenly and sparingly sprinkled with fine reddish brown dots. Incubation probably entirely by female; about 14 days. 1 brood.

Notes: 17 nesting cavities examined by author in California had been laboriously dug by birds themselves. Cracks in walls were caulked with nest material, weatherproofing the cavities. One nest was in end of rotting log lying on ground; entrance 18 in. (45.7 cm) above ground.

BROWN CREEPER *Certhia familiaris* Pl. 20

Breeding range: Washington to Montana, south to Mexico, w. Texas (Guadalupe Mts., rare); also S. Dakota (Black Hills, unc.), ne. and n.-cen. Minnesota, e. Iowa (rare).

Habitat: Coniferous, deciduous, and mixed forests; timbered swamps.

BROWN CREEPER
nest behind loose
slab of bark

WRENTIT chaparral habitat

Nest: Behind loose slab of bark still attached to living or dead tree, av. 5–15 ft. (1.5–4.6 m) above ground. Foundation of twigs, leaves, bark shreds; lined with finer bark, grasses, feathers (occasionally), mosses. Shape of structure conforms to space in which placed; center neatly cupped; sides of nest continue upward, ending in points (crescent-shaped like hammock, half-moon). Female builds, male may carry material. Building prolonged; birds work intermittently up to 1 month.

Eggs: 4–8, commonly 5–6; av. 15.1 x 11.8 mm. Oval to short-oval. Shell smooth, little or no gloss. White or creamy white; peppered, spotted with reddish brown, sometimes wreathed. *Similar to eggs of Black-capped Chickadee.* Both sexes incubate; 14–15 days.

Notes: May occasionally nest in holes in trees if loose bark is not available. Author found nest behind shutter of summer cottage near lake. To attract birds, Californian nailed curled bark strips to trunks of sound trees; 6 pairs nested behind strips in area where 35–40 had been placed.

WRENTIT *Chamaea fasciata* **Pl. 20**

Breeding range: Coastal Oregon and California, also inland in suitable habitat; absent from California's Central Valley and se. deserts.

Habitat: Coastal and lowland chaparral, brushy banks of valley streams.

Nest: Commonly in chaparral, av. 18–24 in. (45.7–61.0 cm) above ground, supported by horizontal or vertical twigs built into or lashed to nest; leafy twigs screen it from view. A compact cup built by both sexes of bark fibers bound with spider silk, lined with fine fibers and sometimes hair or fine grasses. Completed nest often abandoned; another started nearby with much material from 1st nest used. Outside diam. about 4 in. (10.2 cm).

Eggs: 3–5, commonly 4; av. 18.1 x 14.5 mm. Oval. No gloss. Pale greenish blue; no markings. Incubation by female at night, both during day; 16 days. 1 brood; if nests destroyed, bird may lay up to 5 clutches in 1 year.

Notes: Pairs are said to mate for life and are constant companions throughout year. Territories average about 2 acres (0.8 ha) in chaparral.

DIPPER (WATER OUZEL) *Cinclus mexicanus* Pl. 20

Breeding range: Washington to w. Montana, south to Mexico, n. New Mexico; also S. Dakota (Black Hills, unc.).

Habitat: Along swift-flowing mountain streams from foothills to timberline.

DIPPER

Nest: Usually resting on ledge in precipitous rock wall close to rushing water where spray keeps it moist or even wet; sometimes fastened to large boulder in midstream; under streamside roots; many placed on supports under bridges over streams. Bulky domed exterior of living mosses with a few roots and blades of grass interwoven; interior cup of grasses and a few small leaves. Entrance on side 3 in. (7.6 cm) wide, 2 in. (5.1 cm) high during incubation, becoming much larger when nestlings present. Built by both sexes. With repairs, nests may be reused annually.
Eggs: 3–6, usually 4–5; av. 25.9 x 18.5 mm. Oval, sometimes long-oval. White; unmarked. Incubation by female alone; 16 days. Typically 1 brood (2 have been reported).
Notes: Author watched birds building behind a swift-moving cascade in Colorado mountains. Birds approached water on a slanting log, nest material in bill, then dove into the falls. Nest completely hidden from sight. Of 8 Montana nests observed in 1 season, 2 were newly constructed, others were old nests repaired.

HOUSE WREN   *Troglodytes aedon*   **Pl. 21**

Breeding range: All western states except Arkansas, Louisiana; Texas (only in Guadalupe Mts., rare).
Habitat: Thickets, open woods, gardens, farmlands.
Nest: In natural cavity in tree, stump, stub, fencepost; old woodpecker hole; often birdhouse. Male arrives first, establishes territory, builds dummy nests of twigs in many available nest sites. Female may or may not accept prechosen site; may or may not accept male's incomplete twig nest. On base of twigs, female builds cup of grasses, plant fibers, rootlets, feathers, hair, rubbish.
Eggs: 5–8, commonly 6–7; av. 16.3 x 12.6 mm (*T. a. parkmanii*). Oval to short-oval. Shell smooth, has slight gloss. White; thickly speckled with minute reddish or cinnamon-brown dots; colors deepest at larger end. Incubation by female alone; 12–15 days, typically 13. 2 broods.
Notes: In Morton Co., N. Dakota, 106 of 236 boxes erected for bluebirds were used by House Wrens. Unique sites: radiator of unused auto, top of pump, empty cow skull, old boot hanging on side of cabin, leg of workpants hanging on clothesline, flowerpot, pocket of scarecrow, crevice in old Swainson's Hawk nest, Bank Swallow burrow. May destroy nests, eggs, young of same or different species within their territory. Author saw House Wren puncture 4 eggs of Rufous-sided Towhee while female was absent from nest.

BROWN-THROATED WREN   **opp. p. 121**
Troglodytes brunneicollis (or *T. aedon* in part)

Notes: This Mexican species, which many ornithologists believe to be conspecific with the House Wren, nests commonly in mountains of se. Arizona. It was overlooked in the U.S. for years due to its

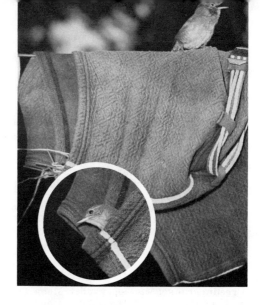

HOUSE WREN
nesting in swim
trunks

close resemblance to the House Wren. Its breeding biology is the
same as the latter's.

WINTER WREN *Troglodytes troglodytes*

Breeding range: Washington south to s. California along Pacific
slopes; east through n. Idaho to w. Montana; also ne. and n.-cen.
Minnesota.
Habitat: Deep coniferous forests with dense undergrowth.
Nest: Most often a well-hidden cavity in upturned roots of fallen
tree; also in or under stumps, live tree roots; in old woodpecker
holes, mossy hummocks, rocky crevices. Cavity filled with moss,
grasses, forb stems, fine twigs, rootlets; lined with hair, feathers.
Occasionally a round mass of twigs and moss with small round
entrance on side, attached to and concealed by branch of coniferous tree. Size of nest varies with space available in cavity; large for
small bird. Unlined dummy nests built by male.
Eggs: 4–7, commonly 5–6; av. 16.4 x 12.4 mm (*T. t. pacificus*).
Oval, less rounded than eggs of Black-capped Chickadee, which
they resemble. Shell smooth, little or no gloss. White; spotted,
dotted with reddish brown, often wreathed. Incubation probably
about 2 weeks.
Notes: Author flushed bird from upturned roots without finding
nest until bird returned to hidden opening.

BEWICK'S WREN *Thryomanes bewickii*   Pl. 21

Breeding range: Washington and Oregon (west of Cascades), ne.
California, east through s. Nevada, s. Utah, sw. Wyoming (unc.),

cen. Nebraska, se. Iowa (rare), south to Arizona, New Mexico, cen. Texas, ne. Oklahoma, cen. Arkansas; also Minnesota (cas.).

Habitat: Thickets, brush piles, open woodlands, farmlands, chaparral, gardens (almost any brushy area).

Nest: Some still in primitive sites: knotholes in fallen trees, natural cavities, old woodpecker holes, brush heaps. Mainly in man-made sites: birdhouses, fenceposts, cans, empty barrels, discarded clothing, abandoned automobiles, crevices in walls, mailboxes, and the like. Bulky mass of sticks, chips, leaves, debris. Lining is deep cup of feathers, hair, moss, dead leaves.

Eggs: 4–11, commonly 5–7; av. 16.5 x 12.8 mm (*T. b. eremophilus*). Oval to short-oval. Shell smooth, little or no gloss. White, irregular brown, purple, gray spots and dots, often concentrated in wreath at larger end. Incubation probably by female alone; about 14 days. Normally monogamous, but polygyny may occur occasionally. Probably 2 broods.

CAROLINA WREN   *Thryothorus ludovicianus*

Breeding range: Mississippi Valley, Minnesota to Louisiana; also se. Nebraska, e. Kansas, Oklahoma, e. and cen. Texas.

Habitat: Brushy forests, woodland thickets, farmlands, parks, suburban gardens.

Nest: Built in natural cavity, woodpecker hole, birdhouse, upturned roots, stone wall, under bridge; nook or cranny around human dwelling or outbuilding. To 10 ft. (3.1 m) above ground, rarely higher. Bulky mass of leaves, twigs, mosses, rootlets, forb stalks, strips of inner bark, debris, generally domed with side entrance; lined with feathers, hair, moss, wool, fine grasses. Both sexes build in about 5 days; female does most of lining. Some building continues after egg-laying starts.

Eggs: 4–8, commonly 5–6; av. 19.1 x 14.9 mm. Oval to short-oval. Shell smooth, little or no gloss. White; typically marked with heavy brown spots, concentrated at larger end. Incubation by female alone; 14 days. Male feeds mate on nest. 2 broods; sometimes 3 in South.

Notes: Time spent on nest during incubation unusually long for songbirds. Incubating House Wren leaves nest 27–43 times daily; Carolina 6–7 times. Like Great Crested Flycatcher, this species often uses cast-off snakeskin as nest material.

CACTUS WREN   *Campylorhynchus brunneicapillus*   **Pl. 21**

Breeding range: S. California, s. Nevada, s. Utah, Arizona, s. New Mexico, w. and s. Texas.

Habitat: Deserts and arid lands of thorny shrubs and trees, cacti.

Nest: Cholla, prickly pear, or other cacti are favorite sites; also mesquite, mistletoe, catclaw, hackberry, yucca; typically 4–9 ft.

(1.2–2.8 m) above ground. Bulky cylindrical to football-shaped mass of straw-colored plant stems and grasses; lining of fine grass, feathers, fur, cotton. Rests horizontally with entrance in one end so that large globular nest chamber is reached by long passageway placed about 3 in. (7.6 cm) above level of chamber floor. Entrance too small to admit hand without forcing it. Overall length about 12 in. (30.5 cm); inside diam. about 6 in. (15.2 cm). Regularly repaired; also used as winter roost.

Eggs: 3, often 4, sometimes 2 or 5; av. 23.6 x 17.0 mm. Mostly oval. Somewhat glossy. Salmon-buff, pinkish white; evenly covered with brown spots, dots, sometimes nearly concealing ground color. Incubation entirely by female, starting before clutch complete; 16 days. 2–3 broods.

Notes: Male commonly builds 1 or more secondary nests while female incubates. These may be used as breeding or roosting nests unless destroyed. Female does not assist with secondary nests until young are fledged.

LONG-BILLED MARSH WREN   Pl. 21
Cistothorus palustris

Breeding range: All western states except New Mexico, Oklahoma, Arkansas. Louisiana and Texas, coastal marshes only; Missouri (rare); e. Kansas (Barton Co., unc.).

Habitat: Freshwater or brackish marshes, banks of tidal rivers, shores of inland rivers, ponds, lakes.

Nest: Lashed to standing cattails, reeds, rushes, sedges, small bushes, trees, commonly 1–3 ft. (0.3–0.9 m) above water. Oblong structure with side opening; *not as globular* as nest of Short-billed Marsh Wren. Woven of wet cattails, reeds, grasses; lined with cattail down, feathers, rootlets, fine plant material. Male builds 1–10 incomplete unlined dummy nests in territory, mostly during 10 or more days before female arrives. Brood nest built by female in 5–8 days; has sill or short tunnel at entrance projecting farther into nest than any other part of lining. Nest cavity small compared to entire structure. Outside height of entire nest 7 in. (17.8 cm); outside width 3 in. (7.6 cm); diam. of opening about 1¼ in. (3.2 cm).

Eggs: 3–6, commonly 5; av. 16.5 x 12.4 mm (*C. p. iliacus*). Oval. Shell smooth, not glossy until well incubated. Dull brown, cinnamon; evenly sprinkled with dark brown dots, spots, often partly or totally obscuring ground color. Rarely may be all white. Incubation by female alone; 13 days. Males monogamous or polygamous. 2 broods.

SHORT-BILLED MARSH WREN   *Cistothorus platensis*

Breeding range: Minnesota through Mississippi Valley south to Arkansas (cas.); also e. and cen. N. Dakota, S. Dakota (prob.), e.

SHORT-BILLED MARSH WREN

Nebraska (rare), ne. Kansas (cas.).

Habitat: Wet meadows, grass and sedge marshes, hayfields. *Prefers drier areas than Long-billed Marsh Wren;* generally avoids cattail marshes.

Nest: Sometimes solitary; sometimes in colonies where conditions favorable. Globular structure, *not oval like Long-billed Marsh Wren's nest.* Of dried or green sedges with entrance, diam. 1 in. (2.5 cm), barely discernible on side. Woven into growing vegetation, 2–3 ft. (0.6–0.9 m) above ground or water. Lined with feathers, fur, soft plant down. Male builds numerous unlined dummy nests, generally easier to find than brood nest built by female. Av. outside height of entire nest 4 in. (10.2 cm); outside width 3½ in. (8.9 cm); front to back 3½ in. (8.9 cm).

Eggs: 4–8, commonly 7; av. 16 x 12 mm. Oval, sometimes pyriform. Shell smooth, thin, fragile, with slight gloss. *Pure white.* Incubation by female alone; 12–14 days. Typically 2 broods; sometimes 1, rarely 3.

CANYON WREN *Catherpes mexicanus*   **Pl. 21**

Breeding range: E. Washington, e. and sw. Idaho, w. and s. Montana, south to Baja, Arizona, New Mexico, w. and cen. Oklahoma, w. and cen. Texas; S. Dakota (Black Hills).

Habitat: Rocky canyons, cliffs, buildings, farms, cities.

Nest: In hollows or crannies in rock walls or crevices in buildings. Base of sticks, grasses, bits of wood; substantially lined with wool, fur, feathers, cocoons, plant down, catkins, spider silk. Somewhat similar to nest of Eastern Phoebe. Outside diam. 4–8 in. (10.2–20.3 cm), height 3–3½ in. (7.6–8.9 cm); inside diam. about 2½ in. (6.4 cm), depth ¾–2 in. (1.9–5.1 cm).

Eggs: 4–6, commonly 5; av. 17.9 x 13.2 mm. Oval to elliptical. White; sparingly marked with reddish brown dots. *Very similar to eggs of Rock Wren* but generally not as heavily marked as other wrens' eggs. Female incubates.

Notes: At one time, 1 or more pairs of Canyon Wrens nested in the dome of state capitol in Austin, Texas. The entrance hole, a broken window, was repaired, and thus "the nation's largest wren house" put out of business.

ROCK WREN *Salpinctes obsoletus* Pl. 21

Breeding range: Washington to w. N. Dakota, south to Baja, Arizona, New Mexico, w. and cen. Texas.

Habitat: Rocky slopes, cliffs, dry washes, in arid and semiarid regions.

Nest: In crevice on rocky hillside, beneath overhanging rock, crevice of building; entrance to cavity generally paved with small

CANYON WREN habitat (California)

stones and bits of rock. Loose cup in shallow space; of grass, bits of wood, bark, moss, hair; lined with rootlets, hair, wool, spider silk. Outside diam. $3\frac{1}{2}$ in. (8.9 cm), height $1\frac{1}{3}$ in. (3.4 cm); inside diam. $2\frac{5}{8}$ in. (6.7 cm), depth $1\frac{1}{8}$ in. (2.9 cm).

Eggs: 4–8, commonly 5–6; av. 18.6 x 14.8 mm. Oval. White; sparingly and irregularly sprinkled with reddish brown dots. *Very similar to eggs of Canyon Wren* but not as heavily marked as eggs of other wrens. Incubation probably by female. 2 or possibly 3 broods.

Notes: Nest found by author on rocky hillside in Pima Co., Arizona, had 142 small stones placed as "pavement" from outside to nest completely hidden under large boulder. Space between rock and nest only $1\frac{1}{4}$ in. (3.2 cm); nest so shallow that only a few bits of grass, dry stems, and hair were included. A California nest contained 1665 objects, from fishhooks to 769 pieces of rabbit, fish, and bird bones.

MOCKINGBIRD *Mimus polyglottos* Pl. 21

Breeding range: Cen. and s. California, Nevada, n. Utah (unc.), se. Wyoming (unc.), S. Dakota, Minnesota (Lutsen, Tofte Cos., prob.), south to Mexico and Gulf of Mexico.

Habitat: Open country with shrubs, scrubby woodlands, parks, gardens, cities, villages.

Nest: In dense shrubbery, tree branches, vines, cholla, prickly pear, sagebrush, 1–40 ft. (0.3–12.2 m), av. 3–10 ft. (0.9–3.1 m), above ground. Bulky, loosely laid outer layer of thorny twigs;

ROCK WREN habitat (Arizona)

inner layer of dry leaves, plant stems, moss, hair; lining of brown rootlets, fine grasses, sometimes horsehair, plant down. Courting male places material in possible sites;. female selects location; both build. Usually new nest for each brood. Outside diam. 7 in. (17.8 cm), height 4½ in. (11.4 cm); inside diam. 3⅛ in. (7.9 cm), depth 2⅜ in. (6 cm).

Eggs: 3–5, commonly 4; av. 24.6 x 18.6 mm (*M. p. leucopterus*). Typically oval, occasionally short- or long-oval. Shell smooth; slight gloss. Shades of blue and green; heavily marked with brown spots, blotches. Incubation by female; 12–14 days. 2 broods.

Notes: Strongly partial to sites near houses; porch vines, foundation and garden plantings favored.

GRAY CATBIRD   *Dumetella carolinensis*   Pl. 21

Breeding range: Washington (east of Cascades), Oregon (prob.), east to Minnesota, south to e. Arizona, n. New Mexico (unc.), e. Texas, n. Louisiana.

Habitat: Brushy thickets, woodland undergrowth, shrubby marsh borders, hedgerows, gardens.

Nest: Built in dense thickets, briars, vine tangles, shrubs, low trees, typically 3–10 ft. (0.9–3.1 m) above ground. Substantial bulky foundation of twigs, grapevine, leaves, grasses, paper, forb stems; deeply cupped; neatly lined with rootlets. Built by both sexes, mostly female, in 5–6 days.

Eggs: 3–5, commonly 4; av. 23.3 x 17.5 mm. Oval to short-oval. Shell smooth, glossy. Deep greenish blue, unmarked; *darker than eggs of American Robin or Wood Thrush.* Incubation by female alone; 12–13 days.

Notes: Rarely parasitized by Brown-headed Cowbird; female ejects cowbird egg. In 1 study of 190 nests, only 5 had 5 eggs. Author found nest containing white shoestring, 8-in. (20.3 cm) strip of white bandage, piece of white napkin, 3 cellophane cigar wrappers, in addition to usual material.

BROWN THRASHER   *Toxostoma rufum*   Pl. 22

Breeding range: East of Rockies: e. Montana to Minnesota, south to New Mexico (cas.), e. Texas, Gulf of Mexico.

Habitat: Thickets, brushy fields, hedgerows, woodland borders.

Nest: On ground under small bush or as high as 14 ft. (4.3 m), av. 2–7 ft. (0.6–2.1 m), in tree, shrub, vine. Loosely constructed foundation of thorny twigs as long as 12 in. (30.5 cm) is base for large cup of dry leaves, small twigs, grass stems, grapevine, inner bark; lined with rootlets. Both sexes build in 5–7 days. Outside diam. about 12 in. (30.5 cm), height 3¾ in. (9.5 cm); inside diam. 3¾ in. (9.5 cm), depth 1 in. (2.5 cm).

Eggs: 2–5, commonly 4; av. 26.5 x 19.4 mm. Oval to short- or long-oval. Shell smooth, has slight gloss. Pale bluish white, some-

BROWN THRASHER

times with greenish tinge; evenly and rather densely covered with small reddish brown spots or fine dots. Incubation by both sexes; typically 12–13 days. 2 broods. May find new mates for 2nd nesting.

Notes: Author found nest on ground under leaning tombstone in old cemetery. Largest passerine known to be parasitized by Brown-headed Cowbird. In 52 nests, 31 had 4 eggs, 13 had 3, 7 had 5, 1 had 2. In 17 nests, 9 hatched in 13 days, 6 in 12 days, 1 in 11 days, 1 in 14 days.

LONG-BILLED THRASHER opp. p. 147
Toxostoma longirostre

Notes: Northern race of a Mexican species; nests in s. Texas, common in Hidalgo and Cameron counties. Its breeding biology is similar to that of the Brown Thrasher, which it closely resembles in appearance; its *eggs are indistinguishable* from eggs of that species.

BENDIRE'S THRASHER *Toxostoma bendirei* Pl. 22

Breeding range: California (San Bernardino Co., rare), s. Utah (rare), Arizona, w. New Mexico.
Habitat: Foothills below 4000 ft. (1220 m), commonly in desert scrub at lower elevations.
Nest: Variety of sites: mesquite, catclaw, mistletoe, saltbush, paloverde, desert thorn, greasewood; 3–10 ft. (0.9–3.1 m) above ground; av. 5 ft. (1.5 m). Compactly built of fine twigs; lined with

170

hair, thread, twine, pieces of cloth, grass, forbs, rootlets, wool. Generally *smaller, more compact,* of finer material than nests of most thrashers.

Eggs: 3 or 4; av. 25.6 x 19.1 mm. Short- to long-oval. Pale gray-green to greenish white; irregularly spotted and blotched with brown, buff.

Notes: Because of its shyness, this species is often overlooked and may be commoner than supposed.

CURVE-BILLED THRASHER   Pl. 22
Toxostoma curvirostre

Breeding range: Arizona to w. and s. Texas; also se. Colorado (unc.), Kansas (Finney, Morton Cos.), Oklahoma (Cimarron Co.).
Habitat: Resident of deserts and arid brushlands.
Nest: Most often in cholla cactus, 3–5 ft. (0.9–1.5 m) above ground; also in yucca, prickly pear, mistletoe, desert thorn, mesquite. Bulky loose bowl of coarse thorny twigs, interlaced and lined sparingly with fine grasses, occasionally horsehair. Nests sometimes built on top of old nests of Cactus Wren.
Eggs: 3, occasionally 2 or 4; av. 29.3 x 20.2 mm. Short- to long-oval. No gloss. Pale bluish green; marked with minute brown specks over entire egg. Incubation by both sexes; about 13 days. 2 broods.
Notes: All nests found by author in s. Arizona were in Teddy Bear or Jumping Cholla Cactus (*Opuntia bigelovii*). Most nests found in s. Texas were in Englemann's Prickly Pear (*Opuntia engelmanii*). Unusually high nest in hackberry tree in Texas was 22 ft. (6.7 m) above ground.

CURVE-BILLED THRASHER

CALIFORNIA THRASHER   *Toxostoma redivivum*   **Pl. 22**

Breeding range: Only in California; from western slopes of the Sierra Nevada and high mountains of s. California to the Pacific, and from head of Sacramento Valley to Baja.
Habitat: Dense shrubs, chaparral, riparian woodland thickets.
Nest: In dense foliage within a few feet of ground; *resembles nest of Mockingbird but larger.* Foundation and body of stiff, rough twigs that project in all directions; lined with rootlets, grasses, forb stems, bark strips. Outside diam. 17⅔ in. (44.9 cm), height 8⅓ in. (21 cm); inside diam. 4¼ in. (10.8 cm), depth 1¾ in. (4.5 cm).
Eggs: 3–4, rarely 2; av. 30.1 x 21.2 mm. Mostly oval. Slightly glossy. Nile blue or pale blue; more or less evenly covered with pale brown spots, flecks, small dots. Larger than and generally not as heavily marked as eggs of Mockingbird. Incubation by both sexes; 14 days. At least 2 broods; nests found from November to July.
Notes: Adults approach and leave nest from ground instead of flying to or away from site.

LE CONTE'S THRASHER   *Toxostoma lecontei*   **Pl. 22**

Breeding range: California (San Joaquin Valley), s. Nevada, sw. Utah (rare), w. and sw. Arizona.
Habitat: Low, hot, barren deserts and valleys; regions of scant vegetation where bird's light color blends with sandy gravel environment.
Nest: Bulky mass of thorny twigs and sticks built by both sexes, often in cholla, commonly 4–8 ft. (1.2–2.4 m) above ground; also in mesquite, paloverde, saltbush, sage, other desert shrubs; lined with leaves, fibers, paper, rootlets. Inside diam. 3 in. (7.6 cm), depth 2–2½ in. (5.1–6.4 cm).
Eggs: 3, sometimes 2 or 4 (22 sets: 6 nests of 4 eggs, 12 of 3, 4 of 2); av. 27.6 x 19.7 mm. Short- to long-oval, somewhat pointed at smaller end. Slight gloss. Light greenish blue; marked with very fine brown dots distributed throughout or concentrated about larger end. *Smaller than eggs of California Thrasher; about same size as eggs of Curve-billed Thrasher; usually less heavily marked than either.* Incubation by both sexes; 14 days or more. 2 broods, possibly 3.
Notes: Study near Maricopa, California, indicated breeding density of 10 pairs per square mile; other areas, 5 pairs or less. Extended breeding season — January to June.

CRISSAL THRASHER   *Toxostoma dorsale*   **Pl. 22**

Breeding range: S. California (unc.), Arizona, sw. Utah (unc.), s. New Mexico, w. Texas.
Habitat: Dense brush along rivers and dry washes, hillsides, canyons, chaparral; in hot, low deserts.

Nest: Of rough thorny twigs supporting a bowl-shaped lining of soft vegetable fiber, sometimes a few feathers, placed 2–8 ft. (0.6–2.4 m) above ground in mesquite, sagebrush, willow, greasewood, and other desert shrubs. Many nests built close under an overhanging limb, making it difficult to examine contents. Outside diam. 15 x 8 in. (38.1 x 20.3 cm), height 6 in. (15.2 cm); inside diam. 3 x 3⅓ in. (7.6 x 8.5 cm), depth 2¼ in. (5.7 cm).

Eggs: 2–3, sometimes 4; av. 26.8 x 19.2 mm. Oval to long-oval. Very little gloss. Bluish green, unmarked; much like color of American Robin's eggs. *Only thrasher that lays unmarked eggs.* Smaller, less glossy, than eggs of Mexican Jay. Incubation by both sexes; 14 days. 2 broods.

Notes: Birds very shy; leave nest well in advance of intruder's arrival; no alarm sounded while nest examined.

SAGE THRASHER *Oreoscoptes montanus* Pl. 22

Breeding range: E. Washington (cas.), e. Oregon, California (San Joaquin Valley), s. Idaho, s. Montana, south to Arizona and New Mexico; w. Nebraska (prob.).

Habitat: Semiarid regions of vast sagebrush and saltbush plains; valleys, mesas, foothills.

Nest: In sage, greasewood, horsebrush, rabbitbrush, saltbush, 1–3 ft. (0.3–0.9 m) above ground; sometimes on ground under bush. Bulky, of coarse twigs, lined with grasses, rootlets, horsehair, animal hair. 6 nests found by author in Weld Co., Colorado, in saltbush, av. 15 in. (38.1 cm) above ground; outside diam. 9¾ in. (24.8 cm), height 4⅛ in. (10.5 cm); inside diam. 3½ in. (8.9 cm), depth 2⅓ in. (5.9 cm).

Eggs: 4–5, rarely 6; av. 24.8 x 18.0 mm. Mostly oval. Quite glossy. Deep greenish blue; spotted and blotched with dark brown; wreathed. Similar to eggs of Mockingbird but with deeper, richer colors. Incubation by both sexes; av. 15 days.

AMERICAN ROBIN *Turdus migratorius* Pl. 22

Breeding range: All western states.

Habitat: Dooryard bird in cities, villages, farms, gardens; also open woods, mountains up to timberline.

Nest: In shrub, tree fork, horizontal branch; almost any substantial ledge, principally on house or outbuilding (less commonly used than by eastern race); rarely on ground. Deep cup of grasses, plant stalks, strips of cloth, string, worked into wet or soft mud; lined with fine grasses. Female carries mud in bill. Outside diam. 6½ in. (16.5 cm), height 3 in. (7.6 cm); inside diam. 4 in. (10.2 cm), depth 2½ in. (6.4 cm).

Eggs: 3–4, rarely 2 or 5; av. 29.2 x 20.7 mm (*T. m. propinquus*). Oval, short- or long-oval. Shell smooth, becomes glossy with incubation. "Robin's-egg blue;" unmarked. Incubation by female; 12–14 days. 2, possibly 3 broods.

Multiple nests of AMERICAN ROBIN

Notes: Lack of orientation may cause female to build nests side by side on long beam, girder, fire escape steps. Author found 13 nests in various stages of construction aligned on a porch beam; eggs were laid and incubated in 1 nest.

VARIED THRUSH *Ixoreus naevius*

Breeding range: Washington, south along coast to Del Norte and Humboldt Cos., California; n. Idaho and nw. Montana.

Habitat: Shady, cool, damp coniferous forests from mountains to seashore in humid coastal belt.

Nest: Bulky, mainly of soft mosses interwoven with twigs; lined with fine grasses and soft dead leaves, commonly placed on branch against trunk of small conifer 10–15 ft. (3.1–4.6 m) above ground. Outside diam. 6½–8½ in. (16.5–21.6 cm), height 4½–5 in. (11.4–12.7 cm); inside diam. 3½ in. (8.9 cm), depth 2–2½ in. (5.1–6.4 cm).

Eggs: 2–5, typically 3; av. 30.5 x 21.3 mm. Oval to long-oval. Pale robin's-egg blue; sparingly but evenly marked with small brown spots or fine dots. Incubation by female; probably 2 weeks. 2 broods probable.

Notes: Desertion common by birds whose nests have been disturbed, even casually, especially during building or laying.

WOOD THRUSH *Hylocichla mustelina*

Breeding range: Mississippi Valley states; also se. S. Dakota (along Missouri R.), e. Nebraska, e. Kansas (unc.), e. Oklahoma, e. Texas.

Habitat: Cool humid forests, mainly deciduous; parks, gardens.

Nest: 6–50 ft. (1.8–15.3 m) above ground, av. 10 ft. (3.1 m) in fork or on horizontal limb of tree. Firm, compact cup of grasses, bark, moss, paper, mixed with leaf mold, mud; lined with rootlets. Similar to nest of American Robin but *smaller,* with *leaves in foundation and lining of rootlets.* Female builds in about 5 days. Outside diam. $4-5\frac{1}{2}$ in. (10.2–14.0 cm), height $2-5\frac{3}{4}$ in. (5.1–14.6 cm); inside diam. $2\frac{3}{4}-3\frac{1}{4}$ in. (7.1–8.3 cm), depth $1\frac{1}{4}-2$ in. (3.2–5.1 cm).

Eggs: 3–4, occasionally 2, rarely 5; av. 25.4 x 18.6 mm. Smaller, generally more pointed at one end than American Robin eggs. Typically oval. Shell smooth, has slight gloss. Pale bluish or bluish green, *slightly paler* than eggs of Robin; unmarked. Incubation by female; 13 days. Typically 2 broods.

HERMIT THRUSH *Catharus guttatus*   **Pl. 23**

Breeding range: Washington to w. and cen. Montana, south to Baja, Arizona, New Mexico, Texas (Guadalupe Mts., unc.); also S. Dakota (Black Hills), ne. and n.-cen. Minnesota.

Habitat: Coniferous forests, aspen groves, typically in high mountains to timberline.

Nest: Unlike eastern race, western form does not usually nest on ground; places nest in low conifers, other bushes or trees, 3–10 ft. (0.9–3.1 m) above ground. Large, well-built, of mosses, plant stems, bark, coarse grasses; lined with rootlets, horsehair, fine grasses (*no mud used*). Built by female alone. Outside diam. 5 in. (12.7 cm), height $2-3\frac{1}{2}$ in. (5.1–8.9 cm); inside diam. $2\frac{1}{2}-2\frac{3}{4}$ in. (6.4–7.1 cm), depth $1\frac{1}{2}-2$ in. (3.8–5.1 cm).

Eggs: 3–5, commonly 4; av. 22.8 x 17.2 mm (*C. g. auduboni*). Oval or long-oval. Shell smooth, has slight gloss. Very pale blue, typically unmarked (rarely spotted). *Similar to eggs of Veery* but paler. Incubation by female; 12 days.

Notes: No record of western race nesting on ground (Bent).

SWAINSON'S THRUSH *Catharus ustulatus*   **Pl. 23**

Breeding range: Washington to cen. Montana, south to Baja, Arizona (rare), New Mexico (unc.); also S. Dakota (Black Hills), nw. Nebraska (cas.), ne. and n.-cen. Minnesota.

Habitat: Coniferous and mixed forests, dense second growth, willow thickets, 6000–9000 ft. (1830–2745 m).

Nest: In small bushes or trees, commonly on horizontal branch near trunk, 2–20 ft. (0.6–6.1 m) above ground, av. 4–8 ft. (1.2–

2.4 m). Female builds bulky, well-made cup of twigs, mosses, cedar and birch bark, grasses, rootlets, wet leaves; lined with lichens, skeletonized leaves, strips of bark, animal hair. Outside diam. 4–4½ in. (10.2–11.4 cm), height 3–3½ in. (7.6–8.9 cm); inside diam. 2¼–2½ in. (5.7–6.4 cm), depth 1½–1¾ in. (3.8–4.5 cm). **Eggs:** 3–4, rarely 5; av. 23.2 x 17.2 mm (*C. u. ustulatus*). Oval. Shell smooth, has very little gloss. Pale blue; evenly *spotted and blotched with brown,* generally heaviest around larger end. Incubation by female; about 14 days.

VEERY *Catharus fuscescens* Pl. 23

Breeding range: E. Washington (unc.) to Minnesota, south to Oregon (unc.), ne. Nevada, Utah (unc.), w. and cen. Colorado, S. Dakota, Iowa (rare).
Habitat: Moist deciduous woodlands, willow thickets along streams, bottomland forests, damp ravines.
Nest: On or close to ground, in low shrubs (willows), often in brush piles. Twigs, forb stalks, grapevine, on pile of dead leaves; lined with soft bark strips, rootlets, grasses. Large nest for size of bird, usually well concealed by surrounding living plants. Building requires 6–10 days. Outside diam. 10 in. (25.4 cm), height 5 in. (12.7 cm); inside diam. 2½ in. (6.4 cm), depth 2 in. (5.1 cm).
Eggs: 3–5, usually 4; av. 22.9 x 16.9 mm (*C. f. salicicola*). Oval. Shell smooth, has slight gloss. Pale blue; unmarked, rarely spotted. *Resemble eggs of Hermit Thrush and Wood Thrush.* Incubation by female alone; 11–12 days.
Notes: Author found 3 nests containing 3 Brown-headed Cowbird eggs, 1 Veery egg; 5 Cowbird eggs, 1 Veery egg; 3 Cowbird eggs, 3 Veery eggs. All females were incubating.

VEERY

EASTERN BLUEBIRD

EASTERN BLUEBIRD *Sialia sialis* Pl. 23

Breeding range: East of Rocky Mts., Montana to Minnesota, south to e. Colorado, e. and cen. Texas; s. Arizona (rare and local).
Habitat: Open farmland, fence lines, open woods, swamps, gardens.
Nest: In natural cavity in tree, old woodpecker hole, birdhouse. Loosely built cup of grasses, forbs. Female usually builds in 4–5 days. Male may carry material. Inside diam. of cup 2½ x 3 in. (6.4 x 7.6 cm), depth about 2 in. (5.1 cm).
Eggs: 3–6, commonly 4–5; av. 20.7 x 16.3 mm. Oval to short-oval. Shell smooth, glossy. Pale blue, bluish white, occasionally pure white; unmarked. *Indistinguishable from eggs of Western Bluebird; darker than eggs of Mountain Bluebird.* Incubation by female; 13–15 days, normally 14. 2 broods, sometimes 3.
Notes: In record of 730 eggs, 40 (5.48 percent) were albinistic. In another record of 774 eggs, 71 (9.1 percent) were white. "Bluebird trails" established in many states phenomenally successful; thousands of birdhouses in use.

WESTERN BLUEBIRD *Sialia mexicana* Pl. 23

Breeding range: Washington to nw. Montana, south to Baja, Arizona, New Mexico, w. Texas (Guadalupe Mts.).
Habitat: Open woodlands, roadside fences, farmland.

Nest: Differs very little from that of Eastern Bluebird. In natural cavity, old woodpecker hole, birdhouse, cavity in building. Filled with grasses and forb stalks; inner cup lined with fine grasses. Built by female; male accompanies her. Much competition between Bluebird and Violet-green Swallows for nesting holes.

Eggs: Commonly 4–6; av. 20.8 x 16.2 mm. Oval to short-oval. Shell smooth, glossy. Pale blue, bluish white, occasionally pure white; unmarked. *Indistinguishable from eggs of Eastern Bluebird; darker than eggs of Mountain Bluebird.* Incubation by female; 2 weeks. 2 broods.

Notes: Author observed 5 species nesting at same time in cavities in 1 large dead tree in Rocky Mountain National Park: Western Bluebird, Pygmy Nuthatch, Common Flicker, Tree Swallow, House Wren.

MOUNTAIN BLUEBIRD *Sialia currucoides*   Pl. 23

Breeding range: Washington to w. N. Dakota, south to Baja, Arizona, New Mexico, S. Dakota (Black Hills), w. Nebraska, w. Oklahoma (cas.).

Habitat: Coniferous and deciduous montane forests, mountain meadows, towns, parks.

Nest: In natural cavities, old woodpecker holes, fenceposts, birdhouses. Built of grasses and forb stems; sometimes lined with a few feathers. Both sexes said to build.

Eggs: 4–7, commonly 5–6; av. 21.9 x 16.6 mm. Oval. Somewhat glossy. Very pale blue or bluish white, occasionally pure white; unmarked. Generally *paler blue than eggs of other bluebirds.* Incubation by female; 14 days. 1 brood at high altitudes, sometimes 2 at lower levels.

Notes: In Wyoming, a pair of Mountain Bluebirds nested in an old Dipper nest under a bridge. The following year, Dippers used the nest. Other unique nesting places: riverbank cavity of Bank Swallow, crevices in cliffs, in a Cliff Swallow's nest within a colony of that species.

TOWNSEND'S SOLITAIRE *Myadestes townsendi*   Pl. 23

Breeding range: Pacific Coast east through Rocky Mt. states; also S. Dakota (Black Hills) and nw. Nebraska (unc.).

Habitat: Open coniferous forests in mountains at elevations up to 10,000 ft. (3050 m); in deeply shaded narrow canyons.

Nest: On or near ground, sometimes sunken into ground, commonly protected from above by overhanging shelter: in cavity at base of tree, under overhanging bank along mountain road or trail, under rock or stump, among tangled roots of fallen tree. Loosely built bulky mass of sticks, pine needles, grasses, bits of bark; lined with fine grass stems molded into a shallow cup. Long "tail" or apron of material often hanging from front of nest.

Eggs: 3–5, commonly 4; av. 23.5 x 17.2 mm. Mostly oval, rarely slightly pointed. Slightly glossy. Dull white or pale blue, evenly covered with small spots, small blotches, or scrawls of various shades of brown, together with an underlay of lavender-gray spots or blotches. *Entirely different from eggs of other North American thrushes.*

BLUE-GRAY GNATCATCHER   *Polioptila caerulea*   Pl. 23

Breeding range: Oregon, s. Idaho, and sw. Wyoming (rare), south to Mexico; also se. S. Dakota and se. Minnesota south through e. Nebraska, e. Kansas, Oklahoma, and Texas.
Habitat: Deciduous woods, brushy streamside thickets; oak, pinyon-juniper woods; wooded swamps; chaparral.
Nest: Saddled to small horizontal tree limb or in fork 4–70 ft. (1.2–21.4 m), av. less than 25 ft. (7.6 m), above ground. Cup-shaped, compactly built of plant down, fiber, oak catkins; bound together with spider silk; covered with bits of lichen, plant down; lined with fine pieces of inner bark, tendrils, plant down, feathers (sometimes). Compares with hummingbird nests in beauty of construction. Both sexes build in 1–2 weeks, preceding egg-laying by 10–14 days. Outside diam. 2–2½ in. (5.1–6.4 cm), height 2¼– 2½ in. (5.7–6.4 cm); inside diam. 1¼ in. (3.2 cm), depth 1¼–1⅜ in. (3.2–3.5 cm).
Eggs: 4–5; av. 14.3 x 11.4 mm (*P. c. amoenissima*). Oval to short-oval. Shell smooth, has little or no gloss. Pale bluish, bluish white; generally covered evenly with a few small reddish brown spots, fine dots. *Indistinguishable from eggs of Black-tailed Gnatcatcher.* Incubation by both sexes; 13 days. Probably 2 broods.
Notes: May tear up completed or partly completed nest and re-use material to build another nearby. Awareness of discovery during building may be cause.

BLACK-CAPPED GNATCATCHER   *Polioptila nigriceps*

Notes: First breeding in U.S. was recorded June 15, 1971, when 3 young with parents were discovered along Sonoita Creek near Patagonia, Arizona. Sight records along Sonoita Creek have been reported before and since that date, but no further breeding has been reported.

BLACK-TAILED GNATCATCHER   *Polioptila melanura*

Breeding range: S. California, s. Nevada, Arizona, s. New Mexico (unc.), w. Texas.
Habitat: Arid country, especially desert washes.
Nest: In buckthorn, Laurel Sumac, sagebrush, cactus, other desert plants. Unlike Blue-gray Gnatcatcher nest, is *invariably low,*

2–4 ft. (0.6–1.2 m) above ground, and does not have extensive lichen decoration. Felted, of hemplike fiber, leaves, plant down, paper, string, spider silk; a deep cup lined with fine fiber, fur, cottony material, few feathers. Outside diam. 2½ in. (6.4 cm), height 3¼ in. (8.3 cm); inside diam. 1½ in. (3.8 cm), depth 1¼–1¾ in. (3.2–4.5 cm).

Eggs: 4, sometimes 3; av. 14.4 x 11.5 mm. Shell smooth, has little or no gloss. Pale bluish or bluish white; generally covered evenly with few small reddish brown spots, fine dots. *Indistinguishable from eggs of Blue-gray Gnatcatcher.* Incubation by both sexes; 14 days. Probably 2 broods.

GOLDEN-CROWNED KINGLET *Regulus satrapa*

Breeding range: Washington to w. Montana, south to Baja, Arizona, New Mexico; also S. Dakota (Black Hills), n. and cen. Minnesota.

Habitat: Dense coniferous forests.

Nest: Firmly fastened to twigs of horizontal limb into which nest is woven; 6–60 ft. (1.8–18.3 m) above ground in conifer, often in spruce. Hanging mass of mosses, lichens, open at top; lined with delicate strips of inner bark, fine black rootlets, feathers. Female builds in 9 days or longer. Outside diam. 2¾–3½ in. (7.1–8.9 cm), height 3–3¾ in. (7.6–9.5 cm), oblong not spherical; inside diam. 1–1½ in. (2.5–3.8 cm), diam. of cup at broadest point 1¾ in. (4.5 cm), depth 1½ in. (3.8 cm).

GOLDEN-CROWNED KINGLET

Eggs: 5-11, commonly 8-9, in 2 layers; av. 13.5 x 10.5 mm (*R. s. olivaceus*). Oval to long-oval. Shell smooth, no gloss. White to cream; spotted, blotched with browns, grays. *Indistinguishable from eggs of Ruby-crowned Kinglet.* Incubation by female; begins before clutch complete. 2 broods.

Notes: Positive identification of nest and eggs not possible without seeing bird. Nest blends well with surrounding foliage; very difficult to see from ground.

RUBY-CROWNED KINGLET   *Regulus calendula*   Pl. 24

Breeding range: Washington to w. and cen. Montana, south to Baja, and in mountains to Arizona, New Mexico; also S. Dakota (Black Hills, unc.), ne. and n.-cen. Minnesota.

Habitat: Coniferous forests.

Nest: Attached to pendent twigs beneath horizontal branch of conifer, often spruce, sometimes fir, pines, 2-100 ft. (0.6-30.5 m) above ground; usually where foliage is thickest; has color and texture like surroundings. Deep pensile cup of moss, lichens, small twigs, inner bark, grasses; lined with abundance of feathers, sometimes fur. Outside diam. at widest point 2½ in. (6.4 cm), height 4-4½ in. (10.2-11.4 cm); opening at top 1¼ in. (3.2 cm) in diameter.

Eggs: 5-11, commonly 7-9; av. 14.0 x 10.9 mm (*R. c. cineraceus*). Oval. Shell smooth, no gloss. Pale buff-white, clear white, dirty white; evenly covered with reddish brown dots, spots, often wreathed. *Indistinguishable from eggs of Golden-crowned Kinglet.* Female incubates, completely concealed in nest.

Notes: Positive identification impossible without seeing bird. Male agitated when intruder approaches; discloses nest area.

WATER PIPIT   *Anthus spinoletta*   Pl. 24

Breeding range: Washington and Oregon to w. and cen. Montana, south in high mountains to Arizona, New Mexico; also California (Mono Co.).

Habitat: Tundra; grassy slopes of Alpine zone.

Nest: Depression in ground among mats of low plants invariably sheltered from above by overhanging moss, grass, rock, roots. Hollow, lined with dry coarse grass and forb stems with cup of same but finer material, sometimes a few strands of hair. Outside diam. 3½-6⅓ in. (8.9-16.1 cm) more or less, determined by size of depression; inside diam. 2½-3⅛ in. (6.4-7.9 cm), depth 1½-2¼ in. (3.8-5.7 cm).

Eggs: 4-6, commonly 5 (39 nests in Colorado: 8 had 4 eggs, 27 had 5, 4 had 6); av. 19.9 x 14.7 mm. Oval. Slight gloss. Grayish white or dull white; chocolate brown spots and blotches evenly distributed over entire egg; markings often obliterate ground color, sometimes form solid wreath at larger end. Incubation by female; about 2 weeks.

WATER PIPIT habitat (Niwot Ridge, Colorado)

Notes: Female sits tight in well-concealed nest. All 9 nests seen by author on tundra in Rocky Mountains found by flushing bird at close range. Horned Lark nests on tundra, but makes nest in open and lays pale gray eggs marked with peppery dots.

SPRAGUE'S PIPIT   *Anthus spragueii*

Breeding range: Ne. and n.-cen. Montana, N. Dakota, nw. Minnesota, nw. S. Dakota.
Habitat: Short-grass prairies.
Nest: On ground, typically in hollow; built of dry grasses packed and woven into firm structure; may be lined sparsely with fine grasses. Often arched with entrance at side.
Eggs: 4–5, rarely 6; av. 20.9 x 15.3 mm. Long-oval. Slightly glossy. Grayish white; thickly, quite uniformly covered with purplish brown spots and small blotches.
Notes: Does not fly directly to nest when approaching; alights several feet away and walks.

BOHEMIAN WAXWING   *Bombycilla garrulus*

Breeding range: Ne. Washington (cas.), n. Idaho, nw. Montana (rare).
Habitat: Coniferous forests, muskeg bogs.
Nest: Often 2 or more nests in same general area. On horizontal branches of conifers of various heights. Made of conifer twigs

intermixed with grasses, mosses; lined with finer grasses, bits of moss and down. Outside diam. 6–7 in. (15.2–17.8 cm), height 2½–4 in. (6.4–10.2 cm); inside diam. 3 in. (7.6 cm), depth 1½–3 in. (3.8–7.6 cm).

Eggs: 4–6; av. 24.6 x 17.4 mm. Pale bluish gray; marked profusely with blackish dots and a few fine irregular lines. *Almost identical to eggs of Cedar Waxwing but larger.*

Notes: Erratic in choice of nesting territory. Abundance or lack of food believed to govern decision to nest or not.

CEDAR WAXWING *Bombycilla cedrorum* Pl. 24

Breeding range: Washington to Minnesota, south to nw. California, Utah, w. Colorado (unc.), Oklahoma (cas.), Missouri.

Habitat: Open woods, orchards, shade trees.

Nest: On horizontal limb of tree, 4–50 ft. (1.2–15.3 m) above ground, av. 6–20 ft. (1.8–6.1 m). Loosely woven of grasses, twigs, forb stems, string, cottony fibers, yarn; lined with rootlets, fine grasses, plant down, mosses, lichens. Both sexes build in 5–7 days. Outside diam. 4½–6 in. (11.4–15.2 cm), height 3½–4½ in. (8.9–11.4 cm); inside diam. 2½–3 in. (6.4–7.6 cm), depth 2 in. (5.1 cm).

Eggs: 4–5, occasionally 3, rarely 2 or 6; av. 21.8 x 15.6 mm. Oval. Shell smooth, little or no gloss. Pale gray, pale bluish gray; lightly, irregularly spotted with dark brown, blotched with pale brownish gray. Incubation by female; 12–13 days, starting before clutch complete. 2 broods. Pair remains mated for both broods.

Notes: Small amount of space demanded for nesting territory results in occasional colonial nestings.

PHAINOPEPLA *Phainopepla nitens* Pl. 24

Breeding range: Se. California, s. Nevada, sw. Utah, Arizona, sw. New Mexico, w. Texas.

Habitat: Mesquite forests, desert scrub, oak foothills, streamside woodlands.

Nest: Built mostly or entirely by *male* in vertical or horizontal fork of tree or shrub — mesquite, catclaw, cottonwood, hackberry, willow, orange, oak, sycamore — 4–50 ft. (1.2–15.3 m) above ground, av. 6–11 ft. (1.8–3.4 m). Often in clump of mistletoe. Shallow, small for size of bird; built of plant stems, blossoms, leaves, cottony fibers, bound with spider silk; thinly lined with down, wool, hair. Outside diam. 3¾–4½ in. (9.5–11.4 cm), height 1½–2½ in. (3.8–6.4 cm); inside diam. 2½ in. (6.4 cm), depth 1–1⅞ in. (2.5–3.8 cm).

Eggs: 2–3, rarely 4; av. 22.1 x 16.0 mm. Spherical to long-oval. Pale gray or grayish white, completely covered with dull violet or black dots, sometimes wreathed at larger end. Incubation by both sexes, mostly by male (at least during daytime); 14–16 days. Probably 1 or 2 broods.

Notes: In Arizona, author watched from one place 4 nests being built at same time, 2 in hackberry, 1 in sycamore, 1 in ash. All construction was by males; females observed from nearby. Several times when female approached nest male drove her away. Both attacked other Phainopeplas that entered immediate vicinity of nest.

LOGGERHEAD SHRIKE *Lanius ludovicianus*   Pl. 24

Breeding range: All western states.
Habitat: Open country with lookout perches; thickets, roadside trees, parks, low scrub, deserts, orchards.
Nest: In dense foliage in tree or shrub, 5–30 ft. (1.5–9.2 m) above ground, av. 8–15 ft. (2.4–4.6 m). Often in mistletoe clump. Bulky, well made of woven sticks, twigs, forb stems, grasses, bark fibers; a well-defined cup lined with cattle hair, rootlets, feathers, bark fibers, cottony materials. Old nests often used succeeding year. Outside diam. 10 in. (25.4 cm), height 4½ in. (11.4 cm); inside diam. 3 in. (7.6 cm), depth 2½ in. (6.4 cm).
Eggs: 4–8, commonly 5–6; av. 24.1 x 18.5 mm (*L. l. gambeli*). Oval to long-oval. Shell smooth, no gloss. Dull white, grayish or buffy; spotted, blotched with browns, grays, often capped. Incubation by female; 16 days (may be less in some races). 2 broods, possibly 3.
Notes: Controversy exists over role of sexes in nest building. Male selects site and may do most of building. Participation of female may vary with individuals. In 32 California nests: 6 had 5 eggs, 16 had 6, 10 had 7. Author found Colorado nest in base of abandoned magpie nest. Recent studies suggest contamination of birds by DDE with eggshell thinning as a result.

STARLING *Sturnus vulgaris*   Pl. 24

Breeding range: All western states.
Habitat: Cities, suburbs, wooded farmlands, swamps, orchards, parks, gardens, cliffs.
Nest: Solitary or in colonies (5 nests found in dead limb of a willow tree). Cavity or hole almost anywhere; prefers natural cavities in trees, old or new woodpecker holes, birdhouses; 2–60 ft. (0.6–18.3 m) above ground, av. 10–25 ft. (3.1–7.6 m). Mass of material: grasses, forb stems, twigs, corn husks, dried leaves, cloth, feathers. Size of nest depends on cavity. Cup formed in trash; lined with fine grass, feathers. Carelessly built, fouled by excrement. Inside diam. 3 in. (7.6 cm).
Eggs: 4–5, often 6, rarely 7; av. 29.2 x 21.1 mm. Shape varies greatly, short-oval to long-oval, sometimes rather pointed. Shell smooth, has slight gloss. Pale bluish or greenish white, unmarked. Incubation by both sexes; 11–13 days, typically 12. Generally 2 broods.

Notes: Dominant species well fitted to survive in competition with other hole-nesting birds. Cannot enter birdhouses with openings less than 1½ in. (3.8 cm). Highway cuts provide nesting cavities among exposed rocks. Author found nesting colony on rocky shore of uninhabited sea island 7 miles (11.3 km) offshore.

BLACK-CAPPED VIREO   *Vireo atricapilla*

Breeding range: Cen. Oklahoma, e., cen., and s. Texas, principally Edwards Plateau; (formerly Kansas).
Habitat: Oak scrub, brushy hillsides, juniper thickets.
Nest: Suspended in fork of 2 slender twigs of tree or shrub, 2–6 ft. (0.6–1.8 m) above ground, usually no higher. Of bark strips, dried leaves, grasses, catkins, spider cocoons, held together with spider silk, lined with grasses, pine needles. Outside diam. 3 in. (7.6 cm).
Eggs: 3–5, typically 4; av. 17.6 x 13.1 mm. Oval, some slightly pointed. Shell smooth, no gloss. Pure white, unmarked. Both sexes incubate.
Notes: Heavily parasitized by Brown-headed Cowbird, which causes many nest failures. In 1 study, 243 eggs found to produce only 43 young (17.6 percent).

WHITE-EYED VIREO   *Vireo griseus*   Pl. 24

Breeding range: Se. Minnesota south to Louisiana; also e. Nebraska, e. Kansas, e. Oklahoma, e. and cen. Texas.
Habitat: Dense shrubby areas, deciduous forest undergrowth, briar thickets, old fields, often along stream banks.
Nest: Cone-shaped, suspended from forked twigs of low shrub or tree, 1–8 ft. (0.3–2.4 m) above ground. Woven of small pieces of softwood, bark shreds, held together with cobwebs; lined with fine plant stems, pieces of fine dry grass. Both sexes build. *Indistinguishable from nest of Bell's Vireo.* Distinguished from round, cup-shaped nest of Red-eyed Vireo by exterior *conelike pointed bottom.* Outside diam. 3 in. (7.6 cm), height 3½ in. (8.9 cm); inside diam. 2 in. (5.1 cm), depth 2 in. (5.1 cm).
Eggs: 3–5, commonly 4; av. 18.7 x 14.0 mm. Oval. Shell smooth, has no gloss. White, with a few widely scattered fine brown or black spots and dots. *Indistinguishable from eggs of Bell's Vireo.* Incubation by both sexes; 15 days.

HUTTON'S VIREO   *Vireo huttoni*   Pl. 24

Breeding range: Washington south to Baja west of Cascades and Sierra Nevada; east through cen. Arizona and sw. New Mexico to sw. Texas (Brewster Co.).
Habitat: Live oak forests, tangles, canyons; chaparral.
Nest: Commonly in oak, typically 7–25 ft. (2.1–7.6 m) above ground; may be up to 60 ft. (18.3 m). Both sexes build nest, a deep,

round, hanging cup anchored to horizontal twigs; of mosses, sycamore down, pieces of paper, spider cocoons, few feathers, held
together with spider silk; lined with fine grasses, occasionally
horsehair. Almost as deep as wide: outside diam. 3 in. (7.6 cm),
height 2¾ in. (7.1 cm); inside diam. 2⅜ in. (6 cm), depth 1¾ in.
(4.5 cm).
Eggs: 4, sometimes 3, rarely 5; av. 18.0 x 13.2 mm. Typically oval.
Shell smooth, no gloss. White, with a few brown dots. Incubation
by both sexes; 16 days. 2 broods. Male often sings while incubating.
Notes: Author found 6 nests in s. Arizona, all but 1 in dense
foliage of Silverleaf Oaks. All were sphere-shaped, woven with
outside of very white cottony material that blended well with
whitish undersides of oak leaves. From ground, nest looked like
baseball hanging from limb.

BELL'S VIREO   *Vireo bellii*   Pl. 25

Breeding range: California, s. Nevada, sw. Utah (unc.), Arizona,
New Mexico, e. Colorado, N. Dakota (Missouri R.), se. S. Dakota,
e. Nebraska, south to Texas; also Iowa south to Louisiana
(Red R.).
Habitat: Streamside thickets, forest edges, mesquite.
Nest: Typically less than 5 ft. (1.5 m) above ground in low mesquite, hackberry, catclaw, oak sapling, willow, ash, cottonwood or
others; built by both sexes. Basketlike cup attached to forked
twigs; built of strawlike stems, small skeletonized leaves, paper,
plant fiber, small pieces of bark; woven together with spider silk;
neatly lined almost invariably with fine yellow grass stems. *Indistinguishable from nest of White-eyed Vireo.* Outside diam. 2¾ in.
(7.1 cm), height 2¾–3⅞ in. (7.1–9.8 cm); inside diam. 1¾ in.
(4.5 cm), depth 1⅝–2 in. (4.1–5.1 cm).
Eggs: 3–5, commonly 4 (in 104 nests in Illinois, no more than 4
eggs per clutch); av. 17.4 x 12.6 mm. Oval, sometimes pointed.
Shell smooth, has no gloss. White; fine brown or black dots scattered mainly about larger end. *Indistinguishable from eggs of
White-eyed Vireo.* Incubation by both sexes; 14 days, may start
before clutch complete.

GRAY VIREO   *Vireo vicinior*

Breeding range: S. California, s. Nevada, s. Utah, and w. Colorado, south to Mexico and Texas (Guadalupe and Chisos Mts.);
also nw. Oklahoma (rare).
Habitat: Pinyon-juniper slopes, scrub oak, chaparral.
Nest: Attached to twigs 3–6 ft. (0.9–1.8 m) above ground in variety of low thorny shrubs or trees. Typical vireo basketlike cup of
dry grasses, leaves, plant fibers, shredded bark, spider cocoons,

BELL'S VIREO

woven together with spider silk; lined with fine grasses, vegetable fibers.

Eggs: 3-4; av. 18.0 x 13.5 mm. Oval or short-oval. White; marked with minute brown dots and spots.

YELLOW-THROATED VIREO *Vireo flavifrons*

Breeding range: Minnesota to Louisiana; also e. and n.-cen. N. Dakota, ne. S. Dakota, e. Nebraska, e. Kansas (rare), e. Oklahoma, e. and cen. Texas.

Habitat: Open woods of oak, maple, other hardwoods; orchards, groves, roadside trees; rarely in conifers.

Nest: Suspended between forks of slender branch of tree, often near trunk, 3-60 ft. (0.9-18.3 m) above ground, commonly over 20 ft. (6.1 m). Thick-walled, deep cup of grasses, strips of inner bark, woven together with spider silk, plant down; decorated with moss, lichens; lined with fine grasses. Nest rim curved in.

Eggs: 3-5, commonly 4; av. 20.8 x 14.9 mm. Oval, some slightly pointed. Shell smooth, without gloss. White to cream-white; strongly spotted with shades of brown, mostly at larger end. Incubation by both sexes; 14 days.

Notes: Ordinarily, but not always, builds nest *near trunk* of tree. Author has never found nest below 30 ft. (9.2 m).

SOLITARY VIREO

SOLITARY VIREO *Vireo solitarius* Pl. 25

Breeding range: Washington to w. and s. Montana, south to Baja, w. Texas; also S. Dakota (Black Hills), w. Nebraska (prob.), ne. and n.-cen. Minnesota.

Habitat: Mixed evergreen and deciduous woodlands, wooded mountain canyons.

Nest: Suspended by upper rim from twig fork on horizontal branch of hardwood or conifer, $3\frac{1}{2}$–20 ft. (1.1–6.1 m) above ground, often less than 10 ft. (3.1 m). Semipensile basket of inner bark strips, soft plant fibers, grasses, forb stems, rootlets, hair; often decorated externally with moss stems, conifer needles, fine grasses. Generally *bulkier* and *more loosely constructed* than nests of other vireos. Male carries material; female does most of building. Outside diam. $3\frac{1}{2}$ x $4\frac{2}{3}$ in. (8.9 x 11.8 cm), height $3\frac{1}{3}$ in. (8.5 cm); inside diam. $2\frac{3}{8}$ in. (6 cm), depth $2\frac{3}{8}$ in. (6 cm).

Eggs: 3–5, typically 4; av. 20.2 x 14.9 mm (*V. s. plumbeus*). Oval, some quite pointed. Shell smooth, without gloss. White, creamy white; sparingly spotted, dotted, with brown, black. Incubation by both sexes, probably 13–14 days. Male often sings while incubating. Possibly 2 broods.

Notes: Of 11 nests found by author in Santa Rita Mts., s. Arizona, only 1 was over 10 ft. (3.1 m) above ground. 9 were built in Silverleaf Oak, 1 in wild cherry, 1 in viburnum. Most decorated outside with paper. One had long strips of facial and toilet tissue hanging several inches below nest.

YELLOW-GREEN VIREO   *Vireo flavoviridis*

Notes: This tropical species is southern counterpart of Red-eyed Vireo, known in the U.S. as a rare and casual breeding species in the resaca woods and thickets of the lower Rio Grande Valley, Texas (Cameron and Hidalgo Cos.). Breeding biology similar to that of the Red-eyed Vireo.

RED-EYED VIREO   Pl. 25 and
Vireo olivaceus   next page

Breeding range: Washington, Oregon (unc.) east to Minnesota, south through e. Wyoming, cen. Colorado to s., cen., and e. Texas, and Louisiana. Absent in southwestern states.
Habitat: Open deciduous woods with thick undergrowth of saplings; occasionally mixed woods.
Nest: Deep cup suspended in horizontal fork of slender tree branch (often sapling), 2–60 ft. (0.6–18.3 m) above ground, av. 5–10 ft. (1.5–3.1 m). Of grasses, paper, bark strips, rootlets, vine tendrils, covered and bound to supporting twigs with spider silk; often decorated with lichens. Built by female in about 5 days. Outside diam. $2\frac{3}{4}$ x 3 in. (7.1 x 7.6 cm), height $2\frac{1}{8}$–$3\frac{3}{16}$ in. (5.4–8.1 cm); inside diam. $2\frac{1}{8}$ x $2\frac{5}{16}$ in. (5.4 x 5.9 cm), depth $1\frac{3}{16}$–$2\frac{1}{8}$ in. (3.0–5.4 cm); wall thickness $\frac{1}{2}$ in. (1.3 cm). *Walls thinner* than in nests of most vireos.
Eggs: 2–4, commonly 4; av. 20.3 x 14.5 mm. Oval, rarely somewhat long-oval. Shell smooth, little or no gloss. White, sparingly marked with fine brown or black dots, spots. Incubation mostly or entirely by female; 12–14 days, may begin before clutch complete. Eggs laid 3–5 days after nest completed. Occasionally 2 broods.
Notes: Measurements of 45 territories averaged 1.7 acres (0.7 ha) per pair. In same area, 87 of 114 nests parasitized by Brown-headed Cowbird. Author found Vireo incubating 4 Cowbird eggs, no Vireo eggs.

PHILADELPHIA VIREO   *Vireo philadelphicus*

Notes: This species nests commonly in the Canadian life zone of s. Canada, and breeds in the U.S. only in n. New England, ne. Minnesota, and rarely in n. N. Dakota. Its breeding biology is similar to that of its close relative, the Red-eyed Vireo. For details see *A Field Guide to Birds' Nests East of the Mississippi River.*

WARBLING VIREO   *Vireo gilvus*   Pl. 25

Breeding range: All western states.

RED-EYED VIREO

RED-EYED VIREO nest with 4 Brown-headed Cowbird eggs; no Vireo's.

Habitat: Open, mixed, or deciduous woods, particularly aspen; orchards; roadside and village shade trees.

Nest: In horizontal fork of slender branch, usually well away from trunk, often in aspen or poplar. Unlike eastern race, western birds *do not nest at great heights,* usually within 12 ft. (3.7 m) of ground in bushes or low trees. Neat cup of bark strips, leaves, grasses, feathers, plant down; fastened and woven with spider webs; lined with fine plant stems, horsehair. Rim overhangs deep cup. Building, by both sexes, requires about 1 week. Greatest outside diam. about $3\frac{1}{2}$ in. (8.9 cm), narrowing to 2 in. (5.1 cm) at top opening, height $2\frac{3}{8}$ in. (6 cm); inside diam. 2 in. (5.1 cm), depth 2 in. (5.1 cm).

Eggs: 3–5, commonly 4; av. 18.4 x 13.2 mm (*V. g. swainsonii*). Oval. Shell smooth, slight gloss. White; sparingly dotted with browns, black. Incubation by both sexes; about 2 weeks.

Notes: Several species of vireos sing while incubating — none more vociferously than this one. Author has found nests by listening for Purple Finch-like song of male.

BLACK-AND-WHITE WARBLER *Mniotilta varia* Pl. 25

Breeding range: N. Dakota (unc.), ne. and n.-cen. Minnesota, south to e. and cen. Texas, Louisiana; also e. Montana (prob.), Iowa (no recent records).

Habitat: Deciduous woodlands, especially hillsides, ravines.

Nest: On ground, commonly at base of tree, stump, rock; under log, fallen tree branch; usually hidden from above in drift of leaves. Built of dry skeletonized leaves; inlaid with grasses, forb fibers, inner bark strips (grapevine), rootlets, sometimes hair. Female builds; male accompanies her. Outside diam. $3\frac{3}{4}$–$4\frac{1}{2}$ in. (9.5–11.4 cm), height $2\frac{1}{4}$ in. (5.7 cm); inside diam. $1\frac{3}{4}$–2 in. (4.5–5.1 cm), depth $1\frac{1}{2}$ in. (3.8 cm); wall of nest 1 in. (2.5 cm) thick; bottom of nest $\frac{1}{2}$ in. (1.3 cm) thick.

Eggs: 4–5; av. 17.2 x 13.3 mm. Oval to short-oval. Shell smooth, slight gloss. White, creamy white; finely sprinkled over entire surface with spots, dots, small blotches of brown. Incubation by female; 11–12 days. 1 brood.

Notes: Record number of 8 Brown-headed Cowbird eggs, 2 warbler eggs found in 1 nest; female incubating all 10.

PROTHONOTARY WARBLER *Protonotaria citrea*

Breeding range: Se. and cen. Minnesota south to Gulf of Mexico; also e. Nebraska (Missouri R. Valley, rare), e. Kansas, e. and cen. Oklahoma, e. Texas (loc.).

Habitat: Forested bottomland, flooded river valleys, swamps.

Nest: *Only cavity-nesting warbler east of Rockies.* In natural cavity, old woodpecker hole (usually Downy), birdhouse, mailbox, 3–32 ft. (0.9–9.8 m) above water or ground, av. 5–10 ft.

PROTHONOTARY WARBLER

(1.5–3.1 m). Male selects nest site, places some material before female's spring arrival. Female does most of building with mosses, rootlets, twigs, leaves. Egg cavity neatly rounded, cup-shaped hollow; smoothly lined with fine grasses, leaf stems, feathers. Nest completed in 6–10 days; several days' delay before eggs laid. Inside diam. 2 in. (5.1 cm), depth 1½ in. (3.8 cm).

Eggs: 3–8, commonly 4–6, often 7; av. 18.47 x 14.55 mm. Oval to short-oval. Shell smooth, somewhat glossy. Creamy; boldly spotted, blotched, with brown over entire egg. Incubation by female; 12–14 days, starting before last egg laid. Typically 2 broods, sometimes 1 in North.

Notes: Of 84 nests observed, 29 were over standing water, 32 over running water, 23 over dry land; of these, 43 were in natural openings, 41 in woodpecker holes. Lucy's is the only other cavity-nesting warbler in U.S.; ranges do not overlap.

SWAINSON'S WARBLER *Limnothlypis swainsonii*

Breeding range: Se. Missouri (cas.), Arkansas (rare), Oklahoma, e. Texas (unc.), Louisiana.

Habitat: In lowlands in wooded swamps and southern cane-brakes; in higher areas in wooded ravines and thickets.

Nest: Difficult to find; often at edge of or even outside singing territory of male. In coastal lowlands, common in cane (*Arundinaria*). In highlands, nest built in shrubs, small trees, masses of vines, briars, rhododendron, laurel, 2–10 ft. (0.6–3.1 m) above ground. Bulky, loosely constructed of leaves, mosses, pine needles; lined with fine grasses. Built by female.

Eggs: 3, sometimes 4, rarely 5; av. 19.5 x 15.0 mm. Elliptical. Shell smooth, has slight gloss. White, rarely spotted. Except for very rare Bachman's Warbler (*Vermivora bachmanii*), Swainson's is only warbler in U.S. that lays *white, unmarked* eggs. Incubation by female; 13 days.

Notes: At nest observed by author for 12 consecutive hours, male never sang within 100 yds. (91.4 m) of nest.

WORM-EATING WARBLER   *Helmitheros vermivorus*

Breeding range: Rare or uncommon Missouri to Louisiana, s. Nebraska, e. Oklahoma, ne. Texas.

Habitat: Deciduous woodlands; dry, brushy hillsides.

Nest: On ground, under drift of leaves, usually protected overhead by shrubs, briars, saplings. Built of skeletonized leaves, lined with reddish hair moss (*Polytrichum*), fine grass, hair.

Eggs: 3–6, commonly 4–5; av. 17.4 x 13.6 mm. Oval to short-oval. Shell smooth, slight gloss. White; dotted sparingly or profusely with shades of brown. Incubation by female; 13 days.

GOLDEN-WINGED WARBLER   *Vermivora chrysoptera*

Notes: Although this is a common nesting bird throughout much of eastern U.S., there are only scattered records of breeding in cen. Minnesota in the West. Nests should be looked for in abandoned fields grown up to saplings and at woodland edges. For details of breeding biology see *A Field Guide to Birds' Nests East of the Mississippi River.*

SWAINSON'S WARBLER

BLUE-WINGED WARBLER   *Vermivora pinus*

Breeding range: Rare or uncommon in se. Minnesota, Iowa, s. Missouri, Arkansas, s.-cen. Nebraska, e. Oklahoma.
Habitat: Overgrown pastures, woodland edges, bottomlands, swamps, stream edges.
Nest: Close to or on ground, among and attached to upright stems of forbs, grass clumps; often very narrow, deep, supported on sturdy foundation of dead leaves. Built of coarse grasses, dead leaves, bark shreds (often grapevine); lined with finer bark shreds, grass, horsehair.
Eggs: 4–5, rarely 6; av. 15.7 x 12.5 mm. Oval to short-oval. Shell smooth, has slight gloss. White; finely dotted, sparingly spotted with shades of brown. *Less heavily marked* than similar Golden-winged Warbler eggs.
Notes: Where ranges overlap, this species hybridizes with closely related Golden-winged Warbler. Habitats also overlap somewhat, but Blue-winged Warbler tends to choose moister situations than Golden-winged.

BACHMAN'S WARBLER   *Vermivora bachmanii*

Notes: This rarest and least known of North American warblers has been placed on the Endangered Species List of U.S. Fish and Wildlife Service, Dept. of Interior. 37 nests have been found in Missouri, Kentucky, Alabama, and S. Carolina, but none since 1937. First nest discovered in Missouri in 1897. Species appears to be continuing its decline.

TENNESSEE WARBLER   opp. p. 199
Vermivora peregrina

Notes: Summer resident in ne. and n.-cen. Minnesota as far south as Duluth and Itasca State Park; rare in nw. Montana. Look for its nest on the ground in open deciduous or coniferous forests, swales, and forest clearings in second-growth timber. For details of breeding biology see *A Field Guide to Birds' Nests East of the Mississippi River.*

ORANGE-CROWNED WARBLER   *Vermivora celata*

Breeding range: Pacific Coast east throughout Rocky Mts.
Habitat: Burns, clearings, thickets, woodland edges of low deciduous growth, overgrown pastures.
Nest: On ground or up to 3 ft. (0.9 m) above ground in shrubs or tangles; built of strips of bark, coarse grass, plant down; lined with fur, feathers, hair, fine grass. Rather large for size of bird. Outside diam. $3–3\frac{1}{2}$ in. (7.6–8.9 cm), height $2\frac{1}{4}–3$ in. (5.7–7.6 cm); inside diam. $1\frac{3}{4}$ in. (4.5 cm), depth $1\frac{1}{2}–1\frac{3}{4}$ in. (3.8–4.5 cm).
Eggs: 3–6, commonly 4–5; av. 16.2 x 12.7 mm. Oval to short-oval. Slight gloss. White, creamy white; speckled, spotted, or

occasionally blotched with reddish brown with underlying shades of light brown-drab. Scrawls may be present on heavily marked eggs.

Notes: One subspecies, Dusky Orange-crowned Warbler (*V. c. sordida*), which breeds on islands off the coast of southern California, rarely nests on the ground. Its nest is usually in bushes or tangled vines, but has been found in trees as much as 15 ft. (4.6 m) above ground.

NASHVILLE WARBLER

NASHVILLE WARBLER *Vermivora ruficapilla*   Pl. 25

Breeding range: Washington to Baja; nw. Montana, Idaho (unc.), nw. Nevada, ne. and n.-cen. Minnesota, Nebraska (Missouri R. Valley, poss.).

Habitat: Slashings, swales, edges of bogs, burns, mixed forest undergrowth, forest edges, particularly aspens.

Nest: Built in mossy depression in ground, often with overhead cover of club moss, Bunchberry, or other low plants. Small, compact, shallow cup of rootlets, bark fibers, grasses; lined with fine grasses, moss stems, hair. Female builds; 7–9 days. Outside diam. 3¼ in. (8.3 cm), height 1¾ in. (4.5 cm); depth 1 in. (2.5 cm).

Eggs: 4–5; av. 15.3 x 12.2 mm (*V. r. ridgwayi*). Oval to short-oval. Shell smooth, has slight gloss. White, creamy white, dotted with shades of brown; markings scattered over egg or wreathed. Incubation by female; 11–12 days.

Notes: Finding well-concealed nest without flushing incubating bird virtually impossible.

VIRGINIA'S WARBLER   *Vermivora virginiae*

Breeding range: California (San Bernardino and Inyo Cos., rare), s. Idaho, Nevada, Utah, w. and cen. Colorado, Arizona, New Mexico, Texas (Guadalupe Mts., prob.).
Habitat: Chaparral in foothills and mountains, scrub oak canyons, pinyon-juniper brushlands.
Nest: On or in ground, often embedded in dead leaves; usually hidden from above by overhanging grass. Built of loosely but intricately interwoven strips of inner bark, grass stems, roots, mosses; lined with similar materials, also fur and animal hair. Outside diam. 3-3½ in. (7.6-8.9 cm); inside diam. 2 in. (5.1 cm).
Eggs: 3-5, typically 4; av. 15.9 x 12.4 mm. Oval to short-oval. Slight gloss. White, with fine dots and spots of reddish brown.

COLIMA WARBLER   *Vermivora crissalis*

Notes: This little-known species nests in the U.S. only in the Chisos Mts., Brewster Co., Texas, where it builds its nest on the ground among small oaks. Colima's summer home can be reached only by packing into the high mountains from a base camp at Boot Spring, Big Bend National Park.

LUCY'S WARBLER   *Vermivora luciae*   opp. p. 121

Breeding range: Se. California, s. Nevada, s. Utah, Arizona, New Mexico, Texas (Trans-Pecos, cas.).
Habitat: Mesquite forests of sw. deserts, mountain foothills, streamside cottonwoods and willows.
Nest: In old woodpecker holes, natural cavities, under loose bark, in abandoned Verdin nests, typically 2-15 ft. (0.6-4.6 m) above ground. Nest small, frail, of grasses, plant fibers and stems; lined with plant fibers, a few feathers, animal hair.
Eggs: 3-7, commonly 4-5; av. 14.6 x 11.4 mm. Oval to short-oval. Very little gloss. White, creamy white; finely dotted with browns. Incubation probably by female alone.
Notes: *Only cavity-nesting warbler other than Prothonotary.* Very shy; does not readily disclose nest site. Difficult to flush; makes no fuss when dislodged from cavity. Reported nesting in holes eroded in stream banks.

NORTHERN PARULA (PARULA WARBLER)
Parula americana

Breeding range: E. Nebraska, Missouri, south to e. and se. Texas and Gulf; also ne. and n.-cen. Minnesota; California (Marin Co., 1977), New Mexico (Sandoval Co., nest attempt, 1977).
Habitat: Chiefly coniferous and deciduous forests where mosslike lichens or bromeliads hang from tree branches. Also in forests without lichens or air plants.

Nest: In North, completely hidden in festoons of *Usnea* lichens hanging from tree branches, 6–100 ft. (1.8–30.5 m) above ground; in South, in Spanish Moss (*Tillandsia usneoides*); elsewhere in conifers, mixed woodlands. Within mosslike "beard," pendent nest of fine grasses, tendrils, hair, plant down; opening at side or top. From ground, nest looks size and shape of tennis ball held in bottom of "beard." Elsewhere, open nests built in accumulated trash, piles of leaves, hanging clusters of twigs, on horizontal tree branches.

Eggs: 3–7, commonly 4–5; av. 16.5 x 12.1 mm. Oval to short-oval. Shell smooth, has slight gloss. White, creamy white; dotted, spotted with browns. Incubation by female; at least 12 days.

Notes: Where *Usnea* and *Tillandsia* not available, nests are extremely varied. Author found nest built within piece of burlap caught in outer branches of hemlock. Other nests: almost entirely of heavy brown wrapping cord and small quantity of wool; entirely of leaf skeletons; chiefly of fine grasses.

TROPICAL PARULA (OLIVE-BACKED WARBLER)
Parula pitiayumi

Notes: This species, abundant in the tropics, breeds in the U.S. only in the lower Rio Grande Valley, Texas, where it is considered rare. Its breeding biology is similar to that of the Northern Parula.

OLIVE WARBLER *Peucedramus taeniatus*

Breeding range: Se. Arizona, sw. New Mexico.
Habitat: High pine forests up to 12,000 ft. (3660 m).
Nest: On horizontal branch of pine or fir up to 70 ft. (21.3 m) above ground; compactly built by female of lichens, mosses, dry flower stalks, bud scales, plant down; lined with fine rootlets and plant down. Outer diam. 4 in. (10.2 cm), height 1¾ in. (4.5 cm); inside diam. 2 in. (5.1 cm), depth 1⅛ in. (2.9 cm).
Eggs: 3–4; av. 17.1 x 12.8 mm. Oval to short-oval. Slight gloss. Grayish, or bluish white; liberally dotted, spotted, blotched with olive-gray or olive-brown overlaid on grayish markings.
Notes: Little is known of the breeding biology of this species because nests are often inaccessible at ends of branches high in tall trees in remote mountainous areas.

YELLOW WARBLER *Dendroica petechia* Pl. 25

Breeding range: All western states but Louisiana, where no definite breeding record has been established.
Habitat: Along waterways, edges of swamps, marshes, brushy bottomlands, orchards, hedgerows, roadside thickets.
Nest: In colonies in ideal habitat, individual territories as small as ⅖ acre (0.16 ha); also single. In upright fork or crotch of shrub,

TENNESSEE WARBLER

MAGNOLIA WARBLER

BLACK-THROATED BLUE WARBLER

BLACK-THROATED GREEN WARBLER

BLACKBURNIAN WARBLER

BAY-BREASTED WARBLER

MOURNING WARBLER

CANADA WARBLER

YELLOW WARBLER nest, opened to disclose buried Brown-headed Cowbird eggs.

tree, briars 2–12 ft. (0.6–3.7 m) above ground, av. 3–8 ft. (0.9–2.4 m). Strong, compact cup of firmly interwoven milkweed fibers, hemp, grasses, plant down; lined with felted plant down, hair, fine grasses. Walls thicker, less neatly built than in American Redstart nest; neater and more compact than nest of Willow Flycatcher. Female builds in about 4 days. Outside diam. 2¼–3 in. (5.7–7.6 cm), height 2–5 in. (5.1–12.7 cm); inside diam. 1¾–2 in. (4.5–5.1 cm), depth 1¼–1½ in. (3.2–3.8 cm).

Eggs: 3–6, commonly 4–5; av. 16.6 x 12.6 mm. Oval to short-oval. Shell smooth, has slight gloss. Grayish white, bluish or greenish white; splashed with brown, gray markings; often wreathed. Incubation by female; 11–12 days.

Notes: Common victim of Brown-headed Cowbird. Has ingenious way of combating parasite: builds 2nd story on top of Cowbird eggs, burying them. Nest may also contain warbler eggs when superstructure is added. As many as 6 stories have been found with Cowbird eggs buried in each layer.

MAGNOLIA WARBLER *Dendroica magnolia*   **opp.**

Notes: Common breeder along northern tier of eastern U.S., but only in ne. and n.-cen. Minnesota in western area. For details of breeding biology, see *A Field Guide to Birds' Nests East of the Mississippi River.*

Opposite: Minnesota Wood Warblers

CAPE MAY WARBLER   *Dendroica tigrina*

Notes: This colorful species nests commonly in Canadian spruce belt and in northern New England; breeds in West only in n.-cen. Minnesota. For details of breeding biology see *A Field Guide to Birds' Nests East of the Mississippi River.*

BLACK-THROATED BLUE WARBLER   opp. p. 199
Dendroica caerulescens

Notes: Breeds only in ne. and n.-cen. Minnesota in western U.S., with largest population in Cook Co., easternmost Minnesota county. For details of breeding biology see *A Field Guide to Birds' Nests East of the Mississippi River.*

YELLOW-RUMPED WARBLER   Pl. 25
Dendroica coronata
(including Myrtle Warbler and Audubon's Warbler)

Breeding range: Washington to Montana, south to Baja, Arizona, New Mexico, w. Texas (Guadalupe Mts.); also N. Dakota (Slope Co., rare), S. Dakota (Black Hills), w. Nebraska (prob.), ne. and n.-cen. Minnesota.
Habitat: Coniferous and mixed forests.
Nest: Typically on horizontal branch of conifer, often near trunk, 4–50 ft. (1.2–15.3 m) above ground, av. 20 ft. (6.1 m). Occasionally in hardwoods: maple, birch, aspen. Neat, deep cup of small twigs, bark strips, plant down, fibers; lined with hair, fine grasses, *many feathers.* Outside diam. 3–3½ in. (7.6–8.9 cm), height 2¼ in. (5.7 cm); inside diam. 2 in. (5.1 cm), depth 1½ in. (3.8 cm).
Eggs: 3–5, almost always 4; av. 17.6 x 13.5 mm (*D. c. auduboni*). Oval to short-oval. Slight gloss. Greenish or cream-white; dotted, spotted, blotched with brown, often wreathed. Incubation by female; 12–13 days. Probably 2 broods.
Notes: Arrangement of feathers is clue to identity of nest. They are woven into rim with *tips inward over cup,* screening eggs when female not incubating. All 8 nests found by author had this arrangement; eggs almost invisible from above.

BLACK-THROATED GRAY WARBLER   Pl. 26
Dendroica nigrescens

Breeding range: Washington, s. Idaho, s. Wyoming, south to Baja, Arizona, n. and w. New Mexico, Texas (Guadalupe Mts., prob.).
Habitat: Coniferous and mixed woods; chaparral, scrub oak, pinyon-juniper forests.
Nest: On horizontal branch of tree (fir, oak) 7½–35 ft. (2.3–10.7 m) above ground, 4–10 ft. (1.2–3.1 m) from trunk; in

shrub near main stem. Built of dry leaves, bits of cocoons, shreds of paper, oak catkins, bark shreds, plant down; held together and fastened to twigs with spider silk; lined with many small feathers, plant cotton, fine grass stems, hair. Outside diam. $2\frac{3}{4}$ x $2\frac{7}{8}$ in. (7.1 x 7.4 cm), height $2\frac{1}{2}$ in. (6.4 cm); inside diam. $1\frac{5}{8}$ in. (4.1 cm), depth $1\frac{3}{4}$ in. (4.5 cm).

Eggs: 3–5, usually 4; av. 16.5 x 12.5 mm. Oval to short-oval. Slightly glossy. White, creamy white; dotted, spotted, sometimes blotched with browns. Some lightly speckled; others boldly marked. Incubation by female.

Notes: Author found nest in Santa Rita Mts., Arizona, lined with 289 (actual count) feathers of Mexican Jay. Of 4 nests found, 3 were in Emory Oak, 1 in juniper; 20 ft. (6.1 m), 30 ft. (9.2 m), 35 ft. (10.7 m), 40 ft. (12.2 m) above ground. 3 were well out from trunk; 1 on limb against trunk.

TOWNSEND'S WARBLER *Dendroica townsendi*

Breeding range: Washington to nw. Montana; w. Wyoming (prob.).

Habitat: Coniferous forests, principally firs.

Nest: Saddled to limb of fir; bulky, shallow (for warbler); built of cedar bark, plant fiber, twigs; lining of moss stems, hair. Outside diam. 3 x $3\frac{1}{2}$ in. (7.6 x 8.9 cm), height $2\frac{1}{4}$ in. (5.7 cm); inside diam. 2 in. (5.1 cm), depth $1\frac{1}{2}$ in. (3.8 cm).

Eggs: 3–5; av. 17.4 x 12.9 mm. Oval. Slight gloss. White; dotted, spotted with browns.

BLACK-THROATED GREEN WARBLER opp. p. 199
Dendroica virens

Notes: An abundant summer resident in eastern coniferous and mixed forests, this species nests in western U.S. only in ne. and n.-cen. Minnesota. For details of breeding biology see *A Field Guide to Birds' Nests East of the Mississippi River.*

GOLDEN-CHEEKED WARBLER *Dendroica chrysoparia*

Breeding range: Cen. Texas, mainly Edwards Plateau.

Habitat: Mature Ashe Juniper (*Juniperus ashei*) and Spanish Oak (*Quercus falcata*) growing in broken terrain in canyons and slopes.

Nest: Most often on horizontal limb of cedar, 5–30 ft. (1.5–9.2 m) above ground, well hidden by leaves and twigs. Exterior of strips of gray cedar bark; heavy-walled, compact. Lined with fine grasses, bits of forbs, some horsehair, abundance of feathers. Built by female. Outside diam. $3\frac{1}{2}$ in. (8.9 cm), height $3\frac{1}{2}$ in. (8.9 cm); inside diam. $1\frac{5}{8}$ in. (4.1 cm), depth 2 in. (5.1 cm).

Eggs: 3–5, typically 4; av. 17.7 x 13.1 mm. Oval to short-oval.

GOLDEN-CHEEKED WARBLER habitat in Edwards Plateau, Texas (*left*); female (*right*).

Slight gloss. White, creamy white; finely dotted, spotted with browns, occasionally mixed with gray. Incubation by female. 1 brood.
Notes: Female characteristically flies to nest at high speed, braking suddenly at side of nest. When intruder near, incubating bird sits tight, completely concealed by foliage.

HERMIT WARBLER *Dendroica occidentalis*

Breeding range: Washington to nw. California and Sierra Nevada; also nw. Nevada (prob.).
Habitat: Mature coniferous forests, often Douglas Fir.
Nest: Saddled on horizontal limb of conifer, 20–40 ft. (6.1–12.2 m), or more, above ground; built of forb stems, pine needles, held together by spider webs; lined with cedar bark, dried grasses, hair.
Eggs: 3–5; av. 17.0 x 13.1 mm. Oval. Slight gloss. Dull white; spotted with shades of red, brown, lavender.
Notes: Forages as high as 200 ft. (61 m) above ground, but nests much lower.

CERULEAN WARBLER *Dendroica cerulea*

Breeding range: Minnesota to Arkansas (rare to unc.); also Nebraska (Missouri R. Valley), e. Oklahoma, ne. Texas (prob.).
Habitat: Tall trees in deciduous forests with little undergrowth.
Nest: On horizontal branch of tree, 20–60 ft. (6.1–18.3 m) above ground; far from trunk, 10–20 ft. (3.1–6.1 m), typically with open area below. Dainty, compactly built, gray, knotlike, shallow structure of fine grasses, plant fibers, bark strips, forb stems, mosses, lichens, neatly interwoven; lined with fine fibers, mosses, hair; bound on outside with spider silk.
Eggs: 3–5, commonly 4; av. 17 x 13 mm. Oval to short-oval. Shell

smooth, slightly glossy. Grayish white, creamy white, greenish white; dotted, spotted, blotched with brown; usually wreathed. Incubation by female; probably 12–13 days.

Notes: From ground, nest resembles those of Wood Pewee and Blue-gray Gnatcatcher in knotlike appearance. Very shallow, not warblerlike.

BLACKBURNIAN WARBLER   opp. p. 199
Dendroica fusca

Notes: This brilliantly colored warbler of the Canadian life zone reaches western U.S. only in coniferous forests of ne. and n.-cen. Minnesota. For details of breeding biology see *A Field Guide to Birds' Nests East of the Mississippi River*.

YELLOW-THROATED WARBLER   *Dendroica dominica*

Breeding range: S. Missouri, e. Oklahoma, south to e. Texas and Gulf of Mexico; also se. Nebraska (rare).
Habitat: Cypress swamps and pine woods festooned with Spanish Moss in deep South; sycamores in North.
Nest: In coastal areas invariably in clumps of Spanish Moss hanging from horizontal branches of trees, 10–120 ft. (3.1–36.6 m) above ground, av. 30–60 ft. (9.2–18.3 m); far out from trunk. Inland nests built in the open, typically saddled to horizontal limb of sycamore, pine. In Spanish Moss, female lines cup-shaped pocket with grasses, forbs, feathers, strands of moss (woven into nest). Open nests built of bark strips, grasses, forb stems, plant down, feathers.

YELLOW-THROATED WARBLER

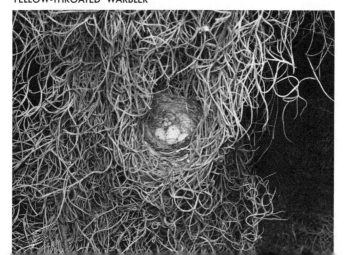

Eggs: 3–5, typically 4; av. 16.9 x 12.7 mm (*D. d. albilora*). Oval to short-oval. Shell smooth, somewhat glossy. Pale green, grayish white; dotted, blotched with dull shades of lavender and gray overlaid with brown, grays; usually wreathed. Incubation by female; probably 12–13 days. 2 broods likely in South.

GRACE'S WARBLER   *Dendroica graciae*

Breeding range: California (San Bernardino Co., poss.), s. Nevada, s. Utah, Arizona, New Mexico, sw. Colorado, Texas (Guadalupe Mts., unc.).
Habitat: Coniferous and mixed mountain forests.
Nest: 20–60 ft. (6.1–18.3 m) above ground on horizontal limb, typically pine, hidden in cluster of needles. Built of vegetable fibers, plant down, string, hair, cobwebs; lined with hair, feathers. Very compact: outside diam. 3 in. (7.6 cm), height 1½ in. (3.8 cm); inside diam. 1¾ in. (4.5 cm), depth 1¼ in. (3.2 cm).
Eggs: 3–4; av. 16.9 x 12.7 mm. Oval to long-oval. Slightly glossy. White, creamy white; dotted, spotted with browns.

CHESTNUT-SIDED WARBLER   *Dendroica pensylvanica*

Notes: Except for its breeding range in n. and cen. Minnesota, this species is rare or absent in western U.S. Old records indicate past nestings in Nebraska, Colorado, and N. Dakota. For details of breeding biology see *A Field Guide to Birds' Nests East of the Mississippi River.*

BAY-BREASTED WARBLER   opp. p. 199
Dendroica castanea

Notes: This boreal warbler finds a summer home in coniferous forests of Cook, Lake, and n. St. Louis Cos. in ne. Minnesota. For details of breeding biology see *A Field Guide to Birds' Nests East of the Mississippi River.*

PINE WARBLER   *Dendroica pinus*

Breeding range: S. Missouri (unc.) south to Louisiana, west to Oklahoma, e. Texas (unc.); also ne. and n.-cen. Minnesota.
Habitat: Open pine woods.
Nest: Saddled to horizontal limb of pine, well out from trunk, 8–80 ft. (2.4–24.4 m) above ground, av. 30–50 ft. (9.2–15.3 m); hidden from below in cluster of needles. Well made, compactly built of forb stems, bark strips, pine needles, pine twigs, spider webs; lined with fern down, hair, pine needles, feathers.
Eggs: 3–5, commonly 4; av. 18.1 x 13.5 mm. Oval to short-oval. Shell smooth, no gloss. White, grayish white, greenish white; dotted, spotted, blotched with shades of brown; normally wreathed. Incubation by female (male suspected of sharing to some extent); probably 12–13 days. 2 broods in South, possibly 3.

PINE WARBLER

Notes: Although nests have been found rarely in cedar and cypress, *attachment* of species *to pine trees* as nesting site is so persistent it is almost useless to look elsewhere. 15 species of pines known to be used; any within breeding range appear to be suitable. S. Carolina nest 135 ft. (41.2 m) above ground is record height.

PRAIRIE WARBLER *Dendroica discolor*

Breeding range: S. Missouri (unc.) south to Louisiana; also se. Kansas (rare), e. Oklahoma, e. Texas (cas.).
Habitat: Dry, brushy clearings, sproutlands, pine barrens, burned-over areas.
Nest: In loose colonies with territories well defined; also singly. Compact cup of plant down, bark shreds, woven with fine grasses, bound with spider silk; interwoven with supporting vegetation (bushes, briars, tree limbs and crotches); lined with hair, grasses, feathers; typically at low sites — 1–10 ft. (0.3–3.1 m) above ground, occasionally higher. Built by female alone.
Eggs: 3–5, commonly 4; av. 15.9 x 12.3 mm. Oval to short-oval. Shell smooth, has slight gloss. White, creamy white, greenish white; spotted, dotted with browns, grays; typically wreathed. Incubation by female; 12–13 days.

PALM WARBLER *Dendroica palmarum*

Notes: Summer resident in ne. and n.-cen. Minnesota and adjacent Marshall and Roseau Cos. Uncommon throughout this range except in extensive open tamarack–black spruce bogs, the preferred habitat of the race *D. p. palmarum.* For details of breeding biology see *A Field Guide to Birds' Nests East of the Mississippi River.*

OVENBIRD

OVENBIRD   *Seiurus aurocapillus*   Pl. 26

Breeding range: E. and cen. Montana to Minnesota, south to cen. Colorado, Oklahoma, Arkansas (absent from Kansas).

Habitat: Forest floors, especially with low undergrowth.

Nest: On ground in depression of dead leaves; *top arched with dead leaves and surrounding vegetation.* Shaped like old-fashioned oven with opening at ground level to 1 in. (2.5 cm) above ground. Invisible from above. Of grasses, plant fibers, forb stems, leaves, rootlets, mosses, bark; lined with fine rootlets, fibers, hair. Female builds in about 5 days. Outside diam. $6\frac{1}{2}$ in. (16.5 cm), height of nest and roof, $4\frac{1}{2}$–5 in. (11.4–12.7 cm); inside diam. 3 in. (7.6 cm); opening $1\frac{1}{2}$ in. (3.8 cm) high, $2\frac{1}{4}$ in. (5.7 cm) wide — narrower than inner cavity.

Eggs: 3–6, commonly 4–5; av. 20.2 x 15.5 mm. Oval to short-oval. Shell smooth, has very little gloss. White; dotted, spotted with reddish brown, lilac; usually wreathed. Incubation by female alone; $11\frac{1}{2}$–14 days, av. $12\frac{1}{4}$ days (information based on observations of 76 eggs in 21 nests). 1 brood.

Notes: Female sits tight on nest; usually will not flush until

almost stepped on. Of 27 nests, 2 had 3 eggs, 6 had 4, 18 had 5, 1
had 6.

NORTHERN WATERTHRUSH   Pl. 26
Seiurus noveboracensis

Breeding range: Ne. Washington (unc.), Oregon (Deschutes Co.,
1977, prob.), n. Idaho, w. Montana, n.-cen. and ne. N. Dakota, ne.
and n.-cen. Minnesota; also Nebraska (Sioux Co., prob.).
Habitat: Wooded swamps, swampy borders of streams, lakes.
Nest: On ground *in upturned roots* of fallen trees or roots of living
trees; in hollows in decaying stumps; sides of overhanging banks
(Louisiana Waterthrush in bank of *running* stream). Built by
female of mosses, small twigs, bark strips, skeletonized leaves;
lined with mosses, hair, fine grasses. Outside diam. varies with
location; inside diam. about 2 in. (5.1 cm), depth 1½ in. (3.8 cm).
Eggs: 4–5, occasionally 3, rarely 6; av. 19.1 x 14.4 mm (*S. n.
notabilis*). Oval to short-oval. Shell smooth, no gloss. White;
dotted, spotted, blotched, sometimes scrawled with browns, grays.
Very similar to eggs of Louisiana Waterthrush and Ovenbird but
slightly smaller. Incubation by female.
Notes: Incubating female sits tight; will not flush until intruder is
very close.

LOUISIANA WATERTHRUSH   *Seiurus motacilla*

Breeding range: Se. Minnesota to n. Louisiana; also Nebraska,
Kansas (unc.), e. and cen. Oklahoma, e. Texas (unc.).

NORTHERN WATERTHRUSH

Habitat: Ravines, small streams, mountain brooks, occasionally wooded swamps with flowing water.

Nest: In hole in steep bank of stream or in overturned roots close to *running water*, hidden by overhanging roots, forbs, or grass (Northern Waterthrush prefers swamps and bogs). Bulky, well-insulated mass of dead wet leaves, packed close together, reinforced by twigs; cup in top; lined with dry grasses, small rootlets, plant stems, hair. Leaves in front create pathway to nest. Both sexes build in 4–6 days; female more active. Size of exterior varies according to cavity filled; inside diam. $2\frac{1}{2}$ in. (6.4 cm), depth $2\frac{1}{2}$ in. (6.4 cm).

Eggs: 4–6, often 5; av. 19.9 x 15.5 mm. Oval to short-oval. Shell smooth, has slight gloss. White, creamy white; dotted, spotted, blotched with browns, grays; usually wreathed at large end. *Similar to eggs of Northern Waterthrush and Ovenbird.* Incubation by female alone; 12–14 days. 1 brood.

Notes: Habitats of this species and Northern Waterthrush seldom overlap even when ranges do.

KENTUCKY WARBLER *Oporornis formosus*

Breeding range: Iowa to Louisiana; se. Nebraska, e. Kansas (unc.), e. and cen. Oklahoma, e. and cen. Texas.

Habitat: Deciduous woodland thickets; moist, shady ravines.

Nest: On or near ground, sometimes in base of shrub, concealed by surrounding vegetation. Cup of grasses, plant fibers, rootlets, on bulky foundation of dead leaves 4–6 in. (10.2–15.2 cm) deep; lined with rootlets, forb stalks, grasses. Like Golden-winged Warbler, but unlike many ground-nesting birds, this species builds nest

LOUISIANA WATERTHRUSH

slightly above ground level.
Eggs: 4–5, rarely 6; av. 18.6 x 14.3 mm. Short- to long-oval. Shell smooth, has slight gloss. White, creamy white; blotched, dotted, spotted with grays, browns, usually concentrated at large end. Incubation by female; 12–13 days. 1 brood.
Notes: 200 leaves counted in foundation of 1 nest. In series of 25 egg sets: 13 nests of 4 eggs, 10 of 5, 2 of 6.

CONNECTICUT WARBLER   *Oporornis agilis*

Notes: This denizen of tamarack–black spruce bogs breeds in U.S. only in n. Michigan, n. Wisconsin, and in our area only in ne. and n.-cen. Minnesota where it is uncommon except in Koochiching Co. and northwestward. The grass nest, sunk in deep moss, is so well concealed in vast bogs of remote wilderness areas that few have been studied. While female is incubating, male sings far from nest and is little help to a searcher. In addition, female sits very tight on 3–5 spotted white eggs.

MOURNING WARBLER   opp. p. 199
Oporornis philadelphia

Breeding range: N. Dakota (Turtle Mts.), n. and cen. Minnesota.
Habitat: Slashings, dry brushy clearings, roadside tangles, swampy thickets.
Nest: On or near ground in tangle of briars or herbaceous plants. Bulky exterior of dry leaves, vine stalks, coarse grasses, forb stalks, pieces of bark; lined with fine grasses, rootlets, hair.
Eggs: 3–5, commonly 4; av. 18.2 x 13.8 mm. Oval to short-oval. Shell smooth, has slight gloss. White, creamy white; dotted, spotted, blotched with brown; occasionally black scrawls. Incubation by female; 12 days.

MacGILLIVRAY'S WARBLER   *Oporornis tolmiei*   Pl. 26

Breeding range: Washington to w. Montana, south to Baja and n. New Mexico; also S. Dakota (sw. and Black Hills, unc.).
Habitat: Low dense undergrowth; shady, damp thickets; forest edges, burns, brushy hillsides.
Nest: In variety of small thick shrubs, 1–5 ft. (0.3–1.5 m) above ground, most often 2–3 ft. (0.6–0.9 m). Carelessly built of coarse grass blades and stems, bark shreds; lined with soft grasses, fine rootlets, hair. Nest usually held upright by several stalks of plant into which it is tightly built. Outside diam. 4½–5½ in. (11.4–14.0 cm), height 2¼–3 in. (5.7–7.6 cm); inside diam. 2–2½ in. (5.1–6.4 cm), depth 1⅛–1½ in. (2.9–3.8 cm).
Eggs: 3–5, most often 4; av. 17.8 x 13.6 mm. Oval. Slightly glossy. White, creamy white; dotted, spotted, blotched with browns, with underlay of light brownish drab. Incubation by female; about 13 days.

COMMON YELLOWTHROAT *Geothlypis trichas* **Pl. 26**

Breeding range: All western states.
Habitat: Wet or dry areas with dense, low cover; fresh- and salt-water marshes, swamps, wet bottomlands; brushy thickets, hedgerows.
Nest: Securely lodged in surrounding vegetation on or near ground in forb stalks, grass tussocks, low bushes. Bulky (large for small bird), built of coarse grasses, reed shreds, leaves, mosses; lined with fine grasses, bark fibers, hair. Built by female alone. Outside diam. $3\frac{1}{4}$ in. (8.3 cm), height $3\frac{1}{2}$ in. (8.9 cm); inside diam. $1\frac{3}{4}$ in. (4.5 cm), depth $1\frac{1}{2}$ in. (3.8 cm). Polygyny has been observed.
Eggs: 3–5, commonly 4, rarely 6; av. 17.5 x 13.3 mm. Oval to long-oval. Shell smooth, has slight gloss. White, creamy white; dotted with browns, grays, black; commonly wreathed at large end. Incubation by female; 11–13 days, av. 12. Normally 2 broods.

YELLOW-BREASTED CHAT *Icteria virens* **Pl. 26**

Breeding range: All western states.
Habitat: Woodland edges, neglected pastures, thick shrubbery, briar thickets, willow thickets, shrubby wet meadows.
Nest: 2–6 ft. (0.6–1.8 m) above ground in bush, briar tangles, vines, low trees. Bulky, built of leaves, vines, forb stems, grasses; lined with fine grasses, plant stems. Outside diam. 5 in. (12.7 cm), height 3 in. (7.6 cm); inside diam. 3 in. (7.6 cm), depth 2 in. (5.1 cm).
Eggs: 3–6, commonly 4; av. 21.8 x 16.6 mm (*I. v. auricollis*). Shell smooth, rather glossy. White, creamy white; dotted, spotted, with browns, lilac, usually over entire egg, sometimes heaviest at large end. *Similar to eggs of Ovenbird.* Incubation by female; 11 days.
Notes: Author's experience is that, while quite shy, the Chat does not desert eggs or young if repeatedly disturbed, despite many claims to contrary. Of 10 nests found by author in Pennsylvania in 1 season, none parasitized by Brown-headed Cowbird. In same area, 11 of 12 nests of Wood Thrush were parasitized.

RED-FACED WARBLER **opp. p. 121**
Cardellina rubrifrons

Breeding range: Cen. and se. Arizona, sw. New Mexico.
Habitat: Montane forests of Douglas Fir, Engelmann Spruce; also oaks and aspen groves at elevations to 9000 ft. (2745 m).
Nest: On ground under tufts of grass, rocks, logs, small bushes, often in depression in litter of fallen leaves on a canyon slope. Built externally of coarse grasses, lined with finer grass, pine needles, hair. Outside diam. $4\frac{1}{2}$ x $4\frac{2}{3}$ in. (11.4 x 11.8 cm), height $2\frac{3}{8}$ in. (6 cm); inside diam. $1\frac{3}{8}$ x 2 in. (3.5 x 5.1 cm), depth $1\frac{3}{8}$ in. (3.5 cm).

Eggs: 3–4; av. 16.5 x 12.7 mm. Mostly oval. Slight gloss. White; finely dotted with browns, frequently scattered over entire egg or concentrated at large end. Incubation by female.

HOODED WARBLER *Wilsonia citrina*

Breeding range: Se. Nebraska (rare), e. Kansas (rare), e. Oklahoma, e. Texas; s. Missouri (rare) to Louisiana.
Habitat: Undergrowth of deciduous woodlands, thickets, wooded swamps (especially in southern areas).
Nest: At low levels, 1–6 ft. (0.3–1.8 m), av. 2–3 ft. (0.6–0.9 m) above ground in small bushes, herbaceous plants, vines, saplings; cane and palmetto in South. Neat, compact; built of dead leaves, grasses, bark strips, plant down, forbs; lined with black rootlets, grasses, plant fibers, hair; often fastened by spider silk to very slight support. Measurements of 84 nests averaged: outside diam. 3 in. (7.6 cm), height 3 in. (7.6 cm); inside diam. 1½ in. (3.8 cm), depth 2 in. (5.1 cm).
Eggs: 3–4, rarely 5; av. 17.6 x 13.6 mm. Oval to short- or long-oval. Shell smooth, slight gloss. Creamy white; blotched, spotted, dotted with browns, lilac; sometimes with underlay of lavender. Incubation by female; 12 days. (Female with unusual amount of black on head may be mistaken for male.) Occasionally 2 broods in South.
Notes: Measurements of heights above ground of 99 nests in Ohio: highest 63 in. (160 cm), lowest 7 in. (17.8 cm); av. 25 in. (63.5 cm).

WILSON'S WARBLER *Wilsonia pusilla*   **Pl. 26**

Breeding range: Washington to w. Montana, south to Baja, Nevada, Utah, w. and cen. Colorado.

WILSON'S WARBLER

Habitat: Thickets along woodland streams, moist tangles, low shrubs, willows, alders; burns growing up in shrubs.

Nest: Compact, in depression on or near ground in dense vegetation. Built of small strips of inner bark (willow), small leaves, plant fibers, grasses; lined with fine grasses, horsehair, deerhair. Av. of 3 Colorado nests found by author: outside diam. $3\frac{1}{8}$ in. (7.9 cm), height $2\frac{3}{8}$ in. (6 cm); inside diam. $1\frac{3}{4}$ in. (4.5 cm), depth $1\frac{5}{8}$ in. (4.1 cm).

Eggs: 3–6, commonly 4–5; av. 15.8 x 12.2 mm (*W. p. pileolata*). Oval to short-oval. Shell smooth, may have slight gloss. White, creamy white; dotted and spotted with reddish brown, usually at large end. Incubation by female; 11–13 days. 1 brood.

Notes: In favorable habitat may nest in loose colonies. Incubating female sits very tight; difficult to flush. In a study of 27 nests made in Inyo National Forest, Mono Co., California, 7 males were polygynous.

CANADA WARBLER   *Wilsonia canadensis*   **opp. p. 199**

Notes: Although breeding as far south as Georgia in Appalachians in East, this boreal warbler nests in our area only in ne. and n.-cen. Minnesota. It has been reported as far west as Itasca State Park and south to Mille Lacs Co. For details of breeding biology see *A Field Guide to Birds' Nests East of the Mississippi River.*

AMERICAN REDSTART   *Setophaga ruticilla*   **Pl. 26**

Breeding range: Washington to Minnesota, south to n. Utah, n. Arizona, w. and cen. Colorado, Oklahoma, Louisiana; also Oregon (Blue Mts., rare), California (Humboldt Co., rare), se. Texas (prob.).

Habitat: Young or second-growth deciduous (mostly) or coniferous woods, roadside trees, thickets, gardens, parks.

Nest: In pronged fork of tree or shrub, 4–30 ft. (1.2–9.2 m) above ground. Firm, compactly woven cup of plant down, bark fibers, small rootlets, grass stems; lined with fine grasses, forb stems, hair, sometimes feathers; decorated on outside with lichens, birch bark, bud scales, plant down; bound with spider silk. Built entirely by female, usually requiring 1 or more weeks. Similar to Yellow Warbler's nest but *is neater,* has *thinner walls.* American Goldfinch nest wider than high; American Redstart nest *higher than wide.* Outside diam. $2\frac{3}{4}$ in. (7.1 cm), height 3 in. (7.6 cm); inside diam. $1\frac{3}{4}$ in. (4.5 cm), depth $1\frac{1}{2}$ in. (3.8 cm).

Eggs: 4, sometimes 2–3, rarely 5; av. 16.2 x 12.3 mm. Oval to short-oval. Shell smooth, has slight gloss. White, grayish white, creamy white, greenish white; dotted, spotted, blotched with browns, grays; often concentrated at large end. Incubation by female 12–13 days. Commonly 1 brood.

Notes: Like Yellow Warbler, sometimes builds nest floor over Brown-headed Cowbird eggs.

PAINTED REDSTART *Myioborus pictus* opp. p. 121

Breeding range: S. Arizona, sw. New Mexico, Texas (Chisos Mts., cas.); also California (Laguna Mts., 1974).
Habitat: Pine-oak canyons, rocky hills covered with sparse oak.
Nest: Almost always on ground, under tuft of grass, projecting rocks, roots of tree or shrub, typically on sloping bank or rocky hillside not far from small stream. Built of grasses, leaves, bark; lined with fine grasses, hair. Outside diam. about 5 in. (12.7 cm), height $1\frac{1}{2}$ in. (3.8 cm); inside diam. $2\frac{1}{8}$ in. (5.4 cm), depth about 1 in. (2.5 cm).
Eggs: Usually 4, sometimes 3; av. 16.5 x 12.8 mm. Oval. Slightly glossy. Creamy white; finely and delicately dotted with browns, underlaid with brownish drab. Markings concentrated at large end but usually not wreathed.
Notes: Nests found by author in Santa Rita Mts., Arizona, were all on sloping sides of narrow canyons or ravines. 1 nest was hidden under clump of blooming Columbine. All incubating birds sat tight, flushing only when intruder was very close.

RUFOUS-CAPPED WARBLER *Basileuterus rufifrons*

Notes: This tropical American species was recorded for the 1st time in the U.S. in May 1977 at Cave Creek Canyon, Arizona. On July 17, 1977, a nest with 4 eggs was found $1\frac{1}{3}$ mi. (2.1 km) from the 1st sighting. The bird disappeared 4 days later leaving unhatched eggs and a question regarding their origin. Only one bird was seen (sexes alike), no male heard.

HOUSE SPARROW *Passer domesticus* Pl. 27

Breeding range: All western states.
Habitat: Cities, villages, farms, parks.
Nest: Commonly in any cavity: birdhouses, porch rafters, holes in walls, billboard braces, tree holes, awnings, behind shutters. Ancestral Weaver Finch-type nest often constructed, especially in rural areas; huge ball of grasses, forbs, trash; opening on side; securely lodged in fork of tree branch. Built by both sexes; mostly of grasses, forbs; lined with many feathers (chicken), some hair, string.
Eggs: 3–7, commonly 5; av. 22.8 x 15.4 mm. Oval to long-oval. Shell smooth, slight gloss. White, greenish white; dotted, spotted with grays, browns. Incubation by female; 12–13 days. Normally 2 broods; perhaps 3 occasionally.
Notes: Birds often carry nest material weeks before eggs are laid, causing unfounded speculation that species breeds most of year.

HOUSE SPARROW

Very aggressive in appropriating nest cavities of native birds, often ejecting occupants: gourdlike nests of Cliff Swallows usurped; have also been observed using holes of Bank Swallows. In 1 season same nest site used by 2 females to raise 4 broods of young.

EUROPEAN TREE SPARROW *Passer montanus*

Notes: This close relative of the House Sparrow was introduced in 1870 into Lafayette Park, St. Louis, Missouri, by a bird dealer who had imported them from Germany. The species, unlike the more aggressive House Sparrow, has not spread far beyond the St. Louis area. It is a cavity-nesting species; lays 4–7 eggs much smaller than those of House Sparrow. Both sexes, which look alike, incubate.

BOBOLINK *Dolichonyx oryzivorus* Pl. 27

Breeding range: E. Washington (prob.) and e. Oregon (unc.) to Minnesota, south to n. Utah (cas.), New Mexico (rare or cas.), cen. Kansas (rare), nw. Missouri (rare).
Habitat: Farmland, open meadows, prairies, hayfields.
Nest: Commonly in dense stands of hay, clover, alfalfa, other forbs. Slight hollow in ground (rarely above ground in low vegetation), natural or scraped by female, loosely filled with coarse grasses and forb stalks; lined with fine grasses. Diam. about $2\frac{1}{4}$–$2\frac{1}{2}$ in. (5.7–6.4 cm); depth $1\frac{1}{2}$ in. (3.8 cm).

Eggs: 4–7, commonly 5–6; av. 21.08 x 15.71 mm. Oval to short-oval. Shell smooth, somewhat glossy. Pale gray, buff, cinnamon; heavily, irregularly spotted, blotched with browns. Some so heavily marked that ground color almost hidden. Incubation by female; 13 days. 1 brood.

Notes: Nest very difficult to find. Female cannot be followed to it or flushed from it. In approaching nest, birds land some distance away and walk through concealing vegetation; run through grass before flying away.

EASTERN MEADOWLARK *Sturnella magna*

Breeding range: Mississippi and Missouri R. valley states; Arizona east to Louisiana; also e. Kansas (w. locally), e. and cen. Oklahoma.

Habitat: Open farm fields, meadows, pastures, prairies.

Nest: *Indistinguishable from Western Meadowlark's.*

Eggs: *Indistinguishable from Western Meadowlark's.*

Notes: Nests and eggs of Eastern and Western Meadowlarks are so similar that positive identification where ranges overlap depends upon hearing male's song, which is decidedly different for each species. Observer must see and *hear* male in whose territory nest and eggs are found. Since male does not visit nest during incubation, singing bird must be related to nest by territory. Problem is further complicated as the 2 species may learn each other's songs.

WESTERN MEADOWLARK *Sturnella neglecta*   Pl. 27

Breeding range: All western states.

Habitat: Grasslands — fields, meadows, prairies, farmlands.

EASTERN MEADOWLARK

Nest: Natural or scraped hollow in ground lined first with coarse dried grasses; inner lining of finer grasses, sometimes horsehair. Dome-shaped roof or canopy constructed of grasses loosely interwoven with and attached to surrounding vegetation. Opening on side. Most have obvious trails leading to nest through surrounding vegetation. Female builds in 3–8 days, often continuing after egg-laying starts; may start 1 or more nests before final site selected. *Indistinguishable from nest of Eastern Meadowlark.*

Eggs: 3–7, commonly 5; av. 28.33 x 20.60 mm. Oval to short- or long-oval. Shell smooth, has moderate gloss. White; profusely spotted, blotched, dotted over entire surface with browns, lavender, especially at large end. Eggs *indistinguishable from Eastern Meadowlark's.* Incubation by female; 13–15 days, av. 14; may begin before clutch complete. Male often polygamous. 2 broods.

Notes: See discussion of Eastern Meadowlark (preceding).

YELLOW-HEADED BLACKBIRD   Pl. 27
Xanthocephalus xanthocephalus

Breeding range: Washington to Minnesota, south to Baja, Arizona, Colorado, Kansas, nw. Missouri.

Habitat: Freshwater sloughs, marshy borders of lakes.

Nest: In large thickly populated colonies, as many as 25–30 nests in an area 225 sq. ft. (21 m²), in aquatic vegetation (cattails, reeds) invariably over water 2–4 ft. (0.6–1.2 m) deep, 6–36 in. (15.2–91.4 cm) above water level. Bulky, built of water-soaked aquatic vegetation woven to upright growing plants; lined with pieces of broad dry aquatic vegetation. Nest shrinks while drying, drawing stems tight around supports. Built entirely by female in 2–4 days. Female often abandons unfinished nests; may build 3–4 before laying eggs. Outside diam. 5 x 6 in. (12.7 x 15.2 cm), height 4 in. (10.2 cm); inside diam. 3 in. (7.6 cm), depth 2½ in. (6.4 cm).

Eggs: 3–5, commonly 4; av. 25.83 x 17.92 mm. Oval to long-oval. Shell smooth, rather glossy. Pale grayish white, pale greenish white; profusely dotted, blotched over entire egg with browns, grays. Incubation by female alone; 12–13 days, sometimes starting with laying of 2nd egg. 1 brood. Males polygamous, may have 2–5 mates.

Notes: Studies suggest that Yellow-headed Blackbirds generally exclude Long-billed Marsh Wrens from immediate vicinity of nests, particularly during incubation. Yellow-headed and Red-winged Blackbirds in same area tend to nest in separate colonies. Typically, Yellow-heads seem to prefer cattails and tules in deeper water than Red-wings.

RED-WINGED BLACKBIRD   *Agelaius phoeniceus*   Pl. 27

Breeding range: All western states.

Habitat: Fresh- and salt-water marshes, swamps, wet meadows, streamside bushes, dry fields, pastures.

Nest: In loose colonies in cattails, rushes, sedges, reeds, bushes (alder, willow), preferably near or over water; also in weeds, grass, tussocks, bushes, low trees, in dry areas (meadows, pastures). Neatly woven but bulky basket of sedge leaves, rushes, grasses, rootlets, mosses, bound to upright stalks of surrounding vegetation; lined with fine grasses; placed 3 in. (7.6 cm) to 14 ft. (4.3 m) above ground or water. Built entirely by female in 3–6 days.

Eggs: 3–4, rarely 5; av. 24.80 x 17.55 mm. Oval. Shell smooth, moderately glossy. Pale bluish green; spotted, blotched, marbled, scrawled, with browns, purples, black; mostly concentrated at large end. *Indistinguishable from eggs of Tricolored Blackbird.* Incubation entirely by female; 10–12 days, av. 11. Often 2 broods. Males probably breed when 2 yrs. old; females 1 yr.

Notes: Males monogamous or polygamous. In Wisconsin marsh, 5 males had 1 mate each, 16 had 2, 4 had 3. In census of 926 nests, clutch size av. 3.5 eggs per nest.

TRICOLORED BLACKBIRD *Agelaius tricolor*

Breeding range: S. Oregon (Klamath marshes) south through Central Valley of California to Baja; sporadic breeding in other areas of California. Statewide survey showed 78 percent of 168 colonies were in Sacramento and San Joaquin Valleys.

Habitat: Freshwater marshes of tules, cattails, sedges.

Nest: In colonies, often crowded (more colonial than Red-winged Blackbird) with nests as close as every 3 sq. ft. (0.28 sq. m); 1–3 ft. (0.3–0.9 m) above water. Of freshly pulled grass, forb stems, lashed to surrounding vegetation, lined with fine grasses. *Indistinguishable from nest of Red-winged Blackbird.*

Eggs: Commonly 4; av. 27.75 x 20.35 mm. Oval. Shell smooth, moderately glossy. Pale green; sharply, sparingly marked with blotches, scrawls of browns, black. *Indistinguishable from eggs of Red-winged Blackbird.* Female incubates; about 11 days.

Notes: In a 6-year California study, Neff noted 36 nests in 1 clump of 4 tall willows growing from same root; 12 nests in 1 small willow. In a stand of cattails, without moving his feet except to rotate, Neff counted up to 36 nests. In 1937, he estimated colonies from less than 100 to over 200,000 nests each.

ORCHARD ORIOLE *Icterus spurius*   Pl. 27

Breeding range: E. Montana (unc.) to sw. Minnesota, south to New Mexico (unc.), Texas, Louisiana; rare in ne. Wyoming.

Habitat: Farms, suburbs, country roadsides, orchards, open woodlands. Shuns heavy forests.

Nest: Hung between horizontally forked branches of trees or shrubs; concealed among leaves, 4–70 ft. (1.2–21.4 m) above ground, commonly 10–20 ft. (3.1–6.1 m). Deeply hollowed, thin-walled, basketlike, with contracted rim, securely woven of grasses; lined with finer grasses and plant down. Depth usually less than

ORCHARD ORIOLE

outside diam.; *not as pendulous* as nest of Northern Oriole. *Invariably uses grasses,* sometimes for entire structure. Built by female in 3–6 days. Outside diam. $3\frac{1}{2}$–4 in. (8.9–10.2 cm), height $2\frac{1}{2}$–4 in. (6.4–10.2 cm); inside diam. $2\frac{1}{2}$–3 in. (6.4–7.6 cm), depth $2\frac{1}{4}$–3 in. (5.7–7.6 cm).

Eggs: 3–6, commonly 4–5; av. 20.47 x 14.54 mm. Oval. Shell smooth, no gloss. Pale bluish white; spotted, blotched, scrawled with browns, purples, grays, over entire egg; sometimes concentrated at large end. Incubation by female; 12–14 days; female fed by male while on nest. Normally 1 brood.

Notes: Often observed nesting in same tree with Eastern Kingbird.

BLACK-HEADED ORIOLE *Icterus graduacauda*

Breeding range: S. Texas (Rio Grande Valley).

Habitat: Dense forests along resacas and sluggish watercourses.

Nest: Semipensile basket (similar to nest of Orchard Oriole) typically about 3 in. (7.6 cm) deep, attached to upright terminal branches of tree, often mesquite, 6–14 ft. (1.8–4.3 m) above ground. Woven of fine wirelike grasses, gathered while green, lined with fine grass tops. Rim somewhat contracted.

Eggs: 3–5; av. 25.02 x 18.29 mm. Oval to long-oval. No gloss. Pale bluish white, grayish white; blotched, streaked, profusely or sparingly, with brown, purples; generally heaviest around large end.

Notes: Heavily parasitized by Bronzed Cowbird.

HOODED ORIOLE   *Icterus cucullatus*   **Pl. 27**

Breeding range: Cen. (rare) and s. California, s. Nevada, sw. Utah (unc.), cen. and s. Arizona, sw. New Mexico, s. Texas (unc.).
Habitat: City parks, suburbs, especially with palms and eucalyptus; also, particularly in Arizona and Texas, in mesquite, cottonwood, sycamore, walnut groves, and woodlands, especially streamside.
Nest: Typically semipensile, swung from overhanging branches or attached directly to underside of live palm leaves 5–45 ft. (1.5–13.7 m) above ground; also in eucalyptus, willow, ash, Avocado (nests sewed to leaves). Built of slender wiry grass or shredded palm fibers; has thick bottom, strong sides, small opening on side or top; unlined or lined with plant down. Av. height 4 in. (10.2 cm); inside diam. 3 x 2 in. (7.6 x 5.1 cm), depth 2½ in. (6.4 cm).
Eggs: 3–5, commonly 4; av. 21.59 x 15.24 mm. Oval. No gloss. Dull white; blotched, spotted, principally about large end, with irregularly shaped markings of dark brown, gray (lines and tracings so evident in most oriole eggs generally absent).
Notes: If available, Spanish Moss is sometimes used in building or concealing nest; mistletoe used as site. Also reported are nests built in Spanish Bayonet in which fibers of the plant are used in construction.

LICHTENSTEIN'S ORIOLE   *Icterus gularis*   **opp. p. 147**

Breeding range: Texas (Rio Grande delta, Cameron and Hidalgo Cos.).
Habitat: Lowlands, hill slopes, woodlands, cultivated areas.
Nest: Long — up to 25 in. (63.5 cm) — pensile pouch placed conspicuously at end of horizontal branch of ebony, tepeguaje, mesquite, willow; 12–50 ft. (3.7–15.3 m) above ground. Of Spanish Moss, palm, and other vegetable fibers; lined with grass, plant down. Starting at top working down, female weaves nest with bill in 18–26 days.
Eggs: 3–4; av. 29.5 x 19.0 mm. Long-oval. Slightly glossy. Bluish white, grayish white; scrawled, irregularly spotted with brown, black, lavender.

SCOTT'S ORIOLE   *Icterus parisorum*   **Pl. 27**

Breeding range: Se. California, s. Idaho (rare), Utah (unc.), s. Nevada, Arizona, s. New Mexico, w. Texas.
Habitat: Intermediate zone between pinyon-juniper foothills and desert mountain slopes (avoids cactus deserts).
Nest: Sturdy basket of twisted, interlaced grasses plucked green, fibers of dead yucca leaves; lined with finer grasses, cottony materials, soft vegetable substances, horsehair; lashed to leaves of

yucca, palm, sometimes in center of mistletoe clump, occasionally in pinyon, oak, sycamore; 8–20 ft. (2.4–6.1 m) above ground. Inside diam. 4 in. (10.2 cm); inside depth 3½ in. (8.9 cm).

Eggs: 2–4, typically 3; av. 23.86 x 16.98 mm. Oval to long-oval. Shell close grained, no gloss. Pale bluish white; small blotches, dots, zigzag markings of black, browns, gray, principally at large end. Incubation by female alone; 14 days. Possibly 2 broods.

Notes: Nest found by author in Santa Rita Mts., Arizona, was attached to 13 different hanging strands in clump of mistletoe 17 ft. (5.2 m) above ground in oak tree. Bound with dry grass.

SCOTT'S ORIOLE

NORTHERN ORIOLE *Icterus galbula*   **Pl. 28**
(including Baltimore and Bullock's Orioles)

Breeding range: All western states.

Habitat: Farms, ranches, city parks, suburbs with shade trees, deciduous woodlands, orchards, roadsides.

Nest: Elms, maples, willows, cottonwoods, sycamores, apples favored; also in many other trees; 6–60 ft. (1.8–18.3 m) above ground, av. 25–30 ft. (7.6–9.2 m), often along streams and irrigation ditches. Attached at rim to drooping branch; intricately woven deep pouch of plant fibers (milkweed, Indian Hemp), hair, yarn, string, grapevine, bark; Spanish Moss in South; lined with hair, wool, fine grasses, cottony materials; opening at top, rarely at side. *More pendulous* than nest of Orchard Oriole; grass abundant in Orchard nest, restricted in Northern nest. Female normally builds new nest each year in $4\frac{1}{2}$–8 days. Outside height $3\frac{1}{2}$–8 in. (8.9–20.3 cm), av. 5 in. (12.7 cm); oval entrance 2 x $3\frac{1}{4}$ in. (5.1 x 8.3 cm); inside diam. $2\frac{1}{2}$ in. (6.4 cm), depth av. $4\frac{1}{2}$ in. (11.4 cm).

Eggs: 3–6, commonly 4–5; av. 23.80 x 15.93 mm (*I. g. bullockii*). Oval to long-oval. Shell smooth, has slight gloss. Pale grayish white, pale bluish white; streaked, scrawled, blotched with browns, black; generally concentrated at large end. Incubation by female; 12–14 days. 1 brood.

Notes: Western race (Bullock's) usually builds less pensile nest than eastern (Baltimore); generally secured more at sides to adjoining twigs as well as by rim. Nests often built in same tree as those of Eastern or Western Kingbirds.

BREWER'S BLACKBIRD   Pl. 28
Euphagus cyanocephalus

Breeding range: Washington to Minnesota, south to Baja, Arizona, w. and n. New Mexico, w. S. Dakota, w. Nebraska, Oklahoma (unc.).

Habitat: Ranches, prairies, farmyards, roadsides, streamside thickets, orchards, marsh edges.

Nest: Singly or in loose colonies, 6–30 pairs; on ground in thick, weedy cover; in cliff crannies; in shrubs or deciduous or coniferous trees as high as 150 ft. (45.8 m) above ground, av. 20–40 ft. (6.1–

NORTHERN (BULLOCK'S) ORIOLE

12.2 m). Sturdy; built of interlaced twigs, forb stalks, grasses; strengthened by matrix of mud or cow dung; lined with rootlets, grasses, hair. Female builds, accompanied by male. In colony, all nests often in identical vegetation. Ground nests more common eastward. Outside diam. 5–6 in. (12.7–15.2 cm), height 3¼ in. (8.3 cm); inside diam. 3 in. (7.6 cm), depth 1½ in. (3.8 cm).

Eggs: 3–7, typically 4–6; av. 25.49 x 18.60 mm. Oval to long-oval. Shell smooth, has slight gloss. Light gray, greenish gray; spotted, blotched with grayish brown, sepia; sometimes ground color hidden by overlay of dark brown markings. Female incubates; 12–14 days. 2 broods. Males monogamous or polygamous (normally 2 mates, occasionally more).

Notes: In Colorado study, Hanka found 50 percent of nests parasitized by Brown-headed Cowbird. In 1 nest he found 6 Cowbird eggs, 3 Blackbird eggs. Nearby (Lake John, Jackson Co.) in colony of Yellow-headed Blackbirds, only 1 nest parasitized.

GREAT-TAILED GRACKLE   BOAT-TAILED GRACKLE

GREAT-TAILED GRACKLE *Quiscalus mexicanus*

Breeding range: Arizona, Texas, sw. Louisiana; presently expanding north to sw. Arkansas, Kansas, Colorado, and west to s. California.

Habitat: Towns, farmlands with trees (Huisache, mesquite, cedar, elm, live oak) and thickets; swamps, marshes with trees, bushes.

Nest: In trees, bushes, man-made structures; marsh vegetation used where no trees or bushes available close to water source. 2 ft. (0.6 m) above water in marshes to 50 ft. (15.3 m) above ground in tall live oaks. Sometimes in heronry. Female builds; tree nests of twigs, forb stalks, Spanish Moss, string, paper, feathers; marsh nests of rushes, cattails, marsh grasses; mud or cow dung often used in foundation.

Eggs: 3–4; av. 32.18 x 21.75 mm. Mostly long-oval. Pale greenish blue, clouded with purple and pale brown tints; marked with coarse irregularly shaped lines and tracings of shades of dark brown, black, gray. Almost if not entirely *indistinguishable from eggs of Boat-tailed Grackle.* Incubation by female; 13 days. Mating promiscuous.

Notes: In coastal sw. Louisiana and se. Texas, range overlaps that of Boat-tailed Grackle, but hybridization is unknown. Females consistently choose mates of own species.

BOAT-TAILED GRACKLE   *Quiscalus major*

Breeding range: Texas, Louisiana, Oklahoma, cen. Kansas.
Habitat: Open coastal areas, islands, fresh- and salt-water marshes.
Nest: In colonies, generally near or over water in willows, cattails, saw grass, bulrushes; 1–4 ft. (0.3–1.2 m) above ground or water; also in trees up to 40–50 ft. (12.2–15.3 m) above ground, av. 10–12 ft. (3.1–3.7 m). Female alone builds bulky, loosely constructed, open cup of grasses, rushes, vines; woven around tree twigs or stems of surrounding vegetation; lined with mud, then with fine grasses, forb stems. Inside diam. usually 4–5 in. (10.2–12.7 cm), depth 2¾–4 in. (7.1–10.2 cm).
Eggs: 3, rarely 4; av. 31.60 x 22.49 mm. Long-oval to oval. Shell smooth, has slight gloss. Light blue, pale bluish gray; boldly spotted, scrawled with browns, grays, purples, black. Almost if not entirely *indistinguishable from eggs of Great-tailed Grackle.* Incubation by female; 13 days. Mating promiscuous. Males may leave when sexual mating accomplished.
Notes: In coastal sw. Louisiana and se. Texas, range overlaps that of Great-tailed Grackle; hybridization unknown. Females consistently choose mates of own species.

COMMON GRACKLE   *Quiscalus quiscula*   Pl. 28

Breeding range: East of Rockies; cen. and e. Montana to Minnesota, south to e. New Mexico (local), ne. Texas, Louisiana.
Habitat: Marsh edges, islands, swamp thickets, coniferous groves, cities, suburbs, farms.
Nest: Usually in small colonies of 20–30 pairs in deciduous or coniferous trees up to 60 ft. (18.3 m) above ground; also shrubs, roadside plantings; natural cavities, ledges; cattail marshes, 1–3 ft. (0.3–0.9 m) above water. Loose, bulky; built of forbs, grasses, Spanish Moss, debris; usually reinforced with mud; lined with fine grasses, moss. Female builds in about 11 days. Outside diam. 7–9 in. (17.8–22.9 cm), height 5–8 in. (12.7–20.3 cm); inside diam. 4–4½ in. (10.2–11.4 cm), depth 3–3¾ in. (7.6–9.5 cm).
Eggs: 3–6, commonly 5; av. 28.53 x 20.89 mm. Oval. Shell smooth, has slight gloss. Pale green or blue; blotched, scrawled,

BROWN-HEADED COWBIRD female removing egg from nest of Chestnut-sided Warbler.

spotted with dark browns, purples. Incubation by female alone; 12–14 days, av. 13, starting with next to last egg. Probably 1 brood.

Notes: Unusual nesting sites: cavity in lower part of Osprey nest; Wood Duck boxes; unit of a 16-apartment Martin house; cavities in deciduous and coniferous trees; bridge, tower, cornbinder, rafters of old buildings.

BROWN-HEADED COWBIRD *Molothrus ater* Pl. 28

Breeding range: All western states.

Habitat: Farms, ranches, open deciduous or coniferous woods, forest edges, suburban gardens, city parks.

Nest: Builds no nest. *Parasitic;* lays eggs in nests of other birds, depending on host to hatch eggs, raise young.

Eggs: 1 egg laid per day until clutch of 6 or more laid, usually in different nests. After interval of several days, 2nd clutch laid. Possibly 3–4 clutches per season; total of eggs probably 11–20. Av. 21.45 x 16.42 mm. Typically oval; vary greatly. Shell granulated, moderately glossy. White, grayish white; evenly dotted with browns; often heavier markings at large end. Incubation by host; 11–12 days.

Notes: Cowbird lays eggs at dawn; usually removes egg of host day before or day after parasitic egg laid. Host may desert nest, build floor over Cowbird egg, throw it out, or accept it. Gray Catbird, American Robin, and Loggerhead Shrike known to throw eggs out. Yellow Warbler and Song Sparrow most heavily victimized. Record numbers of Cowbird eggs in 1 nest: Wood Thrush 9; 4

species each 8; 3 species each 7. Author found Red-eyed Vireo incubating 4 Cowbird eggs, no Vireo eggs.

BRONZED COWBIRD *Molothrus aeneus* Pl. 28

Breeding range: Se. California (prob.), Arizona, sw. New Mexico, se. Texas, sw. Louisiana (rare, 1976 record).
Habitat: Open country, ranches, roadside thickets, open woods, parks, orchards.
Nest: Builds no nest. *Parasitic;* lays eggs in nests of other birds, depending on host to incubate eggs, raise young.
Eggs: 1 egg laid per day, often in nests of orioles, especially Northern, Hooded, and Orchard Orioles. At least 62 species known to have been parasitized. Av. 23.11 x 18.29 mm. Shell finely granulated, rather glossy. Oval to short-oval and elliptical. Pale bluish green, occasionally white, unmarked. *Resemble eggs of Black-throated Sparrow and Blue Grosbeak, but are larger.*
Notes: Multiple eggs in single nest include 7 in Cardinal's nest, 6 in nest of Red-winged Blackbird. Nests have been parasitized simultaneously by Brown-headed and Bronzed Cowbirds. In Texas author found Red-winged Blackbird's nest with 3 eggs of Bronzed Cowbird, 1 of Brown-headed Cowbird, 2 of Redwing.

3 BRONZED COWBIRD eggs and 1 Brown-headed Cowbird egg in nest of Red-winged Blackbird with 2 Redwing eggs.

WESTERN TANAGER *Piranga ludoviciana* Pl. 28

Breeding range: Washington to Montana, south to Mexico, w. Texas (Guadalupe Mts.); S. Dakota (Black Hills), nw. Nebraska.

Habitat: Coniferous and pine-oak forests. In southern part of range mainly in mountains (absent from deserts).

Nest: Usually in pine, fir; occasionally in oak, aspen. Saddled in fork of horizontal branch well out from trunk, 15–65 ft. (4.6–19.8 m) above ground, av. 20–30 ft. (6.1–9.2 m). Shallow, compact saucer of coniferous twigs, rootlets; lined with hair, rootlets.

Eggs: 3–5; av. 22.9 x 16.8 mm. Oval to short-oval. Somewhat glossy. Bluish green; marked with irregular dots, spots, blotches well distributed over entire egg. Markings may be heaviest at large end. Incubation by female; probably 13 days. 1 brood.

Notes: Birds tend to loiter in spring migration; late sight records do not necessarily indicate breeding in area. Fresh egg dates suggest height of season June 10–20. Nests in aspen, sycamore atypical. Incubating female usually reluctant to leave nest when disturbed; has been lifted by hand.

SCARLET TANAGER *Piranga olivacea*

Breeding range: Minnesota south to n. Arkansas; N. Dakota (unc.), e. S. Dakota, Nebraska (Missouri R. Valley), ne. Kansas (rare), e. Oklahoma.

Habitat: Deciduous or coniferous woodlands; groves, parks, orchards, roadside trees.

Nest: 8–75 ft. (2.4–22.9 m) above ground, well out on limb of tree, commonly oak. Small, flimsy, flat cup built by female of twigs, rootlets; lined with forb stems, grasses. Eggs sometimes seen from ground through thin bottom of nest.

SCARLET TANAGER

Eggs: 3–5, commonly 4; av. 23.3 x 16.5 mm. Oval, sometimes short-oval. Shell smooth, moderately glossy. Pale blue, pale green; irregularly dotted, spotted, blotched with browns. Markings often concentrated at large end; generally *not as bold as on eggs of Summer Tanager.* Smaller than eggs of Rose-breasted Grosbeak. Incubation by female alone; 13–14 days.

HEPATIC TANAGER *Piranga flava*

Breeding range: Arizona, New Mexico, Texas (Guadalupe, Davis, and Chisos Mts.); also California (San Bernardino Mts., prob.).
Habitat: Canyons and mountains, generally 5000–7500 ft. (1525–2288 m), in open deciduous or coniferous woodlands.
Nest: In conifers, oaks, sometimes sycamores, 18–50 ft. (5.5–15.3 m) above ground in horizontal fork well out from trunk. Flat saucer of grasses, forb stems; lined with finer grasses.
Eggs: 3–5, commonly 4; av. 24.5 x 17.7 mm. Oval. Moderately glossy. Blue or blue-green; dotted, spotted with browns, generally well distributed over entire egg, may be wreathed. Tend to be *less heavily marked than eggs of Western or Summer Tanagers.*
Notes: 4 nests found by author in Santa Rita Mts., Arizona, were 35 ft. (10.7 m), 40 ft. (12.2 m), 45 ft. (13.7 m), and 50 ft. (15.3 m) above ground; 3 in oak, 1 in sycamore, well hidden in foliage, inaccessible for photography.

SUMMER TANAGER *Piranga rubra*   Pl. 28

Breeding range: S. California (rare), s. Nevada (Clark Co.), sw. Utah (rare), Arizona, s. New Mexico, se. Nebraska, and s. Iowa (unc.), south to Texas and Louisiana.
Habitat: Open, dry, deciduous (mostly) or coniferous woods, groves, orchards, roadside trees; riparian groves in arid areas.
Nest: On horizontal limb (often oak) 10–35 ft. (3.1–10.7 m) above ground, well out from trunk. Flimsy, flat, shallow cup of forb stems, bark, leaves, grasses, Spanish Moss (in South), spider silk; lined with fine grasses. Only female builds, accompanied by male. Outside diam. $3\frac{1}{4}$ x $4\frac{5}{16}$ in. (8.3 x 11.0 cm), height $2\frac{3}{16}$ in. (5.6 cm); inside diam. $2\frac{7}{16}$ x 3 in. (6.2 x 7.6 cm), depth $1\frac{3}{8}$ in. (3.5 cm).
Eggs: 3–4, rarely 5; av. 23.1 x 17.1 mm. Commonly oval, varying to short- or long-oval. Shell smooth, moderately glossy. Pale blue, pale green; dotted, spotted, blotched with brown, faint undertones of gray; markings well distributed over entire egg, sometimes concentrated or capped at large end; *bolder than on eggs of Scarlet and Western Tanagers.* Incubation by female; 11–12 days. 1 brood.
Notes: Where ranges of Scarlet and Summer Tanagers overlap, positive identification of similar nest and eggs should not be made until bird is seen.

CARDINAL   *Cardinalis cardinalis*   **Pl. 28**

Breeding range: California (Colorado R. Valley), Arizona, New Mexico; N. Dakota (unc.) and s. and cen. Minnesota, south to Texas and Louisiana.
Habitat: Woodland edges, thickets, groves, suburban gardens, parks; typically shuns deep forests.
Nest: Placed in dense shrubbery, small deciduous or coniferous tree, thicket, vine, briar tangle, mesquite, 3–20 ft. (0.9–6.1 m) above ground, generally below 10 ft. (3.1 m). Loosely built of twigs, vines, some leaves, bark strips (grapevine), grasses, forb stalks, rootlets; lined with fine grasses, hair. Female builds in 3–9 days, occasionally assisted by male. As long as 6 days may elapse between nest completion and laying of 1st egg.
Eggs: 2–5, commonly 3–4; av. 25.3 x 18.2 mm. Typically oval, sometimes long- or short-oval. Shell smooth, somewhat glossy. Grayish, bluish, greenish white; dotted, spotted, blotched with browns, grays, purples. Some so thickly marked, ground color almost obliterated; others sparingly spotted. *Indistinguishable from eggs of Pyrrhuloxia.* Incubation by female; 12–13 days (male has been observed on nest occasionally). 2–3 broods.
Notes: Similar nest of Gray Catbird invariably contains many leaves in foundation (absent or sparse in Cardinal nest), is generally lined with rootlets (lining of fine grasses in Cardinal nest). Cases of 2 females sharing same nest simultaneously reported several times. 1 nest shared with Song Sparrow.

PYRRHULOXIA   *Cardinalis sinuatus*   **Pl. 29**

Breeding range: S. Arizona, s. New Mexico, sw. and s. Texas, California (San Bernardino Co., 1977).
Habitat: Open mesquite thickets, thorny desert bushes, arroyos, lower portions of canyons, river edges.
Nest: Most often in mesquite, catclaw, condalia, frequently in clumps of mistletoe, 5–8 ft. (1.5–2.4 m) above ground. Small, compactly built of thorny twigs, inner bark, coarse grass, spider silk; lined with rootlets, occasionally fine grass and bark fibers included. Outside diam. 4–4½ in. (10.2–11.4 cm), height 3½ in. (8.9 cm); inside diam. 2¼–2½ in. (5.7–6.4 cm), depth 2 in. (5.1 cm). Generally smaller and more compactly built than Cardinal's nest. Female does most if not all building.
Eggs: 3–4, sometimes 2; av. 23.9 x 17.7 mm (*C. s. fulvescens*). Oval. Somewhat glossy. Grayish white, greenish white; dotted, spotted, blotched with browns overlaid on markings of pale gray; well scattered over entire egg. *Indistinguishable from eggs of Cardinal.* Incubation by female; 14 days.
Notes: Although nesting habits are generally similar, Pyrrhuloxia tends to require denser woodlands in which to nest than Cardinal.

ROSE-BREASTED GROSBEAK

The 2 species do not defend territories against each other. Material used in building often gives Pyrrhuloxia nest a grayish appearance.

ROSE-BREASTED GROSBEAK   *Pheucticus ludovicianus*

Breeding range: E. and n.-cen. N. Dakota, Minnesota, south to e. and cen. Oklahoma (cas.), and Missouri (unc.); also n. Colorado (prob.).
Habitat: Moist, deciduous, second-growth woods, swamp borders, thickets, old orchards, suburban trees, shrubs.
Nest: Generally in fork of deciduous tree, shrub (occasionally conifer), 6–26 ft. (1.8–7.9 m) above ground, av. 10–15 ft. (3.1–4.6 m). Loosely built of small sticks, fine twigs, ornamented with a few skeleton leaves; lined with fine twigs, rootlets, sometimes horsehair. Nest often so flimsy that eggs can be seen through lining from ground. Female builds with some assistance from male.
Eggs: 3–5, commonly 4; av. 24.6 x 17.7 mm. Typically oval. Little gloss. Pale green, blue, or bluish green; dotted, spotted, blotched with browns, purples; generally wreathed or capped. *Indistinguishable from eggs of Black-headed Grosbeak. Similar to eggs of Scarlet Tanager* but usually more heavily marked. Incubation by both sexes; about 14 days. Both birds sing while incubating, especially male. Typically 1 brood, occasionally 2.
Notes: Hybrids with Black-headed Grosbeak sometimes occur where ranges of two species overlap (Nebraska, N. Dakota). Nest found by author contained 757 twigs 1–5 in. (2.5–12.7 cm) long.

BLACK-HEADED GROSBEAK   Pl. 29
Pheucticus melanocephalus

Breeding range: Washington to w. N. Dakota, south to Mexico and through w. S. Dakota, w. Nebraska, w. Kansas to w. Texas (apparently not in Oklahoma).

Habitat: Riparian woodlands, mixed and second-growth forests, willow-cottonwood associations, often in forest edges; orchards, gardens.

Nest: In fork of shrub or small tree 4–12 ft. (1.2–3.7 m) above ground. Height records of 163 California nests averaged 10 ft. (3.1 m). Records show 120 nests placed in 29 plant species, about 80 percent deciduous. Bulky, open cup of interlaced twigs, forb stems, sometimes leaf-bearing twigs plucked green, flower heads; lined rather carelessly with rootlets and grass stems; so thinly made that eggs often can be seen from ground through bottom. Built by female, accompanied by male; 3–4 days. Outside diam. $5\frac{1}{2}$ in. (14 cm), height $3\frac{1}{8}$ in. (7.9 cm); inside diam. $3\frac{1}{8}$ in. (7.9 cm), depth $1\frac{3}{4}$ in. (4.5 cm).

Eggs: 2–5, commonly 3–4; av. 24.7 x 17.7 mm. Typically oval. Little gloss. Pale green, blue, bluish green; dotted, spotted, blotched with browns, purples chiefly at large end. *Indistinguishable from eggs of Rose-breasted Grosbeak.* Incubation by both sexes, alternating during day; female at night. Both sing while incubating, especially male.

Notes: Sometimes hybridizes with Rose-breasted Grosbeak where ranges overlap, mostly Nebraska (Missouri R. Valley) and N. Dakota.

BLUE GROSBEAK   *Guiraca caerulea*   Pl. 29

Breeding range: California, s. Nevada, Idaho (Elmore Co., rare), s.-cen. Montana (prob.), S. Dakota, sw. Minnesota (prob.) south to Mexico, Texas, n. Louisiana.

Habitat: Overgrown fields, streamside woodlands, brushy woodland edges, scrubby thickets, open groves, hedgerows.

Nest: In low tree or bush, tangle of vegetation (vines, briars), 3–8 ft. (0.9–2.4 m) above ground, typically at edge of open area. Compact, rather deep; built of grass, bark strips, leaves, forb stems, snakeskins, paper, cotton; lined with rootlets, hair (sometimes), grasses. Inside diam. $2\frac{3}{8}$ in. (6 cm), depth 2 in. (5.1 cm).

Eggs: 3–5, commonly 4; av. 21.8 x 16.3 mm (*G. c. interfusa*). Typically oval. Shell smooth, has slight gloss. Pale bluish white, unmarked; often fades to near white before hatching. *Unlike other grosbeak eggs; similar to Indigo, Lazuli, and Varied Bunting eggs but larger.* Incubation by female; 11–12 days. Typically 2 broods, especially in South.

Notes: In 23 nests reported in New Mexico, 21 had cast-off snakeskins in foundations. 1 nest reported almost entirely covered with snakeskins. Oklahoma nest built almost entirely of newspaper, but lined with reddish rootlets. Mississippi nest built externally of cotton from nearby field.

INDIGO BUNTING

INDIGO BUNTING *Passerina cyanea*

Breeding range: E. Montana (prob.) east to Minnesota, south to cen. Arizona, New Mexico, n. Texas, Louisiana. 1 nest record for California (Los Angeles, 1958).

Habitat: Open brushy fields, clearings, hedgerows, roadside thickets, woodland edges, overgrown fencerows; avoids mature forests.

Nest: In crotch of bush, shrub, low tree, blackberry tangle; firmly attached by rim and sides to supporting plants 2–12 ft. (0.6–3.7 m) above ground in dense cover. Well-woven cup of dried grasses, bark strips, twigs, forbs, on base of leaves; lined with fine grasses, cotton, rootlets, sometimes hair, feathers. May occasionally use snakeskin in foundation. Shape may be oval or round. Female builds alone.

Eggs: 3–4, occasionally 2; av. 18.7 x 13.7 mm. Oval to short-oval. Shell smooth, has slight gloss. Pale bluish white to pure white; unmarked. *Indistinguishable from eggs of Lazuli and Varied Buntings; similar to Blue Grosbeak eggs but smaller.* Incubation by female; 12–13 days. Probably 2 broods in South.

Notes: Hybridization with Lazuli Bunting reported frequently from Great Plains where ranges overlap. Serious factor in breeding success of Indigo Bunting is parasitism by Brown-headed Cowbird.

LAZULI BUNTING   *Passerina amoena*   **Pl. 29**

Breeding range: Washington east to w. N. Dakota, south to Baja, ne. and cen. Arizona, n. New Mexico (unc.), w. Oklahoma.
Habitat: Broken chaparral, weedy thickets, clumps of bushes, willow thickets, low hillside vegetation, pastures; often along watercourses but not over water or damp ground.
Nest: Coarsely woven cup of dried grasses; lined with finer grasses, horsehair; lashed firmly to supporting stalks or in fork of bush in thicket or tangle (rarely, low in trees); usually 2–4 ft. (0.6–1.2 m) above ground. Outside diam. 4 in. (10.2 cm), height 3 in. (7.6 cm); inside diam. 2 in. (5.1 cm), depth 2 in. (5.1 cm).
Eggs: 3–5, typically 4; av. 18.7 x 13.6 mm. Oval. Slightly glossy. Pale bluish white, unspotted. *Indistinguishable from eggs of Indigo and Varied Buntings; similar to Blue Grosbeak eggs but smaller.* Incubation by female; 12 days. Generally 2 broods.
Notes: In Great Plains, Lazuli and Indigo Buntings frequently hybridize. Possible case of polygamy reported in S. Dakota — male Lazuli observed with 2 females, an Indigo and a Lazuli.

VARIED BUNTING   *Passerina versicolor*

Breeding range: S. Arizona, s. New Mexico, s. Texas.
Habitat: Desert brush (mesquite); avoids heavily wooded areas.
Nest: In thick bush, tangled vine, low tree, 2–10 ft. (0.6–3.1 m) above ground. Compact cup of dry grass, small forb stems, plant cotton, soft materials; lined with rootlets, fine grasses.
Eggs: 3–4; av. 17.8 x 14.3 mm. Short- to long-oval. Pale bluish white, unmarked. *Indistinguishable from eggs of Indigo and Lazuli Buntings.*
Notes: 8 nests in Cameron Co., Texas, in small bushes, 16 in. (40.6 cm) to 5 ft. (1.5 m) above ground. Occasionally cast-off snakeskin in foundation. Birds shy; female difficult to see.

PAINTED BUNTING   *Passerina ciris*

Breeding range: S. New Mexico, Texas, Kansas (west to Clark Co.), Oklahoma, Missouri (rare or cas.), Arkansas (cas.), Louisiana.
Habitat: Bushes, hedgerows, woodland edges, roadsides.
Nest: Firmly attached to twigs or other supporting vegetation at low elevations, commonly 3–9 ft. (0.9–2.8 m), in bushes, vine tangles, low trees. Shallow cup, well made, woven of grasses, forb stems, leaves; lined with fine grasses, rootlets, hair. Built by female in as little as 2 days (may complete lining after 1st egg laid).
Eggs: 3–4, rarely 5; av. 18.9 x 14.5 mm. Oval to short-oval. Shell smooth, has slight gloss. White, bluish white, grayish white; spotted with reddish brown; markings often concentrated at large end. Incubation by female; 11–12 days, often beginning with laying of next to last egg. Normally 2 broods; in South 3 reported occasionally.

Notes: While female tends fledged young unassisted, she carries fresh nesting material to new site for 2nd brood. Just before egg-laying, male suddenly, dramatically, takes charge of 1st brood, which female then abandons. Not all females have 2 broods. Some mate with polygamous males, which may at the same time be mated to double-brooded females.

DICKCISSEL *Spiza americana*   Pl. 29

Breeding range: N. Dakota and s. Minnesota south to Texas and Louisiana; casual in e. Montana, e. Wyoming, e. Colorado, e. New Mexico.
Habitat: Prairies, hayfields, meadows, weed patches.
Nest: On or near ground, typically well hidden in rank growth of grass, forbs, alfalfa, clover. Bulky, substantial, shallow cup of forbs, grass stems, leaves; lined with finer grasses, rootlets, hair; loosely interwoven with surrounding vegetation. Female builds; about 4 days. Av. size 10 nests: outside diam. $4\,^{13}/_{16}$ in. (12.2 cm), height $2\frac{1}{2}$ in. (6.4 cm); inside diam. $2\frac{3}{8}$ x $2\,^{11}/_{16}$ in. (6.0 x 6.8 cm), depth $1\,^{13}/_{16}$ in. (4.6 cm).
Eggs: 3–5, commonly 4; av. 20.8 x 15.7 mm. Oval to long-oval. Shell smooth, glossy. Pale blue, unmarked. *Indistinguishable from eggs of Lark Bunting.* Female incubates; 11–12 days; may start with laying of next to last egg. Typically 2 broods. Male may occasionally be polygamous.
Notes: Nests very difficult to find. Female approaches from distance walking on ground; after eggs hatch shyness diminishes. Species erratic in distribution; may fluctuate from year to year in entire region.

EVENING GROSBEAK *Hesperiphona vespertina*

Breeding range: Coastal forests and mountain chains from Washington to e.-cen. California; Montana to Arizona and New Mexico.
Habitat: Coniferous mountain forests.
Nest: 20–100 ft. (6.1–30.5 m) above ground, on horizontal limb of conifer; occasionally in deciduous tree. Female builds frail loose cup of twigs, lined with rootlets, fine grass fibers, pine needles, moss shreds. Outside diam. about $4\frac{1}{2}$ in. (11.4 cm); inside diam. about 3 in. (7.6 cm), depth 1 in. (2.5 cm).
Eggs: 2–5, commonly 4; av. 23.0 x 16.4 mm (*H. v. brooksi*). Oval to long-oval. Fairly glossy. Clear blue or blue-green; blotched, spotted with browns, grays, purple, with occasional fine black-pencil markings. Resemble eggs of Red-winged Blackbird. Incubation by female; may start before clutch complete.
Notes: In nests found in Yosemite National Park only 1 was less than 40 ft. (12.2 m) above ground; 2 were 100 ft. (30.5 m). Nests similar to those of Purple Finch but of heavier, larger twigs.

California nests have been found from sea level in Coast Range to 9000 ft. (2745 m) in Sierra Nevada.

PURPLE FINCH   *Carpodacus purpureus*   Pl. 29

Breeding range: Washington to Baja in coastal forests; N. Dakota (rare), ne. and n.-cen. Minnesota.
Habitat: Coniferous and mixed woodlands.
Nest: Almost always on horizontal branch of conifer (fork of small tree), 5–60 ft. (1.5–18.3 m) above ground. Female builds neat, shallow cup of twigs, forb stems, bark strips, rootlets; lined with mosses, fine grasses, hair. *Indistinguishable from nest of Cassin's Finch.*
Eggs: 3–5, commonly 4; av. 19.9 x 14.5 mm (*C. p. californicus*). Oval to short-oval. Shell smooth, has slight gloss. Pale greenish blue; dotted, spotted, scrawled in short lines with browns, blacks; markings scattered over entire egg, generally heaviest at large end. *Indistinguishable from eggs of Cassin's Finch.* Female incubates; 13 days. Probably 2 broods in West, 1 in East.
Notes: California race not as likely to choose evergreen for nesting site as eastern form; alders and willows often used. Incubating female sits very tight; may permit intruder to lift her from nest.

CASSIN'S FINCH   *Carpodacus cassinii*

Breeding range: Washington to w. and cen. Montana, south to Baja, n. Arizona, New Mexico (loc., cas.); S. Dakota (Black Hills, poss.).
Habitat: Coniferous forests (lodgepole and yellow pine, fir); typically at high altitudes.
Nest: In colonies or single, almost always in large conifers, usually near ends of limbs, 15–60 ft. (4.6–18.3 m) above ground, av. 30–40 ft. (9.2–12.2 m); occasionally in deciduous tree, particularly aspen. Of dry forb stems, twigs; lined with rootlets, hair, fine grass stems, bark fibers; sometimes decorated with lichens. *Indistinguishable from nest of Purple Finch.* Inside diam. 2⅓ in. (5.9 cm), depth 1⅛ in. (2.9 cm). Female builds.
Eggs: 3–6, commonly 4–5; av. 20.3 x 14.7 mm. Typically oval. Slightly glossy. Bluish green; dotted, spotted with browns, black, often with loose wreath around large end. *Indistinguishable from eggs of Purple Finch.* Incubation by female; 12 or more days. Possibly 2 broods.
Notes: Cassin's Finches found in flocks except during breeding season (May–July). During nest-building and egg-laying, pairs feed away from nest area. Males feed incubating mates on nest. Nonbreeding yearling males when not singing form flocks of up to 50 birds and forage near nesting colony.

HOUSE FINCH   *Carpodacus mexicanus*   **Pl. 29**

Breeding range: Washington to s. Montana, south to Baja, east to w. Nebraska, Kansas (Morton, Ellis, Decatur Cos.), Oklahoma (Cimarron Co.), w. and cen. Texas. Expansion eastward continues.
Habitat: Deserts, chaparral, open woods, farms, cities, suburbs, parks; adapts easily to civilized environment.
Nest: Well-made cup of grass, twigs, debris placed in tree, vine, shrub; on building ledge; in cavity, birdbox — an infinite variety of situations. Nests of other species often taken (orioles, phoebes, towhees, grosbeaks, and others). Female builds in as few as 2 days.
Eggs: 2–6, usually 4–5; av. 18.8 x 13.8 mm. Typically oval. Shell smooth, has slight gloss. Pale bluish green; sparingly dotted with black. *Paler* than eggs of Cassin's and Purple Finches. Incubation by female; 12–14 days, av. 13; may start before last egg laid. 2 or more broods. Male feeds incubating female by regurgitation.
Notes: Tendency to use same nest, not only for 2nd brood, but in subsequent years. Polygamy may occur occasionally. Birds nesting around dwellings may become unusually tame. Instances of Black Phoebes and Robins using same nest simultaneously with House Finch noted. In California, 1 Black Phoebe nest contained 6 eggs of Phoebe, 5 of Finch.

WHITE-COLLARED SEEDEATER   *Sporophila torqueola*

Notes: This Mexican species breeds in the U.S. in the lower Rio Grande Valley, Texas. Difficult to see; most of their activity, including nesting, occurs in forbs and tall grasses. Giant Ragweed is a favorite nesting plant. A delicate cup of fine grasses and hair usually contains 4 or 5 blue-green, brown-spotted eggs.

PINE GROSBEAK   *Pinicola enucleator*

Breeding range: N. and cen. Washington, Oregon (prob.), n. California, east to w. Montana, south to Arizona (White Mts., prob.), New Mexico (Sangre de Cristo Mts.); S. Dakota (Black Hills, poss.).
Habitat: High coniferous forests.
Nest: Bulky; built of mosses, twigs, grasses, lichens; lined with fine grasses, rootlets; on horizontal limb or fork of evergreen, usually rather low — 5–25 ft. (1.5–7.6 m) above ground.
Eggs: 2–5, commonly 4; av. 24.9 x 17.5 mm (*P. e. montana*). Oval to long-oval. Shell smooth, has slight gloss. Bluish green; spotted, blotched with browns, purples, black. Female incubates; 13–14 days. Male feeds incubating mate. 1 brood.

GRAY-CROWNED ROSY FINCH   *Leucosticte tephrocotis*

Breeding range: High mountains of Washington, Oregon

(Wallowa Mts.), California (Sierra Nevada), n. Idaho, nw. Montana, Wyoming (Big Horn Mts.).

Habitat: Rocky outcrops in alpine tundra.

Nest: Bulky; built of rootlets, mosses, lichens, grasses; lined thickly and firmly with fine grasses and occasionally feathers (ptarmigan) and hair; in cavity or on ledge of rocky tundra outcropping.

Eggs: 4–5; av. 24.5 x 17.3 mm. Oval to pyriform. Glossy. White or light creamy white, unmarked. Female incubates; probably about 14 days.

Notes: Breeding range is generally farther west than that of Black or Brown-capped Rosy Finches. Where ranges overlap, hybridization with Black Rosy Finch may occur.

BLACK ROSY FINCH   *Leucosticte atrata*

Breeding range: Rocky Mts. of Idaho, sw. Montana, ne. Nevada, n. Utah, nw. Wyoming.

Habitat: High rocky tundra slopes above timberline.

Nest: In crevice or cavity in vertical cliff (sometimes inaccessible). Base of mosses; cup of grass, mosses, some hair, feathers; inner lining of fine grass, hair. Built entirely by female, accompanied by male; about 3 days.

Eggs: 4–5; av. 22.1 x 16.0 mm. Oval to pyriform. Pure white, unmarked. Incubation by female alone; 12–14 days.

Notes: On breeding grounds males outnumber females, resulting in unusually close attendance of male, who continually drives off others trying to attract his mate. The ratio varies from 1 female with 4 males to 1 female with 6 or even 8 males. The same ratio seems to exist in young birds. This is believed to be main factor limiting increase in population.

BROWN-CAPPED ROSY FINCH   *Leucosticte australis*

Breeding range: Southern Rockies: Wyoming (Snowy Range), w. and cen. Colorado, New Mexico (Sante Fe Co., 1976).

Habitat: Rocky alpine tundra, usually above 12,000 ft. (3660 m).

Nest: On rock shelves or in cavities of precipitous cliffs, sometimes several feet back in narrow fissure, or in shallow crevice on cliff face. Cup of dry grass, flower stems, compactly woven together with fine moss; lined with fine yellow grass, sometimes feathers (ptarmigan, finch), fur, hair. Female builds in 2–3 days. Outside diam. 5⅔ in. (14.4 cm), height 2¾ in. (7.1 cm); inside diam. 2⅔ in. (6.9 cm), depth 1⅝ in. (4.1 cm).

Eggs: 3–5; av. 22.7 x 15.6 mm. Oval to pyriform. Shell thin, fragile; slightly glossy. White. Incubation by female; 12–14 days.

Notes: Though protected from direct wind, sunless crevices and cavities where nests are built are extremely cold. Water running down surface of rock face near nests often freezes at night. Nest on

Mt. Bross, Colorado, was frozen tightly to ice during cold July nights. Fresh eggs have not been found before late June. Several nests have been found built on beams and rafters in abandoned mine buildings high in Colorado mountains.

PINE SISKIN   *Carduelis pinus*

Breeding range: Throughout western U.S. east to ne. and n.-cen. Minnesota, S. Dakota, nw. Nebraska, Kansas (cas.), w. Texas (Guadalupe and Davis Mts.).
Habitat: Coniferous forests; occasionally deciduous trees.
Nest: Siskins are somewhat colonial but may nest as isolated pairs. Typically erratic in choice of nesting area from year to year. Nest concealed in dense foliage well out from trunk on horizontal limb of tree (usually conifer), 10–40 ft. (3.1–12.2 m) above ground. Large (for size of bird), flat saucer of twigs, grasses, mosses, lichens, bark strips, rootlets; lined with rootlets, mosses, fur, hair, feathers. Female builds, accompanied by male. Outside diam. 4 in. (10.2 cm), height 1½ in. (3.8 cm); inside diam. 2 in. (5.1 cm), depth ¾–1¼ in. (1.9–3.2 cm).
Eggs: 2–4, commonly 3, rarely 5; av. 16.6 x 12.4 mm. Oval to short-oval. Shell smooth, very little gloss. Pale greenish blue; spotted, dotted with browns, black, generally wreathed. Incubation by female; 13 days. Said to start with 1st egg, reducing chance of frozen eggs in early nests.

AMERICAN GOLDFINCH   *Carduelis tristis*   Pl. 29

Breeding range: Pacific Coast states to Baja, east to Minnesota, south to cen. Utah, s. Colorado, cen. Oklahoma, n.-cen. Louisiana (rare).

AMERICAN
GOLDFINCH

Habitat: Open country, overgrown fields with scattered trees, forest openings, villages, groves, farms.

Nest: Generally placed in 4 (more or less) upright branches or in fork of horizontal limb of tree, 1–33 ft. (0.3–10.1 m) above ground, av. 4–14 ft. (1.2–4.3 m). Durable neat cup of fine vegetable fibers woven and lined with thistle and cattail down. Female builds in 4–5 days. Av. size of 79 nests: outside diam. 2⅞ in. (7.3 cm), height 2¹³⁄₁₆ in. (7.1 cm); inside diam. 2 in. (5.1 cm), depth 1⅝ in. (4.1 cm). Some nests tend to be deeper than wide.

Eggs: 4–6, commonly 5; av. 16.2 x 12.2 mm. Oval to short-oval. Shell smooth, very little gloss. Pale blue, unmarked. *Indistinguishable from eggs of Lesser Goldfinch.* Incubation by female; 12–14 days. Male feeds incubating mate.

Notes: All races seem to be late nesters (June–Aug.) except Willow Goldfinch (*C. t. salicamans*), a Pacific Coast race that may nest as early as April. Nests found after young have left easily identified by thick rim of excrement left by nestlings.

LESSER GOLDFINCH *Carduelis psaltria* Pl. 30

Breeding range: Sw. U.S.: California east to nw. Oklahoma (Cimarron Co.), w. and cen. Texas; also s. Oregon.

Habitat: Thickets and bushes close to water; pastures, roadsides, hilly slopes, open land with sparse tree cover, suburban gardens.

Nest: In sycamores, live oaks, cypress, shrubs, forbs, sage, willows, figs, grapevines; 2–30 ft. (0.6–9.2 m) above ground. Cup of plant fibers, fine grass stems, fragments of moss; lined with down (cottonwood, thistle, cotton), few feathers, other soft materials; built firmly into concealing bunch of leaves, branching twigs. Female builds with some help from male. Outside diam. 3 in. (7.6 cm), height 2 in. (5.1 cm); inside diam. 1¾ in. (4.5 cm), depth 1½ in. (3.8 cm). Similar to nest of American Goldfinch.

Eggs: 4–5; av. 14.7 x 11.2 mm (*C. p. hesperophilus*). Oval to short-oval. Shell smooth, very little gloss. Pale blue, unmarked. *Indistinguishable from eggs of American Goldfinch.* Female incubates; 12 days. 2 broods, perhaps 3. Male feeds mate on nest.

Notes: Although highly gregarious most of year, generally not so while nesting. Outstanding exception was 22 pairs nesting in 1 summer on Indian School campus in Santa Fe Co., New Mexico.

LAWRENCE'S GOLDFINCH *Carduelis lawrencei* Pl. 30

Breeding range: Cen. and s. California, west of Sierra Nevada.

Habitat: Chaparral, open woodlands, foothills, mountain valleys, usually close to water.

Nest: Generally in single pairs; occasionally may colonize. Construction highly variable, but typically a dainty cup of grasses, lichens, wool, hair, forb stems, feathers, 3–40 ft. (0.9–12.2 m) above ground, av. about 15 ft. (4.6 m). In live and blue oaks, cypress, low trees, bushes. Female builds, accompanied by male. Outside diam. $3\frac{3}{4}$ in. (9.5 cm), height 2 in. (5.1 cm); inside diam. 2 in. (5.1 cm), depth $1\frac{5}{8}$ in. (4.1 cm).

Eggs: 3–6, commonly 4–5; av. 15.4 x 11.6 mm. Oval to elliptical. Very little gloss. White or very pale bluish white, unmarked, typically *paler than eggs of other goldfinches.* Incubation by female; 12–13 days; almost continuous except for short intervals after being fed by male.

Notes: During 57 hours of observation in 13 days, incubating female remained on nest 97 percent of time, making only 27 trips away from nest, and was gone less than 6 minutes on 23 of them. Female fed regurgitated food by mate about once every hour.

RED CROSSBILL *Loxia curvirostra*

Breeding range: Boreal forests of West, east to N. Dakota (irr.), S. Dakota (Black Hills, cas.), n. and cen. Colorado, New Mexico. Minnesota nest observed March 1967 at Moorhead.

Habitat: Coniferous forests.

Nest: Well out from trunk on branch of conifer, often saddled in thick tuft of needles, 5–80 ft. (1.5–24.4 m) above ground, av. 10–40 ft. (3.1–12.2 m). Loosely arranged, bulky; built of twigs, rootlets, decayed wood, bark strips, lichens; well lined with mosses, fine grasses, feathers, fur. Abundance of food may govern choice of nesting site. Outside diam. $4\frac{1}{2}$–$5\frac{1}{2}$ in. (11.4–14.0 cm), height 3–$3\frac{1}{2}$ in. (7.6–8.9 cm); inside diam. 2–$2\frac{1}{2}$ in. (5.1–6.4 cm), depth $1\frac{1}{4}$–$1\frac{3}{4}$ in. (3.2–4.5 cm). *Indistinguishable from nest of White-winged Crossbill.*

Eggs: 3–5, commonly 4; av. 20.4 x 14.8 mm. Oval to long-oval. Shell smooth, has slight gloss. Pale bluish white or greenish white; spotted, dotted with browns, purples; mostly wreathed or capped at large end. Similar to White-winged Crossbill eggs but not as heavily marked. Incubation by female alone; 12–14 days; attentive for long periods of time; fed at nest by male.

Notes: Dates of nesting very irregular, usually in late winter and early spring, less often in summer and fall. Female's olive-green coloring blends with evergreen needles around nest, making detection very difficult.

WHITE-WINGED CROSSBILL *Loxia leucoptera*

Breeding range: Washington (Cascade Mts., cas.), ne. Oregon (Wallowa Mts.), se. Idaho (rare), w. Montana, S. Dakota (Black Hills, poss.), n. Minnesota (Lake and Cook Cos.).

Habitat: Coniferous forests.

Nest: On horizontal limb of conifer 5–70 ft. (1.5–21.4 m) above ground, av. 8–15 ft. (2.4–4.6 m). Deep cup of twigs, rootlets, forb stalks, mosses, lichens, bark strips; lined with fine grasses, feathers, hair, bark shreds. Outside diam. 4 in. (10.2 cm), height 2–$2\frac{1}{2}$ in. (5.1–6.4 cm); inside diam. $2\frac{1}{4}$–$2\frac{1}{2}$ in. (5.7–6.4 cm), depth $1\frac{1}{4}$–

1½ in. (3.2–3.8 cm). *Indistinguishable from nest of Red Crossbill.*
Eggs: 2–5, commonly 3–4; av. 20.9 x 15.0 mm. Oval to long-oval.
Shell smooth, very little gloss. Pale bluish or greenish white;
spotted, blotched, sometimes scrawled with browns, purples. Similar to Red Crossbill eggs, but more heavily marked. Incubation
by female alone, fed on nest by male.
Notes: Erratic nesting; may be Jan. to May. Nesting biology very
similar to that of closely related Red Crossbill.

OLIVE SPARROW *Arremonops rufivirgatus* opp. p. 147

Breeding range: Resident in southern tip of Texas.
Habitat: Scrubby chaparral, weedy thickets, undergrowth near
forest edges.
Nest: In tangles of shrubbery, cacti (prickly pear), low bushes,
usually less than 3 ft. (0.9 m) above ground. Domed, or nearly
round in shape (large for size of bird); built of dried forb stems, bits
of bark, grasses, leaves; lined with fine straws and hair; part of nest
above entrance overhangs it somewhat.
Eggs: 3–5, typically 4; av. 21.8 x 16.2 mm. Oval to short-oval.
Quite glossy. Pure white, unspotted. 2 broods.

GREEN-TAILED TOWHEE *Pipilo chlorurus* Pl. 30

Breeding range: Se. Washington (Blue Mts.), cen. Oregon, south
to s. California; east to sw. Montana, Wyoming, Colorado, n. New
Mexico, sw. Texas (prob.).
Habitat: Montane and high plateau chaparral, sagebrush, alpine
meadow thickets; altitudes to over 10,000 ft. (3050 m).
Nest: On or near ground, up to 28 in. (71.1 cm); large, loosely
constructed, deeply cupped; built of twigs, grasses, bark (sagebrush); lined with fine plant stems, rootlets, hair. Outside diam.
6 in. (15.2 cm), height 3 in. (7.6 cm); inside diam. 2⅜ in. (6 cm),
depth 1 9/16 in. (4 cm).
Eggs: 2–5, commonly 4; av. 21.8 x 16.4 mm. Record of 28 sets: 3
of 2, 7 of 3, 15 of 4, 3 of 5. Oval to short-oval. Moderately glossy.
White; profusely dotted, finely spotted with browns and grays,
often forming cap at large end. Possibly 2 broods.
Notes: In records of 27 nests, 11 were in or at base of sagebrush, 7
in waxberry, 4 in snowbush, 2 associated with scrubby oaks, 1 each
in chokeberry, juniper, gooseberry. In all nests approached, author
noted that female left quietly and secretly or she scurried rapidly
across ground away from nest.

RUFOUS-SIDED TOWHEE Pl. 30
Pipilo erythrophthalmus

Breeding range: All western states.
Habitat: Thickets, hedgerows, chaparral, woodland and roadside
edges, open brushy fields, slashings, suburbs, parks.

Nest: On ground in depression under low bush or in bush invariably within 5 ft. (1.5 m) of ground. Bulky; firmly built of leaves, bark strips, forb stalks, twigs, grasses; lined with grasses, hair (sometimes), bark shreds, pine needles. Built by female in about 5 days.

Eggs: 3–4, sometimes 5; av. 23.6 x 17.8 mm (*P. e. montanus*). Oval to short-oval. Shell smooth, has slight gloss. Grayish or creamy white; dotted, spotted with reddish brown; may be wreathed or capped. Incubation by female alone; 12–13 days. At least 2 broods.

Notes: Large numbers of parasitic eggs of Brown-headed Cowbird reported from nests of Rufous-sided Towhee: Iowa record, 8 Cowbird eggs, 5 Towhee eggs in 1 nest; Illinois, 8 Cowbird eggs, 1 Towhee egg in single nest.

BROWN TOWHEE   *Pipilo fuscus*   Pl. 30

Breeding range: Sw. Oregon to Baja; Arizona, New Mexico, w. and cen. Texas, se. Colorado, nw. Oklahoma (Cimarron Co.).

Habitat: Coastal and foothill chaparral; desert gullies, foothill canyons, dry washes, open woods, suburban gardens.

Nest: Bulky but well-made deep cup of small twigs, forb stems, grasses; lined with fine grasses, rootlets, horsehair; placed in low bushes, vines, small trees, 2–12 ft. (0.6–3.7 m) above ground, commonly 3–4 ft. (0.9–1.2 m). Outside diam. 5⅓–7⅛ in. (13.5–17.9 cm), height 4⅛–4½ in. (10.5–11.4 cm); inside diam. 2⅛–2¾ in. (5.4–7.1 cm), depth 2⅛–2⅝ in. (5.4–6.7 cm).

Eggs: 3, sometimes 4, rarely 2; av. 23.4 x 17.5 mm. Oval to short-oval. Slightly glossy. Eggs of various races highly variable: Canyon Towhee (*P. f. mesoleucus*) off-white with reddish brown spots, blotches, scrawls, scribblings; Pacific Coast race (*P. f. senicula*) pale bluish white with black spots, *indistinguishable from eggs of Abert's Towhee.*

Notes: Author found Brown Towhee to be commonest nesting bird in Florida Wash in desert at base of Santa Rita Mts., Arizona. 6 nests in which eggs were found contained 3 each.

ABERT'S TOWHEE   *Pipilo aberti*

Breeding range: Se. California, s. Nevada, sw. Utah, s. Arizona, sw. New Mexico.

Habitat: Riparian desert thickets, mesquite brushlands, farms, groves, suburban areas, near irrigation ditches.

Nest: Above ground usually in low bushes (mesquite, willow), mistletoe clumps. Bulky, loosely constructed of forb stems, vines, bark strips, green leaves; lined with coiled bark strips (favorite material), dried grasses, horsehair. Outside diam. 5½ in. (14 cm), height 4 in. (10.2 cm); inside diam. 3 in. (7.6 cm), depth 2½ in. (6.4 cm).

Eggs: 2–4, usually 3; av. 23.8 x 17.8 mm. Typically oval. Slightly glossy. Pale bluish or creamy white sparsely marked with black, heaviest around large end. *Indistinguishable from eggs of Pacific race of Brown Towhee (P. f. senicula).* 2 broods.

LARK BUNTING *Calamospiza melanocorys* Pl. 30

Breeding range: California (rare), se. Idaho (unc.), n. Utah, cen. and e. Montana, and N. Dakota south to New Mexico, w. Texas (prob); also sw. Minnesota, nw. Missouri (cas.).

Habitat: Open country, sagebrush, prairie grasslands, weedy pastures.

Nest: In depression in ground with rim level with surface or slightly elevated; may be sheltered by overhead plants. Simple cup of grasses, forb stems, rootlets; lined with finer material, plant down, hair; similar to nest of Dickcissel, but Dickcissel nest commonly low *above* ground. Inside diam. $3\frac{2}{3}$ in. (9.4 cm), height $2\frac{7}{8}$ in. (7.3 cm); inside diam. $2\frac{2}{3}$ in. (6.9 cm), depth $1\frac{1}{2}$ in. (3.8 cm).

Eggs: 3–6, commonly 4–5; av. 21.9 x 16.8 mm. Oval to short-oval. Slightly glossy. Pale blue or greenish blue, usually unmarked but rarely lightly sprinkled with reddish brown dots. Unmarked eggs *indistinguishable from eggs of Dickcissel.* Incubation by female (male's participation reported by some observers); about 12 days. Sometimes 2 broods.

Notes: In 30 egg sets from various collections: 1 nest of 3 eggs, 11 of 4, 15 of 5, 3 of 6, all unmarked. In a series of nests found by author in Pawnee National Grassland, Weld Co., Colorado, 1 set of 3 eggs was sprinkled with reddish brown spots. Polygyny in this species has been observed in Colorado, N. Dakota, and S. Dakota. Quality of male's territory is deciding factor.

SAVANNAH SPARROW Pl. 30
Passerculus sandwichensis

Breeding range: Washington to Minnesota, south to Mexico, Nebraska, Iowa.

Habitat: Prairies, weedy fields, hayfields, salt- and fresh-water marshes.

Nest: In scratched or natural cavity in ground, sometimes slightly elevated; usually hidden from view by natural canopy. Hollow filled with deep cup of grass stems; lined with fine grass, sometimes rootlets, hair, a few feathers (gull or duck in coastal areas). Built by female alone. Outside diam. $2\frac{5}{8}$–$3\frac{1}{3}$ in. (6.7–8.5 cm), height to fill depression in ground; inside diam. 2–$2\frac{1}{4}$ in. (5.1–5.7 cm), depth $1\frac{1}{4}$–$1\frac{1}{2}$ in. (3.2–3.8 cm).

Eggs: 3–4, occasionally 5; av. 19.1 x 14.0 (*P. s. nevadensis*). Oval. Slight gloss. Pale greenish blue, dirty white; heavily spotted, blotched with browns, often wreathed at large end; sometimes dotted over entire egg; wide variation in markings, sometimes within same clutch. Generally smaller than eggs of either Vesper or Baird's Sparrow. Incubation entirely by female; 12 days. 2 broods.

Notes: Author has seen nests in various habitats from saltmarshes of Pacific coast to dry prairies of Colorado and wet meadows of high Rockies, but found uniformity in nest site and construction. Female exceedingly tight sitter; usually does not flush until almost stepped upon. Alternately, may leave nest well in advance of intruder, making nest difficult to locate.

GRASSHOPPER SPARROW   Pl. 30
Ammodramus savannarum

Breeding range: Throughout western states, but distribution, broken by mountains and deserts, is spotty.

Habitat: Prairies, grasslands, cultivated fields.

Nest: In depression in ground, rim typically level with or slightly above ground; well concealed by canopy of grasses, forbs, commonly domed at back. Built by female of dried grasses; lined with fine grasses, rootlets, occasionally hair. Outside diam. $4\frac{1}{2}$–$5\frac{1}{2}$ in. (11.4–14.0 cm), height 2–$2\frac{1}{4}$ in. (5.1–5.7 cm); inside diam. $2\frac{1}{2}$–$3\frac{1}{4}$ in. (6.4–8.3 cm), depth $1\frac{1}{4}$ in. (3.2 cm).

Eggs: 4–5, sometimes 3, rarely 6; av. 18.6 x 14.4 mm. Oval. Slight gloss. Creamy white; sparingly spotted, blotched with reddish browns overlaid on shades of gray, purple; markings scattered over entire egg or concentrated at large end. Incubation by female; 12–13 days. 2 broods.

Notes: Nests difficult to find. Female sits close; when flushed, slips off, runs a short distance through grass, then flies. Approaching nest, does not fly directly to it.

BAIRD'S SPARROW *Ammodramus bairdii*

Breeding range: Ne. and n.-cen. Montana, N. Dakota, S. Dakota (unc.), Minnesota (Clay Co., cas.).

Habitat: Prairie grasslands, wheat fields.

Nest: In tuft of grass, on or near ground, with or without overhead concealing vegetation; often in cavity such as hoof mark, or shallow excavation made by female. Bulky, cuplike; built of dead grasses, occasionally hair or bits of moss in lining.

Eggs: 3–5, sometimes 6; av. 19.4 x 14.6 mm. Oval. Slight gloss. Grayish white; sometimes obscured by reddish brown spots, blotches, dots that cover entire egg; may be wreathed. As a rule, *larger* than Savannah Sparrow eggs, *smaller* than Vesper Sparrow eggs. Incubation by female; 11–12 days.

Notes: May nest singly or form small community in favorable habitat. Female exceedingly close sitter, will not flush until almost stepped upon. Environmental disturbance has caused reduction in number of breeding birds, especially in N. Dakota.

HENSLOW'S SPARROW *Ammodramus henslowii*

Breeding range: Rare or uncommon in e. S. Dakota, s. Minnesota, Iowa, e. Kansas, n. and sw. Missouri.
Habitat: Weedy fields, wet meadows.
Nest: On or in ground, on or near base of grass clump with vegetation often arching over nest to form partial roof. Built of grasses, lined with finer grasses, some hair.
Eggs: 3–5; av. 18.3 x 14.1 mm. Oval. Slight gloss. Creamy white, pale greenish white; thickly, evenly dotted, spotted with reddish brown, often wreathed. Incubation by female, 11 days. Typically 2 broods.

LE CONTE'S SPARROW *Ammospiza leconteii*

Breeding range: N. Montana, e. and cen. N. Dakota, nw. Minnesota, e. S. Dakota.
Habitat: Grassy meadows, prairies, marsh borders.
Nest: Typically placed slightly above ground beneath tangle of dead rushes, grasses, sedges, where dead and fallen vegetation is thickest. Female builds shallow, well-rounded cup of dry grasses interwoven with standing stems. Similar to nest of Henslow's Sparrow.
Eggs: 3–5, commonly 4; av. 18.0 x 13.7 mm. Oval. Has slight gloss. Grayish white; dotted, spotted, blotched with browns, black, generally over entire egg. Incubation by female; probably 12–13 days.

SHARP-TAILED SPARROW *Ammospiza caudacuta*

Breeding range: E. and nw. N. Dakota, nw. Minnesota, ne. S. Dakota (rare).
Habitat: Nelson's Sharp-tailed Sparrow (*A. c. nelsoni*) is only race of this species that breeds exclusively in freshwater habitat: swampy lake borders, overgrown wet meadows, grassy alkaline flats.
Nest: Of coarse grasses; lined with finer grasses; on ground in dense beds of dried grass or in standing vegetation above water. Female alone builds.
Eggs: 4–5; av. 16.5 x 18.3 mm (*A. c. nelsoni*). Oval. Slight gloss. Pale greenish white; dotted, spotted with browns with underlying markings of pale grayish purples; usually well scattered, but may be wreathed. Incubation by female; 11 days. Commonly 2 broods.
Notes: Nests very difficult to locate. Birds shy, wary, very mouse-like in movements.

SEASIDE SPARROW *Ammospiza maritima*

Breeding range: Gulf Coast of Louisiana and upper and cen. Texas Gulf Coast.

Habitat: Saltmarshes.
Nest: In wetter portions of saltmarsh; on ground among marsh grasses above high tide line or 8–12 in. (20.3–30.5 cm) above ground in bushes. Open or globular structure of grass stems, lined with fine grasses. Built by female.
Eggs: Commonly 4, sometimes 3; av. 20.4 x 15.4 mm (*A. m. fisheri*). Oval. Slight gloss. White, pale greenish white; dotted, spotted, blotched with reddish brown; often wreathed at large end. Incubation by female. 1 brood.

VESPER SPARROW   *Pooecetes gramineus*   Pl. 31

Breeding range: Washington to Minnesota, south to Baja, Arizona, n. and w. New Mexico, Kansas (Morton Co.), nw. Missouri (cas.).
Habitat: Open grasslands and sagebrush, mountain meadows up to 12,000 ft. (3660 m), corn-stubble fields, woodland burns.
Nest: Ordinarily in depression in ground under cover of surrounding plants, or in grass tussock. Rather bulky, thick-rimmed, well-cupped but not tightly woven; built of dried grass, rootlets, hair. Outside diam. 4½ in. (11.4 cm), height 1¾ in. (4.5 cm); inside diam. 2¼ in. (5.7 cm), depth 1⅜ in. (3.5 cm).
Eggs: Commonly 4, often 5, sometimes 3 or 6; av. 20.9 x 15.2 mm (*P. g. confinis*). Slightly *larger* than eggs of Baird's and Savannah Sparrows. Oval. Slight gloss. Creamy white, pale greenish white; dotted, spotted, blotched, scrawled with 1 or more shades of brown, gray; considerable variation. Incubation chiefly or entirely by female; 12–13 days. 2 broods.

LARK SPARROW   *Chondestes grammacus*   Pl. 31

Breeding range: All western states.
Habitat: Prairies, weedy fields, pastures, grasslands with scattered bushes and trees.
Nest: Commonly a depression in ground, often in bare or eroded place; filled with grasses and lined with rootlets, hair, fine grasses; usually shaded by a clump of grass or forbs. Sometimes a more bulky structure on foundation of small twigs in low tree or shrub. Female builds in about 3–4 days.
Eggs: 4–5, sometimes 3, rarely 6; av. 20.4 x 16.1 mm (*C. g. strigatus*). Oval. Slight gloss. Creamy or grayish white; spotted, blotched, scrawled with dark browns, black, purple; often capped. Scrawl markings similar to those on eggs of Northern Oriole. Incubation by female; 11–12 days. Probably 2 broods. Male may be monogamous or may mate with 2 females with nests in his territory.
Notes: Although Lark Sparrow is predominately a ground-nesting bird, author discovered female incubating on nest in Pedernales

State Park, Blanco Co., Texas, 25 ft. (7.6 m) above ground well hidden in clump of leaves on horizontal branch of a Cedar Elm.

FIVE-STRIPED SPARROW *Aimophila quinquestriata*

Notes: This Mexican species first nested in the U.S. in the Sonoita Creek area of Pima Co., 4 miles southwest of Patagonia, Arizona, and has now expanded its breeding range in southern Arizona. Its habitat includes brushy, rocky, semidesert slopes.

RUFOUS-WINGED SPARROW *Aimophila carpalis*

Notes: Known to nest in the U.S. only in brush-grass habitat in restricted, isolated colonies in se. Arizona. Nesting appears to be triggered by satisfactory amount of rainfall and suitable temperature levels. The close-sitting female builds her nest of grasses in low bush (mesquite) or cactus. She commonly lays 4 unmarked bluish-white eggs.

RUFOUS-CROWNED SPARROW *Aimophila ruficeps*

Breeding range: California, Arizona, New Mexico, w. and cen. Texas, nw. and cen. Oklahoma; Utah (Zion Natl. Park, rare).
Habitat: Boulder-strewn hillsides, coastal scrub growth, mixture of grass and shrubs, canyon thickets.
Nest: Almost always on ground, usually sunk into small hollow, nest rim level with ground surface, often under grass clump or low shrub. Occasionally low in upward-growing branches of bush or in small tree. Built of grasses; lined with fine grasses and horsehair.
Eggs: 2–5, usually 4; av. 20.0 x 15.6 mm (*A. r. scottii*). Oval. Slightly glossy. Bluish-white, unmarked.
Notes: Nesting dates appear to correlate with annual occurrence of rainfall and amount of rain that falls; thus fresh eggs have been found from March until August.

BACHMAN'S SPARROW *Aimophila aestivalis*

Breeding range: E. Texas, se. Oklahoma (McCurtain Co.), Arkansas, Louisiana.
Habitat: Open pine woods with understory of shrubs, grassy ground cover; weedy abandoned fields, grassy orchards.
Nest: On ground in open or beneath brush, tree, shrub. Built by female of coarse grasses, forb stems; lined with fine grasses. May have dome built by bird, or have natural arch above made by surrounding plants, or lack canopy. May be round or cylindrical.
Eggs: 3–5; av. 19.3 x 15.3 mm. Oval. Slightly glossy. White, unmarked. Incubation by female; probably about 14 days. 2 broods, sometimes 3.
Notes: Birds elusive, shy, nest very difficult to find; neither John J. Audubon nor John Bachman ever succeeded in finding one.

BACHMAN'S SPARROW

BOTTERI'S SPARROW *Aimophila botterii*

Notes: This Mexican species reaches U.S. as breeding bird in extreme se. Arizona, s. Texas, and New Mexico (1977). Habitat is invariably grassland with a scattering of brush or small trees. 2–5, usually 4, *bluish white* unmarked eggs are laid in grass nest on ground. Nest and eggs similar to those of Cassin's Sparrow. A late nester: June–September.

CASSIN'S SPARROW *Aimophila cassinii*

Breeding range: S. Arizona, n. New Mexico, e. Colorado, w. Kansas (loc.), w. Oklahoma, w. Texas.
Habitat: Arid uplands of grass, thornbushes, cacti, yucca; barren rocky areas, sparse mesquite-dotted grassy plains.
Nest: Most often on ground in grass, usually at base of small shrubby plant or low bush. Occasionally in low bush or grass clump, seldom over 12 in. (30.5 cm) above ground; may be in a cholla cactus (*Opuntia leptocaulis*). Of dry grass blades, forb stems, vegetable fibers; lined with fine grass, rootlets, sometimes

hair. Outside diam. 4 in. (10.2 cm); inside diam. $2\frac{1}{2}$ in. (6.4 cm).
Eggs: 4, sometimes 3 or 5; av. 19.0 x 14.6 mm. Nearly oval, somewhat elongated. Slightly glossy. *White,* unmarked. Nest and eggs similar to those of Botteri's Sparrow.
Notes: Nesting dates said to be correlated to wet or dry seasons but observations in some areas contradictory.

BLACK-THROATED SPARROW　　　　　　　Pl. 31
Amphispiza bilineata

Breeding range: California, nw. Nevada, s. Idaho, sw. Wyoming, south through w. Colorado to Mexico, w. and cen. Texas; also nw. Oklahoma (Cimarron Co.).
Habitat: Sparsely vegetated desert terrain, sloping or flat; rocky or gravel desert hills.
Nest: Near ground in small bushes (mesquite, prickly pear, catclaw, hackberry, Crown-of-thorns, cholla, Creosote Bush); occasionally on ground. Sturdy cup of interwoven grasses, plant fibers; lined with finer materials, often hair, wool. Observers mention "whitish lining." Av. dimensions of 3 Arizona nests: outside diam. $4\frac{1}{2}$ in. (11.4 cm), height $3\frac{1}{2}$ in. (8.9 cm); inside diam. $2\frac{3}{8}$ in. (6 cm), depth 2 in. (5.1 cm).
Eggs: 2–4, commonly 3. (In s. Arizona author found 4 sets of 2, 3 sets of 3.); av. 17.3 x 13.8 mm (*A. b. deserticola*). Somewhat glossy. White with slight tinge of blue. Said to have 2 broods.
Notes: Author found this a common nesting species in hot mesquite-cholla desert at foot of Santa Rita Mts. (Florida Wash), Arizona. Female tight sitter; may not leave nest until almost touched. Exterior of some nests very rough, pieces of straw extending in all directions for up to $11\frac{3}{4}$ in. (30 cm).

SAGE SPARROW　　*Amphispiza belli*　　　　　　Pl. 31

Breeding range: West of Rocky Mts., east of Cascades and Sierra Nevada; e. and cen. Washington, e. Oregon, California, s. Idaho, sw. Montana, south through sw. Wyoming, w. Colorado, ne. New Mexico.
Habitat: Sagebrush (particularly *Artemisia tridentata*), chaparral, throughout bush-covered deserts up to base of mountains.
Nest: Usually concealed in sagebrush shrubs, 3–40 in. (7.6–101.6 cm) above ground, av. $16\frac{1}{2}$ in. (41.9 cm). Built of dry sage twigs, sticks; lined with dry grass, forb stalks, wool, hair, fur. Outside diam. 4–7 in. (10.2–17.8 cm), height $2–2\frac{1}{2}$ in. (5.1–6.4 cm); inside diam. $2\frac{1}{2}$ in. (6.4 cm), depth 1 in. (2.5 cm).
Eggs: 3–4, rarely 5; av. 19.47 x 14.56 mm (*A. b. nevadensis*). Oval. Pale blue or bluish white; dotted, spotted, blotched with browns; occasionally black dots, lines; undermarkings of grays; spots may be over entire egg or concentrated in wreath. Much

variation. Incubation probably 13 days. 2 broods.
Notes: Incubating bird sits close; may not leave until forced.
When leaving nest, bird drops to ground and runs off silently,
holding tail up thrasherlike.

DARK-EYED JUNCO

DARK-EYED JUNCO *Junco hyemalis*   **Pl. 31**
(including Oregon, Slate-colored, and White-winged Juncos)

Breeding range: Washington to Montana, south to Mexico,
Arizona; also S. Dakota (Black Hills), nw. Nebraska, ne. and
n.-cen. Minnesota.
Habitat: Coniferous and mixed forest edges, aspen woods, forest
openings, parks.
Nest: Typically on ground in cup-shaped depression, often well
hidden by overhanging vegetation, roots, logs, ledges. Built of
grasses, forb stems; lined with fine grasses, hair. Have been found
in trees, 1 as high as 20 ft. (6.1 m) above ground on horizontal limb
of Douglas Fir. Outside diam. 3⅞ in. (9.8 cm); inside diam. 2 in.
(5.1 cm), depth 1¼ in. (3.2 cm).
Eggs: 4, sometimes 3, occasionally 5; av. 19.3 x 14.6 mm
(*J. h. oreganus*). Oval to short-oval. Slightly glossy. Pale bluish
white, grayish; thickly dotted, spotted, occasionally blotched with

browns, purple, gray, mostly concentrated at large end; much variation in markings. Incubation by female; 12–13 days. 2 broods.

Notes: Unusual nests reported in Montana: in side of straw stack (used 3 years in succession), inside wall of log barn, in old Robin nest on rafter of garage, in woven reed fish basket hanging on garage wall.

GRAY-HEADED JUNCO   *Junco caniceps*   Pl. 31

Breeding range: E. California, s. Idaho, s. Wyoming, nw. Nevada, Utah, Colorado, n. Arizona, n. New Mexico, Texas (Guadalupe Mts.).

Habitat: Coniferous forest edges, aspen groves, at elevations of 7500–12,000 ft. (2288–3660 m).

Nest: Almost always on ground, sometimes in cavity in roadside or stream bank, usually hidden by overhanging tufts of grass, forbs. Occasionally above ground in tree or on building. Built of coarse grasses, dead leaves; lined with fine grasses, hair, feathers (sometimes). Outside diam. $3\frac{1}{2}$ in. (8.9 cm); inside diam. $2\frac{1}{4}$ in. (5.7 cm), depth $1\frac{2}{3}$ in. (4.3 cm).

Eggs: 3–5; av. 19.9 x 15.2 mm. Oval to short-oval. Slightly glossy. White, pale bluish white; dotted, spotted, sometimes blotched with browns; undermarkings of gray. *Indistinguishable from eggs of Yellow-eyed Junco.* Plain bluish white eggs have been found with very few small dots, hardly visible. Incubation by female; probably 11–12 days. Probably 2 broods.

YELLOW-EYED (MEXICAN) JUNCO   opp. p. 121
Junco phaeonotus

Breeding range: Se. Arizona, sw. New Mexico (Hidalgo Co.).

Habitat: Montane pine-oak woods, coniferous forests.

Nest: Usually on ground (sometimes in tree or bush) under tuft of grass, log, stone; in a hollow filled with coarse grass stems, moss strands; lined with finer grasses, hair, sometimes fur. Outside diam. $3\frac{7}{8}$ in. (9.8 cm), height $2\frac{3}{4}$ in. (7.1 cm); inside diam. $2\frac{1}{4}$ in. (5.7 cm), depth $1\frac{5}{8}$ in. (4.1 cm).

Eggs: 3–4, sometimes 5; av. 19.9 x 15.1 mm. Oval. Slightly glossy. Grayish white or pale bluish white; spotted and dotted with reddish brown. *Indistinguishable from eggs of Gray-headed Junco.*

Notes: Despite claims in literature that female alone builds, author watched both birds carry material to nest in Madera Canyon, Santa Rita Mts., Arizona, May 14, 1975. Only the female incubated the 4 eggs.

CHIPPING SPARROW   *Spizella passerina*   Pl. 31

Breeding range: All western states.

Habitat: Open coniferous and deciduous woodlands, conifer plantings, towns, farms, orchards, parks, gardens.
Nest: In trees (often conifers), shrubs, vines, 1–25 ft. (0.3–7.6 m) above ground, av. 3–10 ft. (0.9–3.1 m); rarely on ground. Built of fine dead grasses, forb stalks, rootlets; lined with hair, fine grasses. Resembles nest of Clay-colored Sparrow but *more compact*. Built by female, accompanied by male; 3–4 days. Av. outside diam. $4\frac{3}{8}$ in. (11.1 cm), height $2\frac{1}{4}$ in. (5.7 cm); inside diam. $1\frac{7}{8}$ in. (4.8 cm), depth $1\frac{7}{16}$ in. (3.7 cm).
Eggs: Commonly 4, often 3, rarely 2 or 5; av. 17.6 x 12.9 mm. Oval to short-oval. Slight gloss. Pale bluish green; dotted, spotted, blotched, scrawled with dark brown, black, purple, mainly at large end. *Indistinguishable from eggs of Clay-colored and Brewer's Sparrows.* Incubation by female; 11–14 days, beginning with next to last egg. 2 broods.
Notes: Horsehair alone may line entire nest; if unavailable, human or other animal hair used. In 137 nests, only 4 had 5 eggs.

CLAY-COLORED SPARROW   *Spizella pallida*

Breeding range: Montana to Minnesota, south to e. Wyoming (unc.), n. Nebraska (rare).
Habitat: Prairies, pine barrens, conifer plantings, woodland openings, brushy fields, pasturelands.

CLAY-COLORED SPARROW

Nest: Early nests commonly on or near ground; later nests often in trees and shrubs as high as 5 ft. (1.5 m) above ground, usually lower. Female builds rather bulky, cup-shaped structure of woven grasses, forb stems, rootlets; lined with fine grasses, rootlets, hair (sometimes). Resembles nest of Chipping Sparrow but not as compact. Av. measurements of 34 nests: outside diam. 4 in. (10.2 cm), height $2\frac{5}{8}$ in. (6.7 cm); inside diam. $1\frac{7}{8}$ in. (4.8 cm), depth $1\frac{1}{2}$ in. (3.8 cm).

Eggs: 3–5, commonly 4; av. 17.1 x 12.7 mm. Oval to short-oval. Slight gloss. Pale blue-green; dotted, spotted, blotched with dark brown, black scrawls; sometimes underlaid with gray. *Indistinguishable from eggs of Chipping and Brewer's Sparrows.* Incubation by both sexes, mostly by female; $10–11\frac{1}{2}$ days, starting after 3rd egg laid. Probably only 1 brood.

Notes: One nest contained 384 pieces of grass; another 450.

BREWER'S SPARROW   *Spizella breweri*   Pl. 31

Breeding range: Washington to California, e. of Cascades, east to extreme sw. N. Dakota, w. S. Dakota, nw. Nebraska, w. Oklahoma (Cimarron Co.); south to cen. Arizona, nw. New Mexico.

Habitat: Open brushy areas, principally sagebrush and saltbush; altitude range from 350 to 10,400 ft. (106.8 to 3172 m).

Nest: Usually in sagebrush or saltbush almost always within 4 ft. (1.2 m) of ground. Typically of dry grass stems, rootlets; lined with small, dry rootlets, horsehair. Av. size of 11 nests in California and Colorado: outside diam. $4\frac{1}{2}$ in. (11.4 cm), height $2\frac{2}{3}$ in. (6.9 cm); inside diam. $1\frac{7}{8}$ in. (4.8 cm), depth $1\frac{5}{8}$ in. (4.1 cm). All but 1 lining contained much horsehair.

Eggs: Usually 3–4, sometimes 5; av. 17.0 x 12.6 mm. Oval. Slight or no gloss. Blue-green; marked with dark brown dots and blotches, usually wreathed. *Indistinguishable from eggs of Chipping and Clay-colored Sparrows.*

Notes: In Weld Co., Colorado, author found loose colony of Brewer's Sparrows nesting in open field of saltbush with no sagebrush. 10 nests well concealed within saltbush, av. $11\frac{5}{8}$ in. (29.5 cm) above ground.

FIELD SPARROW   *Spizella pusilla*   Pl. 32

Breeding range: N. Dakota and s. Minnesota south to ne. Texas and Louisiana; also e. Montana and e. Colorado (rare).

Habitat: Brushy pastures, abandoned fields, woodland edges, briar thickets.

Nest: Early nests typically on or near ground; later nests as high as 4 ft. (1.2 m) above ground in low thick shrubs or trees. Cup of grasses, leaves, forb stems; lined with fine grasses, rootlets, hair. Female builds, accompanied by male. In 90 nests: av. outside diam. 5 in. (12.7 cm), height $2\frac{1}{2}$ in. (6.4 cm); inside diam. 2 in. (5.1 cm), depth $1\frac{1}{2}$ in. (3.8 cm).

Eggs: 3–4, sometimes 2 (late nests), rarely 5 (early nests); av. 17.9 x 13.5 mm. Oval. Smooth, slight gloss. Creamy, bluish white, pale greenish; dotted, spotted, occasionally blotched with reddish brown, pale purple; markings sometimes concentrated at large end. Incubation by female; about 11 days. 2 broods, sometimes 3.
Notes: Frequent victim of Brown-headed Cowbird. 182 of 664 nests (27.4 percent) parasitized.

BLACK-CHINNED SPARROW   Pl. 32
Spizella atrogularis

Breeding range: S. California, s. Nevada, sw. Utah, Arizona, New Mexico, Texas (Guadalupe Mts., prob.).
Habitat: Arid chaparral, sage brushlands, brushy mountain ridges.
Nest: Cup of dried grasses; lined with fine grasses, shredded fibers, horsehair; in sage (often) or other shrub. Outside diam. 4 in. (10.2 cm), height $2\frac{3}{4}$ in. (7.1 cm); inside diam. $1\frac{3}{4}$ in. (4.5 cm), depth $1\frac{1}{3}$ in. (3.4 cm).
Eggs: 3–4, sometimes 2 or 5; av. 17.6 x 13.3 mm. Oval. Slight gloss. Pale blue; some unmarked; others have small scattered dark brown spots. In 1 collection: 38 percent unmarked; 32 percent marked and unmarked in same set; 30 percent all marked.

WHITE-CROWNED SPARROW   Pl. 32
Zonotrichia leucophrys

Breeding range: Washington to w. and cen. Montana, south to California, n. Arizona (San Francisco Mts.), n. New Mexico.
Habitat: Clearings, forest edges, alpine meadows, brushy burns, parks, gardens.
Nest: Either on ground or a few feet above ground, under or within dense vegetation. Ground nests may be in tussock of grass, densely matted vegetation; often at base of scrub willow or conifer. In California, av. height above ground of 31 nests was $3\frac{1}{2}$ ft. (1.1 m), range $1\frac{1}{2}$–11 ft. (0.5–3.4 m). Built by female of fine twigs, rootlets, grasses, leaves, forb stems, bark shreds; lined with fine grasses, feathers, various kinds of mammal hair. Av. of 3 Colorado nests measured by author: outside diam. $3\frac{3}{4}$ in. (9.5 cm), height $2\frac{7}{8}$ in. (7.3 cm); inside diam. $2\frac{3}{8}$ in. (6 cm), depth 2 in. (5.1 cm).
Eggs: 4–5, rarely 3 or 6; av. 21.5 x 15.6 mm (*Z. l. leucophrys*). Oval. Slightly glossy. Pale greenish or creamy white; heavily marked with reddish brown spots, blotches. Sometimes markings obscure ground color; in others, markings form heavy wreath. Incubation by female; about 12 days. Probably 1 brood.
Notes: Nest found by author in Colorado tundra at 10,000 ft. (3050 m), was sunk in ground with grassy rim $7\frac{3}{8}$ in. (18.8 cm) wide

at entrance. Nest lined with marmot hair. Occasional polygyny reported.

GOLDEN-CROWNED SPARROW   *Zonotrichia atricapilla*

Notes: Summer resident in extreme ne. Cascades, Okanogan Co., Washington. In its Alaskan summer home, this species nests from sea level to high Hudsonian and Alpine-Arctic zones. Grass nest on ground or in low bush; 3–5 speckled eggs. *Indistinguishable from eggs of White-crowned Sparrow.*

WHITE-THROATED SPARROW   *Zonotrichia albicollis*

Notes: This eastern species breeds in our area only in extreme n.-cen. N. Dakota (Rolette Co.) and in ne. and cen. Minnesota. A ground nester in clearings, brushy thickets at edges of coniferous and deciduous forests. For details of breeding biology see *A Field Guide to Birds' Nests East of the Mississippi River.*

FOX SPARROW   *Passerella iliaca*   Pl. 32

Breeding range: Washington to w. Montana, south to Baja, n. Utah, nw. Wyoming, w. Colorado.
Habitat: Mountain chaparral, brushland, thickets, edges of coniferous and deciduous forests, streamside tangles, logged areas, burns.
Nest: Commonly on ground, may be in bushes or trees. Bulky, well constructed of plant fibers, grass, bark strips; lined with fine grasses, hair. Outside diam. $4\frac{1}{2}$–6 in. (11.4–15.2 cm), height $2\frac{1}{2}$–$4\frac{1}{2}$ in. (6.4–11.4 cm); inside diam. $2\frac{3}{8}$–3 in. (6.0–7.6 cm), depth 2 in. (5.1 cm).
Eggs: 3–4, sometimes 5; av. 22.7 x 16.3 mm. Oval. Slightly glossy. Pale bluish green; boldly marked with spots, blotches, cloudings of reddish brown; considerable variation in pattern and color. Incubation by female; probably 12–14 days. 1 brood.

LINCOLN'S SPARROW   *Melospiza lincolnii*   Pl. 32

Breeding range: Washington to w. Montana, south to Mexico; also ne. Minnesota.
Habitat: Mountain meadows with willow or alder thickets, brushy bogs, marshes, low bushy growth with grassy openings.
Nest: On ground in tussock of grass or sedge, sunk in grass, moss, or lichens, hidden by surrounding vegetation, sometimes just above water. Female alone builds neat cup of grasses, lined with finer grasses. Outside diam. $3\frac{1}{2}$ in. (8.9 cm), height $1\frac{1}{4}$ in. (3.2 cm); inside diam. $2\frac{1}{2}$ in. (6.4 cm).
Eggs: 4–5, sometimes 3, rarely 6; av. 19.1 x 14.5 mm (*M. l. alticola*). Oval to long-oval. Slight gloss. Pale greenish white; dotted, spotted, blotched with reddish brown. Markings

LINCOLN'S SPARROW

sometimes concentrated at large end, sometimes so thick they obscure ground color. *Indistinguishable from eggs of Song Sparrow.* Incubation by female; about 13 days.

Notes: Male does little if any singing during incubation period. Author has found this species most shy and wary of all sparrows he has studied. Rapid flight very low over ground makes bird hard to follow. Nest difficult to find.

'P SPARROW *Melospiza georgiana*

range: Eastern N. Dakota (unc.), e. S. Dakota, n. Minnesota, Iowa (unc.).

shwater marshes, wet brushy fields, meadows, lake-

lonies where habitat is particularly suitable; also of grass, sedge, or in low bush, commonly over large bulky foundation entirely of grass and iner grass.

4–5; av. 19.4 x 14.6 mm. Oval. Slightly fresh, fading to greenish white during spotted, blotched with brown, gray.

Markings vary but usually heavy. *Practically indistinguishable* from eggs of Song Sparrow, except *blotching* and *clouding typically heavier*. Incubation by female; 12–13 days. Sometimes 2 broods.

SWAMP SPARROW

SONG SPARROW *Melospiza melodia*　　　　Pl. 3?

Breeding range: All western states *except* southeast area (Ka sas, Oklahoma, Texas, Arkansas, Louisiana).

Habitat: Farms, cities, suburbs, gardens, yards, roadsides, bru fields, thickets, swamps, hedgerows, woodland edges.

Nest: On ground under tuft of grass, bush, brush pile, or i bush, tree, as high as 12 ft. (3.7 m) above ground, generally 2 (0.6–0.9 m). Cup of grasses, forb stems, leaves, bark fibers with grasses, fine rootlets, hair. Female builds in 5–1 Outside diam. 5–9 in. (12.7–22.9 cm), height 4½ in. (11.4 side diam. 2½ in. (6.4 cm), depth 1½ in. (3.8 cm).

Eggs: 3–5, rarely 6; av. 20.4 x 15.6 mm (av. of 400 eggs races). Oval to short-oval. Slightly glossy. Blue,

SONG SPARROW

gray-green; heavily dotted, spotted, blotched with reddish brown, purple; some underlaid with gray. Markings commonly over entire egg, often obscuring ground color, making eggs appear light brown. Vary considerably in shape, size, intensity of markings. *Eggs indistinguishable from eggs of Swamp and Lincoln's Sparrows.* Incubation by female; 12–13 days. 2 broods, sometimes 3. **Notes:** The American Ornithologists' Union Check-list (1957) recognizes 31 subspecies of Song Sparrow with 3 more races in Mexico. 9 subspecies are found only in California with 8 more reaching that state, totaling 17. This creates some variation in nesting biology, but in general the information above is applicable to all races.

McCOWN'S LONGSPUR   *Calcarius mccownii*   Pl. 32

Breeding range: E. and cen. Montana, w. N. Dakota, Wyoming, ne. Colorado.
Habitat: Short-grass prairies.
Nest: Scraped or natural hollow on grassy prairie lined by female with bits of grass and other plant material; sometimes in open but often at base of prickly pear, grass clump, rabbitbrush, or other prairie vegetation. May contain bits of lichen, shredded bark, wool. Rim of nest typically flush with ground surface. *Similar to nests of Horned Lark and Chestnut-collared Longspur.* Av. size

of 6 nests: outside diam. 3⅜ in. (8.6 cm), inside diam. 2½ in. (6.4 cm), depth 2⅛ in. (5.4 cm).

Eggs: 3–4, occasionally 5; av. 20.4 x 15.0 mm. Oval. Dirty white, gray, or pale olive; marked with various combinations of lines, scrawls, spots, dots of lilac, brown. Some marked over entire surface; in others markings confined to larger end. Incubation by female; 12 days. 2 broods.

Notes: In 52 Montana nests: 24 had 3 eggs, 26 had 4, 2 had 5. In 38 Wyoming nests: 18 had 3 eggs, 18 had 4, 2 had 5. Female is close sitter and generally will not flush until almost stepped on.

CHESTNUT-COLLARED LONGSPUR
Pl. 32
Calcarius ornatus

Breeding range: E. and cen. Montana to nw. Minnesota, south to ne. Colorado, n. Nebraska.

Habitat: Short-grass prairie (slightly taller growth than that preferred by McCown's Longspur).

Nest: Built by female; flush with surface of ground in natural depression or one scraped by bird; under clump of grass, often beside cattle droppings. Principally of dried grasses, occasionally animal hair or feathers in lining. *Similar to nests of Horned Lark and McCown's Longspur.*

Eggs: 4–5, sometimes 3, rarely 6; av. 18.7 x 14.2 mm. Oval. White; spotted, blotched, clouded, scrawled with browns, purple. Incubation by female; reported variously 10–14 days. 2 broods.

Glossary

THE FOLLOWING definitions are the author's intended meanings for terms used in this *Field Guide*. While many are in general use, some are more colloquial.

Clutch: A complete set of eggs laid by one female in one nesting.

Crepuscular: Active at twilight.

Forb: An herbaceous plant that is not a grass nor grasslike.

Gallinaceous: Fowl-like, belonging to the order Galliformes; mainly ground-feeding like grouse, pheasants, turkeys.

Incubation period: The time that elapses between laying of the last egg in a clutch and the hatching of that egg.

Lek: An area used for social display by two or more males of polygamous or promiscuous species. Females are attracted to the area and generally mate with dominant males. Example: "booming ground" of male Prairie Chickens.

Nightjar: A member of the family Caprimulgidae, often called a goatsucker. Examples are nighthawks, Whip-poor-will.

Passerine: A species belonging to the order Passeriformes, the largest order of birds comprising more than half of all species.

Polyandry: A form of polygamy in which a female forms pair bonds simultaneously or sequentially with more than one male. In a polyandrous system, males assume most of the parental duties.

Polygyny: A form of polygamy in which a male forms pair bonds simultaneously or sequentially with more than one female. In polygynous matings, the females assume most or all of the parental duties.

Pothole: A drainage basin, natural wetland pond, or lake in glaciated regions of western prairies. Also a pond containing surface water. Such areas are attractive habitats for nesting waterfowl.

Raptor: Any of the 274 species that make up the order Falconiformes, such as hawks, vultures, eagles. Indicates a bird of prey. Although owls are often referred to as birds of prey, they are members of another order, the Strigiformes.

Resaca: A colloquial term for old river channels created along the Rio Grande when the river overflows its banks.

Riparian: Found along the banks of streams.

Rookery: An Old World term for a colony of breeding birds such as herons, from the name applied to a colony of Rooks.

Sedentary: Nonmigratory.

Scrape: A shallow depression in the ground made by a bird. It may be the base for a nest or it may be the nest itself.

Songbird: A species belonging to the order Passeriformes. Although songs of passerines are considered best among all birds, many nonpasserines have typical songs, some elaborate.

Subspecies: A local population or race of a bird with characteristics different from other populations of the same species.

Stub: A dead tree or dead part of a live tree that provides nest sites well above ground.

Stump: That part of a tree that remains after lumbering or after a tree has broken off near the ground.

Swale: A low, wet, swamplike area surrounded by higher ground, usually brushy, and often choked with vegetation such as alders.

Index

Index

PAGE NUMBERS and plate numbers in **boldface** type indicate species that are illustrated. Boldface type is used only with the common English names of those species; it is not used after scientific names.

Accipiter cooperii, 36
    gentilis, 36
    striatus, 36
Actitis macularia, 67
Aechmophorus occidentalis, 3
Aegolius acadicus, 96
    funereus, 95
Aeronautes saxatalis, 101
Agelaius phoeniceus, 216
    tricolor, 217
Aimophila aestivalis, 246
    botterii, 247
    carpalis, 246
    cassinii, 247
    quinquestriata, 246
    ruficeps, 246
Aix sponsa, 26
Ajaia ajaja, 17
Alauda arvensis, 136
Alectoris chukar, 55
Amazilia beryllina, 108
    verticalis, 108
    yucatanensis, 107
Ammodramus bairdii, 243
    henslowii, 244
    savannarum, 243
Ammospiza caudacuta, 244
    leconteii, 244
    maritima, 244

Amphispiza belli, 248
    bilineata, 248
Anas acuta, 22
    americana, 24
    clypeata, 25
    crecca, 23
    cyanoptera, 24
    diazi, 20
    discors, 23
    fulvigula, 21
    platyrhynchos, 20
    rubripes, 21
    strepera, 22
Anhinga, 9, **10**
Anhinga anhinga, 9
Ani, Groove-billed, 87
Anthus spinoletta, 181
    spragueii, 182
Aphelocoma coerulescens,
    144
    ultramarina, 145
Aquila chrysaetos, 42
Archilochus alexandri, 102
    colubris, 102
Ardea herodias, 10
Arremonops rufivirgatus,
    240
Asio flammeus, 95
    otus, 95

Athene cunicularia, 92
Auklet, Cassin's, 81
  Rhinoceros, 81
Auriparus flaviceps, 156
Avocet, American, 69, **Pl. 9**
Aythya affinis, 28
  americana, 26
  collaris, 27
  valisineria, 27

Baldpate. *See* Wigeon,
  American, 24
Bartramia longicauda, 67
Basileuterus rufifrons, 213
Becard, Rose-throated, 119,
  opp. p. 121
Bittern, American, 16, **16,**
  Pl. 3
  Least, 15, **Pl. 3**
Blackbird, Brewer's, 221, **Pl.**
  28
  Red-winged, 216, **Pl. 27**
  Tricolored, 217
  Yellow-headed, 216, **Pl.**
  27
Bluebird, Eastern, 177, **177,**
  Pl. 23
  Mountain, 178, **Pl. 23**
  Western, 177, **Pl. 23**
Bobolink, 214, **Pl. 27**
Bobwhite, 52, **Pl. 7**
Bombycilla cedrorum, 183
  garrulus, 182
Bonasa umbellus, 49
Botaurus lentiginosus, 16
Brachyramphus
  marmoratus, 80
Branta canadensis, 18
Bubo virginianus, 89
Bubulcus ibis, 12
Bucephala albeola, 29
  clangula, 28

  islandica, 29
Bufflehead, 29
Bunting, Indigo, 231, **231**
  Lark, 242, **Pl. 30**
  Lazuli, 232, **Pl. 29**
  Painted, 232
  Varied, 232
Bushtit, 157, **Pl. 20**
Buteo albicaudatus, 40
  albonotatus, 40
  jamaicensis, 37
  lineatus, 38
  nitidus, 41
  platypterus, 38
  regalis, 40
  swainsoni, 39
Buteogallus anthracinus, 42
Butorides striatus, 11

Calamospiza melanocorys,
  242
Calcarius mccownii, 257
  ornatus, 258
Callipepla squamata, 53
Calothorax lucifer, 101
Calypte anna, 103
  costae, 103
Camptostoma imberbe, 136
Campylorhynchus
  brunneicapillus, 164
Canachites canadensis, 49
Canvasback, 27, **Pl. 4**
Capella gallinago, 66
Caprimulgus carolinensis, 96
  ridgwayi, 98
  vociferus, 97
Caracara, 45
  Audubon's. *See* Caracara,
  45
  Crested. *See* Caracara, 45
Caracara cheriway, 45
Cardellina rubrifrons, 210

Cardinal, 228, **Pl. 28**
Cardinalis cardinalis, 228
  sinuatus, 228
Carduelis lawrencei, 238
  psaltria, 238
  tristis, 237
Carpodacus cassinii, 234
  mexicanus, 235
  purpureus, 234
Casmerodius albus, 13
Catbird, Gray, 169, **Pl. 21**
Cathartes aura, 32
Catharus fuscescens, 176
  guttatus, 175
  ustulatus, 175
Catherpes mexicanus, 166
Catoptrophorus
  semipalmatus, 68
Centrocercus urophasianus,
  52
Cepphus columba, 80
Cerorhinca monocerata, 81
Certhia familiaris, 159
Chachalaca, 48, **opp. p. 147**
Chaetura pelagica, 100
  vauxi, 101
Chamaea fasciata, 160
Charadrius alexandrinus, 62
  melodus, 62
  montanus, 64
  semipalmatus, 62
  vociferus, 63
  wilsonia, 63
Chat, Yellow-breasted, 210,
  Pl. 26
Chickadee, Black-capped,
  152, **Pl. 19**
  Boreal, 154, **154**
  Carolina, 153
  Chestnut-backed, 155
  Mexican, 153
  Mountain, 153, **Pl. 19**

Chicken. *See* Prairie
  Chicken
Chlidonias niger, 78
Chloroceryle americana, 110
Chondestes grammacus, 245
Chondrohierax uncinatus,
  35
Chordeiles acutipennis, 99
  minor, 99
Chuck-will's-widow, 96, **96**
Chukar, 55, **Pl. 7**
Cinclus mexicanus, 161
Circus cyaneus, 44
Cistothorus palustris, 165
  platensis, 165
Coccyzus americanus, 86
  erythropthalmus, 87
Colaptes auratus, 110
Colinus virginianus, 52
Columba fasciata, 82
  flavirostris, 82
  livia, 82
Columbina passerina, 85
Condor, California, 33, **opp.
  p. 35**
Contopus pertinax, 133
  sordidulus, 134
  virens, 133
Coot, American, 60, **Pl. 8**
Coragyps atratus, 33
Cormorant, Brandt's, 9, **Pl. 2**
  Double-crested, 8, **Pl. 2**
  Olivaceous, 8
  Pelagic, 9
Corvus brachyrhynchos, 150
  caurinus, 150
  corax, 148
  cryptoleucus, 148
  imparatus, 151
  ossifragus, 151
Coturnicops noveboracensis,
  59

Cowbird, Bronzed, 225, **225,**
  Pl. 28
  Brown-headed, 224, **224,**
  Pl. 28
Crane, Sandhill, 56, **Pl. 7**
Creeper, Brown, 159, **159,**
  Pl. 20
Crossbill, Red, 239
  White-winged, 239
Crotophaga sulcirostris, 87
Crow, Common, **149,** 150,
  Pl. 19
  Fish, 151
  Mexican, 151
  Northwestern, 150
Cuckoo, Black-billed, 87, **Pl.
  11**
  Yellow-billed, 86, **86, Pl.
  11**
Curlew, Long-billed, 67, **Pl. 9**
Cyanocitta cristata, 143
  stelleri, 144
Cyanocorax yncas, 145
Cynanthus latirostris, 108
Cypseloides niger, 99
Cyrtonyx montezumae, 54

Dendragapus obscurus, 48
Dendrocygna autumnalis, 19
  bicolor, 19
Dendroica caerulescens, 200
  castanea, 204
  cerulea, 202
  chrysoparia, 201
  coronata, 200
  discolor, 205
  dominica, 203
  fusca, 203
  graciae, 204
  magnolia, 199
  nigrescens, 200
  occidentalis, 202

  palmarum, 205
  pensylvanica, 204
  petechia, 197
  pinus, 204
  tigrina, 200
  townsendi, 201
  virens, 201
Dichromanassa rufescens, 12
Dickcissel, 233, **Pl. 29**
Dipper, 161, **161, Pl. 20**
Dolichonyx oryzivorus, 214
Dove, Ground, 85, **Pl. 11**
  Inca, 85
  Mourning, 83, **Pl. 11**
  Ringed Turtle, 84
  Rock, 82, **Pl. 10**
  Spotted, 84, **84**
  White-fronted, 85
  White-winged, 83, **Pl. 10**
Dryocopus pileatus, 111
Duck, Black, 21
  Harlequin, 29
  Masked, 30
  Mexican, 20
  Mottled, 21, **21**
  Ring-necked, 27
  Ruddy, 30, **31, Pl. 4**
  Tree. *See* Whistling-Duck,
    Black-bellied, 19; *see
    also* Whistling-Duck,
    Fulvous, 19
  Wood, 26, **Pl. 4**
Dumetella carolinensis, 169

Eagle, Bald, 42, **43**
  Golden, 42, **43, Pl. 5**
Egret, Cattle, 12, **Pl. 2**
  Great, 13, **Pl. 2**
  Reddish, 12
  Snowy, 13, **Pl. 2**
Egretta thula, 13
Elanoides forficatus, 35

Elanus leucurus, 33
Empidonax alnorum, 129
　　difficilis, 132
　　flaviventris, 128
　　fulvifrons, 133
　　hammondii, 130
　　minimus, 130
　　oberholseri, 131
　　traillii, 129
　　virescens, 129
　　wrightii, 131
Endomychura hypoleuca, 80
Eremophila alpestris, 136
Eudocimus albus, 17
Eugenes fulgens, 107
Euphagus cyanocephalus,
　　221

Falco columbarius, 47
　　femoralis, 47
　　mexicanus, 46
　　peregrinus, 46
　　sparverius, 47
Falcon, Aplomado, 47
　　Peregrine, 46, **opp. p. 35**
　　Prairie, 46, **46, Pl. 6**
Finch, Black Rosy, 236
　　Brown-capped, 236
　　Cassin's, 234
　　Gray-crowned Rosy, 235
　　House, 235, **Pl. 29**
　　Purple, 234, **Pl. 29**
Flicker, Common, 110, **110,**
　　Pl. 14
　　Gilded. *See* Flicker,
　　　Common, 110
　　Red-shafted. *See* Flicker,
　　　Common, 110
　　Yellow-shafted. *See*
　　　Flicker, Common, 110
Florida caerulea, 11
Flycatcher, Acadian, **128,**
　　129

Alder, 129
Ash-throated, 125, **Pl. 15**
Beardless, 136
Buff-breasted, 133
Coues', 133
Dusky, 131, **Pl. 16**
Gray, 131, **131, Pl. 16**
Great Crested, 123, **124,**
　　Pl. 15
Hammond's, 130, **Pl. 16**
Kiskadee, 123
Least, 130, **Pl. 16**
Olivaceous, 125, **opp. p.**
　　121
Olive-sided, 135, **Pl. 17**
Scissor-tailed, 122, **Pl. 15**
Sulphur-bellied, 123, **opp.**
　　p. 121
Vermilion, 135, **Pl. 17**
Western, 132, **132, Pl. 16**
Wied's Crested, 124
Willow, 129, **Pl. 16**
Yellow-bellied, 128
Francolin, Black, 55
Francolinus francolinus, 55
Fulica americana, 60

Gadwall, 22, **Pl. 3**
Gallinula chloropus, 60
Gallinule, Common, 60, **Pl.**
　　8
　　Purple, 59
Gavia immer, 1
Gelochelidon nilotica, 74
Geococcyx californianus, 87
Geothlypis trichas, 210
Glaucidium brasilianum, 91
　　gnoma, 91
Gnatcatcher, Black-capped,
　　179
　　Black-tailed, 179
　　Blue-gray, 179, **Pl. 23**

Godwit, Marbled, 69
Goldeneye, Barrow's, 29
  Common, 28
Goldfinch, American, 237, **237, Pl. 29**
  Lawrence's, 238, **Pl. 30**
  Lesser, 238, **Pl. 30**
Goose, Canada, 18, **Pl. 3**
Goshawk, 36, **Pl. 5**
Grackle, Boat-tailed, **222,** 223
  Common, 223, **Pl. 28**
  Great-tailed, 222, **222**
Grebe, Eared, 2, **Pl. 1**
  Horned, 2
  Least, 3, **3, Pl. 1**
  Pied-billed, 4, **5, Pl. 1**
  Red-necked, 1, **Pl. 1**
  Western, 3, **4, Pl. 1**
Grosbeak, Black-headed, 230, **Pl. 29**
  Blue, 230, **Pl. 29**
  Evening, 233
  Pine, 235
  Rose-breasted, 229, **229**
Grouse, Blue, 48
  Dusky. *See* Grouse, Blue, 48
  Franklin's. *See* Grouse, Spruce, 49
  Ruffed, 49, **49, Pl. 6**
  Sage, 52, **Pl. 7**
  Sharp-tailed, 51, **Pl. 6**
  Sooty. *See* Grouse, Blue, 48
  Spruce, 49
Grus canadensis, 56
Guillemot, Pigeon, 80
Guiraca caerulea, 230
Gull, California, 72, **Pl. 10**
  Franklin's, 73
  Glaucous-winged, 71
  Herring, 72
  Laughing, 73, **73**
  Ring-billed, **25,** 72, **Pl. 10**
  Western, 71, **Pl. 9**
Gymnogyps californianus, 33
Gymnorhinus cyanocephalus, 151

Haematopus bachmani, 62
  palliatus, 61
Haliaeetus leucocephalus, 42
Harrier, Northern. *See* Hawk, Marsh, 44
Hawk, Black, 42
  Broad-winged, 38, **39**
  Cooper's, 36, **Pl. 5**
  Ferruginous, 40, **Pl. 5**
  Gray, 41
  Harris', 41, **Pl. 5**
  Marsh, 44, **Pl. 6**
  Red-shouldered, 38, **Pl. 5**
  Red-tailed, 37, **37, Pl. 5**
  Sharp-shinned, 36
  Swainson's, 39, **Pl. 5**
  White-tailed, 40
  Zone-tailed, 40
Helmitheros vermivorus, 193
Heron, Black-crowned Night, 14, **Pl. 2**
  Great Blue, 10, **Pl. 2**
  Green, 11, **Pl. 2**
  Little Blue, 11, **11**
  Louisiana, 13
  Yellow-crowned Night, 14, **15**
Hesperiphona vespertina, 233
Himantopus mexicanus, 70
Hirundo rustica, 140
Histrionicus histrionicus, 29
Hummingbird, Allen's, 106, **Pl. 13**
  Anna's, 103, **105, Pl. 13**

Berylline, 108
Black-chinned, 102, **Pl. 13**
Blue-throated, 107
Broad-billed, 108, **109, Pl. 13**
Broad-tailed, 105, **105, Pl. 13**
Buff-bellied, 107
Calliope, 106, **Pl. 13**
Costa's, 103, **104, Pl. 13**
Lucifer, 101
Rivoli's, 107
Ruby-throated, 102, **102**
Rufous, 106, **Pl. 13**
Violet-crowned, 108
Hydranassa tricolor, 13
Hylocichla mustelina, 175

Ibis, Glossy, 16
White, 17
White-faced, 17
Icteria virens, 210
Icterus cucullatus, 219
galbula, 220
graduacauda, 218
gularis, 219
parisorum, 219
spurius, 217
Ictinia mississippiensis, 35
Iridoprocne bicolor, 137
Ixobrychus exilis, 15
Ixoreus naevius, 174

Jacana, 61
Jacana spinosa, 61
Jay, Blue, 143, **143, Pl. 18**
Brown, 147
Gray, 143
Green, **98,** 145, **opp. p. 147**
Mexican, 145, **Pl. 18**

Pinyon, 151, **Pl. 19**
Scrub, 144, **Pl. 18**
Steller's, 144, **Pl. 18**
Junco, Dark-eyed, 249, **249, Pl. 31**
Gray-headed, 250, **Pl. 31**
Mexican. *See* Junco, Yellow-eyed, 250
Oregon. *See* Junco, Dark-eyed, 249
Slate-colored. *See* Junco, Dark-eyed, 249
White-winged. *See* Junco, Dark-eyed, 249
Yellow-eyed, 250, **opp. p. 121**
Junco caniceps, 250
hyemalis, 249
phaeonotus, 250

Kestrel, American, 47, **Pl. 6**
Killdeer, 63, **64, Pl. 8**
Kingbird, Cassin's, 122, **Pl. 15**
Eastern, 119, **Pl. 15**
Thick-billed, 122
Tropical, 121
Western, 121, **Pl. 15**
Kingfisher, Belted, 108, **Pl. 14**
Green, 110
Ringed, 109
Kinglet, Golden-crowned, 180, **180**
Ruby-crowned, 181, **Pl. 24**
Kite, Hook-billed, 35
Mississippi, 35
Swallow-tailed, 35
White-tailed, 33, **Pl. 4**

Lagopus leucurus, 50

Lampornis clemenciae, 107
Lanius ludovicianus, 184
Lark, Horned, 136, **Pl. 17**
Larus argentatus, 72
    atricilla, 73
    californicus, 72
    delawarensis, 72
    glaucescens, 71
    occidentalis, 71
    pipixcan, 73
Laterallus jamaicensis, 59
Leptotila verreauxi, 85
Leucosticte atrata, 236
    australis, 236
    tephrocotis, 235
Limnothlypis swainsonii, 192
Limosa fedoa, 69
Longspur, Chestnut-collared, 258, **Pl. 32**
    McCown's, 257, **Pl. 32**
Loon, Common, 1, **Pl. 1**
Lophodytes cucullatus, 31
Lophortyx californicus, 53
    gambelii, 53
Loxia curvirostra, 239
    leucoptera, 239
Lunda cirrhata, 81

Magpie, Black-billed, 147, **147, Pl. 18**
    Yellow-billed, **147,** 148
Mallard, 20, **Pl. 3**
Martin, Purple, 142, **142, Pl. 18**
Meadowlark, Eastern, 215, **215**
    Western, 215, **Pl. 27**
Megaceryle alcyon, 108
    torquata, 109
Melanerpes aurifrons, 112
    carolinus, 112
    erythrocephalus, 113

    formicivorus, 114
    lewis, 114
    uropygialis, 113
Melanitta deglandi, 30
Meleagris gallopavo, 55
Melospiza georgiana, 255
    lincolnii, 254
    melodia, 256
Merganser, Common, 32
    Hooded, 31, **Pl. 4**
    Red-breasted, 32
Mergus merganser, 32
    serrator, 32
Merlin, 47
Micrathene whitneyi, 91
Mimus polyglottos, 168
Mniotilta varia, 191
Mockingbird, 168, **Pl. 21**
Molothrus aeneus, 225
    ater, 224
Murre, Common, 79, **79, Pl. 10**
Murrelet, Ancient, 80
    Marbled, 80
    Xantus', 80
Muscivora forficata, 122
Myadestes townsendi, 178
Myiarchus cinerascens, 125
    crinitus, 123
    tuberculifer, 125
    tyrannulus, 124
Myioborus pictus, 213
Myiodynastes luteiventris, 123

Nighthawk, Common, 99, **Pl. 12**
    Lesser, 99, **Pl. 12**
Nightjar, Buff-collared, 98
Nucifraga columbiana, 152
Numenius americanus, 67
Nutcracker, Clark's, 152, **Pl. 19**

Nuthatch, Brown-headed, 158
    Pygmy, 159, **Pl. 20**
    Red-breasted, 158, **Pl. 20**
    White-breasted, 157, **Pl. 20**
Nuttallornis borealis, 135
Nyctanassa violacea, 14
Nycticorax nycticorax, 14
Nyctidromus albicollis, 98

Oceanodroma furcata, 5
    homochroa, 6
    leucorhoa, 6
    melania, 7
Olor buccinator, 18
Oporornis agilis, 209
    formosus, 208
    philadelphia, 209
    tolmiei, 209
Oreortyx pictus, 54
Oreoscoptes montanus, 173
Oriole, Baltimore. *See* Oriole, Northern, 220
    Black-headed, 218
    Bullock's. *See* Oriole, Northern, 220
    Hooded, 219, **Pl. 27**
    Lichtenstein's, 219, **opp. p. 147**
    Northern, 220, **221, Pl. 28**
    Orchard, 217, **218, Pl. 27**
    Scott's, 219, **220, Pl. 27**
Ortalis vetula, 48
Osprey, 44, **45, Pl. 6**
Otus asio, 88
    flammeolus, 89
    trichopsis, 89
Ouzel, Water. *See* Dipper, 161
Ovenbird, 206, **206, Pl. 26**
Owl, Barn, 88, **Pl. 11**

    Barred, **79,** 92, **93**
    Boreal, 95
    Burrowing, 92, **92, Pl. 12**
    Elf, 91, **91, Pl. 12**
    Ferruginous, 91
    Flammulated, 89
    Great Gray, 94
    Great Horned, 89, **90, Pl. 11**
    Hawk, 90
    Long-eared, **94,** 95, **Pl. 12**
    Pygmy, 91
    Saw-whet, 96
    Screech, 88, **89, Pl. 11**
    Short-eared, 95, **Pl. 12**
    Spotted, 93
    Whiskered, 89
Oxyura dominica, 30
    jamaicensis, 30
Oystercatcher, American, 61, **61**
    Black, 62, **Pl. 8**

Pandion haliaetus, 44
Parabuteo unicinctus, 41
Partridge, Gray, 55
    Hungarian. *See* Partridge, Gray, 55
Parula, Northern, 196
    Tropical, 197
Parula americana, 196
    pitiayumi, 197
Parus atricapillus, 152
    bicolor, 155
    carolinensis, 153
    gambeli, 153
    hudsonicus, 154
    inornatus, 156
    rufescens, 155
    sclateri, 153
    wollweberi, 156
Passerculus sandwichensis, 242

Passer domesticus, 213
   montanus, 214
Passerella iliaca, 254
Passerina amoena, 232
   ciris, 232
   cyanea, 231
   versicolor, 232
Pauraque, 98, **98**
Pedioecetes phasianellus, 51
Pelecanus erythrorhynchos, 7
   occidentalis, 7
Pelican, Brown, 7
   White, 7, **Pl. 1**
Perisoreus canadensis, 143
Petrel. *See* Storm-Petrel
Petrochelidon fulva, 141
   pyrrhonota, 141
Peucedramus taeniatus, 197
Pewee. *See* Wood Pewee
Phainopepla, 183, **Pl. 24**
Phainopepla nitens, 183
Phalacrocorax auritus, 8
   olivaceus, 8
   pelagicus, 9
   penicillatus, 9
Phalaenoptilus nuttallii, 98
Phalarope, Wilson's, 71, **Pl. 9**
Phasianus colchicus, 54
Pheasant, Ring-necked, 54,
   Pl. 7
Pheucticus ludovicianus, 229
   melanocephalus, 230
Philohela minor, 65
Phoebe, Black, 127, **127, Pl.
   16**
   Eastern, 126, **126**
   Say's, 127, **Pl. 16**
Pica nuttalli, 148
   pica, 147
Picoides albolarvatus, 118
   arcticus, 118
   arizonae, 117
   borealis, 117

   nuttallii, 116
   pubescens, 116
   scalaris, 116
   tridactylus, 118
   villosus, 115
Pigeon, Band-tailed, 82
   Domestic. *See* Dove,
     Rock, 82
   Red-billed, 82
Pinicola enucleator, 235
Pintail, 22, **22**
Pipilo aberti, 241
   chlorurus, 240
   erythrophthalmus, 240
   fuscus, 241
Pipit, Sprague's, 182
   Water, 181, **182, Pl. 24**
Piranga flava, 227
   ludoviciana, 225
   olivacea, 226
   rubra, 227
Pitangus sulphuratus, 123
Platypsaris aglaiae, 119
Plegadis chihi, 17
   falcinellus, 16
Plover, Mountain, 64, **65,
   Pl. 8**
   Piping, 62, **63**
   Semipalmated, 62
   Snowy, 62
   Wilson's, 63
Podiceps auritus, 2
   dominicus, 3
   grisegena, 1
   nigricollis, 2
Podilymbus podiceps, 4
Polioptila caerulea, 179
   melanura, 179
   nigriceps, 179
Pooecetes gramineus, 245
Poor-will, 98, **Pl. 12**
Porphyrula martinica, 59
Porzana carolina, 58

Prairie Chicken, Greater, 50, **Pl. 6**
  Lesser, 51
Progne subis, 142
Protonotaria citrea, 191
Psaltriparus minimus, 157
Psilorhinus morio, 147
Ptarmigan, White-tailed, 50, **51, Pl. 6**
Ptychoramphus aleuticus, 81
Puffin, Tufted, 81
Pyrocephalus rubinus, 135
Pyrrhuloxia, 228, **Pl. 29**

Quail, California, 53, **Pl. 7**
  Gambel's, 53
  Harlequin. *See* Quail, Montezuma, 54
  Montezuma, 54
  Mountain, 54, **Pl. 7**
  Scaled, 53
Quiscalus major, 223
  mexicanus, 222
  quiscula, 223

Rail, Black, 59
  Clapper, 57, **57**
  King, 56
  Virginia, 57, **58, Pl. 8**
  Yellow, 59
Rallus elegans, 56
  limicola, 57
  longirostris, 57
Raven, Common, 148, **149, Pl. 18**
  White-necked, 148, **149, Pl. 19**
Recurvirostra americana, 69
Redhead, 26
Redstart, American, 212, **Pl. 26**

Painted, 213, **opp. p. 121**
Regulus calendula, 181
  satrapa, 180
Riparia riparia, 138
Roadrunner, 87, **Pl. 11**
Robin, American, 173, **174, Pl. 22**
Rynchops niger, 79

Salpinctes obsoletus, 167
Sandpiper, Solitary, 68
  Spotted, 67, **68, Pl. 9**
  Upland, 67, **Pl. 9**
Sapsucker, Natalie's. *See* Sapsucker, Williamson's, 115
  Red-breasted. *See* Sapsucker, Yellow-bellied, 114
  Red-naped. *See* Sapsucker, Yellow-bellied, 114
  Williamson's, 115, **Pl. 14**
  Yellow-bellied, 114, **Pl. 14**
Sayornis nigricans, 127
  phoebe, 126
  saya, 127
Scardafella inca, 85
Scaup, Lesser, 28, **Pl. 4**
Scoter, White-winged, 30
Seedeater, White-collared, 235
Seiurus aurocapillus, 206
  motacilla, 207
  noveboracensis, 207
Selasphorus platycercus, 105
  rufus, 106
  sasin, 106
Setophaga ruticilla, 212
Shoveler, Northern, 25, **Pl. 3**
Shrike, Loggerhead, 184, **Pl. 24**

Sialia currucoides, 178
  mexicana, 177
  sialis, 177
Siskin, Pine, 237
Sitta canadensis, 158
  carolinensis, 157
  pusilla, 158
  pygmaea, 159
Skimmer, Black, 79
Skylark, 136
Snipe, Common, 66, **Pl. 8**
Solitaire, Townsend's, 178,
  Pl. 23
Sora, 58, **Pl. 8**
Sparrow, Bachman's, 246,
  247
  Baird's, 243
  Black-chinned, 253, **Pl. 32**
  Black-throated, 248, **Pl. 31**
  Botteri's, 247
  Brewer's, 252, **Pl. 31**
  Cassin's, 247
  Chipping, 250, **Pl. 31**
  Clay-colored, 251, **251**
  European Tree, 214
  Field, 252, **Pl. 32**
  Five-striped, 246
  Fox, 254, **Pl. 32**
  Golden-crowned, 254
  Grasshopper, 243, **Pl. 30**
  Henslow's, 244
  House, 213, **214, Pl. 27**
  Lark, 245, **Pl. 31**
  Le Conte's, 244
  Lincoln's, 254, **255, Pl. 32**
  Olive, 240, **opp. p. 147**
  Rufous-crowned, 246
  Rufous-winged, 246
  Sage, 248, **Pl. 31**
  Savannah, 242, **Pl. 30**
  Seaside, 244
  Sharp-tailed, 244

  Song, 256, **257, Pl. 32**
  Swamp, 255, **256**
  Vesper, 245, **Pl. 31**
  White-crowned, 253, **Pl. 32**
  White-throated, 254
Sphyrapicus thyroideus, 115
  varius, 114
Spiza americana, 233
Spizella atrogularis, 253
  breweri, 252
  pallida, 251
  passerina, 250
  pusilla, 252
Spoonbill, Roseate, 17
Sporophila torqueola, 235
Starling, 184, **Pl. 24**
Steganopus tricolor, 71
Stelgidopteryx ruficollis, 139
Stellula calliope, 106
Sterna albifrons, 76
  caspia, 77
  elegans, 77
  forsteri, 74
  fuscata, 76
  hirundo, 75
  maxima, 77
  sandvicensis, 77
Stilt, Black-necked, 70, **70, Pl. 9**
Storm-Petrel, Ashy, 6
  Black, 7
  Fork-tailed, 5
  Leach's, 6, **6, Pl. 1**
Streptopelia chinensis, 84
  risoria, 84
Strix nebulosa, 94
  occidentalis, 93
  varia, 92
Sturnella magna, 215
  neglecta, 215
Sturnus vulgaris, 184
Surnia ulula, 90

Swallow, Bank, 138, **138, Pl. 17**
  Barn, 140, **140, Pl. 17**
  Cave, 141
  Cliff, 141, **Pl. 18**
  Rough-winged, 139, **139, Pl. 17**
  Tree, 137, **137, Pl. 17**
  Violet-green, 137
Swan, Trumpeter, 18
Swift, Black, 99
  Chimney, 100, **100, Pl. 12**
  Vaux's, 101
  White-throated, 101
Synthliboramphus antiquus, 80

Tachycineta thalassina, 137
Tanager, Hepatic, 227
  Scarlet, 226, **226**
  Summer, 227, **Pl. 28**
  Western, 225, **Pl. 28**
Teal, Blue-winged, 23
  Cinnamon, 24, **25, Pl. 3**
  Green-winged, 23
Tern, Black, 78, **78, Pl. 10**
  Caspian, 77, **Pl. 10**
  Common, 75, **75**
  Elegant, 77
  Forster's, 74, **Pl. 10**
  Gull-billed, 74, **74**
  Least, 76, **76**
  Royal, 77
  Sandwich, 77
  Sooty, 76
Thrasher, Bendire's, 170, **Pl. 22**
  Brown, 169, **170, Pl. 22**
  California, 172, **Pl. 22**
  Crissal, 172, **Pl. 22**
  Curve-billed, 171, **171, Pl. 22**

  Le Conte's, 172, **Pl. 22**
  Long-billed, 170, **opp. p. 147**
  Sage, 173, **Pl. 22**
Thrush, Hermit, 175, **Pl. 23**
  Swainson's, 175, **Pl. 23**
  Varied, 174
  Wood, 175
Thryomanes bewickii, 163
Thryothorus ludovicianus, 164
Titmouse, Black-crested. *See* Titmouse, Tufted, 155
  Bridled, 156
  Plain, 156, **Pl. 19**
  Tufted, 155, **155, Pl. 19**
Towhee, Abert's, 241
  Brown, 241, **Pl. 30**
  Green-tailed, 240, **Pl. 30**
  Rufous-sided, 240, **Pl. 30**
Toxostoma bendirei, 170
  curvirostre, 171
  dorsale, 172
  lecontei, 172
  longirostre, 170
  redivivum, 172
  rufum, 169
Tringa solitaria, 68
Troglodytes aedon, 162. See also *T. brunneicollis,* 162
  brunneicollis, 162
  troglodytes, 163
Trogon, Coppery-tailed, 108
Trogon elegans, 108
Turdus migratorius, 173
Turkey, 55, **Pl. 7**
Tympanuchus cupido, 50
  pallidicinctus, 51
Tyrannus crassirostris, 122
  melancholicus, 121
  tyrannus, 119

Tyrannus (*cont.*)
  verticalis, 121
  vociferans, 122
Tyto alba, 88

Uria aalge, 79

Veery, 176, **176, Pl. 23**
Verdin, 156, **Pl. 20**
Vermivora bachmanii, 194
  celata, 194
  chrysoptera, 193
  crissalis, 196
  luciae, 196
  peregrina, 194
  pinus, 194
  ruficapilla, 195
  virginiae, 196
Vireo, Bell's, 186, **187, Pl. 25**
  Black-capped, 185
  Gray, 186
  Hutton's, 185, **Pl. 24**
  Philadelphia, 189
  Red-eyed, 189, **190, Pl. 25**
  Solitary, 188, **188, Pl. 25**
  Warbling, 189, **Pl. 25**
  White-eyed, 185, **Pl. 24**
  Yellow-green, 189
  Yellow-throated, 187
Vireo atricapilla, 185
  bellii, 186
  flavifrons, 187
  flavoviridis, 189
  gilvus, 189
  griseus, 185
  huttoni, 185
  olivaceus, 189
  philadelphicus, 189
  solitarius, 188
  vicinior, 186

Vulture, Black, 33
  Turkey, 32, **Pl. 4**

Warbler, Audubon's. *See* Warbler, Yellow-rumped, 200
  Bachman's, 194
  Bay-breasted, 204, **opp. p. 199**
  Black-and-white, 191, **Pl. 25**
  Blackburnian, 203, **opp. p. 199**
  Black-throated Blue, 200, **opp. p. 199**
  Black-throated Gray, 200, **Pl. 26**
  Black-throated Green, 201, **opp. p. 199**
  Blue-winged, 194
  Canada, 212, **opp. p. 199**
  Cape May, 200
  Cerulean, 202
  Chestnut-sided, 204
  Colima, 196
  Connecticut, 209
  Golden-cheeked, 201, **202**
  Golden-winged, 193
  Grace's, 204
  Hermit, 202
  Hooded, 211
  Kentucky, 208
  Lucy's, 196, **opp. p. 121**
  MacGillivray's, 209, **Pl. 26**
  Magnolia, 199, **opp. p. 199**
  Mourning, 209, **opp. p. 199**
  Myrtle. *See* Warbler, Yellow-rumped, 200
  Nashville, 195, **195, Pl. 25**
  Olive, 197

Olive-backed. *See* Parula,
Tropical, 197
Orange-crowned, 194
Palm, 205
Parula. *See* Parula,
Northern, 196
Pine, 204, **205**
Prairie, 205
Prothonotary, 191, **192**
Red-faced, 210, **opp. p.
121**
Rufous-capped, 213
Swainson's, 192, **193**
Tennessee, 194, **opp. p.
199**
Townsend's, 201
Virginia's, 196
Wilson's, 211, **211, Pl. 26**
Worm-eating, 193
Yellow, 197, **199, Pl. 25**
Yellow-rumped, 200, **Pl.
25**
Yellow-throated, 203, **203**
Waterthrush, Louisiana, 207,
208
Northern, 207, **207, Pl. 26**
Waxwing, Bohemian, 182
Cedar, 183, **Pl. 24**
Whip-poor-will, 97, **97**
Whistling-Duck, Black-
bellied, 19, **opp. p. 147**
Fulvous, 19
Wigeon, American, 24
Willet, 68, **69, Pl. 9**
Wilsonia canadensis, 212
citrina, 211
pusilla, 211
Woodcock, American, 65, **66**
Woodpecker, Acorn, 114, **Pl.
14**
Arizona, 117
Black-backed Three-toed,
118

Downy, 116, **Pl. 15**
Gila, 113
Golden-fronted, 112
Hairy, 115, **Pl. 14**
Ladder-backed, 116
Lewis', 114
Northern Three-toed, 118
Nuttall's, 116
Pileated, 111, **111**
Red-bellied, 112, **112, Pl.
14**
Red-cockaded, 117, **117**
Red-headed, 113, **Pl. 14**
White-headed, 118, **Pl. 15**
Wood Pewee, Eastern, 133,
134
Western, 134, **Pl. 17**
Wren, Bewick's, 163, **Pl. 21**
Brown-throated, 162, **opp.
p. 121**
Cactus, 164, **Pl. 21**
Canyon, 166, **167, Pl. 21**
Carolina, 164
House, 162, **163, Pl. 21**
Long-billed Marsh, 165,
Pl. 21
Rock, 167, **168, Pl. 21**
Short-billed Marsh, 165,
166
Winter, 163
Wrentit, 160, **160, Pl. 20**

*Xanthocephalus
xanthocephalus,* 216

Yellowthroat, Common, 210,
Pl. 26

Zenaida asiatica, 83
macroura, 83
Zonotrichia albicollis, 254
atricapilla, 254
leucophrys, 253

Notes

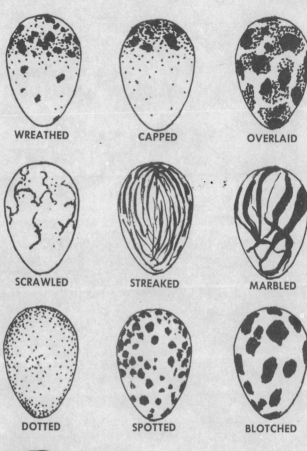

WREATHED   CAPPED   OVERLAID

SCRAWLED   STREAKED   MARBLED

DOTTED   SPOTTED   BLOTCHED

SPLASHED

EGG MARKINGS